Arky

The Baseball Life of
Joseph Floyd "Arky" Vaughan

FRANK GARLAND

McFarland & Company, Inc., Publishers
Jefferson, North Carolina

This book has undergone peer review.

LIBRARY OF CONGRESS CATALOGUING-IN-PUBLICATION DATA

Names: Garland, Frank, author.
Title: Arky : the baseball life of Joseph Floyd "Arky" Vaughan /
    Frank Garland.
Description: Jefferson, North Carolina : McFarland & Company, Inc.,
    Publishers, 2020. | Includes bibliographical references and index.
Identifiers: LCCN 2020028277 | ISBN 9781476669809
    (paperback : acid free paper) ∞
    ISBN 9781476640716 (ebook)
Subjects: LCSH: Vaughan, Joseph Floyd, 1912-1950. | Pittsburgh Pirates
    (Baseball team)—History. | Brooklyn Dodgers (Baseball team)—
    History. | Baseball players—United States—Biography.
Classification: LCC GV865.V37 G37 2020 | DDC 796.357092 [B]—dc23
LC record available at https://lccn.loc.gov/2020028277

BRITISH LIBRARY CATALOGUING DATA ARE AVAILABLE

ISBN (print) 978-1-4766-6980-9
ISBN (ebook) 978-1-4766-4071-6

Front cover: Shortstop Joseph Floyd "Arky" Vaughan
at bat (courtesy Pittsburgh Pirates)

Printed in the United States of America

McFarland & Company, Inc., Publishers
  Box 611, Jefferson, North Carolina 28640
    www.mcfarlandpub.com

To Sandra Brown and Kathleen Johnson Roberts,
whose patience and willingness to share
helped make this project a reality

Table of Contents

Preface

My earliest memories of Joseph Floyd "Arky" Vaughan stretch back more than a half-century, to my childhood days. I was just five years old when my father, a sports fan and athlete in his own right, passed away one day shy of his 33rd birthday, so I don't remember hearing much about baseball—or sports in general—from him. But his three brothers helped pass along his love of sports to my brother and me, and it was one of my uncles who first mentioned the name Arky Vaughan. My memories of that moment are sketchy at best, and it wasn't until I began working on this project that I realized I hadn't put the story together properly.

I remembered, as a young kid, hearing that Arky Vaughan was one of my dad's favorite players, and I found that first name most unusual—and most memorable. I also remember—or at least I think I remember—hearing that Vaughan or someone associated with him had fallen out of a boat. But somehow in my mind I had created the following narrative: my dad was in a boat, listening to a Pirates game on the radio, and when Arky Vaughan hit a home run, my dad stood up to celebrate and fell out of the boat. That, of course, never happened. For one thing, portable transistor radios did not come into wide use until after Vaughan's playing career ended. So there was no way my dad—born in 1927—was listening to Arky Vaughan playing for the Pirates on a transistor radio. In reality, it was Vaughan who fell out of a boat while on a fishing excursion in 1952 and died tragically at the age of 40.

I gave this only sporadic thought over the years until I began searching for a baseball biography project to occupy my summer months. In the spring of 2016, I decided—for three main reasons—to focus on Vaughan. First, as I mentioned, he was one of my dad's favorite players. Second, no one had ever completed a biography of Vaughan before. And as a Hall of Fame player and considered one of the top shortstops of all time, he certainly merited biographical treatment to keep his splendid accomplishments alive forever.

But the third reason was the most intriguing one: Vaughan had an air of mystery about him, both in life and—sadly—in death. In truth I knew

1

very little about Vaughan going into this project beyond his basic baseball numbers and the fact that he led a one-game "mutiny" while playing for Leo Durocher and the Brooklyn Dodgers in the early 1940s. But even that incident was hard to square with the man; he seemed like the least likely candidate to lead such an insurrection, given his quiet, steady nature and his desire to avoid the spotlight. Another mystery surrounded Vaughan's decision to walk away from the game at the age of 31 while performing at an all-star level—and to remain on the sidelines for three full seasons. One might also look at the length of time Vaughan had to wait to gain enshrinement to Cooperstown as a mystery; several baseball historians will weigh in on that wait later in the book. And one final mystery surrounded the event that took Vaughan's life in the chilly waters of a Northern California lake.

Some of those who chronicled the game during Vaughan's career—the 1930s and '40s—maintained that the reason Vaughan did not receive as much notoriety as his numbers might suggest was that Vaughan simply had very little to say, and what he had to say was rather forgettable—and that's why he was rarely quoted. Also, it seemed as though some historians looked at Vaughan as a one-trick pony—all bat and no glove. But a thorough review of the newspapers that covered Vaughan revealed him to be a thoughtful, if not particularly colorful, interview. And to characterize Vaughan as a good-hit, no-field shortstop simply doesn't do him justice. His range in the field was well above average, and his speed—particularly going from first to third—rivaled that of any player in either league. In short, Vaughan never received nearly the credit he deserved for the caliber of baseball he played, and this examination of his career proved as much.

Trying to reconstruct a person's life is never easy; trying to reconstruct the life of a person who was born when William Howard Taft was in the White House and died more than 65 years ago is doubly difficult. The vast majority of his contemporaries, like Vaughan, have passed, so there was precious little opportunity for "live" interviews with teammates or on-field adversaries. Fortunately, the World Wide Web proved to be a boon to my research efforts—entities such as Newspapers.com, Baseball-Reference.com, the Society for American Baseball Research and publications including the *Pittsburgh Post-Gazette*, the *Brooklyn Daily Eagle*, and *The Sporting News* helped flesh out major pieces of his 14-year playing career.

While those sources offered plenty about Vaughan the player on the field, they did not provide much of a glimpse of Vaughan the man off the field. That's where Vaughan's family came in—specifically his granddaughter, Kathleen Johnson Roberts, and indirectly her mother, the late Patricia Vaughan Johnson. Patricia, who was born in 1933 and was Arky Vaughan's oldest child, had been the keeper of all things Arky—boxes and boxes of old newspaper clippings, photos, scrapbooks, correspondence, mementos and much more. Johnson, in fact, in the late 1980s embarked on a journey to interview people who knew her famous father—relatives, former teammates and former opponents—with an eye toward producing a biography of Vaughan. Johnson ultimately wrote a draft of the biography, but was never able to see it published prior to her death in 2015.

However, Roberts—who essentially inherited all of her mother's Arky Vaughan memorabilia—made all of that material available. She even went so far as to take the original cassette tape recordings that her mother made of conversations with family members, old family friends and former players like Frankie Gustine and Dolph Camilli and have them converted to mp3 files. Those recordings contained valuable material that would not have been available anywhere else, as did the unpublished draft manuscript that Patricia Vaughan Johnson produced.

Patricia was more than just the keeper of the Vaughan flame. In fact, she played a key role on a committee that tirelessly lobbied the Veterans Committee to elect her father to the Baseball Hall of Fame in 1985. It was Patricia who gave the Hall of Fame acceptance speech on behalf of her father in July of that year, and in baseball terms, she crushed it. The speech was not a lengthy one, but she eloquently pointed out that while her father never wanted to be famous, his unique skill set and dedication essentially earned him the highest accolade a player can receive—induction into the Hall of Fame. Or, as she poetically put it, "the fame and glory that he never sought are now his forever."

This biographical look at Vaughan is structured chronologically, for the most part, with one exception. Because Vaughan began his major league career in 1932 in Pittsburgh, I wanted to give readers a look at what Pittsburgh was like during the Great Depression. That information is contained in Chapter 3, as several Pittsburgh residents, including Caroline Fellinger and the late Hal Demich, provided their memories, and statistical, employment and attendance figures were also used to paint a picture of the city—and the major leagues—during that time. The final chapter of the book, meanwhile, allows a handful baseball experts and historians to weigh in on where Vaughan ranks among the game's greatest shortstops, and where he ranks among the best players in Pittsburgh Pirates franchise history.

As a longtime journalist, I tried to provide the facts as I found them— hard numbers, recollections of some who played with and against him, family members' memories, expert opinions and the day-to-day reporting that was done during Vaughan's 14 years in the big leagues. My conclusion? Vaughan was an elite player who had the highest of standards—and virtually zero interest in being famous. He would much rather tend to his cattle or spend time with family and friends on or near his various ranch properties in Northern California. He did not open up easily, particularly to those he barely knew, but showed a ready wit to those he trusted and liked. All it took was a couple of postcards that he sent to old friends while traveling west from Pittsburgh at the end of a couple of baseball seasons to see that. In short, based on what little I know of my own father, I could see why Vaughan was among his favorites as a youngster growing up in Pittsburgh in the 1930s. And given the kind of town Pittsburgh is, I could see why Vaughan was a favorite of thousands of Pirates fans for the decade they had him—and why so many of them were saddened when Vaughan died far too soon.

In addition to the aforementioned publications and research sources, significant help and materials were provided by the Baseball Hall of Fame; municipal libraries in Pittsburgh and Fullerton, California; Fullerton High School; and the Richard Nixon Presidential Library and Museum. Dan Hart of the Pittsburgh Pirates' media relations department permitted me to go through some of the club's files. Ken Horn, a fan and collector of Vaughan memorabilia, provided a number of photos. Noted baseball historians and experts including Bill Deane, Bill Felber, Donald Honig, Jay Jaffe, Mark Langill, Jim McConnell, Rob Neyer and Richard Tourangeau, along with experts and historians from the Pittsburgh area—David Finoli, Sam Reich and Ronald Waldo—offered much-needed insight and opinions. In addition to Kathleen Johnson Roberts, Vaughan's son, Timothy Vaughan, provided a unique look at his father while family friends Audrey Smith Ifft, Tom Smith and Joyce Espil Volney were able to share their observations of the man they came to know and appreciate off the field. Special thanks go to Eric Compton, a long-time sports journalist, who provided invaluable editing services, and Gannon University, which offered much-appreciated research funding.

For those of you who played a part in this project but I inadvertently forgot to name, I appreciate your help and contributions. While only one name appears as the author of this book, it wouldn't have happened without the work of many.

Where It All Started

Nothing in the record shows that Joseph Floyd Vaughan and Theodore Roosevelt ever crossed paths. But if anyone ever embodied Roosevelt's slogan of "speak softly and carry a big stick," it was Vaughan. The Arkansas native, who embraced the nickname of "Arky" and later in life had his name legally changed from Floyd Ellis Vaughan to Joseph Floyd Vaughan, swung his stick in the big leagues like few others before or since. A batsman of the highest order, Vaughan never hit below .300 in his first 10 seasons in Major League Baseball, playing for the Pittsburgh Pirates, and finished his Hall of Fame career with a .318 lifetime batting average, an on-base percentage of .406, and a .453 slugging percentage—this despite sitting out his age 32, 33 and 34 seasons in order to run his California cattle ranch during World War II. No less an authority than Bill James ranked Vaughan as the second-best shortstop ever to play the game.[1]

Yet Vaughan remains mostly a mystery to all but the staunchest of baseball fans. Several reasons come into play in that regard; first and foremost, he played the bulk of his career in Pittsburgh, hardly a media mecca then or now. Second, Vaughan did not seek out publicity and in fact went out of the way to avoid being noticed—to the point where he would send his brother to sign autographs in his place after games at Pittsburgh's Forbes Field. And third, Vaughan lost his life in a tragic and mysterious boating accident in 1952 at the age of 40, missing out on decades of old-timers' games and post-career interviews and retrospectives. In short, Vaughan was out of sight, out of mind.

But Vaughan was no two-dimensional character. And he was hardly a wallflower. He did not mind getting into a scrape now and then on the field, and he led what nearly became a team mutiny while playing for the Brooklyn Dodgers in 1943. He was known to have a good time with his close friends, both those he played with and those he grew to know off the field. He was a devoted family man who loved nothing more than to be at home on one of his California ranches, tending to his cattle. Or, if the weather kept him indoors, you could find him reading quietly or listening to music—or even playing the harmonica.

The vast majority of Vaughan's contemporaries have passed, but the records that remain tell the story of one of baseball's greatest—and least-known—players.

Vaughan's story has its roots far from any Major League Baseball diamond. It began in Wales, where Vaughan's great-great-great grandfather, William Vaughan, was born. Later, William moved to Ireland before sailing to America in 1775. He landed in Virginia, but by the time Vaughan's father, Robert Michael (Bob) was born in 1874, the Vaughans had relocated to the town of Clifty, Arkansas. In 1893, with the nation in the midst of a financial panic that would stretch for several years, Bob Vaughan—who later would be referred to by many in the Vaughan family as Daddy Mike—set his sights on moving west to California, and specifically a small town 120 miles north of San Francisco known as Ukiah. There, Bob's uncle, "Bub" Gibson, had a dentistry practice and also owned a small ranch in nearby Potter Valley.[2]

After arriving in Ukiah, Bob Vaughan found work at a ranch/resort on the Eel River in the mountains above Potter Valley called Jerry Lierly's Mountain Resort. When he wasn't working, young Bob Vaughan enjoyed the outdoors—hunting and fishing—and liked to have a good time as well. But after 10 years in California, Vaughan chose to head back to Arkansas. He wasn't there long before he married Laura Denny, a sturdy, strong-willed woman of Scotch/Irish descent. At 19, she was 10 years younger than her husband, and the two set up house on a farm in Clifty. Their first child, a daughter named Blythe, was born in 1905 and two years later, a second daughter—Zella—was born. All the while, though, Bob Vaughan couldn't let go of what he'd seen in California, and he convinced Laura to return with the family to Potter Valley. They went, and Bob found work on one of the local ranches. In 1909, the couple had their first son, Kenneth—known to family members as Teak. But it wasn't long before Laura began having second thoughts about life in California. She missed her home, and her husband's drinking had begun to cause problems. Laura stuck with it for two more years before deciding to return to Arkansas with her three children—while expecting a fourth. Bob, aware of how dire the situation was, vowed to reform and give up drinking for good—a promise he would keep from that day forward. After the family resettled in Clifty, they welcomed their newest member—a son, named Floyd Ellis Vaughan, born on March 9, 1912.[3]

The Vaughan family's stay in Clifty would be short-lived, though; life there wasn't as Laura had remembered it or hoped it would be, so the Vaughans opted to return to Northern California once more. Seven months after young Floyd joined the fold, the family headed back to Potter Valley, but Bob Vaughan found work hard to come by. Oil had been discovered in the southern portion of California's vast Central Valley, a 450-mile swath of land that eventually would become one of the most productive agricultural areas in the world. Young men throughout California were heading to the oil fields, and Bob Vaughan chose to join them. The entire family packed up and headed to Coalinga, a dusty, hot enclave 60 miles southwest of Fresno. Life was entirely different—and not in a good way—as the surroundings were not nearly as beautiful as the Potter Valley area. But Bob Vaughan had found a job with Standard Oil, and the family decided to stay. Their decision paid off two years later, as Bob was transferred to Standard Oil's Coyote Hills fields in Southern California, near the town of Fullerton. The town experienced good times in those days and into the 1920s; in addition to the oil fields, which provided many jobs, Fullerton became an agricultural center thanks to its climate and the nearby railroad connections.

The Vaughan family continued to grow, as a third son, Glenn, was born in 1917. Added mobility in the form of a car enabled Bob Vaughan to live at home with the family and indulge in one of his true passions—going to ballgames. According to Patricia Vaughan Johnson, Arky Vaughan's oldest daughter, there were few things Bob Vaughan enjoyed more than taking his children to local baseball or softball games. Despite his small stature, he had no problems being heard from the grandstand and in fact he had earned the nickname of "Warwhoop" Vaughan from local fans.[4]

Young Floyd had settled into life in Fullerton, attending Ford Street School and forging friendships that would last the rest of his life. He grew close to three boys in particular—John "Skeet" Steele, Jack Hatfield and Arch Carpenter. They shared several common interests—most notably sports and a love of the outdoors—and they were virtually inseparable.

The boys grew particularly close to the Steele family; Skeet's mother and dad were known as Cap and Onie, and they had no problem with Skeet's friends making themselves at home at the house on Balcom Avenue. Cap and Onie grew particularly fond of Vaughan and enjoyed having him around. Years later, in an interview with Steve Grimley of *The Register* in Orange County, Skeet's sister, Louise, was quoted as saying, "Mrs. Vaughan used to tell my mom, 'I have my son Teak [Kenneth], but Arky, he's your boy.'"[5]

It was those young friends, upon hearing young Floyd's drawl and learning of his Arkansas roots, who bestowed upon him the nickname of "Arky." Years later, when Vaughan had become one of the Major Leagues' best players, various stories made the rounds of how he got his name. One indicated that it was a fellow Fullerton High School product named Johnny Hawkins, who went on to quarterback the University of Southern California football team in the mid–1920s, who pinned the nickname on Vaughan when he was a young boy. Yet another story noted that Vaughan had been given the nickname even before he had left his home state of Arkansas. Patricia Vaughan

Johnson, though, gives the credit to Arky's lifelong friends—Steele, Hatfield and Carpenter—and believes her father was only too happy to get it. "He had never been overly fond of his given name," Johnson wrote in an unpublished biography of her father. "His mother often called him 'Floydy Boy' and that was just a little too sissified to suit him." Another nickname that some tried to use was "Pretty Boy"—the same moniker used by a high-profile gangster of the late 1920s and '30s, Charles Arthur "Pretty Boy" Floyd. But Floyd Vaughan despised any reference to his appearance—despite how handsome he was—and that made him embrace the "Arky" nickname all the more.[6]

Although more than 500 miles separated Fullerton from Potter Valley, Bob Vaughan's original California home never lost its attraction to him—or to the family. On many a vacation, Bob would pile his wife and children into their car and make the long trek north—through the Tehachapi Mountains, which separate Southern California from the Central Valley, through the valley and then west to San Francisco before boarding the car ferry for the trip across San Francisco Bay to Marin County. That was hardly the end of the journey, though, as the group still had another 150 or so miles to go to reach Potter Valley. It was customary for the Vaughans to stay at Bob's former place of employment, the Lierly Resort, or with friends who lived in the valley. The Vaughan children—and particularly Floyd and Glenn—grew to love the area and the freedom they had there to hunt, fish and generally explore the rugged area.

The Vaughan boys also got involved in team sports—including basketball and softball leagues sponsored by a local Presbyterian church. Arky, despite being two or three years younger than the rest of the boys, was often among the first players selected when captains would "draft" teams. His prowess continued to grow as he got older; while he was in elementary school, the team he played on defeated the Fullerton High School freshman team, and Arky delivered the deciding blow—a bases-clearing double that won the game in the ninth inning. Teak Vaughan, playing center field for the freshman team, had the misfortune of having to track down the ball.

While Floyd might have outshone his big brother on the field, the same was not true in the classroom. Floyd kept a "C" average—enough to remain eligible for interscholastic sports—while Kenneth had his sights set on a college education, and ultimately secured one at the University of Southern California, where he studied geology. Floyd had no such desires. Whenever anyone asked him what he wanted to do when he grew up, he never hesitated to respond: He would be a professional ballplayer.[7]

For the most part, Vaughan enjoyed his time at Fullerton High School. He tried his hand at several high school sports and excelled in all of them throughout his four years. In football, he made his name as a junior by being a sure tackler on defense and on kickoff and punt coverage teams. He was among the top scorers on the Fullerton High School basketball team, helping the Indians win the Orange League title before bowing to Long Beach in the unofficial Southern California championship game. In baseball, Vaughan and old friend Archie Carpenter teamed with a boy named Willard Hershberger, who was a year older than Vaughan and would go on to join him in Major League Baseball before tragically taking his own life in 1940. In the spring of Arky's junior year, he and Hershberger joined Carpenter and Hatfield on a team that ultimately would play for the Southern California championship.[8]

Vaughan's senior year at Fullerton High was a banner one in several respects. Off the athletic fields, Vaughan served as vice president of the senior class and vice president of the Redmen's Club, a school organization aimed at promoting sportsmanship. On the field, he excelled in all three of his sports. Fullerton High's football team went unbeaten in Foothill League play, with Vaughan playing a key role at halfback. He was one of three members of Foothill League champion Indians to earn a spot on the all-league football team. When fall turned to winter, Vaughan traded his cleats for basketball shoes, as he and Carpenter helped lead the team to an unbeaten Foothill League season. He saved the best season of his high school career for last, as he displayed the hitting that would make him one of the greatest offensive shortstops in Major League Baseball history. He collected 28 hits in his first 54 at-bats and nearly kept up that pace throughout the season, finishing with a .476 average in 82 at-bats. The highlight of Vaughan's senior season came in late May in the Foothill League championship game against Whittier when he went three for four, doubled home the tying run with two outs in the ninth inning and then scored the pennant-clinching run one batter later on Carpenter's single.[9]

In addition to all the time they spent playing sports, Vaughan and his close group of friends managed to get away for hunting or fishing trips in the countryside surrounding Fullerton. Occasionally they would venture south of the border into Mexico, where their favorite spots were the beaches below Ensenada and in particular a place known as Punta Banda. There, they would drive along the beach at low tide, then fish around the clock to catch as many as possible before the tide changed and they would be unable to leave. Vaughan loved the beach—surf fishing and swimming—and so did his friends. But he enjoyed baseball even more and would often stay home in Fullerton to play for one of the local teams while his friends would go off to the beaches.

In addition to the beaches of Mexico and the countryside around Fullerton, one other area continued to attract Vaughan: Potter Valley. In his younger days, he would accompany his father on vacations there, but as he became more self-sufficient, he would make the trip north by himself and stay for longer stretches while working a summer job. A hard-working young man could land a position at one of the local cattle or sheep ranches, vineyards, orchards, farms or dairies, and Vaughan had no aversion to hard work—in fact, he enjoyed it, particularly if it was outdoors. While working in the summer, he also found time to hone his baseball skills, playing for teams in Potter Valley. When his parents were visiting, they'd often come out to watch their son play, and Laura and ol' "Warwhoop" would make their presence known. Arky, though, tended to keep his emotions bottled up—a trait he would exhibit throughout his life. But if pushed to the limit, either on the field or off, he would not hesitate to stand up for himself. Indeed, he did not mind a good scrap—something he would show on more than one occasion once he reached the big leagues.[10]

Following Vaughan's graduation from Fullerton High School in June 1930, he still had only one goal in mind—to be a big-league ballplayer. Vaughan attempted to get a tryout with the Hollywood Stars of the Pacific Coast League, since the club had trained in Fullerton, but Stars manager Oscar Vitt never gave Vaughan much of a shot. Undeterred, Vaughan played wherever he could. He had a stint in a night baseball league in Fullerton, for example, but his fate was sealed after he joined a local semi-pro team, the Cypress Merchants of the Orange County Baseball League. Among his teammates on the Merchants was Hershberger, who played second base and also caught, and would occasionally play with a town team in nearby Long Beach.

The Cypress Merchants ended their 1930 season on December 29, recording a 2–1 win over Laguna Beach to run their record to a perfect 14–0. Vaughan led the way, hitting .500 and attracting the attention of local scouts. Several stories made the rounds in subsequent years regarding Vaughan's "discovery," and while they differed on the details, they were similar in that it was essentially a quirk of fate that allowed Vaughan to become Pittsburgh Pirates property rather than that of the New York Yankees. According to Vaughan's daughter, Patricia, Jim Bouldin, who happened to be the chief of police in nearby Anaheim, had tipped off his friend, Bill Washburn, a scout for El Paso of the Arizona State League, about Vaughan and Hershberger. Hershberger, in fact, had played for El Paso during the 1930 season, and was interested in rejoining the team. Vaughan, too, was interested—as was the club, which sent Vaughan a contract and waited for his signature. But a neighbor of Vaughan's named Chester Parks, who had played in the Pittsburgh organization and knew Pirates owner Barney Dreyfuss, tracked down Art Griggs, who had done some scouting for the Pirates in addition to serving as president-manager of the Western League club in Wichita. Parks urged Griggs to take a look at Vaughan.

Griggs recalled his first impressions of Vaughan for *Pittsburgh Post-Gazette* sportswriter Edward F. Balinger, who also reported for *The Sporting News*:

This youthful shortstop fielded smashes that few others his age could reach ... always throwing to the proper base ... straight to the target. He braced himself carefully at the plate and unless the ball passed through the strike zone he would not offer at it. [He had] an eye like an eagle, an arm like a rifle and the legs of an antelope. He is polite at all times and is not given to rough tactics, although he will not run away if somebody threatens to harm him. He ... loves to play and wants to be the first on the field for practice and the last to exchange his uniform for street clothes.[11]

It wasn't just Washburn and Griggs who were hot on the trail of Hershberger and Vaughan—"Vinegar" Bill Essick, a longtime Yankees scout, also had his eyes on the two. Essick, who lived in nearby Los Angeles, made plans to see the two players in person, but on one particular day, he had to choose between going to Long Beach to watch Hershberger or Fullerton to see Vaughan play for Cypress. He opted to make the trip to Long Beach, figuring he could attend a Cypress Merchants game later that same week and catch Vaughan in action. Griggs, meanwhile, took in Vaughan's game that day in Fullerton.

There's no telling how much of an impact Essick's decision that day ultimately had on Vaughan's decision to sign with Pittsburgh. During his final season as a major-league player, in 1948, Vaughan told the *Pittsburgh Press*' Les Biederman that the Yankees wanted both him and Hershberger. "They sent me a contract for $175 for the El Paso team, but I didn't sign it right away," Vaughan told Biederman. "Then Art Griggs, who scouted for the Pirates, sent me a contract calling for $250 a month."[12] So, for what amounted to $75 a month, the vaunted Yankees, whose lineup already included the likes of Babe Ruth, Lou Gehrig, Bill Dickey and Tony Lazzeri, missed out on yet another Hall of Famer.

Arky Vaughan, in his earlier days with the Pirates, follows through with a warmup swing (courtesy Pittsburgh Pirates).

As 1930 gave way to the following year, area media outlets began to speculate on where local talent would be lining up on the baseball fields. The *Santa Ana Register* reported in mid–January that Orville Schuchardt, Santa Ana's junior college basketball star, would try his hand at professional baseball in the spring and likely would join El Paso of the Arizona State League. Schuchardt, a talented outfielder, reportedly would not sign a professional contract until after basketball season ended, so as not to jeopardize his college eligibility.[13] The article also noted that other Orange County players were expected to break into professional baseball that season and four players were named, including "Arky" Vaughan, who was said to be "lined up for Wichita."

That "lining up" became a reality early in 1931. Vaughan had been working in nearby Buena Park, cutting corn out in a field when word reached his family and friends that the Pirates wanted to sign him for Griggs' Wichita club. "Skeet" Steele borrowed a car to go tell Vaughan the news and bring him back home to sign the deal. Vaughan was thrilled to finally be getting the chance to do what he wanted all along—be a ballplayer—and he would only have to wait a couple of months to show what he was capable of doing.

The *Fullerton Daily News Tribune* reported Vaughan's signing on January 10, noting that his contract was with the Pittsburgh Pirates and that the document was "in the mails back to Pittsburgh." The story noted that major and minor league scouts from all over the country were attending the Cypress Merchants games in recent weeks. The story reported that Chet Parks, "Union Oil man in this section who is an old time friend of Barney Dreyfuss," was largely responsible for bringing Vaughan the special opportunity." The *Daily News Tribune* reported that Vaughan likely would be "farmed out" to one of the Pirates' minor league clubs after Pittsburgh brass had a chance to look at him in spring training in Paso Robles.[14]

Vaughan first caught the attention of the Pittsburgh sportswriters in late February of 1931 while the Pirates were filtering into Paso Robles for spring training. Balinger, writing for the *Post-Gazette*, noted that new Pirates coach Otis Crandall, who lived in the Los Angeles suburb of Bell, was there waiting for a group of Pirates players and coaches on their way north to Paso Robles. The story mentioned that Crandall was joined by Griggs, who had brought two of his Aviator players—outfielder Forrest Jensen and infielder Vaughan, who was referred to as "Floyd" in the story. Vaughan, it was noted, was a 19-year-old shortstop who made his home in Fullerton and was "enlisted as a member of the Wichita team and as the Witches are owned by the Pittsburgh club, Vaughan will be looked over at the Pirate camp. Crandall no doubt will capture several Corsair rookies for development on the Kansas farm when the training period ends."[15]

Vern Kennedy, who would go on to pitch 12 years in the big leagues for several teams, was a rookie like Vaughan during that first spring training in

Paso Robles. But he said it was clear that Vaughan had what it took. "Anyone could tell that Arky was a major league prospect," he told Vaughan's daughter, Patricia. He also noted that while Vaughan could hit both right-handed and left-handed, Griggs made him give up hitting from the right side.[16]

Not much is known of Vaughan's first spring training trial with the Pirates, as a little more than two weeks after his arrival in Paso Robles, he was given a railroad ticket back home to Southern California. The day before his departure, he was pictured in the *Post-Gazette* with catcher Rollie Hemsley; both men were shown holding seven baseballs in one hand—Hemsley's favorite trick. According to the photo caption, Vaughan—whose last name was misspelled, a common occurrence throughout Vaughan's playing days and beyond—had seen Hemsley perform the feat one time and then did it himself.[17] The *Post-Gazette* reported that Griggs was "satisfied" with Vaughan's showing and that Vaughan would report for Griggs' Wichita team when the Aviators began spring training.[18]

Griggs offered to take Vaughan along for the ride to Wichita and Vaughan gratefully accepted, as it would help defray expenses. But on their first night on the road, in Vaughan's first overnight hotel stay, he left his wallet under his pillow—a transgression that he didn't notice until the two had made it a ways out of town and had stopped for breakfast. A call to the hotel revealed that the wallet—and all of Vaughan's money—was gone. It was quite a start to his life as a professional ballplayer.[19]

Spring training consisted of the usual activities—running, hitting, intrasquad games and instruction. Players were not paid; they received only room and board, and most of them—including Vaughan and Kennedy—stayed at the Hamilton Hotel on Main and English streets. But the Depression had gripped Kansas and the rest of the nation, and no one complained about the baseball life. "Good wages then were about a dollar a day, ten hours a day," Kennedy told Patricia Vaughan Johnson. "Men fought to keep a job. They couldn't quit, because there were plenty of people to take their place." Spring training, Kennedy said, "was tough, but we didn't mind it. All of us liked baseball and wanted to get to the big leagues, and we did our best to stick with the Pirates next year."[20]

Vaughan, at age 19, opened the Western League season on the bench, as Pep Young—who would later become his teammate with the Pirates—started at shortstop. Vaughan did see action on Opening Day in an extra-inning win over Denver, though, as a pinch hitter, and his double off the center field fence off Caveman Ed Greer—a huge right-hander—helped the Aviators pull even late in the game.

After starting the season with 11 straight home games—all of which they won—the Aviators went on a seven-game road losing streak. When they returned, the club sent third baseman Felix Vigare to Omaha, and that left an opening at third for Vaughan. He took the opportunity and ran with it. He went on to have a spectacular season with the Aviators, hitting .338 and slugging .573 in a league where the average hitter was six to seven years older. In 132 games, Vaughan scored a league-leading 145 runs and collected 167 hits, including 21 doubles, 16 triples and 21 home runs. He led the league with 43 stolen bases—he was caught just five times—and his 283 total bases were third in the league—yet he did not make the league's all-star team. At shortstop, he wound up with a .952 fielding percentage in 91 games, and his fielding mark at third base was .926 in 38 appearances there. He also set a league record by collecting nine consecutive hits—seven singles and two home runs—over two September games against St. Joseph, Missouri.

Vaughan's club finished first over the first half of the season, compiling a 44–27 record, and then met the Des Moines Demons—the league's second-half champs—in the playoffs. There, Des Moines came out on top, four games to two.[21]

Going into the series, which would be played entirely in Des Moines, reporter Sec Taylor of the hometown *Des Moines Register* gave the Demons a slight edge based on the team's overall stronger infield, but he conceded that Vaughan—referred to as a "dangerous walloper" in a photo caption—was stronger at shortstop than Des Moines' Jimmy Cronin. Vaughan, playing in his first season of professional baseball, "wields his bat more effectively and with more deadly effect than Jimmy Cronin of the locals," Taylor noted. Taylor also pointed out that Vaughan's 136 runs scored were only four behind league leader Stanley Keyes. Taylor wrote that league managers voted Vaughan the Western League's No. 2 shortstop behind Gus McIsaac of Pueblo. "However, if the votes were to be taken at this time both Vaughan and Cronin no doubt would place ahead of the Pueblo star."[22]

Although the Demons prevailed in six games, Vaughan had his postseason moments. In the series opener, won by Des Moines, 11–6, on September 25, Vaughan went two for five and scored a run.[23] In game two, he collected three hits in three at-bats, scored three times and drove in two in the Aviators' 8–7 win in a game that was halted by fog after 7½ innings.[24]

The turning point in the series came the next day, on September 27, when Des Moines swept both ends of a doubleheader, 6–1 and 6–3, to go up three games to one. Vaughan did his part to keep the Aviators aloft with two hits in each game. His solo home run accounted for the club's lone run in the opening game of the twinbill, and he delivered an RBI single and a two-run double in the nightcap.[25] Wichita staved off elimination by taking the next game, 3–1, as Vaughan collected two more hits.[26]

The Demons finished off the series with a 6–4 victory on September 29, despite Vaughan's solo home run. His effort in the field wasn't as stellar, however, as he committed a pair of errors, the first of which came when he juggled

Baseball

Frank Robinson

Baseball

Frank Robinson

First Black Manager

Baseball managers are hired and fired with little fanfare. But when the Cleveland Indians decided to dismiss Ken Aspromonte on Oct. 4, 1974, the press conference was important enough for Baseball Commissioner Bowie Kuhn to attend. That's because the man hired to replace Aspromonte was Frank Robinson, who, on that day became major league baseball's first black manager. Robinson brought superstar credentials to the job. He had been one of the top sluggers in baseball in a career that spanned 19 seasons in both the National and American Leagues. Until 1947, when Jackie Robinson came to the major leagues with the Brooklyn Dodgers, organized baseball barred black players. And, until 1974 when the Indians hired Frank Robinson, no black had ever managed a major league team.

Robinson was a player-manager with the Indians and made a dramatic debut on April 8, 1975, hitting a home run in his first at-bat before 55,000 fans at Cleveland's Municipal Stadium. Indian fans later voted that the most memorable moment in the team's history. The Indians posted a 79-80 record, finishing fourth in 1975 and were 81-78 and fourth again in 1976. On June 19, 1977, with the team record at 26-31, Robinson was dismissed as manager. He was quickly hired as a coach by the California Angels and then moved to the Baltimore Orioles as a coach for 1978. When Baltimore's International League farm team at Rochester lost its manager, Ken Boyer, to the St. Louis Cardinals, Robinson was named as the replacement. The team finished in sixth place with a 68-72 record.

Including his two years of part-time duty with the Indians, Robinson spent 21 years in the major leagues and is among the top ranking players of all time in 10 categories including home runs, where he stands No. 4 with 586. He is the only man in history to win the Most Valuable Player Trophy in both leagues. Now he'd like to be Manager of the Year some day, too.

FRANK ROBINSON

Born, Aug. 31, 1935, in Beaumont, Tex.

AWARDS AND RECORDS

NL, Rookie of the Year, 1956
MVP, NL 1961; AL, 1966
Triple Crown, 1966
MVP, 1966 World Series; 1971 All-Star Game
Established record for hitting home runs in the most major league parks, 32

Leading the way

a ground ball by Earl Johnson, which eventually led to two Des Moines runs in the opening frame.[27] For their efforts, members of the winning Demons each took home $177.05 while Vaughan and his Wichita teammates each pocketed $104.92 for the best-of-seven series, which drew a total of 17,529 fans for the six games.[28]

While Vaughan's first season as a professional was an eventful one, his off-season was anything but routine. During his days at Fullerton High School, Vaughan was a popular—and handsome—young man, as his curly brown hair and brown eyes made him the object of many a young girl's desire. As Patricia Vaughan Johnson put it, some of Arky's female classmates just about swooned in his presence. He wasn't perfect; he was self-conscious of the fact that his teeth were not perfectly straight, and this perceived defect affected his willingness to smile—particularly for photographs. The closed-mouth approach extended beyond photo situations; he tended to keep his inner-most thoughts to himself. It was a trait that many—even those closest to him—would bring up throughout his life and long thereafter.[29]

While a student at Fullerton, Vaughan met an attractive young classmate named Margaret Ann Allen. They were in the same year of school and lived in the same neighborhood. Athletic but quiet, Margaret—known as "Sissie" to her family—appeared to be a fine match for Vaughan. They had a few other things in common; both came from relatively large families that traced their roots back to Arkansas. Margaret had three brothers—Billy, John and Max, who was called Buddy—and sisters Betty, Nettie and Mary. The Allens hailed from Farmington, Arkansas, a small town near Fayetteville. Three generations of Allens had farmed land there, including Margaret's father, Max, and Sissie thrived there. A loner, she loved nothing more than to explore the countryside with her dogs. But when Sissie was 10, her family left the farm for the town of Farmington proper, where Max opened a small general store known as The Red Onion. He also had a hand in the cattle business, but issues with alcohol caused problems for him and his family. To help alleviate the situation, Max decided to leave Arkansas and headed for Colorado with oldest son Billy and a cousin, and they opened a small restaurant there. Eventually, the rest of the family joined them, but later the crew relocated to Idaho and finally to Southern California, where they landed in Whittier—home of future U.S. president Richard M. Nixon—before ultimately settling in Fullerton.[30]

Although Margaret left school during her junior year to help earn money for the family, she and Vaughan continued seeing one another, and their common interests and values—their Arkansas roots, their love of sports and the outdoors in general and their relative shyness—bound them even tighter. Margaret's sister, Betty Allen Wagner, recalled that on the couple's first real date, Vaughan took Margaret to a professional wrestling match at the Olympic Auditorium in Los Angeles. On the way home, Vaughan took the thin paper band off a cigar and placed it on Margaret's finger. "And that was her wedding ring," she joked.[31]

The real wedding, though, wouldn't come until Vaughan completed his first year of professional baseball. Vaughan had made up his mind to ask Margaret to marry him after he returned home from Wichita—to the surprise and dismay of Vaughan's parents. "The Vaughans were so against him getting married—to anybody," Margaret's sister, Betty, said.[32]

So, the couple chose instead to elope. Arky and Margaret piled in the Vaughans' touring car and were joined by Betty and three others—Margaret's best friend, Edith Christensen, and Edith's sister and brother-in-law, Helen and Jack Pollack. They headed to Yuma, Arizona, where the marriage laws were different and the young couple would not need to wait to get a marriage license, as they would have had to do in California. Just like that, the Vaughans officially became man and wife—unbeknownst to Daddy Mike and his wife—and when Arky and Margaret returned to Fullerton, they each went back to their respective families, keeping the marriage a secret for the time being. That did not last long, though. "I don't know how the Vaughans found out about it," Betty said. "I remember Daddy Mike coming to our house in his little Model T Ford. He wanted to see that marriage license. He was very unhappy."[33]

But once the reality of the situation sank in, the Vaughans accepted Margaret and welcomed her as part of the family. She and Arky often joined them at regular Sunday dinners—fried chicken and other traditional Southern fare would often be on the menu—but during the week they continued to live apart, with their respective families, as they couldn't afford their own place.[34]

Vaughan's name popped up in late November—albeit a misspelled version once again—in the *Pittsburgh Press* as Pirates followers speculated who might replace Jewel Ens, who departed after three seasons as manager. Dreyfuss said he was not opposed to a player-manager, and later in the same story noted that he was pleased with the season that Vaughan had in 1931 at Wichita. Dreyfuss also noted that he had been offered $50,000 for Vaughan, an offer he declined.[35] The following day, the *Press* reported that club secretary Sam Watters said Vaughan—described as "the sensational young shortstop of the Wichita Club farm"—would not be traded or sold, regardless of the "fabulous" offers coming in from other big-league clubs. Watters told the *Press* that Vaughan would be taken to spring training and if his play warranted it, he would be kept on the club's payroll. "We don't sell players," Watters said.[36] However, Dreyfuss later said he wouldn't rule out the idea of trading for a shortstop to challenge holdover Tommy Thevenow.[37]

Although Vaughan's reputation began to get established, his backstory remained somewhat of a mystery, if not downright inaccurate. A small write-up in the *Pittsburgh Post-Gazette* noted that Vaughan was discovered playing scholastic baseball in San Francisco and recommended by Joe Devine while Devine was scouting for the club on the Pacific Coast.[38] In reality, Vaughan made his presence known on the amateur fields 400 miles to the south, where he had caught the attention of Griggs and Essick.[39] It would only be a few more months before Vaughan, still just 19, began impressing the Pirates organization as a whole—and making it exceptionally difficult to keep the Arkansas native off the big league roster.

♦♦ 2 ♦♦

The Early Years

As the Pittsburgh Pirates prepared for another spring training on the West Coast, the franchise was dealt a major blow. Club owner Dreyfuss, under whose guidance the team had won six National League pennants and a pair of World Series championships, died on February 5, 1932, at Mount Sinai Hospital in New York, and the franchise's future was uncertain. Dreyfuss had previously owned a National League franchise in Louisville, but when the league contracted, he bought the Pittsburgh franchise and merged the two clubs in 1900. He was a major mover in the creation of the World Series and proudly watched his ball club play in the first one—a losing effort against Boston in 1903—and later capture titles in 1909 and 1925.

A story in the *Pittsburgh Press* indicated that Dreyfuss, 67, had undergone a series of major operations and was unable to rally "although recent reports of physicians had predicted his recovery."[1] Some said the loss of his only son, Sam, a year earlier, was a blow from which he could not recover. Sam Dreyfuss, who was the team's vice president and treasurer and was being groomed to take over the club, was just 35 when he succumbed to pneumonia, leaving a widow and a three-year-old son. Said Jewel Ens, the former Pirates manager who was a coach with the Detroit Tigers at the time of the elder Dreyfuss's passing: "Barney took the death of Sam so hard that for at time I feared he would break completely under it. He carried on bravely, but I could see how he grieved constantly. Beside him, at his office, he kept Sam's picture at all times. He built up the club for Sam. Barney Dreyfuss was a great power in the game. At any baseball meeting he attended, he was always a dominant figure. The game has lost a great man."[2]

Dreyfuss's death raised speculation that the ball club might be sold, but for the time being, Sam Watters, the team's secretary and Dreyfuss's right-hand man for 25 years, told the press it was too soon to think about the club's fate. "All we can do today," Watters said, "is to carry on. As to what is to happen to the baseball club, that is a question for Mr. Dreyfuss' family."[3] Ultimately, Dreyfuss's widow, Florence, tapped her son-in-law, William

Benswanger, to become team president, and he took control despite having just a year of experience in a baseball front office.

Prior to Dreyfuss's death, he had decided to make a managerial change, letting Ens go after two consecutive fifth-place finishes and replacing him in late November with George Gibson, who had spent 14 years in the big leagues as a catcher, the first 12 of which came with the Pirates. This would be Gibson's second managerial go-round with the Pirates; he guided the club for two full seasons—1920–21—and half of the 1922 season before resigning.

The Pirates convened in Paso Robles, California, for spring training, and once again Vaughan was among those getting a look by virtue of his association with Art Griggs, who had moved his Western League franchise from Wichita to Tulsa, Oklahoma. Edward F. Balinger, covering the team for the *Pittsburgh Post-Gazette*, referred to "Vaughn" as "the fine youthful prospect who worked out with the Pirates one year ago and then played sensationally in the Western league." Balinger predicted that Vaughan would be "reclaimed by the Pittsburgh club before the championship race is far advanced."[4]

Balinger proved prescient, but it would be a few more weeks before Vaughan—who had not yet turned 20 years old—would lock up a roster position. In the meantime, he went about impressing those who watched him in action. A *Pittsburgh Press* reporter remarked in mid–March that Vaughan could "go get them with the best of them" around second base.[5] In the final scrimmage of the camp between the Pirates regulars and the reserves, Vaughan went four for six with a home run, scored twice, and performed sensationally at shortstop.[6]

Vaughan continued his stellar work as the Pirates moved up the California coast, playing exhibition games against some Pacific Coast League clubs. On March 13, Vaughan subbed for starting shortstop Tommy Thevenow in a doubleheader with the Oakland Oaks and collected four hits—including a triple—in seven at-bats while making "a number of sensational fielding plays."[7] The *Pittsburgh Press* noted that Gibson was "particularly elated" with the performance of three of his players—Vaughan and pitchers Bill Harris and Larry French—and the United Press story lauded Vaughan for both his fielding and his "stick work."[8]

Vaughan collected 10 hits in his first six exhibition games, and the *Pittsburgh Press* referred to him as "the hard-working youngster whom the Bucs are looking over after his banner season last year with Wichita. … Rangy, dependable, this Vaughan lad appears to have little of bluster about him but much of quiet confidence and ability."[9] Balinger wrote that Vaughan was being tried out at shortstop "and is making a pretty satisfactory job of it. If he fails to crowd Tommy Thevenow from that berth this spring, it is almost certain that he will get another opportunity." Balinger referred to Vaughan as "gifted with great speed, a fine throwing arm and a pair of sharp batting eyes" and noted that since the Pirates transferred their farm interests from Wichita to Tulsa, the question was whether Vaughan would be sent to Oklahoma for additional work or would remain with the big-league club. "He looks so good right now that the fans are beginning to think he may make the grade—if not as a regular, to be used as a substitute infielder," Balinger wrote.[10]

Although Vaughan hardly needed any help, his main competition for the starting berth—Thevenow—was less than 100 percent physically, as he was still rounding into form after suffering a major leg injury the previous September. While Thevenow attempted to come back from that injury, Vaughan was rolling in Paso Robles. Havey J. Boyle of the *Pittsburgh Post-Gazette* noted that Vaughan was getting special mention from the new Bucco manager. Boyle said that Gibson had no doubt that Vaughan had a brilliant future, but wasn't sure if he was ready to hold down a starting job. Still, Boyle noted that Gibson "stresses Vaughan more than any other member of the Pirate cast."[11] And for good reason, as the youngster continued to hit as spring training progressed. He went four for five in a 10–9 win over the San Francisco Missions on March 17 and was batting .391 through the first 16 exhibition games. Many were predicting that Vaughan would make the club. Gibson wasn't ready to announce any such thing, but did not deny that Vaughan was making an impression, saying that he liked him more and more every day. "I've never seen any recruit who so closely resembles Hans Wagner in his actions upon the diamond," Gibson said. "Before Vaughan had been at Paso Robles a week, he convinced me that he possesses a wonderful amount of natural ability." Although Vaughan was property of the Tulsa club, the Pirates actually owned that franchise, so it would only be a matter of some simple paperwork to transfer Vaughan's contract to Pittsburgh if Gibson and the front office decided he merited a space on the roster.[12] When the club's spring training tour headed south to Los Angeles in the final week of March, Vaughan managed to squeeze in a visit to his hometown of Fullerton—an item duly noted by the Fullerton newspaper. A brief story noted that Vaughan—referred to as "Arkie"—was the first Fullerton High School baseball product to "get to first base" in the big leagues since the immortal Walter Johnson went East as a 19-year-old with the Washington Senators in 1907.[13]

That same month, Vaughan first attracted the attention of what was considered the bible of the baseball world—*The Sporting News*. He merited mention in a pair of stories in the March 24 edition. In the first, writer John B. Foster noted that Vaughan was "so good that a major league manager will not have cause to regret that he can report to him for three meals a day and all the working hours between breakfast and dinner." Foster wrote that Vaughan "draws pictures around shortstop" that were reminiscent of Honus Wagner and made plays that Wagner made when Gibson and McGraw were young.

He added: "No infielder on the Coast who was seen on the trip to the big league camps could surpass [Vaughan] in going behind second base to get the ball. He made one think of Wagner with his wide-spread arms, hands close to the ground and easy manner of picking up ground hits and throwing an astonished batter out."[14] As March wound down, the *Santa Ana Register*—located about five miles from Vaughan's hometown of Fullerton—weighed in on Vaughan's spring training performance. "Best kid to join the Pittsburgh Pirates in 10 years" is the way Gibson described Vaughan to the *Register* reporter, noting that he was the most promising Pirates infielder since Harold "Pie" Traynor a dozen years earlier.[15] His exploits even caught the attention of National League President John Heydler, who talked about Vaughan while touring the West Coast. "In the East, I've been hearing a great deal of favorable comment concerning this clever youth, and he appears to be generally regarded as one of the best finds of the year," Heydler said of the rookie shortstop.[16] At the end of the first week of April, Vaughan was hitting .351 with 27 hits in 77 at-bats—good for third on the club behind veteran outfielder Paul Waner (.366) and his brother, Lloyd (.360).

On April 7, following a 10–9 loss to a Fort Worth Texas League team in Fort Worth in which Vaughan went hitless, he received word that he had been transferred from the Tulsa club to the Pirates, and he signed a big-league contract that was presented to him by club president William Benswanger.[17] He went out the next day and contributed a home run and a double with four RBIs in a 14–8 win over host Dallas. By the time the exhibition campaign had concluded, Vaughan was sporting a .358 average—good for No. 2 on the club behind Paul Waner at .372—and was leading the team in home runs with three.

Vaughan was not in the starting lineup when Opening Day arrived on April 12, but the local press certainly was high on the California youngster. "If Thevenow fails at short, young Floyd Vaughan is ready to step in," wrote Chet Smith, the *Pittsburgh Press* sports editor. "Vaughan has no major league experience, but he shapes up as the best piece of infielding machinery the Corsairs have gobbled up in a long time."[18] In the *Post-Gazette*, Balinger noted that while Vaughan had been performing brilliantly all spring, Gibson believed that he would be "taking some risk by sending the clever kid into a contest of this sort." Balinger said the team would be better served by using the veteran Thevenow at short and allowing Vaughan to "watch the big league stuff for a time at least."[19]

That week's issue of *The Sporting News* highlighted Vaughan on the front page, noting that he was a "sensation" at shortstop during spring training, hitting the ball hard and often and showing the fielding instincts of a veteran. "Vaughan has shown so much class at short, and especially at the bat, where Thevenow is weak, that Floyd seems to have an excellent chance of displacing

Tommy as a regular, and unquestionably will be retained to fill the role of utility infielder."[20] Vaughan never made it onto the field during the Pirates' season-opener at St. Louis, a game that the Pirates lost 10–2. Thevenow went one for four that day, and in his first five games he collected seven hits in 22 at-bats, a .318 average.

While Vaughan was slowly becoming acclimated to the big leagues, his young bride, Margaret, also was attempting to get comfortable in her new surroundings. Margaret's sisters accompanied her to the train station in Fullerton, where she started her journey east. "She was awfully nervous about it," Betty recalled of her sister. "This was a whole new life for her—living in a big city, staying in hotels. Riding a train all by herself. Arky just accepted such things. He wouldn't want anybody to know he was scared, if he was. I mean, you would never know it."[21]

Vaughan finally made his first major-league appearance in the Pirates' sixth game of the season, a 4–3 win over the Cincinnati Reds in the Queen City. Vaughan batted for Thevenow in the ninth inning and struck out against Reds pitcher Larry Benton. However, Vaughan did his job in the field, starting a double play "without which the ball game might have been at least deadlocked," wrote Ballinger. "Heath followed with a dangerous bounder to short but Vaughan came up with the ball like a veteran and passed it quickly to Piet who fired it to Suhr and two men were gone."[22] The *Pittsburgh Press* referred to Vaughan's defensive effort as a "pretty play on Heath's hot smash in the last half of the ninth."[23]

Vaughan continued to serve as Thevenow's understudy during the early going, but he got his work in, staying late to field grounders with manager Gibson. His second big league at-bat came in another pinch-hitting role, this time against St. Louis on April 22 in a 5–3 loss at Forbes Field. Batting for Larry French, Vaughan

Arky Vaughan, in one of his earlier seasons with Pittsburgh, prepares to field a ground ball at his shortstop position (courtesy Pittsburgh Pirates).

struck out again. "But young 'Poker-face' somehow creates the feeling he's going to be quite all right as a player before he's done," the *Press* reported.[24]

Vaughan finally earned his first start on April 28 when the Pirates hosted the Reds in what proved to be a 7–6 loss at Forbes Field. His first at-bat as a starter came with two outs in the bottom of the second inning and the Bucs trailing 2–0. Vaughan tripled to right field, scoring Adam Comorosky, who had reached on error, to cut the lead to 2–1. In the fourth, batting against Biff Wyson, Vaughan popped out to first, and then he flied out to right field in the sixth off Jack Ogden. In his fourth and final at-bat of the day, Vaughan slugged his second triple of the day, this one off Ogden, and drove in both Traynor and Suhr to trim the deficit to 7–5.

Vaughan's starting debut was well-chronicled by the local press. The *Post-Gazette* featured a sizable photo, complete with a caption that read "Off to a Great Start," while the *Press* featured a huge photo depicting Vaughan's first triple, complete with a dotted line showing the route of the ball from home plate to right-center field. *Press* reporter Fred Wertenbach wrote that Gibson, "the round-faced peppery pilot, delved into his bag and presto— brought out a real shortstop in the youthful person of 'Poker Face' Floyd Vaughan, late of the Wichita Club of the Western League." Wertenbach said that Vaughan appeared to have punch, referring to his two booming triples. And the compliments didn't end there, as Wertenbach noted:

> He has a fine throwing arm, as the three double plays in which he participated, can prove. He has the willingness to go from here to Hoboken after a drive, as his Traynor-like dive for pitcher Ray Kolp's single over second in the third inning showed. And he doesn't curl up in a pinch, as witness his first triple, with Comorosky on second, and his second three-bagger with Traynor and Suhr on the sacks, in the eighth inning. Too fulsome praise of this latest Bucco may be unseemly, for a thimbleful of Bourbon doesn't make a highball and one game doesn't make a season, but coming on top of laudatory reports from the training camp and on the exhibition jaunt, it looks like Floyd, after the initial hubbub subsides, may develop into a mighty fine shortfielder.[25]

Vaughan earned his second start the following day, and again went two for four in a 6–4 loss to the Reds. He remained a fixture in the lineup throughout the month of May, and more than held his own during the first half of the month, going 10 for 33 with six RBIs. Following a 7–5 loss to the Reds in which Vaughan had two hits and drove in a pair, Wertenbach wrote that it would take "a crane or derrick of some sort" to displace Vaughan from the starting lineup. "'Poker Face,' besides getting his two hits, a mighty nice habit he seems to have developed, turned in an errorless game in the field, handling seven chances."[26] A couple of days later, Wertenbach discussed the club's inexperience, particularly as it applied to Vaughan, who made a couple of miscues in an 8–6 loss to the Cubs. "Vaughan may toss away a few ball games, but he looks like too good a player to do otherwise than make good," Wertenbach wrote. "In the big leagues, as in other lines, experience is quite a factor, and when Floyd gets a bit more, he should prove a wiz."[27] Vaughan was making an impression on the opposition, as Cubs first baseman Charlie Grimm liked what he saw during his team's series with the Bucs in early May. "There is a coming star, a great kid who doesn't sag when he makes mistakes," Grimm said of Vaughan. "What if he does throw one away occasionally? That's the rookie in him. I wish we had him around for our club."[28] On May 6—a 4–2 loss to the Phillies—Vaughan collected two more hits and turned in what Balinger described as a "clever" game at short, handling eight chances without an error and "figuring in two lightning double plays."[29] Boyle focused on one of Vaughan's defensive gems, which came in the first inning: "The ball hit Harris' leg and caromed dizzily, but Vaughan made a wild stab, came up with the ball, and retired the left-handed batting Hurst. It was young Vaughan's sterling piece of the season. Speaking of Vaughan, there are some who believe he is as fast as Lloyd Waner. He could be something less than that and be entirely satisfactory."[30]

Twenty games into the season, Pittsburgh was limping along with a 7–13 record, good for last place in the eight-team National League, one and a half games behind seventh-place Brooklyn. While Vaughan started off hot at the plate during his first month as a starter, the hit tool that would prove to be his calling card throughout his career was more like hit-or-miss for the month as a whole. Vaughan started 25 games, made 105 plate appearances and drove in a respectable 12 runs, but batted just .208 with a .550 on-base plus slugging percentage. He wasn't having much more luck in the field, as he continued to make errors from his shortstop position. In a 6–5 loss to the Braves on May 9, Vaughan booted two balls that figured into the scoring. Pirates starter Larry French, who was victimized by his team's shoddy defensive play, tossed his glove across the foul line and then kicked it several times on his way to the bench. Boyle noted that some of the fans on hand at Forbes Field were inclined to give Vaughan "the well-known Bronx cheer, but Vaughan shouldn't worry too much about that. The same fans used to turn thumbs down on Joe Cronin, too, so that their judgment is not always perfect."[31]

Vaughan's fielding woes continued as the month wore on. The club committed four errors in an 11–1 loss to Brooklyn on May 16, including one by Vaughan that led to a deluge of five straight hits in the ninth inning. Wrote Wertenbach: "Four misplays in a game isn't big-league baseball and that's how many the Bucs turned in yesterday. The pitching naturally seems poor, but when an infield looks like a sieve the hurling suffers accordingly."[32] In a 6–5 win over the Cubs on June 3, Vaughan committed a pair of errors but did drive in a run. The following day, Boyle wrote that Thevenow "should give a series of lectures on the art of throwing to young Vaughan. ... Vaughan is still green, but most experts think he will come through in great style as time rolls on. One thing in his favor he does not allow fielding lapses to bother his work at the plate."[33] However, Vaughan's average by that time was only .227. His troubles had spawned some disagreement among the scribes covering the team as to whether Gibson should pull the plug on the young shortstop in favor of the veteran Thevenow, his balky ankle notwithstanding. Smith, in his June 6 "The Village Smithy" column, wrote: "The pro–Vaughaners say Gibby did the right thing and will be smart to keep the lad in the game no matter how many he boots. On the other hand, the antis are claiming Tommy Thevenow ought to be put back to give the infield more defensive strength. Here's a vote for Vaughan. Let him boot 'em if he wants to. That baby's headed straight for big stuff. Paderewski didn't play the Prelude and Fugue in A Minor the first time he parked himself in front of a piano, did he?"[34] Vaughan might have been sputtering, but by the first week of June the Pirates as a team were playing solid baseball, and after reeling off 15 wins in a 21-game span, they held down third place in the National League. This, despite ranking last in fielding and next to last in hitting in the NL.

Vaughan's most productive date to that point came on June 7 in a 7–4 win over the Philadelphia Phillies in the City of Brotherly Love. Vaughan collected five hits in five at-bats, including a double, scored once and drove in a run. The *Pittsburgh Press* noted that Vaughan "is going to be a real star some day; at least that is the impression Philly fans got yesterday."[35] That came on the heels of a three-for-five day that included two runs scored and two RBIs in a 12–4 win over the Cubs. Those two games helped Vaughan hike his average from .226 to .272, and he was clearly on the rise, offensively speaking.

Vaughan continued to see his batting average climb as the month of June progressed. For the 20-game stretch that ran from June 3 to June 30, Vaughan batted .410 with an OPS of 1.004, collecting five doubles and three triples, and driving in 12 runs for the Bucs, who went 14–6 during that span. In early July, he was the centerpiece of a brouhaha that erupted in the first game of a doubleheader against the Cubs at Forbes Field. Vaughan banged out three hits in the first game, a 9–6 win, and three more in the second, the last of which fueled a 6–5, 11-inning victory. Vaughan ignited a "fistic encounter" in the opener of the July 4 twinbill as he took a throw from pitcher Bill Harris to force Chicago's Marvin Gudat at second base. Gudat came in with his cleats high and spiked Vaughan on the left foot, eliciting some grumbling from Vaughan. Gudat retaliated by throwing a punch and, as Wertenbach put it, "'Poker Face,' the last fellow in the world to hunt an argument, propelled a few fists right back, until Tony Piet, stirred to righteous wrath by the attack on his fellow infielder, picked up Gudat bodily and held him, while Umpire Cy Rigler kept Vaughan from renewing the battle."[36] It wouldn't be the last time Vaughan would flash his temper. Gudat did more damage with his foot than his fists; Vaughan had to retreat to the bench for treatment of the spike wound, but returned to the game after a 10-minute delay. Later, it was Vaughan's speed that enabled him to beat out an infield hit with two outs in the bottom of the 11th inning to drive home Tommy Padden with the winning run.[37]

By July 7, the Pirates—at 40–29—owned a three-and-a-half-game lead over the Cubs in the National League. By that time, Vaughan had lifted his average to a robust .319, where it would hover for most of the rest of the season. Vaughan's exploits were being chronicled back in his hometown area, as Eddie West devoted a portion of his local sports column in the July 12 edition of the *Santa Ana Register* to the young shortstop. West noted that Vaughan's insertion into the lineup on an everyday basis triggered the run that boosted the club into first place in the National League. He also pointed that his rookie salary—which he estimated in the neighborhood of $2,500—would likely be topped by a winning share of the World Series if the Pirates were fortunate to get that far. West recounted an interview that *New York Times* sports editor John Kieran had with Pie Traynor, and the two men began talking about Vaughan. Traynor referred to Vaughan as "just a kid" and said he was hands-down the fastest man in the National League. "Was he faster than Estel Crabtree of the Reds?" Kieran asked.

"He is," Traynor replied.

"Was he faster than the Waner boys?"

"I think so," Traynor responded.

"Could he beat out a foul fly to the catcher?"

"He doesn't hit many foul flies to the catcher," Traynor said.

"And that's that. The vagaries of baseball are many. Here is a lad who is a major league sensation, a star in his own right. And two years ago this summer he was dubbing around with Fullerton's night baseball team, getting exactly nowhere."[38]

Vaughan continued to impress in mid–July, stroking a pair of hits in a 6–1 win over the Boston Braves. He finished the month with a .317 average and the Pirates, at 59–40, owned a seemingly healthy five-and-a-half-game lead over the second-place Cubs heading into August. Vaughan turned heads just about everywhere he went, but he left a particular impression on the New York press contingent when he hit .357 with two home runs and four RBIs in a seven-game set the Pirates had with the New York Giants July 26–29. *New York Sun* reporter Frank Graham called him "one of the most remarkable recruits to come up in years." Gibson, the Pirates skipper, told Graham that Vaughan hadn't been in baseball "long enough to learn what it's all about, but he knows, just the same. How? By instinct, I guess. I have no other explanation for it." Graham noted Vaughan's physical stature—5-foot-11, 170 pounds—and said his weight is "so smoothly and evenly distributed that it is deceptive. For instance, he weighs two pounds more than Pie Traynor but, seeing them shoulder to shoulder, you'd be willing to bet Pie outweighed him by fifteen pounds or more." Graham said that on the bench before a game, Vaughan is quiet—shy, almost—"and he makes no fuss whatever on the field." But, Gibson said, "Don't get him wrong. He's not as meek as he looks. In fact he's not meek at all. There's no brag in him, but he knows he's a good ball player and nobody is going to make him believe otherwise, even for a minute." Gibson told Graham that in Vaughan's first at-bat against the Cubs the previous week, Chicago's Guy Bush made him look bad on a screwball. "Next time he started for the plate he said to me: 'Screwball, eh? I'll knock that screwball down his throat.' Well, he didn't do that exactly. But he doubled to right." Graham said the brevity of Vaughan's dossier as a player was amazing, noting his "leap from obscurity to a key position on a team that is out in front in the race for a major league pennant."[39]

Vaughan told Graham that he was born in Clifty, Arkansas, but his family moved when he was seven months old to Fullerton, where he attended grade school and high school and still lived there. For as long as he could remember, he told Graham, the only thing he wanted to be was a major league baseball player. He noted that he played before school, at recess and then again after school, staying out until it got too dark to play—or until his parents came looking for him. Vaughan noted that the Southern California climate definitely worked in his favor, as he was able to work on his game year-round. "I used to spend my Christmas vacations playing ball," Vaughan told Graham. He also told Graham that he played the outfield for two years in high school and was playing shortstop with the Cypress Merchants when he was offered a professional contract. He still wasn't sure if he wanted to be a shortstop or an outfielder. "But now, as then, I just ask to be allowed to play. Where I play doesn't matter much," he said. The rookie said he was enjoying his first big-league season. "I think it's great up here. Now I know I had a great idea when I was a kid and set my heart on being a ball player." Graham, pointing out Vaughan's .320 batting average at the time, said there wasn't a shortstop in either league that "has an edge on him in playing that difficult position."[40]

Not to be outdone, the hometown *Pittsburgh Press* took stock of Vaughan's meteoric rise, noting that he had played his first big league game at shortstop just three months earlier to the day against the Reds at Forbes Field, and after smacking two triples and fielding flawlessly, he had supplanted Thevenow as the starting shortstop. "Today, Vaughan is a big cog, offensively and defensively, in the fast-traveling Pirate machine. He has made numerous misplays, but the bulk of these were when he was finding his feet, as it were, earlier in the season, and were due in part to inexperience." At the time the article appeared, on July 28, Vaughan was on a .366 tear over his most recent eight games. He was compared with the Pirates' most recent standout shortstop Glenn Wright, who was the starter on the 1927 pennant-winning team. Rangy and gifted with what some thought was the best arm in the league, the clutch-hitting Wright was lauded as the best Bucco shortstop since Honus Wagner. The unnamed writer pointed out Vaughan's attributes—he was among the fastest players in baseball at the time, a gift that enabled the left-handed hitter to beat out more than his share of infield hits: "And his mates refer to him as 'Poker Face' due to his calmness under fire. In the smartness that comes through experience and for his remarkable punch in a pinch, the Wright of 1927 had an edge. But the fact that there is even a question as to his superiority in one of his greatest years over Vaughan is the best commentary on the newcomer's ability."[41]

In the space of two weeks, though, the Pirates' lead in the National League evaporated. The club went on a 1–11 skid while the Cubs got hot and vaulted a half-game in front of Pittsburgh. Vaughan's bat cooled off during that stretch, as he batted just .275 with only three RBIs. Vaughan, in his first major league season, was bothered by two sore feet, and club trainer Doc Jorgensen pronounced the problem as corns. "'Doc' smeared salve on the ailing tootsies and he says Floyd will be going at full speed in the Flatbush bargain," Balinger reported on August 4.[42] If the corns weren't enough, Vaughan was reported to have ptomaine poisoning and had to sit out one full game and appeared only as a pinch hitter in another.[43] When Vaughan returned, so did his shaky fielding from earlier in the season, as he committed two costly errors that resulted in a 2–1 loss to Brooklyn on August 6 and a 7–6 loss to Boston the following day. Tony Piet, the young second baseman, also was guilty of a fielding miscue in the loss to the Braves. "Early in the year the fear was expressed the Buccos lacked sufficient experience at the important shortstop-second base stations, and it begins to look like the experts, for a change, may have known whereof they spake," the *Press* reported on August 8.[44]

On August 11, the Pirates returned home from Boston in first place—but just barely after losing 10 of their previous 11 games. Gibson denied that his team was cracking under pressure, and backed Vaughan despite his sometimes-shaky defensive play. "Vaughan is our shortstop and will continue to stay there. I think as much of him as I ever did." Wertenbach concurred, saying that Vaughan "at short looks just as good from this corner as ever. Floyd should stay in there until the cows come home. What the Bucs need to help out a valiant pitching staff is a few more hits."[45]

But the slide continued, as Pittsburgh lost three more in succession and four of its next five to fall two games in back of the Cubs and just a half-game in front of Brooklyn. Boyle, the *Post-Gazette* columnist, on August 11 published an "imaginary talk" that Gibson had with the young Pirates shortstop:

Vaughan, I, like Pie Traynor, think you are going to be one of the best shortstops in history. Without you this season we would have no doubt finished in the second division. We may even finish there with you, but no matter where we finish you are going to play shortstop day in and day out, regardless of how you slump in hitting or fielding, or both. I'm telling you this to remove the strain that you may be under now. I don't think we can win the pennant with you on the bench, so we will keep you out there on the chance that you will get back in the stride that stamped you as one of the finest young brilliants of the game and which made possible the difference between this year's team and last year's.[46]

That very same day, Vaughan's wild throw in the 10th inning led to the Pirates' 3–2 loss. Vaughan, under much scrutiny from fans for his recent fielding woes, tried to make up for it at the plate by going three for four with an RBI. That triggered a seven-for-15 spurt, but the club lost three of its next four. The slide continued into the third week of August, as Vaughan committed three errors in a 10–4 loss to the New York Giants, but the Bucs were still in the thick of things in third place, two and a half games behind the Cubs. However, a 3–6 stretch proved deadly, as the Pirates fell seven games in back of Chicago at 64–60 on August 25. It wasn't all doom and gloom for Vaughan during that time, however; in the opener of a doubleheader with New York, Vaughan hit the game-winning home run and put on a "really satisfying" fielding performance, according to the *Press*' Wertenbach. It was in that story that the first mention was made of Vaughan's nickname—spelled "Arkie."[47]

The August 22 edition of the *Press* featured a fairly lengthy story and illustration on Vaughan with the headline "Hero or Goat—No Middle Course for Him." The illustration read, "At present, the prize 'off-again-on-again' member of the Buccaneer squad—one day's hero—next day's bum—never mind Floyd—even the great Honus has heard the Bronx Cheer." The lead of the story read:

> He makes costly errors but he follows with a remarkable stop and throw on almost the next play. He fails at the plate; then he comes back the next time with a bingle in a pinch. And neither his misplays nor his failure at bat ever gets him, in baseball parlance, down. And, to make his record stand out all the more, he's not yet 21, had had only a year's experience in organized baseball and the job is all the more trying because he's on a club that is in a heated pennant chase. There you have Floyd Vaughan, iron-nerved Arkansas lad with the Pirates, who gives promise of someday ranking with the greatest shortstops in the major leagues. He has a strong arm, a keen eye and is exceptionally fleet of foot; so fast, indeed that he can beat Lloyd Waner, his mates on the Bucco team assert. But it isn't these physical qualities alone that are his chief virtues: it's the heart in the face of adversity.[48]

The story chronicled some of Vaughan's recent failures in the field but noted his attitude:

> A little over five feet 10 and weighing about 170, Floyd gives no quarter to no rival player. Recently he upset Lombardi when the giant Red catcher blocked the plate.

He figured in the near-fistic lash with Marvin Gudat of the Cubs July 4 morning at
Forbes Field. His spikes ride high, too, when he goes into a bag. That's the way he
plays, no quarter. ... One of these days Floyd is going to be ranked among the best.
But right now he goes quietly about his shortstopping business—a hero one day, a
goat the next, but always with his head up.[49]

On August 27, Vaughan sustained his first significant injury, one that
would keep him out of action until September 10. In the first inning of a
game against Boston at Forbes Field, Vaughan fielded a grounder, stepped
on second to force a runner there and threw to first in an attempt to complete the double play. But Fritz Knothe, the runner heading for second, struck
Vaughan's left calf on his slide, upending the young shortstop. Vaughan had
to be carried off the field. He underwent X-rays, and Pirates doctor W.L.
Marks termed Vaughan's injury a "very severe bruise."[50]

The Pirates went on a 9–2 run during Vaughan's absence but still remained six games in back of Chicago when the young shortstop returned to
duty on September 10. The Bucs went 10–5 the rest of the way, but finished
in second place, four games back of the Cubs with an 86–68 mark. Gibson
earned praise in his first season back as skipper, although some fans believe
the club might have been better off with the old hand Thevenow manning the
short field position when Vaughan began to experience difficulty in the field.
But Smith wrote that Gibson was right to stick with Vaughan: "Gibby has to
look to the future strength of his infield, and when he permitted Vaughan to
gain the experience you get only by actually playing, he was only following
the plan every wise baseball head thought was correct. Throughout the circuit
Vaughan is recognized as the best recruit to come up this year. He will pay his
manager manifold for the confidence he has shown him this season."[51]

Gibson's treatment of Vaughan also was applauded by the national
media. Ralph Davis of *The Sporting News* wrote that Gibson's refusal to bench
the rookie shortstop when he fell into a pronounced slump during the height
of the summer heat triggered some criticism, but that the skipper was looking out for Vaughan's best interests—and the future—by retaining confidence
in Vaughan when things "were breaking badly. Arky, as his mates call the
Wichita recruit, as a result is a more confident youth today than he would
have been had he been lifted under fire, and Gibson predicts that in a season
or two he will be ranked with the best short fielders in the game."[52] Vaughan
finished his rookie season in style, going three for five with two runs scored
in a 7–1 win on the road against St. Louis on September 25. His totals for the
season were more than respectable—a .318 batting average and a .787 OPS
mark to go with 15 doubles, 10 triples, four home runs, 10 stolen bases and
61 RBIs. The Pirates went 71–58 in games in which Vaughan appeared and
69–56 in his games started. Defensively, Vaughan finished with 46 errors in
696 chances over 1,124 innings, good for a .934 fielding percentage.

More than a month after the season ended, people were still talking baseball in Pittsburgh. Balinger, in his "Baseball Gossip" column, reported that former Pirates manager Bill McKechnie, who was then skippering the Boston Braves, called Vaughan "the greatest infielder I have seen since Hans Wagner was playing short field for the Pirates."[53]

Wagner, speaking at a reception in the Pittsburgh neighborhood of Crafton, weighed in on the youngster's rookie season: "When Vaughan was booting many chances, some persons thought he should have been placed on the bench and at the time, I was inclined to believe that perhaps a rest might benefit him. Now I feel that Gibson was right in keeping him in the game. It is not always best to take a young fellow out if he is trying, no matter if he is making a lot of misplays. To remove him might discourage him and perhaps after that he would be of little use to his club."[54] Wagner noted that Vaughan loved the game "and with the experience he gained this year, he should have a great season in 1933. You'll not hear of any rival pilot who wouldn't wade through fire to get such a find."[55]

1933

With his first big league season behind him, Arky and Margaret headed west to spend their first off-season together in Fullerton. The new year brought significant change, and none of those changes was bigger than the one that occurred in the White House, where Franklin Delano Roosevelt replaced the embattled Herbert Hoover as president of the United States. Roosevelt hung his hat on a series of economic and social changes that fell under the umbrella of the "New Deal," with the goal of easing the economic hardships brought on by the Great Depression.

Arky and Margaret, meanwhile, rented an apartment near Malvern Avenue and prepared for the arrival of their first child. The blessed event would take place in late February—the same time the Pirates would report to spring training at Paso Robles.

Although pleased with Vaughan's rookie season, the Pirates took a major step in trying to shore up some of the California youngster's leaky defensive tendencies. While some clubs were cutting back on coaching personnel in the face of the Depression, the Pirates in early February added an iconic name to their staff in the form of Honus Wagner, the greatest shortstop the game had ever known and the best player in club history. Wagner retired as an active player in 1917 and had been involved in several endeavors, including running a sporting goods store in Pittsburgh. But when offered the chance to return to the Pirates in a coaching capacity, he eagerly accepted—and expressed joy to be back in the Bucco fold. "Why shouldn't I be happy?" he told the *Press'*

Volney Walsh. "Baseball has been my life; there is nothing I like so well. To
put on a Pittsburgh uniform again will be one of the happiest moments of
my life."[56] Wagner was hired to instruct the Pirate infielders, which included
Vaughan and his equally young double-play partner, Tony Piet. Wagner said
he believed the two would become one of the greatest keystone combinations
in the National League but stressed that he would be available to all of the
Pirate players and assist in any way manager Gibson saw fit.

As the players prepared to leave for Paso Robles, Vaughan took care
of some important business—signing his contract for the 1933 season. The
Santa Ana Register reported that the club doubled Vaughan's 1932 salary, and
"Fullerton street corner gossip" pegged the young shortstop's salary in the
neighborhood of $7,500 for the year. "There will be no depression in Floyd
Vaughan's bankroll this year," the story noted.[57] Experienced baseball men
were not shy about singing Vaughan's praises heading into his second season.
McKechnie, the Boston Braves manager, once again lauded Vaughan, saying
he had everything it takes "to be a world beater, except experience and the
polish that comes with it." McKechnie noted Vaughan's natural hitting prowess and said he had great fielding possibilities. "He will not be merely a good
shortstop, in my opinion but an amazingly great one—the greatest of all since
Wagner."[58]

The Pirates were set to arrive in Paso Robles on February 22, but Vaughan
was elsewhere—in the waiting room of Fullerton Community Hospital, where
Margaret was preparing to have the couple's first child—a girl named Patricia
Ann.[59] Vaughan could not stay long, as he needed to report to camp, where he
would begin what would prove to be a most productive relationship with the
greatest Pirate shortstop of all time—Wagner. The *Post-Gazette* reported on
March 2 that Vaughan was "the happiest boy in the world" when he was told
that Wagner had been assigned to room with him. Wrote Balinger:

> He was not many minutes in writing home to tell the folks how he is the pal of the
> famous shortstop. The Dutchman was also delighted for it always has been one of his
> hobbies to chum with some young player and try to teach him new tricks in the art
> of diamond strategy. Both became acquainted last spring and their friendship was
> mutual. "I look for Vaughan to be the greatest infielder in the National League," said
> Hans tonight, "and nothing would please me more than to see him play twice as well
> as I did in my best days."[60]

Early in camp it appeared as though Wagner's work with Vaughan was paying dividends. In mid–March, the *Press'* Volney Walsh noted that Vaughan
made a couple of plays in an exhibition game that "made old Honus Wagner
turn somersaults. In fact, they have a new nickname for Arky and it's 'Little
Honus.'"[61] On April 2, Vaughan had a chance to visit with some hometown
friends, as more than a hundred Fullerton fans traveled to Los Angeles'
Wrigley Field to watch the Pirates' 8–7 exhibition win over the Chicago

Cubs. Vaughan went two for three and flawlessly handled four chances at short.

As the Pirates made their way east, so did Margaret and new addition Patricia. They were accompanied this time by Margaret's sister, Betty, and her presence enabled Margaret to watch many of her husband's games at Forbes Field. Vaughan was becoming more established and more well-known in Pittsburgh, and occasionally his name would appear in stories in the local papers that had nothing to do with the action on the field. For example, on April 19—one day before the season opener—Smith noted that players would be busy house- and apartment-hunting. The Larry Frenches, for instance, would be on the lookout for a spot that would accommodate the family poodle, "and they also must not be too far away from the Floyd Vaughans. Mr. French and Mr. Vaughan spend many an evening trumping each other's aces to the unalloyed delight of the little women."[62] Betty, in an interview with Vaughan's daughter, Patricia, recalled the Vaughans also spending time with players like Gus Suhr, Earl Grace and the Waner brothers, Paul and Lloyd, as well as Doc Crandall, one of the coaches: "I remember Arky telling stories about Paul Waner and this one night they were out in St. Louis really whooping it up and somehow they got in a little boat that had an outboard motor and oars. They were out there on the Mississippi River, going with the motor, but they were rowing, too. And everybody thought they could really row."[63]

The 1933 season proved to be another successful one for both Vaughan and the Pirates. The sophomore shortstop batted .314—down four points from his rookie batting average, but still good for fifth in the National League. He also packed more wallop in his at-bats, as his OPS mark jumped nearly 100 points to .866—fourth in the league. He collected 29 doubles, a league-leading 19 triples and nine home runs to go with 97 RBIs—fourth in the league

Arky Vaughan, shown during one of his early seasons with Pittsburgh (courtesy Pittsburgh Pirates).

and 36 more than his rookie total. His 85 runs scored left him tied for fourth in the league with teammate Traynor, and his 180 hits were good for fifth in the league. Although Vaughan was not known for his power, his nine home runs were tied for sixth with Spud Davis. He finished second in the league in drawing walks with 64. He even garnered a vote in the Most Valuable Player tally, finishing 23rd among 25 players listed. However, his WAR—wins above replacement—figure of 7.0 ranked second among position players and fourth overall behind only MVP Carl Hubbell (9.2), Lon Warneke (7.9) and Chuck Klein (7.5).

As a team, the Pirates again finished in second place, five games in back of the NL pennant winners that year—the New York Giants—with a one-game improvement over the '32 campaign at 87–67. Vaughan's best day of the season came on June 24 as he went five for five with five RBIs in a 15–3 pounding of Brooklyn. The young standout singled twice, doubled, tripled and homered for his first cycle. His line drive in the second reached the right field stands, and in the next inning he beat out a bunt for a hit. His base hit in the fifth drove home Traynor, and he doubled and scored in the seventh. He closed out his first-ever cycle with a triple in the eighth.

In the field, Vaughan had his problems in the early going, as he committed 18 errors in the Pirates' first 38 games—this after committing only two miscues in 30 spring training contests. But he settled down to some degree in the field as the season wore on. The *Press*' Volney Walsh called Vaughan the National League's most improved player from mid–April until mid–July, specifically noting his defensive improvement. Walsh wrote that while Vaughan gave you the jitters when he went after a ground ball in April, "now [he] makes you want to toss your hat in the air on the same plays." Walsh pointed out how manager Gibson had been criticized in 1932 for not pulling Vaughan out of the lineup when he ran into a rough patch late in the season. "Gibby had a reason. He wanted Vaughan to gain confidence in himself. He has done that very thing for he now goes about the business of playing shortstop with more sureness than he ever has shown in the big league."[64]

Vaughan gave the veteran Thevenow—now playing second base—credit for his standout defense in mid-season. As for his work at the plate, Vaughan did not offer much of an explanation, as he told Al Abrams of the *Post-Gazette*: "You either hit them safe or you don't. Luck has a lot to do with it. I can hit 20 balls right on the nose and think they're going for base hits only to see someone step in front of them. Then again, I'll probably plunk one over somebody's dome and I've got a hit when I least expect it. That's the way it goes in this game."[65] Vaughan said left-hander Bill Clark of the Giants gave him more trouble than any other pitcher, but also noted that left-handers didn't give him any more trouble than right-handers when he was going well. "When I'm hitting, I hit them all, and when I'm not, they're all tough."[66]

One of the season's most memorable series came the first few days of August when the Pirates—still in the thick of the NL pennant race—hosted St. Louis at Forbes Field. On two successive days, the teams wound up brawling, and Vaughan was at the center of one of them. The first game's combatants were Pittsburgh pitcher Steve Swetonic and St. Louis outfielder "Watty" Watkins, who exchanged blows after they exchanged words. In the second of those games, which the Pirates ultimately lost 4–3, in 12 innings, Vaughan collided with Cardinals pitcher Bill Walker, who was covering first, and the two ended up swinging at one another. Vaughan said after the game that he harbored no ill feelings toward Walker or the Cardinals. "Walker and I just reached first base about the same time, collided, and when I put out my arms to prevent falling we clinched. After wrestling a moment, he made a swing at me and I came right back. It was all over quickly and is just one of those things which happen in a heated moment."[67] Gibson was not pleased afterward that Walker threw the first blow. "What else could the kid [Vaughan] do when Walker hit him?" Gibson asked. "We won't play rowdy baseball, but we also won't stand for the kind of stuff they pulled on us yesterday without swinging back."[68] Frankie Frisch, the Cardinals' 34-year-old skipper, not surprisingly blamed Vaughan, saying that Walker was only trying to get away from Vaughan to make a play on Paul Waner at the plate. "Vaughan was wrong," Frisch said. "He had already been called out and when he grabbed Walker, the umpires should have called both runners out because of interference."[69] Still, Frisch insisted there was no bad blood between the two teams, a sentiment that Walker echoed: "I have no bone to pick with Vaughan. I want to see him get along. He merely grabbed me after he was called out in order to prevent a play at the plate. I guess I would have done the same thing for my club. Anyway, I wrestled to get loose, and it got a bit rough. He was already out of the play when he grasped me, for I had taken one step over the bag. I think it was interference. But as far as being angry at Vaughan, there's nothing to it. There is no cause for a big rumpus in the papers."[70]

While Vaughan's play was praised by many, not all were enamored with the young shortstop, particularly when it came to his defensive play. In the final weeks of the season, Havey J. Boyle of the *Post-Gazette* wrote that Vaughan's hitting produced a complacency about his shaky fielding that was detrimental to the best interests of the team. Added Boyle:

> What he needed was a little of the failings at the plate from which Blondy Ryan suffered. Blondy was such a terrible hitter that he knew he had to be extra good, and an extra hustler, in the field to make up for his weakness at the plate. On the other hand, young Arky was such a dandy hitter that he couldn't take his fielding lapses with any great seriousness. He was not careless, but he was not as ambitious or as determined to improve in the field as he would have been with a lesser batting mark. Perhaps, without knowing it, Arky slid into the mental state where it was a pretty good day for

him if he got three out of four, but if the Pirates lost, 5 to 1. How this can be corrected is something the doctors of the team will have to take up at one of their clinics.[71]

1934

At home in Fullerton for the winter, the Vaughans rented a small house, and Arky would occasionally get together with his boyhood friends. At one point, Vaughan and Jack Hatfield made plans to visit one of their old fishing haunts—Punta Banda, on Mexico's Baja Peninsula. The two drove their car to their usual camping spot along the beach, but this time the sand gave way, and their only choice was to try to dig the car out of the sink hole. It took the pair two days and by the time they were finished, the hole was as big as a good-sized bedroom. They managed to free the car but were too exhausted to do any fishing, so they headed home with no fish and a tale of woe to share. According to Arky's daughter, Patricia, when the group went back to Punta Banda, the room-sized hole was still there on the beach.[72]

Back in Pittsburgh, fans were looking forward to the 1934 season. Word got out that the National League would put a livelier ball into play—a prospect that Pirates skipper Gibson did not mind. Gibson said he had six players who would benefit from the new ball, including Vaughan. In Chicago, Cubs pitcher Guy Bush agreed that Vaughan and a dozen or so other sluggers would likely be happy with the new ball. But he said he was looking forward to throwing it, noting that the lower seams might result in less of a break but they should help hard throwers like him. "The pitchers who rely on slow breaking curves probably will be chased right out of the park," he said.[73]

As players prepared to embark for Paso Robles, contract signings were reported for all but two team members—Vaughan and pitcher Bill Swift. The *Santa Ana Register* reported on March 2 that Vaughan had returned his contract unsigned four times "and is one of the season's most determined holdouts." The story claimed the Pirates had offered him a contract that was less than what he made in 1933 and that Vaughan threatened to remain at home in Fullerton before he accepted a pay cut.[74] On March 8, though—a day before his 22nd birthday—Vaughan "catapulted from the ranks of the holdouts" and signed a new contract, then immediately put on a uniform and joined his teammates for the morning workout. Contract details were not available, but Vaughan "announced himself as highly satisfied," Walsh reported.[75] The *Santa Ana Register*, meanwhile, reported on March 13 that Vaughan's contract dispute wasn't over his actual salary, but about bonus checks amounting to $2,500, which had been promised to Vaughan if he hit higher than .300. It was also reported that Vaughan's annual deal called for a salary of $8,000.[76]

The new livelier ball was a topic of some discussion in spring training, as players were asked what they thought of it. From a defensive standpoint, several players said the ball carried much better than the previous one. "That ball certainly skips through the infield," Vaughan said. Outfielder Paul Waner noted that he was fooled on several balls hit during a spring training game. "Some drives, when they left the bat, looked like easy outfield catches, but the ball sailed farther than I expected," he said.[77] At the plate, Vaughan found the new sphere to his liking, as he slammed five home runs in a five-game stretch at one point and finished the spring with a .366 batting average to go with nine home runs and 26 RBIs. He continued his torrid hitting into the regular season and just about the entire year, except for the month of July when he batted just .252—one reason why the Pirates stumbled to an 11–19 mark that month under new player-manager Pie Traynor, who was hired to replace Gibson as skipper on June 19. At that point, the Pirates—picked by some to challenge for the pennant—were 27–24 and seven and a half games in back of first-place New York. The managerial change didn't help—and in fact, the club's record got worse under Traynor—47–52 compared to Gibson's 27–24. The overall mark of 74–76 put the Pirates in fifth place, 19½ games behind the Frankie Frisch–led St. Louis Cardinals, who went 95–58 and edged out the previous year's pennant winners, the Giants, by two games.

Individually, Vaughan continued to rank among the top batsmen in the National League during the 1934 season. He led the league in on-base percentage and walks, tied for fourth in batting average (.333), was fourth in runs scored (115) and OPS (.942), fifth in RBIs (94) and slugging percentage (.511), seventh in hits at 186 and ninth in home runs with 12. Overall, his WAR rating of 6.6 put him fourth in the league. On the defensive side, he started particularly well, committing just six errors in his first 40 games. Some attributed it to a new glove that he acquired during spring training at the behest of Traynor, who had seen his glove and couldn't understand how he ever fielded a ball with it: "How many balls do you see get away from him now when he gets his hands on them? Very few, in fact, you can't recall three or four to be exact. The answer is that glove. ... Last season, ground balls were hitting Vaughan's gloved-hand and bounding into the outfield. That's why he made a lot of errors. He couldn't hold the ball once he got his hands on it."[78]

Vaughan did end up with 41 errors, but that was five fewer than each of his first two seasons.

He also found the spotlight on several occasions, although not necessarily to his liking every time. In a game in late May at Philadelphia's Baker Bowl, Vaughan was attempting to turn a double play when the Phillies' Dick Bartell—like Vaughan, a shortstop—came barreling into second in an attempt to disrupt things. Vaughan, who early in his career made every throw from an overhand motion, was learning to throw from different angles depending on the occasion, and this time his sidearm throw to first base struck Bartell in the

Arky Vaughan displays the glove that he used to play shortstop during his rookie season with Pittsburgh in 1932. Vaughan used the old mitt for his first two seasons. Finally, at the behest of his manager, Pie Traynor, Vaughan employed a new mitt during the 1934 season. Traynor maintained the new leather made the offensive-centric Vaughan a more reliable fielder (courtesy National Baseball Hall of Fame Library, Cooperstown, New York).

head, knocking him flat and leaving him motionless on the field. Bartell was removed from the game. Vaughan, meanwhile, went four for five with a double and a home run to raise his batting average to a league-leading .381. Not much was said after the game about the Bartell-Vaughan play, but three days later, Bartell told reporters that he thought Vaughan hit him on purpose and that the Pirates had taunted him earlier in the game. "They wanted to get me out of there and they got their man," Bartell was quoted as saying in an article written by Chet Smith. Vaughan, meanwhile refuted Bartell's claim; he was quoted as calling it "unqualifiedly and atrociously false." Gibson said Bartell always went to great lengths to try to break up a double play "and Vaughan told me Dick ran directly into the line of throw when it was too late for him to hold up."[79] A month or so later, when the Phillies visited Forbes Field, the dispute flared up again, as there were reports that Bartell and Vaughan had words—and even shook fists at one another—before a Sunday game, but nothing further developed. Smith asked several players in the dugout, "What did Bartell say to Vaughan Sunday?" For a while, no one spoke up, but then reserve catcher Art Veltman said he thought it would be "extremely unhealthy" for Bartell to pick a fight with Vaughan. "Those quiet babies are always tough when someone touches them off," Veltman said.[80]

Vaughan's exploits on the field had caught the attention of the national media, as the Baseball Writers Association of America, in a special ballot that was tied to the upcoming All-Star Game, voted Vaughan as the National League's top shortstop, outpointing backup Travis Jackson of the Giants, 119 to 88. Charles J. "Chilly" Doyle, a writer for the *Pittsburgh Sun-Telegraph*, said that the vote was a good indication that Vaughan was now considered the best shortstop in the league. Doyle pointed to Vaughan's plate prowess as well as his ability to run the bases as the high points of his game.[81] Two other Pirates were selected by the writers as well—Traynor at third base and Paul Waner in the outfield. Vaughan, who had received plenty of writers' votes the previous year but was not named to the inaugural NL All-Star roster, was officially named on July 3 when league manager Bill Terry announced his squad. Vaughan started the game and went zero for two while playing solid defense.

Vaughan had difficulty getting untracked after the All-Star Game, as he batted just .256 for the rest of July and fell out of the league lead in hitting. He picked it up in August, hitting .342 for the month, and turned it up a notch in September with a .354 mark, but the Pirates never made a serious run at the flag that year. Vaughan finished at .333, which reminded the *Post-Gazette*'s Al Abrams of a remark that the young infielder had made at one point that summer. Several players were discussing the topic of batting averages, and specifically what would be considered a mark each player could live with. "I'll take 'one for three' [one out of every three times at bat] for a whole season any day," Vaughan said.[82]

This remark would resurface the following season, which would prove to be the high mark—at least individually—in Vaughan's illustrious career.

◆◆ 3 ◆◆

Hard Times
in Pittsburgh

Vaughan's ascendance to Major League Baseball's elite coincided with the deepening of the nation's worst economic disaster, the Great Depression. Sparked by a stock market crash in October 1929, America's financial fabric was stretched thin until it reached the breaking point for thousands of families in Pittsburgh and millions throughout the nation. Makeshift Depression villages sprang up in Pittsburgh, including one between Penn and Liberty avenues from 17th Street to nearly 11th Street that housed scores of displaced residents. In a six-year stretch that ended in 1933, industrial production fell by more than 50 percent and 270,000 manufacturing jobs were lost in Pennsylvania alone, the third biggest job loss in the United States. Bituminous coal production dropped from 144 million to 75 million tons, and pig iron production fell 86 percent. The total cash receipts of state farmers plummeted 46 percent to $175 million. The number of families seeking relief in Pennsylvania had risen to 324,000—the largest figure in the nation.[1]

Caroline Fellinger doesn't need history books to recall the impact the Depression had on her family. "I remember because I was starving," she recalled. Fellinger's father had worked at a Jones & Laughlin steel mill in Ambridge—about 20 miles northwest of Pittsburgh—but when the Depression worsened, he and thousands like him lost his job. "We didn't have any food," Fellinger said. "There was no welfare—you had to make do with however you could. You had to work on your own." Born in 1924, Fellinger remembers her family losing its home and moving in with her grandmother. A little while later, her family moved again. "I was too young to remember why we had to move out, but we did," she said. Her father began heading down to the Strip District, where he would help pack and unpack boxes that came in on railroad cars. "Cans of food would come in with the labels missing or they would be dented, and they'd throw them out. People were allowed to pick the cans up and bring them home. He had a burlap sack and he would fill that sack with canned goods and then he would walk home." People worked however they could—they didn't sit around and wait for help. Once when Fellinger was about six years old, she and her sisters found a rail car full of bananas on some nearby tracks—and the door was open. Her sister Josie crawled inside and pulled out a big stock of bananas, and the girls took off running. "The railroad cop caught up with me because I couldn't run as fast as they could," Fellinger recalled. "I was crying. What could he do to me? Nothing. My sisters hid there until he let me go and we took the bananas home. We got beat, but at least we had something to eat."[2]

After a while, Fellinger's family moved into its own apartment, and her father got a job working at Dick's Meat Market in the Strip District. "They didn't pay him in money—they paid him in chickens," she said. "We had chicken for breakfast, lunch and dinner." Fellinger's father would scour the produce yards in the Strip after work and bring home what he could. "People would throw away half-rotten tomatoes and carrots and my mother would cut away the rotten parts and make vegetable soup or whatever she could make." She would also make use of the label-less canned goods that Fellinger's father would bring home, although they didn't know what was in the cans until they were opened. "Sometimes you'd go through five or six cans before she'd find tomatoes or corn or whatever she was looking for. But you'd still eat whatever was opened. If it was peaches, you ate the whole can of peaches." Sometimes during the day, Fellinger would walk to St. Augustin's School on 37th Street in the summer and get a bowl of vegetable soup and a slice of apple butter bread. "Sometimes," Fellinger said, "that's all you had all day."

At one point, Fellinger contracted diphtheria and was treated by a doctor whose office was next door to her family's apartment. "He was nice enough to take me into his house," Fellinger said. "We were so undernourished, he sent my sister and me to a camp—Camp Carondawanna, which was on a farm. My first meal, I thought I had died and gone to heaven. Mashed potatoes, sliced tomatoes, corn on the cob and a slice of butter bread. I thought that was the most wonderful meal I ever had. Occasionally today I will make that meal for myself."[3]

Back home, Fellinger's mother found a job in a cigar factory in the Strip District, walking from their apartment on 37th Street and Penn Avenue. Her two older sisters left school after the eighth grade to help support the family, but Caroline and her younger sister were able to finish high school. Still, things didn't improve until the late 1930s. Franklin D. Roosevelt, who succeeded Herbert Hoover as president after winning the 1932 election, enacted policies that helped put some people back to work, and with war looming abroad, the nation's arms factories came to life. Still, unemployment figures were frighteningly high. According to the U.S. Bureau of the Census' Historical Statistics of the United States, Colonial Times to 1957, nearly one in four people, or roughly 12.8 million, were without a job in 1933. That proved to be the high point—or the low point, depending on your vantage point—in terms of unemployment. With each succeeding year, the number dipped a bit, falling to 21.6 percent in 1934, 20 percent in 1935, 16.8 percent in 1936 and 14.2 percent in 1937. The nation saw a spike in unemployment again in 1938 as a result of a recession, jumping to 18.9 before falling to 17.1, 14.5 and 9.7 percent over the following three years.[4]

In Allegheny County, relief cases grew as the recession worsened. In September 1934, the *Pittsburgh Post-Gazette* reported that nearly 70,000 relief cases were on the books, with the number of new applications growing faster than ever that year. The number of people unemployed had increased to upward of 170,000 with between 80,000 and 90,000 employable people on relief roles. This did not include dependents—wives and children—of those out of work.[5] In November that year, the *Post-Gazette* reported that 274,933 people in Allegheny County were receiving on the average of $1.73 a week in state or federal grants—money that had to be used to pay for food, clothing, rent, fuel and medical care. A total of $30 million had been expended since January 1, 1933. Still, things were actually brighter than they were the year before in some respects, as private employment had improved 29 percent in Western Pennsylvania in the first 10 months of 1934 compared with the same time frame in 1933.[6]

By March 1935, the relief roles had grown even larger, with 305,000 people in 854,000 families—or about one-fourth of the population—receiving either direct relief or work-relief pay. The county Emergency Relief Fund had expended more than $37 million in its first two years of existence. By late 1937, the relief role numbers had decreased to 200,000—down from the peak period of February 1935, when 326,000 people were being supported by direct and work relief. But the 1937–38 recession triggered a bump in aid in the Pittsburgh area and the state as a whole. Statewide, more than 173,000 relief cases—affecting more than 550,000 people—were on the books in February 1938, compared with 142,891 cases, or 431,700 dependent individuals, just two months earlier. By October 1938 more than 100,000 Allegheny County households—and 320,000 people—were on relief of some sort. That amounted to about 23 percent of the total population and a new all-time high.[7]

While the unemployed received some assistance, Fellinger's family did not because of her father's job at the meat market. "My dad kept bringing home those chickens and my mom would do the best she could," she said. Occasionally, she would bring one of the chickens her dad brought home over to her friend's house, and would trade it for a can of what she called "welfare beef"—two-pound cans of corned beef. "It was wonderful," she said.

Although she realized times were difficult, "everybody was poor, so you didn't realize you were poor. Everyone was in the same boat, so what was the use talking about it?" Still, some memories stand out. "I remember I was about 5 or 6 years old, walking all the way into [downtown Pittsburgh] from 37th Street because I was going into first grade and I needed shoes. My shoes were very small—my toes were practically bent." She and her mother walked into the Frank & Seder Department Store building on Smithfield Street and headed for the shoe department. "I took off my old shoes, she cut the string on the new shoes and we ran out of the store. No one was around—she made sure. I threw my old shoes under the table that the new shoes were on."[8]

As Fellinger got older, she started walking the streets in search of empty cigarette packs, which she would take apart and scavenge the aluminum foil. She would roll those foil sheets into a ball and then walk down to a junkyard on 24th Street. There, a man would weigh the ball and give her a dime, or sometimes 15 cents, depending on how heavy the ball was—how much aluminum foil she had. "Then I'd go across the street to Wards Baking Company, give the lady a nickel and she'd fill a bag with stale doughnuts, cakes and breads," Fellinger said. "We were so happy—I'd bring it home and we were all thrilled. It was like Christmas—a bag of stale doughnuts, bread and cake." All of the Fellingers grew to be resourceful. Caroline, who made her own clothes all the way through high school, once turned an old sheet into a tennis dress. Her sister resorted to something similar when she got invited to a formal dinner—and the family could not afford to buy her a gown. "So she took the lace curtain off the living room window, and we sewed a dress for her just for that night. She came home, we took it apart and we hung the curtain back up. Her boyfriend used to ask, 'When are you going to wear that dress again?' You had to be ingenious to live in those days."[9]

Fellinger eventually finished high school, got married at age 18, earned her bachelor's degree in industrial engineering at night at what was then Carnegie Tech, and had a 29-year career at H.J. Heinz, eventually rising to become general manager of trade relations. It was a position that offered her travel to the nation's biggest cities while staying in some of the most lavish hotels around. "I'd walk into the Ritz Carlton in Chicago and they'd say, 'Hello, Mrs. Fellinger, how are you?' Everybody knew me. In the afternoon, I'd take a shower to get ready for a party that night, and there would be champagne, strawberries and cheese in my room." It was quite the contrast to running away from the railroad police with stolen bananas. "After you grow up, you think of the good times," she said. "You sort of close your mind to the bad times you had and the hunger that you had. It just goes away."[10]

The late Hal Demich was eight years old when the stock market crashed in October 1929. He grew up in Sagimore, a small mining town about 60 miles northeast of Pittsburgh. He remembered using baseball to help get through some difficult times—and he particularly took a shine to Arky Vaughan. "He was one of my heroes—and a wonderful ballplayer," said Demich, who passed in March 2019. He recalled his first trip to Pittsburgh's Forbes Field to see his Pirates. It came during the 1936 season, and the Pirates beat the Cubs, 4–2. In that game, Paul Waner went four for four with three line drives—one to each field, as he recalled: "On the fourth trip up he laid a bunt down the third base line that Stan Hack couldn't handle. I was all eyes. I just thought that was wonderful to see. Lloyd Waner caught the last out—a line drive into right center. He raced over, grabbed the ball on the fly and kept running into the locker room. That was my first experience in Forbes Field."[11]

Sagimore had its own baseball heritage, having produced several big leaguers, including Mike Goliat of the famed 1950 Philadelphia Phillies "Whiz Kids" club. And every couple of years, the mighty Homestead Grays of the Negro Leagues would stop in town during their barnstorming tours when Demich was a youngster. But he never got to see them—his mother wouldn't let him go. As he recalled: "She said it would be a problem. I would cry and make a big fuss, but she didn't care—she wasn't impressed. Could you imagine seeing all those great Grays players—Satchell Paige, Josh Gibson? One of the greatest sins baseball ever committed was not letting the black man play baseball."[12]

Demich eventually left Sagimore to attend college in 1940 but after the Japanese bombed Pearl Harbor in December 1941, his days as a civilian were numbered. By the following June he was drafted, and he spent the rest of the war overseas. He saw service in Italy and in four years, he never got so much as a scratch. "It seemed to me the good Lord was always watching over me," he said. After the war, Demich earned his degree from Penn State and spent his adult life in education. He never lost his love for baseball, a love that he passed down to his children and grandchildren, many who have played the game. "I remember so many wonderful moments," he said. "When you're a kid and you idolize these guys as players, and then you get to see them in the flesh, it's just so wonderful. They gave me memories I've never lost."[13]

Pittsburgh's corps of the unemployed made national headlines in early 1932 when the Reverend James R. Cox, a Catholic priest and the pastor of Old St. Patrick's Church, led a jobless army of more than 1,000 automobiles and trucks to Washington, D.C., to seek relief from the federal government. On January 5, more than 6,000 people left Pittsburgh, and thousands more were added to the ranks as the caravan made its way through Johnstown and the state capital in Harrisburg. There, the group was fed—and heard—by Pennsylvania Governor Gifford Pinchot before it moved on to its ultimate destination. On January 7, the group—which by that point numbered some 15,000—made it to Washington, where Cox addressed a group from the steps of the Capitol building, demanding work for all. In a reception room at the White House, President Herbert Hoover met with Cox and told him he believed the Depression was nearly over.[14]

The Pittsburgh contingent returned home on January 8, crossing into town shortly after noon and reaching Old St. Patrick's Church, where the marchers received a hearty welcome. "Boys and girls in patched, ragged clothing clung to the trucks and autos while the throng surged forward for a glimpse of the men who had marched almost constantly for three days and nights on their way to and from the Capitol to present a job relief petition to President Hoover and Congress."[15]

Baseball was hardly immune to the difficulties brought on by the Great Depression. Major League players had their salaries cut on the average of 25 percent during the first part of the Depression. The slight pickup in the economy that started in 1934 enabled some salaries to go up, but they never fully recovered until after World War II. Still, in comparison to the average U.S. worker, the big-league ballplayer was fortunate, as a player earning $3,000 in 1932 was still bringing home twice the pay as your average industrial worker who was fortunate enough to have a job. Babe Ruth—baseball's biggest star at the time—was among those who had to get used to a completely different salary structure, as he had seen his annual contract go from $80,000 in 1931 to $52,000 in 1933—the same salary he earned each year from 1922 through 1926—and $35,000 in 1934. Lou Gehrig, Ruth's longtime Yankees teammate, was the game's highest-paid player in 1935 at just $31,000. Team salaries fluctuated throughout the Depression years. In Pittsburgh, the total team payroll including players, coaches and managers, came in at $136,864 in 1929, increased to $220,776 by 1933 but then dropped to $173,383 for the 1939 season.

As a whole, the industry saw a reduction in 32 jobs for the start of the 1932 season, as rosters had been trimmed from 25 to 23. A proposal to slice that number to 20 for the 1933 season did not gain approval from club owners.[16]

The cuts even went beyond the active player roster. In early 1932, the St. Louis Cardinals announced that assistant trainer Kirby Samuels was let go. Dr. Harrison J. Weaver, the team's trainer, would have to take care of the job on his own for the defending world champions. In 1933, a half-dozen or so clubs eliminated one coach as a cost-cutting move. Still, supporters of the great American pastime were doing what they could to boost morale. *The Sporting News*, in its December 31, 1931, edition, acknowledged the existence of the Depression but said:

> [T]here will be no depression in 1932 in home runs. There will be no depression in expert pitching as Lefty Grove strikes out the third man in the last half of the ninth inning with three runners on the bases. There will be no depression in marvelous catches in the outfield, as Tris Somebody skims over the turf, leaps into the air and grabs the ball with one hand when it seemed physically impossible that any one should touch it. There will be no depression in the stolen base that is taken away from the team in the field under the very eyes of the pitcher and the catcher.... Baseball is not a game of depression. It is a game of elevation. What floor, please?[17]

Still, there was no denying that times were tough. Only two teams, the Chicago Cubs and New York Yankees—the National and American League pennant winners respectively—made money in 1932. The Cubs saw their attendance dip by more than 500,000 from two years earlier, and the Cardinals, who had won the 1931 World Series, attracted only 20,000 or so more fans than did their minor-league club in Columbus, Ohio. Attendance overall dropped each year from 1930 through 1933 in both leagues, falling by 31 percent in the National League and 38 percent in the American League. The 1934 season saw a slight uptick in the NL and a fairly sizable jump—28 percent—in the AL, and from that point until 1940, the numbers continued to climb—although somewhat modestly—in the senior circuit. The American League saw a slight dip from 1934 to 1935 and then again from 1938 to 1939, but like the NL, attendance figures otherwise were on the increase.[18]

In Pittsburgh, attendance tended to fluctuate somewhat prior to the Depression, but for a five-year stretch in the mid–1920s, when the team was competitive on the field, it finished no worse than third in attendance in the eight-team National League. The Pirates suffered at the gate during the heart of the Depression, though, as did many teams. In 1930, the first year after the stock market collapse, Forbes Field ranked seventh among eight NL venues in attracting fans and in 1931, the Pirates finished dead last in attendance, sinking from 357,795 to 260,392—a decline of 27 percent. Throughout the decade of the '30s, the Pirates finished no better than fourth in the league in attendance, and that occurred only once, in 1937. Even when the Pirates nearly won a National League pennant in 1938—falling just short of the Cubs—the club finished fifth in terms of drawing patrons through the turnstiles. That likely was the result of a recession that took hold in mid–1937 and lasted throughout the following year—a setback that had wiped out many of the gains of the previous few years.[19]

Two staples of today's game—night baseball and radio broadcasts—either came into existence or grew in popularity during the Depression, with the idea of appealing to a broader audience and ultimately increasing gate receipts. Baseball games had been broadcast on the radio since the early 1920s, but it finally took hold on a larger scale the following decade—despite the fact that some owners continued to have their doubts about its effectiveness. It wasn't until 1939 that all teams broadcast their games. Night baseball, meanwhile, had appeared in the minor leagues in the early 1930s, and it finally reached the big leagues on May 24, 1935, when the Cincinnati Reds hosted the Philadelphia Phillies at Crosley Field. Pittsburgh, meanwhile, would not play under the lights at Forbes Field until June 4, 1940.

The economic scene began to brighten during the second half of the 1930s, and that was reflected in baseball's attendance figures as well as the attendance figures in other sports. The 1936 Indianapolis 500, for example, attracted 168,000 people and the fourth game of the World Series that year drew nearly 67,000 people to watch the New York Giants and Yankees go head to head. A panel of experts, responding in an Associated Press query in December 1936, agreed that the larger crowds and gates in all sports was the top sports trend for that year, with the growth of night baseball coming in at No. 5 in the poll.[20] National League President Ford Frick, in an opinion piece that ran in several newspapers nationwide in January 1937, wrote that the fact that what transpired during the 1936 season, highlighted by the World Series attendance and record-setting per-game receipts, "means to me that not only baseball but the United States as a whole is entering into a year of renewed national health and prosperity."[21] Baseball attendance figures jumped by 10 percent for 1937 and those numbers increased again in 1938. The Depression was far from over, as the recession of 1937–38 proved, and serious challenges loomed in the form of wartime baseball. But the sport had survived its darkest economic decade and gave millions of fans something to take their minds off the grim realities they faced on a daily basis.

◆◆ 4 ◆◆

Hittin' Up a Storm

With the nation still in the throes of the Great Depression, Roosevelt launched a second "New Deal," and in the spring of 1935 he created an entity known as the Works Progress Administration (WPA), whose goal was to put the unemployed to work. The WPA completed dozens of public works projects including parks, bridges and public buildings such as post offices. Later in the year, Roosevelt would sign the Social Security Act, which guaranteed retirees a pension and also provided a safety net for the disabled and dependent children.

Vaughan was among the lucky ones, as his position with the Pirates guaranteed him a fairly comfortable income, even just a few years into his career. After playing his first season under a contract that paid him $2,500, Vaughan was earning an estimated $7,500 by his third season in the big leagues—more than fair compensation during the depths of the Depression. After the 1934 season ended, he and his family returned to Fullerton for the winter, where they purchased their first real home—a Spanish-style split level model set in the foothills outside of town. The white stucco house with a red-tiled roof featured a spacious den that was off-limits to children. Vaughan made heavy use of the room, which featured some photographs as well as hunting and fishing memorabilia, as a place to escape, as he would read there or listen to music—two pastimes that seemed to relax and renew him, his daughter Patricia Vaughan Johnson believed. Vaughan had a great appreciation for music, and counted Bing Crosby—who would later become a part-owner of the Pirates—as one of his favorites. Patricia remembered her father as being quiet by nature and even moody at times, and on occasion would go for hours without speaking. She remembered one time after her father got into the ranching business that he asked her to accompany him on a trip to take some cattle out to the Eel River in Northern California. "We got up way before daylight, packed a lunch, and left. I don't think he spoke to me the whole day. I remember just riding along real quiet." On another occasion, Vaughan invited Patricia to go hunting with him, but again, he hardly said a word. "So why did he let me go and hang around? I would just like to know that. Did he just not know how to talk to kids or what?" He gave the same silent treatment later to Patricia's husband, Kenny, when the latter would accompany Vaughan on trips to San Francisco's Seals Stadium when he was playing his final professional season in the Pacific Coast League in 1949. Kenny would ride along in silence unless he could think of something to ask Vaughan. "I don't know why he scared the hell out of Kenny so bad, but it seemed like he did it on purpose," Patricia said.[1] Whatever the reason, Vaughan enjoyed his privacy, and did not particularly relish the public notice that was coming his way. He felt some stress from this growing fame. He sought refuge on the golf course, playing a round nearly every day during the off-season.

He would get even more attention in the 1935 season; in fact, the attention started coming well before the season started. For the first time since his rookie year, when word got out about teams wanting to purchase his contract for somewhere in the neighborhood of $50,000, Vaughan's name began being mentioned in the annual hot-stove trade rumors. *Post-Gazette* reporter Edward F. Balinger, in a story that ran on January 12, mentioned an Associated Press dispatch from St. Louis that said Cardinals team exec Branch Rickey had conferred with Pirates manager Pie Traynor and was willing to swap one of his catchers for either Vaughan or Paul Waner. But Pirates President Bill Benswanger quickly shot down that idea, saying that he hadn't spoken with Traynor in a week or so. "One thing I will say, however, and that is we will not trade either Arky Vaughan or Paul Waner."[2] Vaughan definitely would not be swapped or sold, and Balinger pointed to Vaughan's improvement in the field as one of the reasons why Vaughan wasn't going anywhere. Balinger noted that while Vaughan committed 41 errors, he also handled 850 chances and pointed out that two shortstops with fewer miscues—Bill Urbanski of Boston, who had 31 errors, and Leo Durocher of the World Champion Cardinals, who had 33, took care of 786 and 760 chances, respectively. Balinger also reported that the Giants' Travis Jackson, who joined Vaughan on the NL All-Star team the previous season, committed 43 errors in 784 chances. "The Pirate star follows the footsteps of his distinguished predecessor, John Honus Wagner, by going after everything," Balinger concluded. "No player can do that without making foozles."[3] Even some of the fans were speaking out in favor of Vaughan, despite his error numbers. In a letter to the *Pittsburgh Press* sports editor, a writer identified as "The Dopester" wrote: "He tries for every ball that is anywhere near the position, and at the same time is a heavy hitter, and may at any time place one up in the right field stands. When looking at the [fielding percentages], one notices that he is well down in the list, but this is only because he attempts to get balls which other shortstops would let go by as base hits, instead of taking the chances of lowering their fielding averages."[4]

With the start of spring training drawing near, talk of Vaughan's contract status heated up, as he was one of two players who hadn't signed their annual deals as of mid–February. The *Santa Ana Register* reported earlier in the winter that the Pirates sought to slash Vaughan's salary, but that the budding star returned his contract unsigned—just as he did the previous winter.[5] Details were scarce, however; the *Register*'s Willie Q. Pryor said Vaughan revealed next to nothing about his baseball business—even to family members. However, he came to terms in the final days of February, driving to the Pirates' new spring training home in San Bernardino to complete his deal after about 15 minutes of

A youthful Arky Vaughan, at age 20, snares a throw during pregame practice at Forbes Field in 1932 (courtesy National Baseball Hall of Fame Library, Cooperstown, New York).

discussions. He then promptly headed back to Fullerton for one more week of rest and relaxation before reporting to camp for good.

Elsewhere, players were rounding into shape in other camps across the league. In Miami Beach, New York Giants shortstop Dick Bartell, who had a couple of run-ins with Vaughan the previous season, announced that he was seeking to clean the slate with all of his combatants and would-be combatants. The *Press*' Chet Smith, in his "Village Smithy" column, noted that Vaughan was never mad at Bartell or anyone else, and that when Bartell came to Pittsburgh, any thoughts of an altercation came to an end when "someone had slipped Dickie the information that Arky spent his spare time straightening bent pokers and horseshoes and should not be trifled with."[6]

Nothing unusual transpired during the Bucs' stay at San Bernardino. Vaughan's bat was robust, as usual, and he concluded exhibition play with a three-hit performance in the Pirates' win over Chattanooga on April 14. Traynor saluted Vaughan for the play of the spring when Arky scored all the way from second base on Gus Suhr's bunt in that final spring training game. Traynor also said he hoped to get a bit more from Vaughan in the RBI department, despite the fact that Vaughan had driven in 94 runs the previous season. Traynor told the *Press'* Volney Walsh that he wanted to see Vaughan swing more frequently at "pay balls"—pitches thrown when Vaughan was ahead in the count. Vaughan took too many of those pitches to suit Traynor, Walsh reported.[7]

Vaughan got off to a blistering start, producing 23 hits in his first 53 at-bats for a whopping .434 batting average through the end of April. He also collected 11 walks for an on-base percentage of .531, and three of his 23 hits left the park. He slowed a bit in May, but still compiled a .385 mark for that month, leaving him at .404 entering the month of June. In the field, he continued to have his struggles, which mirrored the Pirates' defensive woes as a team. Through 20 games, the club had committed 36 errors—most in the National League—and Vaughan had 11 of them, including three in one game at Boston. Vaughan's difficulties prompted some to call for a move to third base. Smith wrote that as great a hitter as Vaughan was, he "has never appeared at home in the shortfield. Perhaps at third he would find a better niche. It certainly wouldn't harm his hitting and it might make him more valuable defensively."[8] Traynor, though, rejected that idea and said even if he would consider making such a move, it would have to take place during spring training—not in the middle of a season.

The highlight of the month of May came not from a Bucco player, but from one of the Pirate opponents. On May 25, the great George Herman "Babe" Ruth, playing for the Boston Braves, left his mark on Forbes Field when he crushed three home runs in an 11–7 Pirates win. He struck his first round-tripper off Red Lucas in the first inning, a long, towering fly ball to right that found a seat in the lower deck. His second home run came in the third inning off Guy Bush, described as a tremendous drive into the second deck in right-center field. Ruth saved his best for last, though, as he smashed a drive off Bush that cleared the right field roof—the first such ball hit in Forbes Field, which opened in 1909. Vaughan recalled the sight years later when he was playing for the San Francisco Seals of the Pacific Coast League. "I have never seen three home runs hit harder than the Babe hit them that day," he told *San Francisco Chronicle* writer Art Rosenbaum in the spring of 1949. "Especially that last one."[9]

Vaughan's season hit a snag on June 13 when he injured his left leg while sliding into first base in a game against Brooklyn. Traynor had hoped to have him back in the lineup in a day or two, but that wouldn't be the case. Vaughan ended up missing 14 games in all, and didn't return to the lineup until June 29 when Pittsburgh visited Chicago. When Vaughan left the lineup, the club was 31–21 and trailed first-place New York by four and a half games. When he rejoined the team, the Pirates were 38–28, still in second place but now seven and a half games behind.

Shortly after Vaughan returned from his injury, he penned an article for the *Pittsburgh Press* in which he discussed the art of playing shortstop. "A shortstop has to be able to do more things well than any other man on the ball field. He is the busiest fellow in the inner works," he wrote in the first paragraph of the story, which appeared on July 6. Vaughan talked about his good fortune in learning from the great Honus Wagner and noted how slowly hit balls had always given him so much trouble. "That was my most pronounced weakness when I came into the National League in 1932—not that I didn't have others, too," he wrote. He said he asked Wagner how to play those kinds of balls. Wagner responded that the only way to play it is to "run as fast as you can for the ball, pick it up and throw the batter out." Vaughan wrote that he believed he had overcome that old weakness. "There's only one chance to get the batter on those teasing, slow rollers," he said. "Race in, pick up the ball with your bare hand and let heave."[10]

When Vaughan returned from his injury, he went on a defensive streak that was among his best ever, going 20 straight games and handling 105 chances without an error. That streak came to an end on July 11. In the meantime, Vaughan made an appearance in his second All-Star Game, receiving 208 out of a possible 222 votes to nail down the starting shortstop job. He went one for three in the game, walking and doubling off Lefty Gomez in the fourth inning and scoring the NL's only run in a 4–1 loss that was witnessed by 69,812 fans at Cleveland Stadium. He played flawlessly in the field at short, with two putouts and two assists, including a throw home to nail Jimmy Foxx, who tried to score on Rollie Hemsley's hard-hit ball to Vaughan.[11]

By the time play resumed after the All-Star Game, Vaughan's average had dipped below the coveted .400 mark—one that no major league hitter had reached since Bill Terry hit .401 for the Giants in 1930. At that stage, Vaughan was hitting .391, but he got hot in the second half of July and pushed his average up to .401 by the end of the month. He continued to win over new fans, like 10-year-old Walter Bethem of Charleroi, who came to watch the Pirates play the Boston Braves on July 19. That day, Arky went two for five, with one of those hits being a two-run homer into the right field stands that young Bethem outwrestled a pack of other spectators to pocket. The *Pittsburgh Press'* "Sports Stew" column reported what happened after Bethem returned home: "He walked into the house, shirt torn, face dirty and had to tell his mother the truth. There were a couple of thousand other kids after the same ball, but young Walter snagged it. The older kids in the stands that afternoon tried to kid Walter and told him he'd have to return it because the boys got in free. But they'd have to tear his arm off to get that ball."[12] Years later, Bethem related that story to his son, Dennis, recounting his catch of the ball and the fight that ensued. "As I remember, there were adults involved in trying to get the ball—not just other kids," Dennis Bethem recalled. "He talked about it more than once; otherwise, I wouldn't have remembered it. I don't think he had any idea it was ever written up in the papers."[13]

As the calendar flipped to August, Vaughan continued his push for .400 and found himself either just above it or a few percentage points below it for the entire month. His flirtation with that mark certainly made him a target of much local press coverage. Walsh noted that with 55 games to play, "it begins to appear very possible indeed that he may conclude the season of more than .400."[14] Vaughan's success started rekindling stories of his discovery as a youth on the sandlots of Fullerton. One story, which ran in the *Milwaukee Journal* in July, noted that Lin Storti—a former member of the St. Louis Browns who lived in Long Beach, about 10 miles away from Fullerton—had taken note of Vaughan and suggested that the Browns send a scout out to look him over. But St. Louis management waited too long and by the time the club showed interest, Vaughan had already signed his deal with the Pirates. "I guess Vaughan got the best break in his young life when he missed the Browns," said Storti, referring to the team's lengthy history of underachieving. *Journal* reporter Sam Levy called Vaughan "a rare major league gem, possessing all the requisites of a top-notcher ... around his position there is no one, major leaguers claim, who can outthrow him. On the bases he is as fast as Mercury."[15]

Even other players around the league were weighing in on Vaughan's attributes. "The sweetest hitter in the league," Billy Herman told Al Abrams of the *Post-Gazette*. Said Bill Jurges: "Why that so-and-so just stands out in the field itching for the inning to be over so he can get up to that plate." Stan Hack said that Vaughan "loves to hit 'em and it's a pleasure to watch him even though it hurts sometimes." Pitcher Larry French wisecracked, "The secret of a pitcher's success in stopping Arky lies in the speed of his outfielders in chasing his drives!"[16] That same day, Vaughan helped sink the Cubs with a grand slam off Lonnie Warneke to help Pittsburgh to a 6–5 win over the visitors from Chicago. Dazzy Vance, pitching for Brooklyn in the final season of his long career, said he could see why Vaughan was flirting with .400. "He guards the plate like no other hitter we've had in the league since I joined it," said Vance, who appeared in his first major league game in 1915—with the Pirates—and went on the play 16 seasons. "He hits to all fields, left, right and center, with the same ease."[17]

Vaughan was asked by reporters to share his own hitting philosophy, and although he wasn't exactly talkative with the press, he did offer a few tidbits. "The main idea," he said, "is not to hit too far ahead of the ball and not to let it go by you." Vaughan told Harry Grayson of the Newspaper Enterprises Association that good hitters are born and that the art of hitting could not be taught—although "certain faults may be straightened out here and there."

Vaughan said he was not a guess hitter—in other words, he did not try to
guess which type of pitch the pitcher would throw—and he acknowledged
that he wasn't afraid to take a strike if the pitch wasn't to his liking. Vaughan
said his advice to young players was to come to the plate relaxed, not think too
much about their stance and to pick out a good pitch. He said he had no particular baseball idol as a youngster and never tried to mimic an older player.
In fact, Vaughan had never seen a major league game until he played in one
and maintained that his biggest thrill came that day when he drove in Adam
Comorosky in his first game as a starter against Ray Kolp of the Cincinnati
Reds. Vaughan also told Grayson that it was Johnny Hawkins, captain and
quarterback of the University of Southern California football team of 1924,
who tagged Vaughan "Arky" when Vaughan was a young boy in Fullerton.[18]

Vaughan noted that he had been a switch-hitter as a youngster but that
he became strictly a left-handed swinger at Wichita on the advice of Art
Griggs, who told him the extra step he'd gain from the left side of the plate
would come in handy in beating out a few infield hits. Vaughan was hardly a
slap hitter, though, as his first three seasons' slugging and OPS figures would
indicate. And in 1935, his power came to the forefront. On August 17, against
the Philadelphia Phillies, Vaughan smacked his 18th home run of the season,
tying the Pirates' franchise record set by fellow shortstop Glenn Wright in
1925 and tied in 1930 by infielder George Grantham. He had 39 games left to
establish the record on his own.

The national media certainly picked up on Vaughan's chase for .400 that
season, as stories appeared in various publications. Many of them picked up
on his disdain for notoriety. A publication known as Young America did a
feature on Vaughan in mid–July and noted that he didn't enjoy talking about
himself—and that he let his bat do all of his talking. The writer added:

> He's shy, doesn't like to be photographed, throws right-handed and bats left. Not
> the phenomenal shortstop Wagner was, Arky is, however, steadily improving as an
> infielder. Arky has a unique batting style that isn't duplicated by any other player. He
> plants himself firmly in the batter's box, rather far back, and stands with his legs wide
> apart. He doesn't stride into the ball like most hitters, but gets his balance and lever-
> age like a golfer by bending his right knee inward. The result is a smooth, easy, flat
> swing that spells death for any type of offering.[19]

Vaughan's batting style also caught the attention of Tommy Holmes, a
sportswriter for the *New York Herald Tribune*. Holmes wrote that Vaughan's
stance was all his own:

> Vaughan stands far back in the batter's box and as much directly behind the home
> plate as the law allows. In fact, opposing clubs frequently emit raucous squawks
> about the position of Arkie's left foot on the rear chalk mark and sometimes perhaps
> a bit behind it. His position so far back enables him to hit a curve after it breaks.
> His position behind the plate enables him to see the break of a curve better and

results in his swinging at remarkably few bad balls. You'd think with that stance that Vaughan would hit an inside pitch on the handle. But he doesn't. The stride of his right foot—away from the plate—takes care of that. On the other hand, Vaughan has the power in his 175-pound frame to pull even an outside pitch into right field. Most ball players just couldn't hit that way. They'd be meeting the ball on the handle and popping 'em up all afternoon. Just as other right-handed batters couldn't adapt Rogers Hornsby's style to their own hitting. Hornsby stood so far away from the plate that it didn't seem possible for him to hit an outside pitch. But he did and Vaughan can lay the business end of his bat against an inside pitch. That leaves him virtually without a weakness as Hornsby was a few years ago. Our Dodgers hope to beat the Pirates for the seventh straight time when they meet them in a single game at Ebbets Field this afternoon, but they have just about given up worrying about Vaughan.[20]

Some of the sporting press went to the ol' master—Wagner—to get his thoughts on his young protégé. Jack Cuddy, a United Press writer based in New York, said that some of the players referred to Wagner and Vaughan as "dad and the kid." Wagner told Cuddy that Vaughan was "a fellow with a closed mouth and an open mind" and added that Vaughan worked hard to improve his fielding. "After we got together in 1933, I told him all the short-stop tricks I knew, and it was great to see the way he picked them up. We've been talking baseball and eating baseball almost all the time since we started rooming together." Wagner said the hardest thing for Vaughan to master was getting the jump on the ball off the bat. Offensively, Wagner said, Vaughan didn't need much in the way of help. "I think he's the greatest natural hitter I ever seen," Wagner said. "And now he's doing so well at bat and in the field that in a couple more seasons he'll be the greatest shortstop that ever played baseball. He's faster now than I ever was—and a better hitter."[21]

Vaughan's high point in the season—at least in terms of his batting average—came on August 18, when he was at .407. The attention began to get ratcheted up as the season wound down. Grantland Rice, one of the nation's elite sporting journalists, checked in on Vaughan the first week of September, and Vaughan downplayed the .400 chase. "In the first place, I haven't finished the season over .400 yet," he told Rice. "There are still a flock of fast balls and fast curves coming my way before the show is over." Rice asked Vaughan's teammate, Paul Waner, about Vaughan, and Waner said Vaughan was "about the best hitter I ever saw, bar nobody. I mean by that that he has the best natural swing and hits the ball more solidly on a general average than anyone else now playing. Every batter is supposed to have some weak spot, but no pitcher has been able to find Arky's yet. High or low—in or out—it's all the same with him."[22] Vaughan said he did make one change that season that might have helped him become a better hitter—he changed his bat model, going with a smaller or thinner handle. This, he said, allowed him to use his fingers to better effect. "A thicker handle calls for more of a palm grip," Vaughan said. "When you use your fingers you get much better wrist action—and wrist action is a big detail in swinging any sort of club, from golf to baseball, polo or tennis. I found this change a big help from the start." Vaughan also talked about his batting stance, standing as far back in the batter's box as possible so he could time the break of a curve ball. And his open stance, which allowed him to face the pitcher, enabled him to "look things over in a better way." He noted that Waner stood with his feet more on an even line in the batter's box. Vaughan also said it's important to not "hit or swing too quickly—a common fault due largely to too much tension. Keeping as relaxed as possible is always a big help."[23]

Throughout the season, Vaughan had been a model of consistency, going hitless in just 25 games from April through August. Vaughan's manager, Pie Traynor, joked that Vaughan's .400 average somehow wasn't spectacular because of Vaughan's steady production: "Vaughan never has a big day at bat. Usually a .400 hitter comes up with four or five hits a game a couple of times a month. But Vaughan just gets his two a day, month after month. Sure I'm tickled to death that the boy is going as he is. But I do wish he could get that big day once in a while. Then, my friends and oh, my foes, he'd be a lovely sight."[24]

Traynor said that he had read some stories recently that indicated he had been giving Vaughan advice that helped him improve as a hitter, but that wasn't the case: "Neither I nor anybody else helped him. He just stuck to his natural style and is sticking to it. Doing pretty well for a twenty-three-year-old kid, too. I don't think anybody in the league will come close to him for the next five years. He is and will be the best there is. And if he ever learns to go after those big days…"[25]

A year earlier, Vaughan had been chatting with Honus Wagner and a few players before a game and talking about hitting—and specifically batting averages. Wagner told them his goal was to try to get two hits every day, but Vaughan said he'd be satisfied if he went one for three every game. That's when veteran Freddy Lindstrom piped up. "That's where you're wrong, Arky. A fellow who could hit as well as you should get as many base hits as possible, and even shoot for that .400 figure. I'm willing to bet you'll be able to make it some day."[26]

Vaughan finally established a new club record for home runs on August 30 when he picked out a pitch from "Fidgety" Phil Collins and lined it into the right-field stands. Walsh described it as a "typical Vaughan smash" and it helped the team win its ninth straight game in what would become a 10-game winning streak before it was snapped on September 1.[27]

Vaughan did not disappoint during the streak, as his average was at .399 when it started and .399 when it ended. However, he batted "only" .333 during a 12-game stretch that reached the end of the month, causing his average to drop from his high-water mark of .407 to .399 on the final day of the month. Some pitchers began to work around him; for example, in a game against the

New York Giants on September 9, the great Carl Hubbell walked Vaughan with a man at third and two outs in the first inning and then gave him a free pass with four straight balls in the eighth inning with two on and two out. "He didn't want to get the ball in a spot where Vaughan could click one," wrote Walsh, noting that the Pirates would need to find someone better to hit behind Vaughan the following season.[28]

Vaughan's final day above .400 came on September 10, when he finished the first game of a doubleheader against New York at .401. He went zero for four in the second game, and from that point on he batted just .229 to finish at .385 for the season. The *Pittsburgh Press* referred to his late-season slump as a "toboggan ride" but his final mark of .385 proved plenty good enough to win the batting title, as runner-up Joe Medwick wound up at .353.[29] Vaughan became the fourth Pirate to claim a batting crown, joining Wagner, Paul Waner and Clarence Beaumont. Vaughan was remarkably consistent with regard to home and road splits, as he batted .386 at Forbes Field and .384 on the road. The only team that gave him difficulty was the Giants, against whom he batted just .243 at Forbes Field and .250 at the Polo Grounds. Vaughan's .246 mark against the Giants was the lowest by far against any team. He hit better than .400 against three clubs—Boston (.450), Brooklyn (.434) and Cincinnati (.425) in 58 games combined. Vaughan dominated a number offensive categories, leading the NL in WAR at 9.2, on-base percentage at .491, OPS at 1.098, slugging percentage at .607, walks at 97 and runs created at 147. He drove in 99 runs, good for sixth in the league, scored 108 times (tied for eighth) and slugged 10 triples. He accomplished all this in 499 at-bats—nearly 200 fewer than the league-leader in that category and more than 100 fewer than the two players who finished tied for ninth in at-bats that year. Defensively, Vaughan finished ninth in the league in fielding among NL shortstops with a .950 mark, committing 35 errors—his best total yet in his big-league career. For Vaughan's efforts, a national committee of sportswriters named him the National League's Most Valuable Player as announced by *The Sporting News* on September 30, outpolling Cardinals pitcher Dizzy Dean by 10 points.[30] Hank Greenberg, Detroit's hard-hitting first baseman, won the American League voting. *The Sporting News* handled the MVP voting since the American and National leagues discontinued their official awards in 1929 and 1930, respectively. The Baseball Writers Association of American, meanwhile, awarded its National League MVP to Chicago Cubs catcher Gabby Hartnett, with Vaughan finishing third in the voting.

The local press never asked Vaughan if he felt disappointed to finish under the .400 mark after hovering around it or being over it for most of the season. But Vaughan's daughter Patricia later asked pitcher Mace Brown, one of Vaughan's closest friends on the Pirates, if Vaughan ever said anything about failing to hit .400 that season. Brown told her that her father said he wasn't at all disappointed, adding, "They would have just expected me to do it again next year."[31]

With the season completed, Vaughan headed back to California in a new car, taking teammate Earl Grace and New York Giants outfielder Hank Leiber with him. Folks in Vaughan's hometown of Fullerton planned to honor their hero with a banquet on October 8, at which time they would present him with a six-foot-long balsa wood bat made by Hillerich & Bradsby Company, in Louisville, Kentucky. The bat featured a replica of Arky's autograph and the inscription of "Leading Hitter Major Leagues 1935." The event, sponsored by the Fullerton 20–30 Club, would be held at the Fullerton Masonic Temple and limited to 200 seats—at 65 cents per seat. "Join in this big welcoming event marking the success of a 'Home-Town' Boy!" read a full-page advertisement in the *Fullerton Daily News Tribune* on October 7. "We are glad to number 'Arky' among outstanding Fullertonians."[32] Nearly 300 people attended the event, including the guest of honor and his wife Margaret, Vaughan's parents and his brothers and sisters. Afton Reinert of the 20–30 Club presented the large balsa wood bat to Vaughan and said that it "would give some idea of what Arky's bat looked like to opposing pitchers during the past season." Oscar Reichow, general manager of the Los Angeles Angels of the Pacific Coast League, told the gathering that people don't realize what it means to bat .385 in the National League. "Many players would give a year of their lives to lead the league in hitting. Few ever reach the .400 mark. It requires a great deal of skill and courage to finish a season with .385. Every time Arky stepped to the plate the opposing pitcher knew he was the leading hitter and that he had to put everything he had on the ball."[33] Reichow also pointed out that Vaughan, at just 23, was the youngest player in major league history to win a batting title. "Most of the players have reached 27 or 28 with years of experience before they attain such a record," Reichow said of Vaughan, whom he also described as "one of the greatest players of all time."[34]

Vaughan, who had plans to go on a hunting trip with boyhood friend Bob Williams as soon as the banquet was finished, was not thrilled with the idea of being honored at such a public event. In fact, he nearly skipped it. Years later, Williams told Patricia Vaughan Johnson that when Vaughan got to town and realized what was being planned, he contacted Williams and tried to talk him into leaving *before* the banquet. "I knew his dad, Bob, would never forgive me if I agreed, much less the rest of the town," Williams recalled. "So I finally talked Arky into waiting until after, but the minute it was over we were in the car and gone!"[35]

Vaughan spent the winter relaxing with his family in Fullerton, but did manage to sneak in a few hunting and fishing trips with his friends and family. In addition to hunting and fishing, Arky kept in shape for part of the off-season by playing plenty of golf with the local pros at the Hacienda

Country Club in La Habra. He shot a career-best 71 in early January. Art Roux, the club pro, said Vaughan could be a professional golfer if he put his mind to it.[36] Roux told the *Los Angeles Times* the same day that Vaughan "had what it takes, from swing to temperament. His best suit is driving. No less than four times today he was 300 yards off the tee." Roux said he'd never had anybody under his wing who possessed the ability to relax at all times and to conserve energy as Vaughan did. "Never ruffled, Vaughan works with the ease and perfection of a machine," the *Times* correspondent wrote. "Vaughan has the happy faculty of being able to concentrate on the situation at hand, never allowing his thoughts to wander back several holes or ahead."[37]

Back east, thoughts were already turning to the 1936 season and what the Pirates could do to retool after finishing the '35 campaign in fourth place at 86–67, 13½ games in back of the pennant-winning Cubs. Trade rumors were beginning to swirl, and just about everyone wanted Vaughan. Walsh declared that Vaughan wouldn't be traded "under any circumstances. And if he were to be placed on the market, what value would be placed on him? Right now Arky is a better shortstop than Joe Cronin, and the Red Sox put out a quarter-million for Joe."[38] In late October, *The Sporting News* did a large feature on Vaughan, recounting once again the story of how scouts Art Griggs and Bill Essick both had their eyes on Vaughan but that Griggs got to him first and inked him to a contract with the Pirates. Balinger, writing for *The Sporting News*, also talked about the Vaughan family's connection to Potter Valley, in Mendocino County, and how Vaughan spent summers there working on ranches and playing baseball when time permitted. Balinger described Vaughan as type of player any manager would want on his ball club. He added:

> He is polite at all times and is not given to any rough tactics, although he will not run away if somebody threatens to harm him. He has the respect of all the umpires, in spite of the fact that he does not hesitate to protest when he feels certain a decision has been called the wrong way, but he is not the type of athlete to lose his head and cause some official to order him out of a game. He is one of those youngsters who loves to play and wants to be first on the field for practice and last to exchange his uniform for street clothes.[39]

As October gave way to November, trade talk continued to simmer on the hot stove, and once again Pirate officials told local writers that Vaughan would not be traded. However, one Philadelphia scribe—Bill Dooly of the *Philadelphia Record*—suggested that Vaughan be moved to the outfield, a position change that had been put forth several times in previous years due to Vaughan's defensive difficulties at shortstop. Traynor, in town in November to meet with team officials Benswanger and Watters before the annual minor-league meetings later that month, said he thought there would be relatively little dealing going on that off-season, based on the unrealistic expectations that some general managers had in talking trade. "Everybody seemed to think the Pirates should be willing to give them Paul Waner and Arky Vaughan in exchange for some worn-out veteran or a couple of rookies who were not needed," Balinger wrote in the *Post-Gazette*.[40] The Pirates did figure to get younger, though, and the start of that movement occurred when veteran Tommy Thevenow, 32, whom Vaughan had supplanted from the shortstop position in 1932, was dealt in December. That opened the door to a potential infield of Harry Lavagetto or Bill Brubaker at third, Vaughan at short, Pep Young at second and Gus Suhr at first. Only Suhr would be older than 30 when the season started, while Vaughan would not turn 24 until early in spring training.

Some members of the national media spent the off-season speculating on Vaughan's future with regard to his place among baseball's upper crust. Grantland Rice acknowledged Vaughan's fabulous 1935 season but said he had a long way to go before comparisons with the great Ty Cobb had any merit. Rice's discussion wasn't so much a knock on Vaughan as it was an illustration of the kind of production Vaughan would need—and over an extended period of time—before he began challenging any of Cobb's records. Those marks included 4,191 career hits, 2,244 runs scored and a career batting average of .368 in 11,429 at-bats over 3,033 games. Rice noted that Vaughan would need at least 18 more seasons at a pace similar to the one he had set over his first four big-league campaigns to "even have a faded chance at any of Ty's figures." That would put Vaughan at age 41 in his 22nd season.[41]

As was his custom, Vaughan was not among the first Pirates players to sign his contract for the 1936 season. Club president Benswanger wouldn't call Vaughan a holdout in late January because he said no player could be placed in that category until March 2—the first day of spring training.[42] Balinger reported on the same day that the Pirates offered Vaughan a salary increase, but not enough to suit him, although he said it's doubtful that the difference between the two parties was all that great.[43]

In early February, Traynor, who was in Northern California receiving treatment for an arm injury that had sidelined him as a player for most of the 1935 season, headed to Southern California to try to sign Vaughan. Arky, meanwhile, when asked about his run at .400 the previous season, said he believed he would have hit the coveted mark had the "old" sacrifice fly rule been in effect. From the 1926 season through 1930, a more liberal sacrifice fly definition was on the books, one that spared hitters from an official at-bat any time a runner advanced after a putout on a fly ball—not just when a runner scored on a fly ball. That definition was narrowed to today's interpretation in time for the 1931 season.[44]

By mid–February, Vaughan remained a holdout; he was among an estimated 50 major-league players who had yet to submit a signed contract. Other holdouts included American League batting champion Buddy Myer and Tigers slugger Hank Greenberg. On February 12, Vaughan penned a story for the *Pittsburgh Post-Gazette* in which he recounted his biggest thrill in baseball—the grand slam he hit off Lonnie Warneke of the Cubs on August 1 of the previous year. Vaughan wrote: "A homer at any time is sweet music to a ball player. A homer with three men on base is sweeter. A homer with three men on base which turns a ball game is better still and a homer with three men on base which turns a ball game and made after the pitcher has dusted off the preceding batters is par for any course."[45]

Vaughan recounted how Warneke had hit Paul Waner and knocked down brother Lloyd Waner and another player before Vaughan stepped to the plate. "I got hold of one of Lonnie's fast ones and cracked it into the upper deck of the right field stands and it was a thrill to see Swift, Jensen and Paul Waner cashing in ahead of me because I had hit the jack pot," Vaughan wrote.[46]

By February 18, Vaughan was in the fold, confirming that his signed contract would be sent to the club office within a couple of days. Terms of the contract were not disclosed in any of the Pittsburgh papers at the time, but a month later the *Pittsburgh Press* reported his salary at $15,000—an increase of $5,000 over his 1935 pay grade.[47] Vaughan told the *Post-Gazette* that he was "well-satisfied" with the deal, which called for a salary that ran "well into the five-figure column." Vaughan said he never considered himself a holdout but did turn down two or three contract offers that the club had submitted earlier. As for the club's prospects for the 1936 season, Vaughan said he hated to see Earl Grace leave via trade, but added that the acquisition of Al Todd figured to be a big help to the club behind the plate "and might provide the spark that we have been lacking for a couple of seasons."[48] After training in San Bernardino the previous season, the club moved its spring training headquarters to San Antonio, Texas, but the change of scenery didn't seem to affect Vaughan, as the *Post-Gazette* reported on March 13 that Vaughan was "damaging fences in practice."[49] In addition to sharpening his batting eye, Vaughan used camp to become more familiar with his double-play partner, Young, at second base, as Traynor made turning more double plays a point of emphasis. The team turned just 94 in 1935—seven fewer than the last-place Boston Bees, who finished with an astoundingly poor 38–115 record and wound up 61½ games behind the pennant-winning Cubs.

Vaughan opened the season April 14 against Cincinnati with his customary two hits in five plate appearances, but then had just two hits in his next 24 at-bats and batted .232 for the month of April. The local press certainly picked up on the fact that Vaughan was uncharacteristically struggling. "Gus Suhr is more at ease than I have ever seen him," a fan told Chet Smith. "On the other hand, Arky Vaughan seems to me to be as tight as a drum every time he faces the pitcher." Vaughan was hitting .174 at the time, and Smith said he had no doubt that if you asked Vaughan if he had changed anything with regard to his approach to hitting, he would have said no. "One of these days Vaughan will discover that he is driving the ball with old-time venom," Smith wrote. "He will have loosened up without being conscious of it."[50] Havey J. Boyle of the *Post-Gazette* wrote the next day that box scores "do not always tell the complete story of a batter's work. Take Arky Vaughan. He has been hitting the ball right on the nose—and right into the hands of a fielder, when he has not been victimized by spectacular fielding. The combination which has worked against him will not continue."[51]

Although he was mired in the worst slump of his career, Vaughan did not let it affect his defense. He handled his first 65 chances of the season without an error before finally committing his first on April 30, the team's 12th game. In May, he went 17 straight games—88 chances—without a miscue. He continued to room on the road with Wagner, and many thought Wagner's influence was finally paying dividends in the field.

Vaughan had no explanation for his hitting difficulties, though, when asked about it by members of the local press corps. "Darned if I know," he told Balinger in mid–May. "I think I'm hitting the ball as sharply as ever. Last year I seemed to have magic in my hits. No one was around when I hit them through the infields. This year, why even the daisies seem to jump up and rob me of sure hits."[52] Traynor said Vaughan was connecting with the ball just as well as he had done during his 1935 batting championship season. He told Jack Cuddy of United Press: "The pitchers aren't fooling him at all. And he's getting plenty of power into his drives. But he isn't getting the base hits. Wherever that ball goes, seems like there's always someone to grab it. He just isn't getting the breaks. The way he's connecting, Arky ought to be a way over .300. This is the first time he ever hit under .300 in the majors."[53]

Vaughan was also puzzled, telling Cuddy: "I've figured it out from all sides and there's only one answer—luck. I'm using the same stance and the same model bat as last year, a modified Chuck Klein model that hefts about 37 ounces and is 35 inches long. And I'm trying to place my drives just the same as last season. But those balls just don't find the blind spots. Somebody always gloms onto them and I don't get the hits."[54]

Vaughan even admitted to resorting to good luck charms in his bid to shake his slump, saying that he took a little black cat luck charm to the ballpark just to see if something would happen. Vaughan said he wasn't superstitious, but when a player gets desperate, he'll try almost anything—even if he doesn't believe in what he's trying. "There's always that little glimmer of hope that maybe you're wrong about those charms and that maybe your luck will change," Vaughan said. "I guess that's the reason."[55]

Whether it was the black cat charm or some other talisman, Vaughan slowly began pulling himself out of his slump—and trade rumors began to swirl. This time, the press reported that the Dodgers were interested in Vaughan and would be willing to give up Van Mungo, a tall right-handed pitcher who had won at least 16 games in each of the previous three seasons and led the league in innings pitched with 315⅓ in 1934. Smith wrote that while Vaughan would be missed, the Pirates would be able to fill the gap at shortstop with Wilbur Brubaker, who had been playing at third, and insert Cookie Lavagetto at third. "And Mungo would look right smart as the No. 1 casting gentleman for the Pirates, wouldn't he?" Smith wrote. "What the team has needed for a long time is a strong-arm fast-baller who can walk out and whale the onion under hostile noses in a crisis."[56]

Arky Vaughan, in his early years with the Pirates, leans on the bat that made him one of the most feared hitters in all of major league baseball. Vaughan's .385 batting average in 1935 earned him the National League batting title and stands as the highest single-season batting mark in Pirates franchise history (courtesy National Baseball Hall of Fame Library, Cooperstown, New York).

Vaughan hit a more than respectable .291 for the month of May, but overall, he took a .278 mark into June. As a group, the Pirates were muddling along in third place at 21–20, six games behind league-leading St. Louis. Vaughan continued to pick up the pace at the plate, putting together a 19-game hitting streak that ended on June 8 and brought his average up to .299. Boyle wrote that Vaughan remained the league's most valuable shortstop, pointing out his tremendous arm strength, his keen batting eye and speed on the basepaths. "On top of this is a phlegmatic disposition that does not permit a slump now and then to get him down. He is quiet on the field, being in this like that other fine workman of calm disposition, Charley Gehringer of the Tigers, the best second baseman in baseball."[57]

That .299 batting average would be Vaughan's

high-water mark until July 23, when he finally reached the .300 level, and after dipping below that by a point or two until the final days of July, he went up for good on July 29 when he rapped out three hits against Boston and followed with four more hits in the next two games to move to .309. Despite his somewhat pedestrian batting marks, Vaughan earned his third straight berth in the All-Star Game, which would be played July 7 in Boston and ended in a 4–3 win for the National League. But Vaughan did not start the game and never made it off the bench, and neither did Bucs first baseman Gus Suhr. Fans—as well as Pirates front office personnel—were not pleased with NL manager Charlie Grimm. "It was a rotten deal all the way," said Sam Watters, the club's vice president. "They failed to pick our players in the first place. Then when they were forced into accepting some of them, they failed to use them." Watters said he believed the margin of victory could have been greater if the National League had played Vaughan. Phil Weaver, a fan from the Crafton neighborhood of Pittsburgh, told the *Press* that there had to be a good reason why Vaughan didn't get into the game. "Grimm probably has an explanation, but it would have to be a good one to satisfy me—and probably a lot of other fans." Added Pirate booster Mike Cullen, "It was the rottenest thing I've ever heard of. I was so disgusted with the opening lineup that I turned off the radio."[58] Vaughan admitted after returning to Pittsburgh that he was slightly embarrassed to be called before his teammates and fans and presented with a watch for being the league's Most Valuable Player in 1935 and then having to "ride the mahogany" all afternoon. But he would not criticize Grimm for failing to get him into the game.[59]

After the All-Star break, Vaughan saw his average rise steadily, but he began to consider taking a somewhat drastic measure—hitting right-handed. He was spotted hitting from the right side during batting practice in mid–July and "swears he'll turn over to the other side of the plate if he hasn't raised his average over the .300 mark shortly," Smith reported.[60] Nothing came of it, though, and Vaughan continued to swing away from the left side. He also continued to be among the most accommodating players, when it came to working with the media—even if he rarely delivered stop-the-presses material. An unnamed writer, penning the "Sports Stew" column for the Press, wrote: "His teammates, opponents and newspaper photographers and baseball writers agree on that. In contrast to some surly remarks made by a few of the Yankees, here for the exhibition with the Bucs Monday, Vaughan went out of his way to make things easier for the focus boys, yet Arky had more of a right to complain than the New Yorkers, what with his batting slump getting on his nerves."[61]

Even though some characterized it as a slump, Vaughan was hitting .298 by July 22, and was at .309 at the end of the month. He never characterized his hitting performance during the season as a "slump" and continued to chalk things up to bad luck. "The only difference I can see is that a good many more of my drives are now being caught that went for hits last year," he was quoted as telling a sportswriter who employed the byline "The Old Scout" but who was reputed to be Herb Goren of *The New York Sun*. "I don't think I've been in a real slump all year. Even when I was as low as .250, I was still hitting as hard as I was when my mark was around .350 a year ago."[62]

Vaughan only got hotter during the last two months of the season. He regained his cleanup spot in the batting order—he had been dropped to fifth earlier—on August 11 and three days later he started an 18-game hitting streak that pulled his average up to .315. Vaughan's offensive turnaround was saluted by local scribes, particularly those who had heard some folks in the league dismissing Arky's 1935 showing as something of an anomaly. One such pundit was Cincinnati Reds manager Chuck Dressen, who earlier in the season was quoted as saying, "Vaughan will not be much account anymore as a hitter 'cause the pitchers has got onto him." But by September 17, Vaughan was hitting at a .331 clip and was busting Reds pitchers at a .309 clip.[63]

He hit a sizzling .429 in 98 September at-bats to finish at .335, which put him fifth in the National League for the season. He amassed a .474 slugging percentage and a .927 OPS—good for sixth in the league. He drew 118 walks, had an on-base percentage of .453 and scored 122 runs, leading the league in all three offensive categories, and also led all NL players in times on base with 313. He struck out just 21 times and drove in 78 runs. He also led the NL in offensive WAR (7.7) and trailed only Carl Hubbell (9.9) and Mel Ott (7.8) in overall WAR, according to Baseball Reference. From July 29 through the season's final game on September 27—a period of 62 games—Vaughan batted .388 with a .998 OPS, 52 runs scored and 39 walks for an on-base percentage of .489. For an even larger piece of the season—125 games from May 23 to the final game—Vaughan batted .353 in 561 plate appearances, with 96 runs scored. Defensively, Vaughan showed improvement during the first half of the year, as he finished the month of June with 15 errors, but he wound up with 47 on the season. Still, he was ranked as the league's fourth-best shortstop among those who played at least 100 games. The Pirates, meanwhile, finished in fourth place with an 84–70 mark, eight games in back of the pennant-winning Giants.

No sooner had the season ended and Vaughan headed back to California did the trade rumors start. One had Vaughan going to the New York Giants in exchange for two players and cash. But Traynor said it would take more cash than any team would be willing to pay to get Vaughan.[64] Another had Vaughan going to the Cubs for shortstop Billy Jurges, pitcher Roy Parmelee and a bundle of cash. But after signing a new contract to manage the team for the 1937 season, Traynor came out at the end of October and tried to squelch all those rumors when he said, "I'll trade anyone on the ball club—except Arky Vaughan."[65] But the trade talk continued unabated. The *Santa Ana Register's* John Neubauer reported that Vaughan might end up a Yankee in 1937, but Vaughan's father, Robert, laughed at that. Neubauer also reported that Vaughan had spent a day with family after arriving from Pittsburgh but promptly "packed his shooting irons yesterday and headed for the tall timber this morning," accompanied by brother Glenn and a few baseball players. Neubauer reported that an elaborate homecoming had been planned for Vaughan but it had to be postponed to accommodate his annual hunting trip. "Vaughan isn't talkative," Neubauer wrote. "He is one of the hardest celebrities to interview. Modest, almost bashful, he never talks about himself. Vaughan holds the unique distinction of being in the public limelight without tooting his horn. He never did and probably never will. He just smiles, and his answers are all yes or no."[66] Vaughan wasn't exactly a recluse in his hometown, though; he even spoke briefly when he was introduced by Fullerton Mayor Harry Maxwell before a semipro game at Fullerton's ballpark that off-season. Nationally as well Vaughan had received some recognition when he was featured on a Wheaties cereal box, touting the "Breakfast of Champions." The box featured a quote from Vaughan: "Wheaties with lots of milk or cream, sugar and some kind of fruit—I thought to myself, by gosh, there's a dish that's sure to make good in any league." His endorsement would even be used in grocery store advertisements that ran in the *Pittsburgh Press*.[67] Vaughan was not above endorsing other products—even competing ones—as he lent his name to a new breakfast cereal made by General Foods known as Huskies. "There's no doubt about it," says Arky, "that delicious new cereal is right down the old groove with me!" read a newspaper ad that appeared in the *Pittsburgh Press* on June 25.[68]

In late November, another trade rumor surfaced—this one sending Vaughan to St. Louis with Cy Blanton for star pitcher Dizzy Dean. Cardinals president Sam Breadon said he didn't want to talk about any trade rumors. Boyle reported that it would take four members of the Pirates' big-league roster—including Vaughan—plus three minor leaguers and $175,000 in cash to land Dean, whom Boyle called "the game's most celebrated pitcher." Traynor admitted he and club president Bill Benswanger had discussed the deal. "If we could talk the Cardinals out of the Vaughan angle, we could swing the deal," he said. "The cash consideration is not the drawback. The door is still open. I consider the deal still on the fire. We will make a counter proposal to him, but I feel safe in saying that we won't give up Vaughan."[69] Benswanger was even more to the point, saying he wouldn't trade Vaughan for Dean straight up. Traynor said Vaughan hadn't even reached his prime yet and he was able to shake off a slow start at the plate to have a fine year. "Had the season lasted a few weeks longer, I believe he would have led the league," Traynor said. "At any rate he made a remarkably fine showing. He has a brilliant future in front of him and I would not be surprised to find him carrying off the batting honors in 1937 and perhaps continuing the performance. It would be foolish to think of using him in a deal."[70]

Back in Fullerton for the winter, Vaughan settled into his usual routine of fishing and hunting with friends, and playing golf. He also found time to visit his favorite haunt—Potter Valley—where he spent time with an assortment of friends that included a man named Julius Rottluff, a longtime area melon farmer who would often accompany Vaughan and his father on hunting expeditions. Rottluff told Patricia Vaughan Johnson that her father, despite his accomplishments in baseball, didn't care to talk about the sport all that much. Rotluff said,

> The only one he talked baseball to was his mechanic in town, Angelo Grilli. Angelo had played in the minor leagues—he was a good hitter and he could field. But he stood still running. And when you play baseball, you've got to be quick. Your dad was one of the fastest men in baseball. On a ranch, he was the slowest man I ever saw. Cutting wood? When you got him on the saw, he'd look this way and that way, trying to get every piece just as near even length. You can't do it that way if you're doing it to make money on it. He'd look both ways and then he'd cut that stick.[71]

Vaughan began to enjoy his annual forays to Potter Valley so much that he began to seriously contemplate the idea of buying property there, and moving the family from Fullerton. He discussed the idea with his father, and they agreed to go in on a partnership. That settled, the two told their Potter Valley friends to keep an eye out for any ranching property that might come up for sale.

Unlike previous off-seasons, Vaughan wasted no time in getting his contract signed, as he submitted it in late January. But people still spoke about possible trades or position switches to third base or the outfield as the Pirates prepared to head to San Bernardino for spring training. Sportswriters both locally and nationally reported that Traynor was growing weary of the suggestions that Vaughan should be moved to the outfield or third base. "Vaughan will play shortstop and no place else," he said after the club reported to San Bernardino in February. He shot down the idea of Vaughan moving to right field to replace the unsigned Paul Waner, saying he had other outfielders who could hit, but no other hitting shortstops. He downplayed Vaughan's fielding difficulties. "He's improving greatly as a fielder, with his slowness on double plays his only real weakness. For straight-away fielding, I claim Arky is just as good as Leo Durocher, Bill Jurges or any other National League shortstop. At least he was that last year."[72]

Vaughan was a popular figure during spring training in 1937, as reporters sought to get his explanation for the 50-point decline in his batting average between 1935 and 1936. He maintained that a lot of it had to do with luck—and hitting the ball right at fielders. He said he was confident he'd be back in the thick of the batting race in '37. "But only if luck is at my elbow and not with Paul Waner or Joe Medwick or Frank Demaree," he said. "They topped me last year and if you want to hear more about luck, look them up. They'll tell you all about it—probably too much in June or July."[73] Local writers looked forward to what figured to be another battle for the NL batting crown between Vaughan and Paul Waner; the latter had won titles in 1934 and '36 while Vaughan prevailed in '35.

But the heated battle never materialized, in large part due to injury. Vaughan got off to another slow start, and by May 4 was batting just .150. A collision with umpire George Magerkurth left him woozy and nearly dislocated Vaughan's jaw. He was unable to eat solid food for four days. But Vaughan recovered and picked up his hitting, too, as a 10-for-14 stretch over a three-game period boosted his mark to .308, and by the end of May he was sailing along at a .379 clip. During one eight-game stretch, Vaughan went 16 for 33—a .485 average—with eight extra-base hits and seven RBIs.

One of the more noteworthy games of the 1937 season occurred on May 6 at Brooklyn's Ebbets Field. It was noteworthy not so much for what took place on the field, but above it. In the sixth inning, fans and players alike looked toward the sky to see the huge hydrogen-filled air ship known as the *Hindenburg* floating overhead, less than 1,000 feet over the playing field, on its way to Lakehurst, New Jersey, some 75 miles away. The German airship, which displayed Nazi swastikas on its tail fins, was in the final stages of a three-day transatlantic trip from Frankfurt, Germany. Those taking in the sight would find out later that the zeppelin had exploded, burst into flames and crashed to the earth, killing 36 people.[74]

Vaughan had gained the reputation of being a steady player over the years and by 1937 he was extremely relaxed. Woody English of the Dodgers said Vaughan was so relaxed he would whistle while playing shortstop. "That's a fact," he said. "I've heard him lots of times. A whistling shortstop, that's what he is."[75] He was obviously relaxed at the plate as well. He continued to hit well through June, which was highlighted by a 19-for-39 burst in the latter part of the month that left him at .359 going into July. His strong first half enabled him to snare his fourth straight appearance in the All-Star Game, which would be played July 7 at Griffith Stadium in Washington. Joined by teammates Paul Waner and Cy Blanton, Vaughan started at third base for the NL club—Bartell was the starting shortstop—and had two singles in five plate appearances in an 8–3 loss to the American League. While the game proved inconsequential for Vaughan, it would prove to be the beginning of the end for a player who had trade ties to Vaughan—Dizzy Dean. The standout pitcher, who had won 82 games in the previous three seasons combined and had chalked up another 12 victories by the All-Star break, earned the start for the National League team. In the third inning, Cleveland's Earl Averill lined a shot off Dean's foot, breaking his toe. Dean tried to rush back into action too soon, changing his throwing mechanics to compensate for the injured toe. Those changes resulted in serious arm problems, and he never was the same pitcher again, as he won just 17 more games before retiring at age 31.

Play resumed after the All-Star break on July 9, and two days later, Vaughan sustained a major knee injury in a collision with teammate Johnny Dickshot. Playing the Cubs at Forbes Field, Vaughan was pursuing a short fly ball hit by Phil Cavarretta and snared it in his glove when Dickshot, the left fielder, cut him down. Both went down in a heap, with Vaughan still clutching the ball, and the perennial All-Star had to leave the game. Vaughan received immediate attention from team trainer Dr. Charles Jorgensen and limped off the field. X-rays showed no fracture, but Vaughan tore ligaments in his right knee and would be sidelined for an undetermined length of time. At the time, the Pirates stood 40–31 and were in third place, four and a half games in back of pace-setting Chicago.[76] Vaughan came back to pinch-hit in back-to-back games on July 17–18, but would not make another appearance until July 25, when he pronounced himself fit for fulltime duty. Vaughan played both ends of a doubleheader that day, but committed two errors in the second game that led to a 7–5 loss to the Boston Bees. He also went hitless in eight plate appearances, although he did reach once in each game on a walk and a hit-by-pitch. "It was evident Vaughan was not ready to use his injured leg, and in the seventh he went to the bench," Balinger reported.[77] Afterward, Traynor second-guessed himself for penciling Vaughan into the lineup. "This was a costly series for us, not because we lost those three games but because Vaughan may have a long layoff as a result."[78]

Vaughan finally returned to action on August 3 against Brooklyn, but only as a pinch hitter. He would be relegated to pinch-hitting duty for more than two weeks, as he wouldn't get more than one at-bat in a game until August 20. Somehow, despite missing one of the game's best hitters, the Pirates held their own, posting a 59–49 record and lurking in fourth place, seven games behind the Cubs, who held just a two-game edge over second-place New York. Young, who had taken over at shortstop during Vaughan's absence, was playing well with second base partner Lee Handley. In fact, it was to the point where fans, writers and even Traynor had to consider the previously unthinkable and move Vaughan off shortstop. Boyle asked Vaughan how he would feel about moving to third base or the outfield. Vaughan responded:

I would like that very much. Understand, though, I have nothing against playing the shortstop position. I like to play there, and in fact, would play any position Traynor asked me to play, if it would help the team to win. I have played third base and have had a whirl of the outfield in the minors, and I can play either position. I don't know what Traynor has in mind for me as soon as this leg gets better, but if he wants me

to switch, I am ready. If not, I will go back to my old position, although Pep Young is
playing a great game there.[79]

Boyle wrote that putting Vaughan at third would plug a major infield hole,
but his strong throwing arm would be a major weapon in an outfield that
was considered weak in that area.[80]

Vaughan appeared ready to resume full-time action on August 17, but
Traynor continued to use him as a pinch hitter—or not at all—for a few more
days. Then on August 20, he made a start in left field against St. Louis, playing
the first six innings before giving way to Woody Jensen. Vaughan went one
for three, scored two runs and made three putouts in left field. In his second game back, Vaughan went three for five with two triples and two RBIs
and made what *Press* reporter Les Biederman termed a "miraculous" catch
of Jimmy Brown's fly ball near the left-field line. "Vaughan made a running,
half-diving catch and barely saved himself from crashing into the wall. It was
the fielding feature of the afternoon."[81] Elsewhere in the *Pittsburgh Press*, it was
reported that when Vaughan returned to his position after retiring Brown, he
shouted over to Lloyd Waner in center, "Hey, Lloyd, if you need any help, just
let me know."[82]

Vaughan played at least parts of a dozen games in left field before returning to shortstop fulltime on September 1. But from that point on, he
never again ventured into the outfield that season. He batted .274 during that
stretch, and saw his average drop from .340 on September 11 to a final mark
of .322 with a .395 on-base percentage and a .463 slugging mark, good for
an OPS of .858. He scored 71 runs in 126 games, collected 17 triples—tops
in the National league—and struck out only 23 times in 469 official at-bats.
The Pirates went 22–11 down the stretch to finish 86–68, good for third place
in the NL but 10 games behind the pennant-winning Giants. It wasn't long
after the season-finale doubleheader on October 3 that Vaughan departed for
Fullerton.

Four days later, the first off-season trade rumor found print—the Cubs
wanted to ship Jurges to Pittsburgh for Vaughan. Boyle said there was little
substance to that talk but acknowledged the Pirates were anxious to make a
few deals over the off-season.[83] The Jurges-for-Vaughan talk persisted into
the year's final month, with Biederman reporting that the Pirates "very definitely" offered Vaughan, an outfielder believed to be Woody Jensen, and a
pitcher thought to be Bill Swift to the Cubs for Jurges and outfielder Frank
Demaree, but the Cubs rejected that deal. Biederman reported that baseball
men believed the Cubs would have gotten the better of that deal, largely on
the basis of Vaughan's bat, and that the Pirate shortstop was too valuable to
ship out of town.[84] The Pirates talked trade the entire month of December,
including hours of conversation at the winter meetings in Milwaukee, but no

major moves were made. "We did everything possible … but got nothing out of it," Traynor said. "Everybody we talked to wanted Paul Waner and Arky Vaughan, and were willing to give us second-rate ballplayers in exchange for these stars."[85]

While some were talking trade, others were still dissecting the recent season. Waite Hoyt, who spent part of the '37 season in Pittsburgh, offered several critical comments regarding the Pirates in an article published in *The Sporting News*. "When the Pirates open the season, they immediately start counting the days until they can return home to resume hunting, fishing, or whatever their off-season diversion happens to be," Hoyt was reported to have said on a New York radio program. He added: "From top to bottom, the members of the club are disinterested ball players and have a defeatist attitude toward the game. Arky Vaughan could be the greatest shortstop in baseball if he were a hustler, but the only thing that worries Arky, once the season starts, is how soon he can return to California and resume his hunting."[86]

Vaughan had other things on his mind. His wife, Margaret, had given birth to the couple's second daughter, Michaela Elizabeth—who would be known as Mikie—on September 1 back home in Fullerton. By the time Vaughan returned to the West Coast, he'd gotten word that his friends in Potter Valley had found some property they thought might be of interest, and Vaughan and his father went to take a look. The land—part rangeland and part bottomland—was just outside the town itself, which by this time consisted of an elementary and high school, a grocery store and meat market, a bar and restaurant, a post office and a garage. The Vaughans liked what they saw, and on December 14, they purchased the 400-plus acre property in the area where Bob Vaughan had first settled upon leaving Arkansas more than 20 years earlier. The purchase price was $15,000—equal to about one year of Vaughan's salary with the Pirates. The Vaughan men returned to Fullerton and broke the news to the rest of the family. Patricia later said that her mother was not exactly thrilled, given that she had just had her baby three months earlier and had grown fond of the Spanish-style home they had been living in the past several years in Fullerton. "But she accepted Arky's wishes and began to prepare for the move to a country life," Patricia wrote later.[87]

◆◆ 5 ◆◆

Falling Just Short

The disappointment of the 1937 season gave way to hope for the following one, as fans in Pittsburgh began contemplating what awaited them as soon as the calendar turned to 1938. But before they could completely digest the previous campaign, the sour taste of Waite Hoyt's comments from the month before returned, thanks to a column written on January 5 by the *Pittsburgh Press'* Chet Smith. He summarized Hoyt's comments, which were made on a New York radio station, saying that the former Pirate pitcher accused his old teammates of having no real interest in the game other than carousing on the road, and that the team needed a major house-cleaning if it expected to be competitive in the future. Smith, though, said Hoyt was off-base and accused him of "scattering his fire and hitting a lot of innocent victims who may not be fitted in championship molds but at least can't be accused of not trying." Smith said the overwhelming majority of players gave it a professional effort—they just happened to be average players, for the most part.[1]

Back in California, the Vaughan family had made the move from its comfortable home in Fullerton to the rugged ranch property that Arky and Margaret—along with Arky's parents—had purchased in Potter Valley. The Vaughans' two-vehicle caravan contained the usual array of people and property along with a most unusual piece—a sow pig that a women's group had given to Margaret as a going-away present. The pig—named Salome—would be a fixture on the ranch property for several years. When the Vaughans arrived, Margaret was in for a bit of a shock. The "house" more closely resembled a cabin, as it had no indoor plumbing, no electricity and no running water. It did have a small living room, dining room, two small bedrooms on the first floor, and a large kitchen that featured a huge cast-iron wood-burning stove that not only handled the cooking chores but also served as the house's main heat source, along with a fireplace in the living room. A well supplied water to the house, and the pump handle was located near the kitchen sink. It wasn't nearly as convenient as turning on a tap, but it paled in comparison to having to use an outhouse behind the regular house. But the family did its best, knowing that by that same time next year, the house would be remodeled and outfitted with modern conveniences.[2]

Although the start of spring training was two months away, Pie Traynor was already pondering the merits of his squad with local reporters in mid–January, telling Havey Boyle of the *Post-Gazette* that despite Arky Vaughan's brief foray into the outfield the previous season, he would be ensconced at shortstop. "Gus Suhr is a fixture at first base and I have given up on the idea of experimenting with Arky Vaughan at other positions but short," he said. "Arky has played there five years and belongs at that spot."[3] Vaughan's roommate, Honus Wagner, heartily endorsed the idea of leaving Vaughan be at shortstop, saying it would be a mistake to convert him to the outfield or third base. Wagner said people complained that Vaughan didn't take part in as many double plays as some of the other top shortstops in the league. "But that wasn't his fault," Wagner told a reporter known as "The Old Scout." "Our soft-ball pitching forced batters to hit up instead of into the dirt. Naturally there were fewer chances for double-play making." Wagner pointed out that Vaughan ranked second among shortstops in double plays in 1936. "Arky does a good job where he is. I can see no reason why he should move to a different position at this time in his career."[4]

Outside of the world of baseball, President Franklin D. Roosevelt gave his annual State of the Union address in early January and made note of the nation's ability to remain at peace despite rising tensions in various spots around the world:

> It is our traditional policy to live at peace with other nations. More than that, we have been among the leaders in advocating the use of pacific methods of discussion and conciliation in international differences. We have striven for the reduction of military forces. But in a world of high tension and disorder, in a world where stable civilization is actually threatened, it becomes the responsibility of each nation which strives for peace at home and peace with and among others to be strong enough to assure the observance of those fundamentals of peaceful solution of conflicts which are the only ultimate basis for orderly existence.[5]

On the home front, he said it would be unreasonable to expect drastic pay increases for the common worker, "only legislation to end starvation wages and intolerable hours; more desirable wages are and should continue to be the product of collective bargaining."[6]

Back in the world of baseball, front-office and field-management types were discussing the ball itself, as a change was to be implemented for the '38 season. Traynor said the changes would not be radical, but that the ball's cover fit more loosely than did the previous model. Traynor speculated it might result in pitchers throwing better breaking balls and the ball having less carry than in past seasons.[7] In early February, Pirates club president Bill Benswanger said trade talks with the Cubs, Reds, and Dodgers that began at the minor-league meetings in Milwaukee and the major-league meetings in Chicago in late 1937 heated up again. Specifically, the Pirates were interested in shortstop Jurges and outfielder Demaree from the Cubs. "I think we've made a little progress," Benswanger told Les Biederman of the *Press*. "But a deal is still far from closed." Benswanger would not divulge the names of the Pirate players involved in the talks, but Biederman said it was believed to be Vaughan, a veteran pitcher and one of two outfielders—Paul Waner or Woody Jensen.[8]

The first group of Pittsburgh players was expected to arrive at the club's San Bernardino spring training quarters on March 5, and Benswanger was scheduled to meet shortly thereafter with the Pirates' West Coast contingent—Vaughan, Gus Suhr and Bill Brubaker—to discuss contract terms. The local press continued to discuss the trade that ultimately wasn't made, with Smith saying the Pirates' Traynor would rather have Vaughan hitting *for* the Pirates than *against* them. He also said that while Vaughan continued to have difficulty in the field, he believed veteran infielder Tommy Thevenow, who was returning to the club, might be able to show Vaughan a few tricks. In the same article, Smith talked about the need for the Pirates to step things up in the hustle department for the coming season: "There is no denying that the Corsairs were the sleeping beauties of the league last year. It was a characteristic so marked that other clubs joked about it and Traynor was accused of being too lenient a master. At the end of the campaign, Pie had made up his mind that 1938 would not witness a recurrence. It won't be long now until it will be reported from San Bernardino that he has laid down the law and intends to make it stick."[9]

Vaughan headed for spring training around the second week of March, and his wife and children headed south to Fullerton, where they would remain until they joined Arky in Pittsburgh at the start of the season. Vaughan signed his contract on March 12, and although no specific dollar terms were announced, it was believed that Vaughan received a pay increase that made him one of the team's highest-paid players.[10] Smith opined that Traynor's planned infield of Brubaker, Vaughan, Young and Suhr, from third to first, needed tinkering. He called it no better than the third-best infield in the league and had little in the way of kind words for Vaughan's defense. "Vaughan is a hitting fool with a grand throwing arm, but he is the poorest shortstop in the league on double plays and utterly lost at handling topped hits that dribble down the infield," he wrote.[11]

As the club prepared for the regular season, players talked about the teams they figured would provide the stiffest competition, and they agreed that it would be the Cubs, based on their all-around strength. One Pirate player told Biederman that Chicago had the best infield, a strong, hard-hitting outfield and a solid pitching staff. "Yes, sir, the Cubs are the team to beat," the unnamed player summarized. "The Giants have had too much luck to last."[12] The national media agreed, as the Cubs were chosen to finish ahead of New York in the National League in a poll of 500 baseball writers that was conducted for Liberty Magazine. The Pirates, meanwhile, were chosen to finish fourth.[13] The *Post-Gazette* reported that Vaughan apparently found the ranching life to his liking, although the unnamed reporter noted that Vaughan was kept busy picking off wolves and coyotes that had their eyes on some of the All-Star shortstop's flock. The report stated that Vaughan's 400-acre sheep ranch included 40 acres set aside for alfalfa and a productive vineyard. He also had plans for an orchard featuring apples, peaches and cherries and also intended to grow corn. The off-season work of keeping up the ranch appeared to leave Vaughan in excellent physical condition, the reporter noted, and he promised to "improve on the .322 batting average he compiled the previous season."[14]

One of the highlights of spring training was the Pirates' visit to Vaughan's hometown of Fullerton. There, Pittsburgh took on the Portland Beavers of the Pacific Coast League, who made Fullerton their spring training home. It marked the first time that a major league team had visited Fullerton. The *Daily News Tribune* of Fullerton devoted an entire 12-page section to Vaughan's homecoming, which was set to take place March 31 at Amerige Park. "Few players on record have crowded as much brilliant baseball into their early 20s as Vaughan has done for the Pirates. Just turned 26, this fleet-footed and hard-hitting shortstop has been a top-flight star for several seasons," the *Daily News Tribune* reported. In addition to highlighting Vaughan's career, the section featured stories on a number of other subjects, including Honus Wagner, Fullerton's ballpark, Gus Suhr, the cost of spring training, and a brief history of baseball in Fullerton, which numbered among its products the great Walter Johnson, another Fullerton High School graduate.[15]

Much of the town shut down when the Pirates and Beavers squared off the next day, as a crowd estimated from 1,000 to 2,000 people showed up to watch their hometown hero. He did not disappoint, as he came up in the first inning with runners at second and third and promptly deposited an offering from southpaw George Darrow over the right-field wall for a three-run homer. Vaughan, who was hitting .450 for the spring, also drew two walks and flied out deep to right in his other plate appearances in a 5–1 Pirates win.[16]

After the Fullerton stop, the Pirates embarked on a spring training tour that took them to California's central valley with stops in Fresno, Taft and Barstow before moving on to Winslow, Arizona, and Clovis, New Mexico. By mid–April, the tour had reached Shawnee, Oklahoma, where Vaughan cracked two home runs in one game, both of which sailed over a large white advertisement that read "Sock one over this sign and we'll give you a five dollar hat." The *Post-Gazette* reported that Vaughan planned to send one of them to his father.[17] On April 14, the Pirates battled the Chicago White Sox in Wichita, Kansas, the same city where Vaughan broke into professional ball in 1931. As he did in Fullerton, Vaughan gave some 6,000 fans—including the governors of Kansas and Michigan—a thrill by collecting two hits and scoring twice.[18] Through 10 exhibition games against major-league competition, Vaughan—who made a habit of entertaining his teammates with a harmonica on the tour—piled up 18 hits in 35 at-bats, including five home runs, two triples and a double for a whopping .516 average. It appeared as though he was more than ready to get the regular season started.

When the Pirates took the field in St. Louis on Opening Day, their lineup looked nearly identical to the 1937 model. Only one spot was occupied by a different player—Johnny Rizzo, obtained from the Cardinals, made his major-league debut in left field. Also making his major-league debut that day would be the Cardinals' Enos Slaughter, who coincidentally would be inducted into the Baseball Hall of Fame on the same day as Vaughan, 47 years later. But Traynor believed the 1938 edition of the Pirates was stronger overall thanks to a better bench and a few new arms in Bob Klinger and Kenny Heintzelman. The latter didn't do much, but Klinger wound up going 12–5 in 21 starts.

The season opener ended in storybook fashion, as Vaughan came to the plate in the top of the ninth with Rizzo at second and the Cardinals clinging to a 3–2 lead. Vaughan worked left-hander Bob Weiland to a 3–1 count, then roped a 400-foot shot that came down on the roof of the right-field pavilion and bounced onto Grand Avenue to put Pittsburgh on top, 4–3. Klinger, in his first major-league appearance, retired the side in the bottom of the inning to pick up his first victory.[19] Vaughan and the Pirates got off to a solid start, with Vaughan clubbing three home runs in April, including a grand slam that was part of a three-for-three day in a 6–5 win over the Cubs on April 27. The slam, which came on a full count with two outs in the seventh inning off Larry French, made the difference. "The ball had started on a line and fell into the upper deck of the right field stands," Biederman wrote afterward. "It was a tremendous wallop." When Vaughan reached home plate, the runners he'd just driven in grabbed him, shook his hands and even took off his cap to make him take a bow to the fans.[20] Vaughan characteristically showed little emotion afterward, saying, "French just gave me a good pitch and I hit it right."[21]

The Pirates stumbled late in the month of April and couldn't get untracked in May, ending the month with a 17–18 record, good for fifth place, seven and a half games behind league-leading New York. Vaughan held up his end offensively, as he carried a .316 batting average into June. He finished the month of May by inviting a young guest into the Pittsburgh dugout before the May 30 doubleheader with the Cardinals at Forbes Field. The guest was 12-year-old Robert Albert Arke of Pittsburgh, who several years earlier had been a patient at Children's Hospital and passed his time there listening to Pirates games on the radio. He became enamored with Vaughan, and hospital workers began calling Robert "Arky," partly due to Vaughan's heroics and partly because of the young boy's surname. Vaughan heard about the story and invited young Robert to come to the dugout before the doubleheader, where he received a ball autographed by Vaughan.[22]

The Pirates turned things around in June, compiling a 16–7 mark to pull into a tie for second with Cincinnati and climb within four games of front-running New York at 33–25. Vaughan scuffled a bit, batting just .253 for the month to drop his average to .291 heading into July. Early that month, with Pittsburgh rolling, Vaughan was named to play in his fifth straight All-Star Game, which took place in Cincinnati on July 6, but for the second time in three years, he did not get into the game, a 4–1 NL victory. Leo Durocher, who would become Vaughan's manager several years later, earned the start at shortstop for the winners. Mace Brown and Lloyd Waner also represented the Pirates in the annual mid-summer game. The day play resumed, Pittsburgh won its eighth straight game, 6–2, over host St. Louis, with Vaughan collecting two hits and two RBIs while scoring twice. The streak

Arky Vaughan, an established big leaguer but still relatively young in the late 1930s, enjoys a brief respite on a bench at Forbes Field (courtesy National Baseball Hall of Fame Library, Cooperstown, New York).

would reach 13 games before Brooklyn snapped it on July 13, but by that time the Pirates had pulled into first place, albeit just two percentage points in front of the Giants at 44–26. Even though the Bucs saw their streak end, the heads-up play they displayed caught the attention of Smith, who pointed out two instances by Vaughan in particular that merited praise. The first saw the speedy shortstop tag up from first on a short fly out to left and beat the throw to second from Buddy Hassett, whom Vaughan knew did not have an accurate throwing arm. Vaughan followed by moving to third on a fielder's choice that scored Rizzo and when Brooklyn first baseman Dolph Camilli held the ball, Vaughan roared all the way around to score himself. "Camilli is astonished, and so are 5,500 customers who did not see the Corsairs do things such as that earlier in the year," wrote Smith.[23]

A few days later, as Vaughan's bat continued to blaze, he nearly came to blows with the Reds' Alex Kampouris, who apparently took exception to a comment Vaughan made toward old nemesis Dick Bartell. But cooler heads prevailed and no fisticuffs ensued in the game, which attracted a throng of 43,241—the largest crowd for a regular-season game in Pirates history up to that point. By July 20, Vaughan's climb up the NL batting race had reached the top with a .318 average. Yet it was Vaughan's fielding that some said was the key reason for the Bucs' surge to the top spot. "The hard-hitting husky is playing the best shortfield of his career with the Pirates, and has helped considerably along with Handley, Young and Suhr to tighten the inner defense, considered weak in the past," Al Abrams of the *Post-Gazette* wrote on July 23. Abrams noted that Vaughan had taken part in 60 double plays in 80 games after having figured in just 58 in 106 games the previous season.[24] Vaughan's speed also was a factor in several games, most notably a 4–2 win over Philadelphia on July 27. Vaughan turned a walk into a run in the second inning when he stole second and scored on Young's single. Then in the ninth, he walked again, took second on a fielder's choice, stole third and beat the throw home on an infield roller. In the field that day he handled nine chances flawlessly and saved what would have been the tying run in the sixth when he dashed behind second, fielded Phil Weintraub's smash and threw him out at first.[25] For the month of July, Vaughan raked at a .370 pace with 23 RBIs and an on-base percentage of .511, and during a 21-game stretch that reached into the first week of August, he was hitting at a .432 clip with 32 hits in 74 at-bats. The club went 24–7 over the month of July to improve to 57–32—a .640 winning percentage—and owned a five-game lead over New York with two months to play.

Vaughan's sparkling fielding continued into August as the Pirates kept rolling. He and Young turned five double plays in a 2–0 win over the Cubs on August 14, including one to end the game. With the bases loaded and one out in the ninth, Gabby Hartnett cracked a Mace Brown pitch toward left field.

It looked like a sure RBI single but Vaughan—playing a bit deep and to the right of his usual positioning—made a diving stab of the hard grounder and tossed to Young, who then avoided a tumbling Augie Galan to throw out the slow-moving Hartnett at first and end the game. "It isn't often that a home run, one of the two runs made in the game, can be put in the shade by fielding work, but that was what Arky and Pep did yesterday as the Sunday crowds moved out into the streets happily singing their praises," Boyle wrote. The win was particularly big for Pittsburgh, which had dropped the first two games of the series to the second-place Cubs.[26]

The Pirates kept rolling through the first three weeks of August and on August 21, the club sat 66–42, five games in front of second-place New York, despite just dropping a doubleheader that day to the third-place Cubs, who were lurking seven games behind. Vaughan had been credited with driving in the game-winning run in 12 of those first 66 victories—tops on the team.[27] Over the last third of the month, Pittsburgh kept up its pace, stretching its record to 73–48, good enough for a 6½-game lead over New York and Cincinnati heading into September after splitting a doubleheader against the Giants before a record crowd of 43,586 on the final day of August.

Local reporters showed no restraint in their praise of Vaughan as the season wound down. Biederman said Vaughan ranked as the best shortstop in the major leagues—and not just for his hitting. He described the 1938 model of Vaughan as "streamlined" and a "greyhound in the field." He noted Vaughan's penchant for throwing runners out from deep short and said that few balls were getting past him overall. Vaughan's best fielding play, Biederman wrote, was grabbing a sizzling grounder behind second and beating the runner to first base with a perfect throw. Biederman said Vaughan cleaned up two former weaknesses—a tendency to uncork the occasional wild threw and fumble slow-rolling grounders. "Today the fellow plays like an automaton—his throwing is almost perfect and only on rare occurrences do grounders now give him any trouble."[28] Biederman went on, noting:

> He talks with sort of a drawl. His humor is dry. He likes to tell jokes but usually kills the jokes by laughing before he is finished. ... He is a very plain fellow. He drives around town in a tan "station wagon," the same car he uses on his ranch. It seats nine persons and looks like a bus. He bought a gaudy sports coat recently and wonders what the boys back in Potter Valley will say when they see it. His biggest boosters are his teammates and practically all the opposing players in the league—which makes it unanimous.[29]

Vaughan was hitting .331 at the time, good for second in the NL batting race behind Ernie Lombardi. He told Abrams he thought he had a chance to catch Lombardi, although he acknowledged that base hits were getting hard to come by. Vaughan said the new less-lively ball introduced that season had made a big difference both at the plate and in the field, saying:

That ball is plenty dead and don't let anyone tell you differently. The ball will travel plenty if you meet it squarely on the nose, in fact, any ball will, but the difference lies in the point, that those drives through the infield are much easier to handle than in other years. That is why you see so many double plays. Why, I believe that nearly every team in our league has a hundred or more double plays to date. The ball used to come at you like a rifle shot, and before you could get down to pick it up, it would be past you and out in the outfield. A lot of those drives that used to be hit between the outfielders, because the ball traveled faster, are now being caught. There's all the difference in the world between the balls used in the past few years and the one in use now.[30]

No one was about to say the Pirates were a lock to win the NL crown and take on the vaunted Yankees in the World Series, given that a little over a full month of play remained, but Boyle reported that the Giants' Bill Terry said the Pirates "ought to quit if they don't win the flag now and he was speaking words of the wise. There will be pitfalls, and dark days yet, until the flag is unfurled, but barring a catastrophe, the local club can start contemplating the Yankees—whether they are men or beasts."[31]

A week into September, the Pirates remained atop the NL standings with a 76–52 mark and a five-game cushion over Chicago. Smith endorsed Vaughan as the National League's most valuable player "whether the Pirates finish first, second, third or fourth." Smith added:

For the first five years of his major league life, Vaughan was a great hitter, a fast but sloppy base-runner and a jittery fielder. He is still the batsman he always has been, but all of a sudden, he has become as sure-handed as a veteran juggler and by far the most unpredictable runner in the circuit. Vaughan is just beginning to realize that seven rivals fear his speed and break into a cold sweat when he is on base. Owning the best throwing arm in the league, he has acquired the ability to snap a ball out of his possession instead of winding up to let it go like a pinwheel. He learned to push a hit into left field two years ago when it became evident that the defense was ganging up on him and now he is as hard to play as a phony daily double.[32]

Vaughan sustained a right thumb injury in a game against New York on September 1 when the Giants' George Myatt spiked him on a slide at second base. The injury forced Vaughan to sit out the Pirates' next two games—back-to-back losses to St. Louis, 11–10 and 6–0, the latter of which left Pittsburgh's lead at five games over Cincinnati. Vaughan, who had played the previous two weeks with a leg injury, returned to the lineup on September 4 in a 5–3 win over St. Louis, but a stiff neck and sore back forced him out of the lineup the next day after just three innings of the first game of a doubleheader with the Cubs. He appeared in the clubhouse with his back taped up "like a prize fighter's hands just before he puts the gloves on," as Boyle wrote. He took a heat treatment before the game, but had to exit the first game early. The Bucs dropped both games, 3–0 and 4–3, and saw their lead over Cincinnati trimmed to four games. "There is nothing radically wrong with the Pirates at the moment," wrote Biederman. "But one thing is certain, Arky Vaughan happens to spell the difference between victory and defeat when he's on the bench."[33] Said Traynor: "The present slump shows how important Vaughan has been to the club. Things will get right when he gets back."[34]

Vaughan would not return to the lineup until September 10 in a 14–7 win over the Cardinals in St. Louis. He walked, singled and scored a run as the Pirates maintained a four-and-a-half-game lead over both the Cubs and Reds. "Vaughan's apparent recovery naturally acts like a shot of confidence into the Corsair arteries," Balinger wrote. He also noted that a "squeaky tendon" in Vaughan's back had healed and that Vaughan could now "wiggle his neck without gritting his teeth. The cut on his right thumb has healed and a new coat of skin has grown over a patch of hip that was peeled in a base sliding mishap."[35]

But a Pittsburgh loss and a Chicago win the following day left the lead at three and a half games, and a rainout on September 13 resulted in a doubleheader with the Giants on September 14—the first of four doubleheaders to come in an eight-day stretch. The Pirates dropped that first twinbill, 3–0 and 10–3, and saw their lead reduced to two and a half games with 21 games to play. Vaughan managed just one hit in nine at-bats in the two games. The team rebounded with back-to-back wins, though, before dropping the second game of a doubleheader to Boston, 5–4, on September 16. The Cubs stood just three games back now, with 18 games to play, and were in the midst of a torrid pace that would see them win 20 of 24 games—and ultimately break the hearts of the Pirates and their legion of fans.

The strain on the Pirates was beginning to tell. Dan Parker, sports editor of the *New York Mirror*, wrote in *The Sporting News* on September 22 that the Pirates were among the tightest clubs he'd ever seen in a pennant race. He referred to them as the "jitterbucs" and added: "If ever a club tightened up like a Scotch trap drum under pressure, it's the not-so-bold Bucs. There's more tension on Pie Traynor's team than in Ringling's big top. Traynor himself looks like a pie from which all the filling has been extracted. ... Right now, Manager Traynor is so thin the Pirates can use him for a pennant pole, if they win."[36]

Rain entered the picture in the third week of September. Wet weather—triggered by a hurricane that had pummeled the New England coast—washed out a scheduled doubleheader at Brooklyn on September 20, and more rain forced the postponement of the next day's activities. Although some Pirates officials later would claim the rainouts and subsequent doubleheaders contributed to the Pirates' demise, it also reduced the number of games remaining that the teams chasing the Pirates—namely the Cubs and the Reds—had to catch them. As of September 21, Pittsburgh held a three-and-a-half-game lead on the Cubs with just 12 games remaining.[37] The Pirates returned to action on September 22 and swept a pair from Brooklyn, 6–0 and 11–6. Vaughan went a combined six for 10 in the two games, smacking three doubles and a single in the second game to drive in three runs and hike his batting average to .329. The Cubs, though, would not go away, as they, too, swept a double-header from the Phillies to remain three and a half games back with 10 games to play.

As Pittsburgh prepared to open a three-game set at home with the Reds, the press once again spoke out on behalf of Vaughan in the Most Valuable Player race. A column titled "Pirate Patter"—a regular feature in the *Press*—noted that if Vaughan wasn't voted the NL's MVP, "the boys who cast the deciding ballots will have done a great player a great injustice." The column also noted that when Vaughan was told he had crept to within six percentage points in the batting chase, Vaughan replied, "Don't tell me that. All I'm interested in is winning games and winning that pennant. Hits that I make don't mean a thing unless we win the game." The column pointed to Vaughan's team-first attitude and recalled a moment after a recent game in which Vaughan rode to the ball park with a certain reporter and happened to get four hits that day. The reporter accosted him the next day and said, "Now that you got four hits yesterday, you'll probably want to ride to the ball park every day with me in a taxi?" … "No. I don't," Vaughan replied. "We lost, didn't we?"[38]

The opening game of the series with Cincinnati ended in a 5–4 loss in 12 innings, and compounding the problem, the Cubs—on a 16–3 tear—swept a pair to pull within two games. The Pirates rallied to take the last two games of the series, 4–1 and 5–3, with Vaughan homering in the second game to aid the cause. Although the club's lead was still tenuous at two games with seven to play, some national writers already were talking about a Yankees-Pirates World Series. Grantland Rice, in a column printed in the *Post-Gazette* on September 26—the day before the start of the three-game series with the Cubs—wrote that the Yankees would be "top-heavy favorites to flatten the Pirates." He gave Pittsburgh no chance to beat the Yankees, whom Rice rated as one of the greatest teams ever assembled, putting them in a class with the famed '27 Yankees, who swept the Pirates in one of the most lopsided World Series of all time.[39]

On the same day, Boyle talked about Vaughan's spirit, calling it a "revelation." Boyle wrote that Vaughan had always been a capable shortstop and a good hitter but "a complacent fellow on the ball field. This season he has been the chief spark of the club, and through the closing days he has been a wild man hungry for victory. No ball player has ever changed so suddenly, and the results speak for themselves."[40] Boyle noted that Vaughan not only had been handling his own assignments but had "given off sparks of leadership for his comrades to follow." He added: "In a field where every man is bearing down with his last ounce of resourcefulness, Vaughan still towers, partly because of the contrast to an earlier attitude, and partly because the sight of the victory goal has given him the air of a Bancroft or a Bartell fighting for every point. … If he does not capture the most valuable player award, even if he doesn't lead the league in hitting, those who have watched him closely all season will be disappointed."[41]

It was now down to a two-team race, with the Reds and Giants being eliminated from contention. Both the Pirates and Cubs had seven games remaining, and if the Pirates went 4–3, the Cubs would need to win all seven to capture the pennant. If Pittsburgh could take two of three in Chicago, it would then need to win just one of its final four with Cincinnati even if the Cubs swept their final series against St. Louis. A three-game sweep of the Cubs in Chicago would clinch the pennant for the Pirates.

The Cubs made it 17 wins in their last 20 starts when they wrapped up a sweep of St. Louis, 6–3, on September 26 to narrow idle Pittsburgh's lead to one and a half games going into their epic head-to-head showdown that started the following day at Wrigley Field. On that same day, while the Cubs and Pirates prepared to do battle, Adolf Hitler called for peace talks to be held in Munich with representatives from Great Britain, Italy and France. Just three days later, it was announced that Hitler signed a pact with those three nations promising that their people "never would go to war with one another again and promised to work jointly for the solution of the general European problems." Neville Chamberlain, British prime minister, returned to London and read the joint statement over the radio shortly after arriving. "The importance which Mr. Chamberlain attached to the Hitler document was emphasized when he descended from the plane and waved it aloft for all to see like a trophy." The press reported that Chamberlain and his wife visited the King and Queen of England at Buckingham Palace, and the four of them appeared for four minutes on the balcony, "waving in response to the thunderous cheers of the crowd."[42]

Back in Chicago, the Cubs took the opening game of the showdown series with Pittsburgh, 2–1, behind the "slow ball and great heart" of veteran pitcher Dizzy Dean, a win that "sliced the Pirates advantage as thin as delicatessen bologna"—specifically to one-half game.[43] Dean, throwing only one or two fastballs, held the Pirates hitless from the second to the sixth, and Pittsburgh's lone run came on a wild pitch in the ninth after Dean was relieved by Bill Lee. "Dean walked off the mound, tears running down his cheeks, while the standing room crowd of 42,238 gave him a tremendous ovation," Biederman wrote.[44] It was the Cubs' 18th win in their last 21 starts. Meanwhile, back in Pittsburgh, Mrs. Barney Dreyfuss, the majority stock owner of the Pirates and chairman of the board, was too nervous to listen to the game on the radio during the middle innings but turned it on in the ninth. Her mood brightened after Jensen scored on the wild pitch but she could only muster a weak smile when the game ended. She said of her club's standing in the pennant race: "Oh, it would be terrible if they lose now. They've led for so long and we've done so much work getting ready for the World Series. It's hard to lead for such a long time, you know. It's better to come up from second or third. It would be a dreadful disappointment now if they were beaten out."[45]

The game of September 28 would go down as perhaps the single most excruciating loss in the long history of the Pirates franchise, and one that turned the pennant tide in favor of Chicago. The Cubs jumped to a 1–0 lead in the second on a base hit by Ripper Collins, an error on Pirates third base-man Jeep Handley and a fielder's choice. But Pittsburgh would come back to take the lead, 3–1, in the sixth on Johnny Rizzo's solo homer, a base hit by Vaughan, a pair of walks and Handley's two-run single. The Cubs answered in the bottom of the sixth with two runs to tie it at 3–3.

Pittsburgh threatened in the seventh when singles by brothers Lloyd and Paul Waner left runners at first and third with one out. With the slugging Rizzo at the plate and the count 2–1, Cubs pitcher Vance Page started his motion and then stopped, and first base umpire Dolly Stark started toward the mound to call what the Pirates believed was an obvious balk. Boyle wrote the next day that Pirates third base coach Jewel Ens wildly threw up his hands and started running toward the home plate umpire, George Barr, to ask for the balk call—and to tell Rizzo to step back. But Page quickly delivered the pitch and Rizzo hit into an inning-ending double play, leaving the score tied at 3–3. Pirates personnel argued vociferously with all four umpires, but none would change the call. A balk would have brought Lloyd Waner home from third with the go-ahead run, but it was not to be.[46]

The game remained deadlocked until the top of the eighth when a walk to Vaughan, Gus Suhr's single and RBI singles by Heinie Manush and Hand-ley made it 5–3 in favor of Pittsburgh with just six outs remaining. But Pirates starter Bob Klinger was pulled after issuing a leadoff single to Collins in the bottom of the eighth, and he was replaced by Bill Swift, who promptly gave up a walk, an RBI double to pinch hitter Tony Lazzeri and a run-scoring single to Billy Herman. Mace Brown then came on to relieve Swift, and he induced Frank Demaree to hit into a double play to leave the game tied at 5–5.

Darkness had descended upon Wrigley Field, but the game continued. Balinger reported that it was so dark that the umpires went into a brief con-ference to consider calling the game "but decided to let the two contenders fight it out" although many had trouble following the ball throughout the ninth inning.[47] The Pirates did not threaten in the top of the ninth after Paul Waner singled with one out and was caught stealing. In the bottom of the inning, Brown induced Phil Cavarretta to fly out to center and got Carl Reyn-olds to ground out to second. That brought up the Cubs catcher-manager, Gabby Hartnett. By this time, darkness was "blotting out the playing field," as Biederman wrote later that day. "It was obvious that if Hartnett couldn't come through somehow the game would have to be called." Brown "pulled his cap down, hitched his belt and wound up."[48]

He jumped ahead 0-1 with a curve, then got Hartnett to swing and miss on a low and outside offering to make the count 0-2. "The crowd groaned and virtually gave up hope," Biederman wrote. Brown then wound up and delivered his third pitch. Hartnett swung and connected "and the moment the bat struck the ball there was no doubt about its destination," wrote Biederman. He continued: "Still, the crowd, seemingly not believing what was happening before its eyes, sat breathlessly until a thousand hands in the left field bleachers reached up for the ball. Then bedlam broke loose. Newspapers, score cards, straw hats, felt hats, women's hats—all kinds of hats—sailed into the playing field and behind them came a rushing stream of humanity—all dashing toward home plate to grab Gabby's hand or touch some part of him as he lumbered across the plate."[49]

Brown, meanwhile, "brushed his hand across his eyes as he walked through the shadows to his clubhouse, head bent. The Pirate infielders and outfielders seemed to remain glued to their positions—stunned by the dramatic suddenness of it all. Then they walked slowly off the field—and, perhaps, right out of a World Series."[50]

Later, Hartnett admitted he had sold out on his swing and "gambled on a home run or nothing." Brown, meanwhile, had difficulty getting over the shock in the Pirates' clubhouse. "He tossed his sweatshirt in a corner and tramped on it ... 'had him in a hole, too,'" Brown moaned. "Two strikes, no balls. Why couldn't that curve break for me instead of him?" Pirates players and coaches still were bemoaning what they felt should have been a balk call in the seventh. Manager Pie Traynor said first base umpire Dolly Stark rushed in past Collins with his hand almost upraised, but when Rizzo hit into the double play, Stark went back to his position. "Most of the writers saw it," the *Pittsburgh Press'* "Pirate Patter" column reported. National League president Ford Frick, who was in the press box, was asked for his opinion later but said he didn't see the balk. "To overrule the umpires in a situation like that would be folly," the column stated.[51] Chilly Doyle of the *Sun-Telegraph* minced no words, saying that the non-call was the difference in the game. "Ladies and gentlemen, and children, too, I saw that balk committed, and I am convinced that one of the four umpires in charge of the game saw it plainly and was rushing toward the slab to call the illegal pitch when something happened that caused him to change his mind."[52]

Boyle wrote that no baseball fiction ever matched the reality of the Cubs' 6–5 win, which knocked the Pirates out of first place for the first time since July 12: "It must have been written ages ago by the baseball gods that come September 28, in the year 1938, the Pirates at all costs were not to win the ball game. When the sun was first hung out to light the earth it must have been timed so that at a certain second the earth's revolving would bring on the mantle of approaching dusk to doom the Pirates."[53]

Boyle wrote of the bedlam that ensued after Hartnett's blast, which came to be known for all time as the "Homer in the Gloamin'," but also focused on the man who had yielded the titanic blast: "At the precise split second Hartnett's bat hit the ball, Brown's gloved hand and his right hand shot to his face. His head came down to meet the hands. It was the perfect picture of a man suddenly shocked into abject horrors. He knew, without looking, that the jig was up. He stood stunned for a few seconds and then walked off the mound— the personification of complete dejection."[54]

Outfielder Paul Waner later told author Lawrence Ritter that he feared Brown might harm himself after the game. He said he found Brown sitting in front of his locker "crying like a baby. I stayed with him all that night, I was so afraid he was going to commit suicide."[55]

Pirate fans back home who listened to the game on the radio reacted accordingly. Kaspar Monahan said that after Hartnett's game-winning homer he got up with the idea of walking to his kitchen, but wound up in a clothes closet by mistake. "I know I was in the wrong place because there are two windows in the kitchen, and where I was it was dark," he explained to Chet Smith. "Then, for no reason he can think of," Smith said of Monahan, "he put on his hat and went upstairs. An hour later Mrs. Monahan found him there. He told her he was waiting for a street car but consented, finally, to come down for dinner."[56] Smith recounted the goings-on of several others but said the saddest involved the head of a house in Carrick who "threw the radio out the window, pinched his 11-month-old son until the little codger broke into tears, told his wife he never intended to work again and stalked out of the house. If he reads this, I hope he'll go back to his family. There is still an outside chance for the Pirates."[57]

Mathematically speaking, Smith was correct, as the Cubs held a half-game lead with five games to play. But Hartnett's home run essentially was the beginning of the end for Pittsburgh, which could win just one of those remaining five games—a 4–2 decision over the Reds in the second game of a September 30 doubleheader in Cincinnati. The Pirates dropped the last game of the three-game set with the Cubs—the day after Hartnett's backbreaking home run—by a lopsided 10–1 count. Boyle wrote after the Cubs finished off the sweep that he tried to "engage a prominent Chicago undertaker to write my column tonight on the heels of listening today to the death wheeze in the Pirates' throats, but he said … he wasn't that morbid so he declined with thanks." Boyle said that even one win in Chicago likely would have given the Pirates the pennant, but that did not happen. "And to make the death certificate of the Pirates official, after two well-fought games, the Cubs went out today and scored 10 runs against the Pirates' one."[58]

Mathematically, the Pirates remained alive at that point. But the team dropped its last two games to the Reds, managed by former Buc skipper Bill McKechnie, while the Cubs split, leaving Chicago with a two-game edge as the season came to a close on October 2. For all his heroics on the season, Vaughan faded in the final week, collecting just four hits in 20 at-bats, and drove in just one run as the Pirates went 1–6. The following day, Traynor and team president Bill Benswanger were expected to head back to Chicago for some league meetings, but before leaving Traynor said several Pirates had played their last games in a Pittsburgh uniform. He would not name names, but Biederman surmised that two outfielders, two infielders and several pitchers would go, either via trade or outright release.[59]

When the Most Valuable Player votes were tabulated, Vaughan wound up third behind winner Ernie Lombardi and runner-up Bill Lee of the Cubs—a tally that didn't do Vaughan's season justice, at least according to Smith. "I have a deep-rooted conviction that it was largely because of Vaughan that the Pirates—logically a third or fourth-place team—were first until four days before the race was over."[60] Smith quoted his colleague at the *Press*—Biederman—as saying that the season was a huge disappointment for Vaughan. "He wanted to make it his biggest season and if there was one Pirate who hustled and gave everything it was Vaughan," Biederman said. He also said the hard-hitting shortstop had been called on the carpet several times by the front office for not hustling and when he talked to Benswanger about his contract that spring, Vaughan was told he'd have to hustle more. Smith quoted Biederman as saying: "Vaughan is a peculiar type. He's quiet and doesn't show off, but goes about his work in his own way. You don't hear him shouting and yammering out there at shortstop, but there isn't a pitcher on the team who would trade him for any other shortstop in either league. Arky was a little hurt by the insinuation that he didn't hustle. So he dedicated the 1938 season to the idea that he'd show his bosses a thing or two."[61]

Biederman said Vaughan put forth a tremendous effort all season, adding: "He wanted to be a member of a pennant-winning team before his career came to an end and he figured this was the year. He didn't especially care about leading the league in batting, except that if he could help the team to the pennant by so doing, that was okay with him. On the day the Pirates finally lost the pennant, when they dropped that Saturday game to the Reds as the Cubs beat the Cards, Vaughan was the picture of dejection. His dream had gone."[62]

He wasn't alone. Pirate ownership missed out on a major payday by failing to reach the World Series, as some 150,000 requests for World Series tickets—valued at over $1.6 million—had been submitted and would need to be refunded. Hotel and restaurant owners also failed to cash in on what they figured would be handsome returns if Pittsburgh had hosted the Series.

One chain store had purchased 50,000 live turtles with the names of Pirate players printed on the shells, figuring that Pirates fans would snap up the tiny reptiles. "Now these officials are wondering what one does with 50,000 live turtles."[63]

Statistically, Vaughan turned in another standout season for the Pirates, as he finished second among all major league players in WAR at 8.6 and was fifth in the big leagues in on-base percentage at .433. Among National League players, Vaughan finished third in walks at 104, struck out just 21 times, tied for fourth in stolen bases at 14, fifth in batting average at .322, eighth in OPS at .876 and ninth in runs scored at 88. Defensively he was among the best in the game; later advanced statistics would show that he was the top defensive player in baseball that year based on a 2.8 WAR rating, according to Baseball Reference. In terms of conventional statistics, he tied with Leo Durocher for the top fielding percentage among NL shortstops with a .961 mark. He committed 33 errors, but handled 85 more chances than any other shortstop, led all shortstops in putouts and assists and took part in more double plays than any other shortstop, as his 107 twin-killings were 17 more than the next closest competitor.[64]

As the year wound down, word reached Pittsburgh of the death of Art Griggs at the age of 53. Griggs, who had won a football letter for his play at fullback at the University of Pittsburgh in 1905, was president of the Tulsa club in the Texas League at the time of his passing. But in Pittsburgh, he was remembered better as the scout who made the right choice some eight years earlier, when he decided to go see the Cypress Merchants play a Sunday baseball game in Southern California and came away enamored with one Floyd Vaughan.[65]

◆◆ 6 ◆◆

Closing Out
the Decade

Amid more trade rumors that had Arky being shipped to Chicago or perhaps Brooklyn, the Vaughans retreated to their "new" old ranch home in Potter Valley. The house had been renovated and now had running water and electricity. Young Patricia began first grade in a small white schoolhouse that contained three rooms to house pupils in grades one through eight. The local one-room high school, meanwhile, had an enrollment of 12 students. When Vaughan bought the ranch property, it was set up for sheep, but he soon found that sheep were not to his liking. Patricia would later write that her father's distaste for sheep "stemmed from his observance of their lack of initiative and their inability to think for themselves. These were qualities he detested, in animals as well as in people." As a result, Arky vowed to get rid of the sheep and instead use the ranch to raise cattle, which he would start doing the following off-season.[1]

Unlike other winters, when Vaughan was late to sign his annual contract, he was among the first to ink his deal for the 1939 season, which local reporters estimated to be in the range of $15,000. And although club president Bill Benswanger had said in December that he would not tear the club apart just because it failed to win the NL pennant, his '39 team would feature several new faces, including catcher Ray Mueller, who was obtained from the Boston Bees for fellow catcher Al Todd, outfielder Johnny Dickshot and $30,000 cash. Several rookies also figured to be in the mix, including outfielders Maurice Van Robays and Fern Bell and infielders Jack Juelich and Frankie Gustine, the latter of whom would eventually find his way to Pittsburgh in September and would become a fixture as Vaughan's double-play partner at second base the following year.

Pirates manager Pie Traynor said on a stop in town in January that his biggest job would be to make his players forget what happened down the stretch the previous season. "He must, owing to the reluctance of other clubs to trade with the Pirates, build up a new morale, or rebuild that which carried the Pirates just to the edges of the pennant," wrote *Post-Gazette* columnist Havey Boyle.[2]

Traynor started out full of hope in April, noting that the club had led the NL for 10 weeks in '38 and that it couldn't be subjected to the same bad breaks down the stretch that sunk the team's hopes the previous season. He told local reporters just before the April 17 season opener in Cincinnati that the '39 club was superior to the '38 edition in every area, pointing out that Mueller was an upgrade defensively at catcher, his infield was one of the best in the game defensively, his outfield was one of the best in club history and his starting pitching staff of Cy Blanton, Russ Bauers, Jim Tobin, Bobby Klinger and Mace Brown would be improved over the previous year. Vaughan appeared to be rounding into form nicely in the spring, as evidenced by a two-homer, six-RBI game against the White Sox in one of the final exhibition games.

But the club stumbled out of the gate, dropping 13 of its first 23 games over the opening month of the season, and sat in seventh place, three and a half games behind the front-running Cardinals in a tightly bunched NL race. The team was hampered by several injuries, most notably a sore arm that shelved Blanton for most of the year and a beaning that Lee Handley suffered in an exhibition game—an injury that kept him out of the lineup for the entire month of April. No sooner did he return than Pep Young, the standout second baseman, left the lineup due to a twisted knee. Vaughan's start mirrored the club's, as he batted just .256 during that opening stretch, driving in nine runs. The Pirates picked up the pace slightly by Memorial Day and were now above .500 with a 19–18 mark, but they also saw their deficit grow, as they trailed first-place Cincinnati by five and a half games in fourth place.

Vaughan was still scuffling with a .265 batting average and just 14 RBIs—and no home runs. He showed some signs of life on May 29 when he nearly tangled with Dizzy Dean of the Cubs. Dean had dumped a blooper to left that Pirates outfielder Johnny Rizzo claimed he had caught, but the umpires ruled it a trap. While a discussion ensued, Dean and Vaughan began arguing, but no punches were thrown.[3] Boyle wrote that it might behoove Vaughan to get mad more often. Boyle maintained that the easy-going shortstop "would improve his natural talents by several degrees if he could get stirred up." Boyle added: "He is good enough as it is, as is shown by the way every club mentions his name first in any trade talk, but keyed to a high pitch Arky might cut himself new records. He was the chief factor in last year's drive and he took the loss of the pennant as a personal one. No one worked harder for the success that just missed the Pirates' eager fingers. His argument with Dizzy Dean yesterday may be the signal that Arky is ready for another great drive."[4]

The *Pittsburgh Press*' Les Biederman reported some specifics of the conversation that Dean and Vaughan had. Biederman wrote that Dean, stationed at second base, pointed to his stomach and shouted at Vaughan, "You guys don't have it down here. Never did. What a bunch of louses." Vaughan started after Dean but had to be restrained. "Say, you big four-flusher, I'll show you whether I have any fight," Vaughan was reported to have told Dean. "I'll take you anywhere, anytime, anyplace. Just meet me under the stands after the game. I'll tear you to pieces." The next time Vaughan batted, he clubbed a two-run triple off Dean.[5]

The Pirates had the opportunity to participate in a "first" of sorts on June 1 when they visited Philadelphia to play in the first night game at the Phillies' Shibe Park. Only 9,858 spectators turned out for the contest, due largely to a driving rainstorm, as Pittsburgh beat its cross-state rivals, 5–2. Under the lights, Vaughan doubled and walked off

Arky Vaughan follows through on the swing that made him a perennial All-Star with the Pittsburgh Pirates. Note the misspelling of Vaughan's last name on the photo signature; it was not uncommon for Vaughan—despite his star status—to see his last name misspelled by the press during his playing days (courtesy National Baseball Hall of Fame Library, Cooperstown, New York).

Kirby Higbe and scored a pair of runs in the win. Biederman noted that the majority of big-league players "detested" night baseball. "They feel they had their fill of night ball in the minors, but as long as baseball under the lights continues to draw some fans for the magnates, they won't squawk."[6]

A few weeks later, the National Baseball Hall of Fame and Museum was dedicated in Cooperstown, New York, as part of a baseball centennial celebration, and a couple of Pirates were on hand for the event. Honus Wagner was part of the inaugural class of inductees that included Babe Ruth, Ty Cobb, Connie Mack, Napoleon Lajoie and Walter Johnson, while Vaughan and Lloyd Waner were selected to represent the National League in a seven-inning exhibition game against a team of American League stars. Wagner and Eddie

Collins, general manager of the Boston Red Sox, served as manager/captains
and took turns choosing players for their respective teams. Wagner, not surprisingly, chose Vaughan, who wound up playing shortstop. He went one for
two and scored a run, as the Wagner bunch took a 4–2 win before a sellout
crowd of more than 10,000 at Doubleday Field. The highlight of the afternoon
came when Ruth appeared as a pinch hitter for the Wagner team. "The Babe,
far off his old-time form, popped weakly to catcher Art Jorgens after missing
one strike by a country mile and fouling off another," read an article in the
June 13 edition of the *Pittsburgh Post-Gazette*.[7]

While the Hall of Fame dedication served as one of the high points of a
mostly forgettable—at least for Pirate fans—season, perhaps the lowest point
arrived a few weeks later when the playing career of Lou Gehrig, baseball's
"Iron Horse," officially came to an end. Leslie Avery, a United Press staff
writer, wrote on June 22 that Gehrig would "pull himself out of the Yankee
dugout and plod over to the umpire with the lineup for today's game, knowing that his own name never again will be written on those little pieces of
pasteboard." Added Avery: "He can never play again. The truth has now come
out. He is suffering from a form of infantile paralysis. For the fans, it marks
the breakdown of the most extraordinary physical machine sports ever produced. It means that 'Locomotive' Gehrig, a household word, has been rav-
ished by disease, practically before their eyes."[8]

Gehrig had broken into the Yankees lineup on June 1, 1925, and played
2,130 consecutive games until May 2, 1939, when he voluntarily benched himself. "If this is the finish," Gehrig said, "I'll just have to take it. You've got to
take the bitter with the sweet. At least I know what is the matter with me now.
I haven't the slightest idea where I picked up such a germ. Nobody ever finds
out, I guess." Gehrig was undergoing tests at the Mayo Clinic from June 13
to 19, and the clinic issued a statement noting that Gehrig was found to be
suffering from amyotrophic lateral sclerosis, an illness that affects the motor
pathways of the central nervous system. The illness would come to be known
as "Lou Gehrig's Disease."[9]

Gehrig had gone to the stadium that day to meet with manager Joe Mc-
Carthy and team president Ed Barrow, and afterword Barrow came out and
told reporters he had bad news. He proceeded to read the physician's report
and then took questions. "I can't believe it," Barrow said. "Imagine what kind
of a constitution he has, to have played all last year. It must have started a couple of years ago. It hits me hard. Lou is one of my favorites," he added, shaking
his head.[10] On July 4, Gehrig—the model of consistency in a career that included two Most Valuable Player awards, six straight All-Star Game appearances and 12 consecutive seasons of .300 or better, including a career average
of .340—would stand at home plate at Yankee Stadium and deliver his formal
farewell before a crowd of nearly 62,000 people. "A couple of big men cried

unashamed tears and several thousand fans had lumps in their throats at the Yankee Stadium yesterday," wrote the *Brooklyn Daily Eagle*'s Jimmy Wood in the July 5 edition.[11] Gehrig delivered one of the most famous speeches of all time that day, a portion of which can be found on the National Baseball Hall of Fame website. "Fans, for the past two weeks you have been reading about the bad break I got. Yet today I consider myself the luckiest man on the face of the earth. Look at these grand men. Which of you wouldn't consider it the highlight of his career to associate with them for even one day? Sure I'm lucky."[12]

As June gave way to July, Pittsburgh occupied sixth place in the NL with a 27–31 mark, nine and a half games behind league-leading Cincinnati. Vaughan, meanwhile, began to see his average climb, as he batted .326 for the month—albeit with just three RBIs—to hike his overall average to .289. In the field, he continued his fine play, as evidenced by this snippet from Boyle's "Mirrors of Sport" column on July 5: "...the only few times we have to cheer is when the swell Arky Vaughan is tumbling all around the infield, making plays that should not be made." On that particular day, Vaughan also came through with the bat, as he singled home the winning run in the bottom of the ninth inning of a 4–3 Pirates win, salvaging a split with the Reds before a huge gathering of 41,937 on a Fourth of July holiday doubleheader.[13]

Vaughan began hitting like the Vaughan of old; a highlight in early July was a four-hit game against the Cubs on July 7. Following Vaughan's four-hit game against Chicago, which gave him hits in 18 of his past 20 games, Biederman wrote: "Gabby Hartnett saw his National League all-star shortstop in action yesterday.... Arky Vaughan is his name and if he doesn't start for the National Leaguers in Yankee Stadium Tuesday, then there just isn't any justice." Vaughan's four hits raised his average to .312.[14] Vaughan indeed was named to the National League All-Star team's starting lineup for the game, which was played on July 11 before nearly 63,000 people in New York's Yankee Stadium. The American League, getting excellent relief pitching from young Bob Feller, came away with a 3–1 win. Feller, the fireballing Iowa farm boy, hurled 3⅔ innings of scoreless relief, allowing only one hit and one walk while striking out two.[15] Vaughan singled, walked, and scored a run and figured in two key plays of the game. First, his error on a grounder hit by Joe Gordon allowed the American League to score what proved to be the deciding run. Then, trailing 3–1 in the sixth, the NL squad mounted a rally, loading the bases with one out against Detroit's Tommy Bridges. The American League team had three pitchers warming up in the bullpen, but Yankees manager Joe McCarthy—who started six of his own players that day—called for Feller, who hadn't even turned 21 yet. Feller threw only one pitch, which Vaughan smacked right at second baseman Gordon, who started a 4–6–3 double play—a rarity for Vaughan, who had hit into only eight double plays the entire 1938 season.

At least one member of the media had no difficulty in placing the blame for the NL's loss. "It is no trick whatever to pick out the All-Star goat," wrote Tommy Holmes of the *Brooklyn Daily Eagle*. "It was this same chunky Mr. Vaughan. This was the first time the Pittsburgh shortstop ever saw the Yankee Stadium. He'll see it in a hundred nightmares from now on." Vaughan scored his team's only run, after beating out an infield hit, but Holmes said that Vaughan "held first base like a man in a trance" when Stan Hack followed with a base hit down the left field line. As a result, Vaughan only got as far as second base. If Vaughan had read the ball correctly, Holmes wrote, he would have reached third and Hack would have wound up with a double—and both men would have scored on Lonnie Frey's double to right.[16]

Vaughan and several of his teammates took time out to take in a boxing match in New York, as they watched Pittsburgh's Billy Conn dethrone Melio Bettina on July 13 at Madison Square Garden to take the light-heavyweight title. Vaughan and Conn would become friends over the next few years, a friendship that would include Conn's future father-in-law, "Greenfield" Jimmy Smith, a former major-league player, and Smith's brother, Tom Smith. In fact, Vaughan and his wife, Margaret, became particularly close friends with Tom and Helen Smith, and their respective families would often get together for picnics or to play cards and games. The two men spent lots of time golfing when the opportunity arose. Vaughan would often stay with the Smiths early in the baseball season, before Margaret and the children would make the trip back east from California, and also stay there in the final month or so of the season, after Margaret and the girls would head back to Potter Valley. Later in Vaughan's career, after he was traded to the Dodgers, he received permission to stay with the Smith family in the Squirrel Hill section of Pittsburgh when Brooklyn came to play the Pirates, rather than have to stay at the team hotel.

"My dad and Arky were the best of friends," recalled Audrey Smith Ifft, the daughter of Tom and Helen Smith. "Arky was such a nice guy—he was always in a good mood and very friendly. He was like part of the family. He would just park his car and move in for the weekend."[17] Audrey Smith Ifft recalled the Vaughans and her parents sitting around talking and the subject of religion popping up. Recalled Ifft: "My mother was a great Catholic—and we are too. Mother said something to Margaret about her religion, and Margaret said, 'We are no religion.' My mother said, 'Margaret, you have to be something,' but [Margaret] said, 'We're not—we just never decided to join anything.' So, Mother started working on her, the good Catholic that my mother was."[18]

Vaughan began to give this more thought; his parents had been members of the First Christian Church in Fullerton, but as an adult, Vaughan did not participate. According to his daughter, Patricia, Vaughan admired the way the Smiths lived. "Their principles and moral values, their social responsibility and their devotedness to family corresponded with the way Arky felt about these things," Patricia would write later. "His Irish blood, of which he was very proud, was 'called' by this Catholic faith."[19] Arky and Margaret began to study the religion through a friend of the Smiths, the Reverend Thomas Dearing, as well as the Reverend J.S. Garahan, a Catholic priest who was close to many Pittsburgh sports figures and was a rabid sports fan himself. He and Vaughan had become close friends. Finally, on August 20, 1939, Vaughan— referred to in the Diocese of Pittsburgh's official records as Joseph (Floyd) Vaughan rather than Floyd Ellis Vaughan—was baptized in St. Paul's Cathedral in Pittsburgh under the sponsorship of Thomas P. and Helen C. Smith. Also baptized were Margaret Vaughan and the couple's two daughters—Patricia and Mikie. According to Dennis Wodzinski of the diocese's archives and records center, since neither of Vaughan's original names—Floyd or Ellis (his middle name) was a saint's name, he may have had to choose one for his baptism—hence the name "Joseph" on the baptismal record.[20] Patricia said that her father would often sign his name as "Joseph Floyd Vaughan" thereafter, but it would be another 10 years before Vaughan officially changed his first name. A legal notice that appeared in the *Ukiah Republican Press* on March 16, 1949, contained an application for a change of name to switch from Floyd Vaughan to Joseph Floyd Vaughan.[21] Audrey Smith Ifft said her mother in particular was delighted that the Vaughans converted to Catholicism at that time of their lives. "They all got baptized," she said. "I thought that was nice— they're up there all together in heaven."[22]

Audrey Smith Ifft's brother, also named Tom Smith, recalled the times that Arky would stay with his family while playing for Brooklyn: "One of our neighbors owned a bakery, and every time Arky came to town, we would have more cakes, pies, doughnuts, and rolls than you could shake a stick at. We had just the best time. I was little, but I can still see Arky's face. I can remember him. And I was the big shot on the block when Arky Vaughan came to stay with us. A professional ballplayer!"[23]

Tom Smith recalled that Vaughan and some of his teammates were not exactly choirboys in their after-hours following games. Smith's father, Tom, and his uncle "Greenfield" Jimmy Smith had an interest in an after-hours speakeasy known as the Bachelor's Club, which featured illegal gambling, alcohol and entertainment. "Guys like Dean Martin and Jerry Lewis got their start here," Tom Smith said. It was a popular hangout for athletes and people in general; "Greenfield" Jimmy had political connections that enabled him to run that type of club, although occasionally a raid would occur—and that would put young Tom Smith into action. His job was to take all of the gambling paraphernalia and quickly lower it through a trap door into the cellar.[24]

It wasn't uncommon for ballplayers to spend their evenings there on off days or when games were scheduled during the day. Vaughan would stay with the Smiths while in town and then go out to the club at night—and then have to play a game the next day or night. "The first thing he'd say was 'Helen, give me a couple of aspirin.'" One morning when Vaughan was playing for Brooklyn and staying with the Smiths, Tom's father decided to play a trick on Vaughan, and when Vaughan asked Helen Smith for an aspirin, the elder Tom Smith told him he had something better than an aspirin, and he handed Vaughan some blue pills. Before the game started, Vaughan went to relieve himself and got a major surprise. "He's peeing blue and he has no idea what the hell it is," Tom Smith said, chuckling at the memory. "He is scared to death; he thinks something's wrong with him." Vaughan played that day, but committed two errors and went zero for four at the plate. Recalled Tom Smith:

> He went to make a play at home and threw it over the catcher's head and the Dodgers lost the ballgame. The manager chews Arky up one side and down the other, "What the heck is wrong with you; you cost us the ballgame." So Arky comes over to the house afterward and he said, "Tom, you have to call Dr. Worthly right away. Something is wrong and I don't want anyone to find out—and I need to get checked out." My mom and dad start laughing like mad and he says, "What are you laughing at? I could be dying." My dad told him he'd given him a pill that was just a dye for an X-ray. And Arky said, "Tom, no more blue pills—I want aspirin from now on."[25]

The elder Tom Smith went out to visit Vaughan on his Potter Valley ranch once a few years later and had an experience to remember. His son recalled:

> My dad was a city boy from Pittsburgh but Arky told him, "C'mon, we're going for a ride." My dad thought they were going in a car, but Arky said, "You're going to ride this horse. It's a very good horse. Gentle. All you have to do is hold on." My dad was very dubious of this—in the back of his mind he's thinking about those blue pills, and thinking that horse was going to buck him. So he gets on the horse; the horse is fine and everything is good. They start up this mountain. By the time they're halfway up, the trail narrows to about as wide as the horse. If you look over to your right, it's a sheer drop—a sheer drop. My dad starts sweating bullets. Arky says, "Let's turn around." My dad says, "Where the hell can we turn around? I'm getting off and walking." But Arky says, "Thomas, this horse is more sure-footed than you are. Don't touch the reins. Just hold on to the horn and don't kick him, don't knee him, let the horse do it." They rode for a good hour. My dad came back and said he'd never get on another horse for as long as he lived. That's how Arky got even for those blue pills. My dad was scared to death thinking that horse would fall off a cliff.[26]

It was not uncommon for Vaughan to spend time with Billy Conn when Vaughan was in Pittsburgh. Conn ended up marrying "Greenfield" Jimmy Smith's daughter, Mary Louise—much to the chagrin of her father. So the get-togethers would occur either at Tom Smith's home or Jimmy Smith's.

These get-togethers weren't exactly tame, as the younger Tom Smith recalled. "They weren't afraid to drink, let's put it that way," he said. "They loved their hooch. But Arky was more laid back than everybody else. At my Uncle Jimmy's, he'd be more quiet—even when everyone was drinking, he'd be more quiet than anyone else."[27]

Vaughan put together an outstanding month of July in 1939, batting .361 over 119 at-bats to raise his overall mark to .311. His best day of the month was a five-for-five explosion on July 19 against the Giants in New York, as he hit for the cycle for the second time in his career. He started his day with a home run and then followed with a triple, double and two singles, jumping his batting average 12 points to .311. Vaughan told reporters later that he'd had several five-hit games in the big leagues but never a six-hit game. He also recalled going nine for nine—including two home runs—in a doubleheader while playing for Wichita in the Western League in 1931.[28] Vaughan's big day gave him a string of 15 hits in 33 at-bats over his last eight games—a .455 clip. On that same day, the *Ukiah Republican Press* near Vaughan's home in Potter Valley reported that Vaughan's father, Robert, had retired after 25 years of service with the Standard Oil Company in Fullerton and had come to reside on Arky's Potter Valley ranch with his daughter, Blythe, and her daughter, Laura Lee.[29]

Vaughan ended the month of July with a .311 mark, and Pittsburgh had climbed to 46–42, good for a tie for third place with Chicago, but still trailed Cincinnati by 13 games. The season fell apart for good in August, though, when the team slumped to an 8–22 record that left the Pirates 54–64 and in sixth place, 19 games in back of the Reds. From that point on, the Bucs merely played out the string, and their effort—or lack thereof—resulted in Traynor's resignation on September 28—a year to the day after Hartnett's "Homer in the Gloamin'" effectively ended Pittsburgh's 1938 pennant hopes. Traynor's resignation ended 20 years of continuous service with the Pirates, first as a player and the last six as manager. Club president Bill Benswanger said the club had accepted Traynor's resignation "with keen regret" and added that it would find a place for Traynor within the organization. No immediate successor was named, but speculation focused on Jimmy Wilson, a coach with Cincinnati, and former St. Louis manager Frankie Frisch.[30]

Two days earlier, Traynor was among those who turned out to watch Vaughan's pal, Billy Conn, defend his light heavyweight boxing crown for the first time by decisioning Melio Bettina, from whom he'd taken the crown earlier in the year, in 15 rounds before a crowd of 18,422 at Forbes Field. Vaughan and teammate Jimmy Tobin dropped in to congratulate Conn "and that doubly pleased Billy because Tobin and Vaughan happen to be his favorite baseball players," reported the *Pittsburgh Press*.[31]

Club president Benswanger made it official on October 1 when he announced that Frisch had accepted the job as manager of the Pirates—the 19th skipper in franchise history. He met with Traynor and Benswanger in New York the day after the season ended to go over personnel. Traynor, whose final Pirate team skidded to a sixth-place finish at 68–85, 28½ games behind pennant-winning Cincinnati, appeared to hold no grudge; he referred to Frisch as "the best man you could have signed."[32] Frisch said he was satisfied with the Bucs' second base combination of shortstop Vaughan and second baseman Pep Young but acknowledged the team would have to "go to work" on the catching and pitching. He also said he hoped to instill more of a fighting spirit on the ball club. "I don't want this job if I can't make these players put on a fighting show for two and a half hours," he said. "I want a colorful, aggressive club. Baseball is short and sweet and it's a grand life. I hope the players appreciate that."[33]

Vaughan finished the season with a somewhat pedestrian .306 batting average, an on-base percentage of .385 and a slugging percentage of .424, but his offensive WAR mark of 5.1 was the fourth-best in all of baseball. He collected 182 hits and managed to score 94 runs and his runs-created figure of 95 was good for a tie for eighth among all major leaguers. He also tied for eighth in the majors in total bases with 252.

Vaughan and Frisch were not strangers; in fact, the two had been involved in a dustup of sorts during Vaughan's second year in the league when Vaughan tangled with Cardinals pitcher Bill Walker following a collision at first base. Frisch blamed Vaughan for the brief outburst and said he was wrong for not letting go of Walker when the two fell in to a clinch. It would be worth watching how Vaughan's temperament would mesh with Frisch's "Gas House Gang" approach to the game.

While the transition from Traynor to Frisch was beginning, Vaughan was already en route to California, this time with a physician friend of his named Dr. James Wilson, a Canonsburg resident who was one of the team doctors. They stopped in Cheyenne, Wyoming, where Vaughan sent Tom and Helen Smith a postcard that was dated 12:30 a.m. October 5. "Bingo," he used as a salutation, "Arrived in Cheyenne all safe and sound, still going strong. Just had one for you [Old Grand Dad]. I miss you two 'lugs.' Will write later. 'Arky.'" Two days later from Reno, Nevada, Vaughan wrote, "Dear 'Toots' & 'Toots,' Arrived in Reno tonite, will be home tomorrow. I still have the champagne but am running low on 'Old Grand Dad.' Hope I make it to Potter Valley. I'll be seeing you. 'Arky.'"[34]

It wasn't long before talk of possible trades began to waft across the baseball landscape, and many felt that Frisch might be inclined to make some moves before assembling his first edition of the Pirates in 1940. Brooklyn was said to be among the clubs interested in Vaughan.[35]

After arriving in Potter Valley, Vaughan managed to squeeze in a few hunting trips in addition to taking care of his ranch. He also found time to answer a few letters from fans, including one dated November 2 in which he sent an autographed baseball and a silver dollar to a fan named Jackie. Vaughan's note read: "We don't have many paper dollars here. I know that silver dollars are very rare in the East, so thought you might like one. I received your cards and the gum, appreciated them very much. I intended sending the baseball sooner, but have been so busy. I had kinda forgotten; it doesn't have all the autographs, as I didn't get it until after the last game and some of the boys had left before I could get them. Hoping to hear from you again, I remain—Sincerely Yours, Arky Vaughan."[36]

The next day, Vaughan wrote a letter to Tom and Helen Smith, greeting them as "Dear Down the Middle Once in Awhile Smith." Vaughan wrote: "I've enjoyed all the letters you haven't written, as a letter writer you are a 'faker,' the same as in golf. I wish you would practice both a little more, so you could give me a little competition. We have enjoyed Helen's letters, tho'. Margaret was right when she said that Helen wrote like she talks, of course we miss all the gestures, etc. Tell her I'm sorry that she broke her fingernails, but they were too long, anyhow. Margaret thanks you two 'lugs' for the champagne, she enjoyed it very much (I didn't get any of it)."[37] Vaughan talked about the trout fishing he'd been doing and the venison he'd been eating "so I haven't gone hungry, like I did when I stayed with you. I kinda miss you tho' at that. ... Give my regards to your big brother, & all the gang up at the club. Write a brief note, once in awhile. Sincerely Yours, 'Satchel' Vaughan."[38]

Patricia thought the letter showed a lot about her father's personality. She wrote years later:

He loved to tease the people he liked. He loved the joking and camaraderie that came along with his golf games with his friends. If Arky liked you he was a warm and loving friend, unlike the coolness and aloofness that he could show to people he had no use for. His idea of "fun" was being with friends and family, sharing drinks and food and often, games like bingo.[39]

Sportswriters often made comments about Vaughan's personality—or specifically the lack thereof—saying that he lacked color. Those who knew him, though, often took exception to that characterization. Barbara Dawson Maple, who grew up in Fullerton with Vaughan, took the time to write a letter to the editor of the *Los Angeles Times* after an article appeared in that publication in the summer of 1985 following Vaughan's induction into the Hall of Fame. The *Times* article quoted a line from a *Fullerton Daily News Tribune* article that read, "He lacked only one thing—a colorful personality." Dawson Maple wrote: "Well, I'm here to tell you he was handsome enough to make us girls swoon when he walked by with that shy smile and he was colorful and popular enough to get elected freshman class president, and later student body vice president at Fullerton Union High School.... Maybe he didn't make smart-aleck remarks to the press or enjoy talking about himself, but he was colorful enough for me and just about everyone else in Fullerton. Not only that he was loved and respected—someone to look up to—but a hero!"[40]

Vaughan was featured in a movie titled *Play Ball, America!*, which was put together by the National League and released in mid–November of 1939. Vaughan was used in a segment that focused on base running and sliding. "Arky Vaughan shows how to use the straight-leg method without breaking any bones," a story in *The Sporting News* noted.[41] At the movie's release in New York City, Pirates president Benswanger said he was still opposed to night baseball, as he regarded the sport as "something which belongs to the sunshine." However, he admitted that conditions might prompt him to look at the situation differently in the future.[42] In a little more than six months, the Pirates would play their first night game at Forbes Field.

As December rolled around, and club executives held their annual winter meetings, trade talk heated up. Brooklyn sought Pirates slugger Johnny Rizzo and the Cubs made their annual bid to pry Vaughan away from Pittsburgh, "but Frisch didn't allow the Bruins to get very far," reported Biederman. "He didn't even listen to the proposition and merely said no when Vaughan's name was mentioned."[43]

Boyle reported that while the Cubs were rejected in their bid to get Vaughan, the Pirates did show some interest in acquiring second baseman Billy Herman—"but not at the price of giving up Vaughan."[44] Later in the month, the *Post-Gazette*'s Al Abrams reported that the Cubs had offered Herman and outfielder Augie Galan for Vaughan and Johnny Rizzo, but nothing came of it.[45]

The new year brought more post-mortems on the disappointing 1939 season, and some members of the press pointed to Vaughan's subpar—at least by his standards—year as a key reason why the team tanked. Chet Smith of the *Pittsburgh Press* wrote that he disagreed with those who said the Pirates had only three worries—catching, pitching and the outfield—because that would insinuate the infield had no issues. "But what about shortstop?" he wrote. "The thought occurs that Arky Vaughan's bog-down last year was a contributing cause in the great el foldo that dropped the team into the second division. Vaughan should outrank any man at his position in the league— but it remains that he didn't."[46] Smith did note, though, that new manager Frisch—known in his playing days as the "Fordham Flash"—didn't seem overly concerned and that Frisch believed if the rest of the team picked up the pace, Vaughan would follow. "In other words, the Flash has a hunch that Arky is not the type that exudes inspiration, but rather he flourishes from it. The Pirates' biggest years have been Vaughan's best, it is pointed out, which is true—and may provide the right answer."[47] Not everyone took kindly to

Smith's criticism of Vaughan. A reader identified only as "C.L.M." said he was angered by Smith's January 8 column and said a closer comparison of Vaughan's numbers from 1939 with those from the near-pennant season of 1938 would show that he played a better shortstop in '39—and that his fielding was improving every year. "As for spirit, Arky tried to play ball last year, which is more than some of the other Pirates did. Don't blame the downfall of the team on Arky, blame it on the pitching. Here's hoping the Pirates go places under Frisch this year and that Arky is the captain."[48]

Biederman wrote that a rebound from second baseman Pep Young would greatly improve the Pirates' chances and added that Lee Handley at third would work just fine—just as it did in the near-pennant winning season of 1938. "[T]hat was the perfect combination and the play of these two fellows gave Arky Vaughan the impetus that almost crowned him the Most Valuable Player of the season and almost transformed a third or fourth place team into a pennant winner," Biederman wrote.[49]

Major news broke in the dead of winter when the ball club announced that it would play seven night games at Forbes Field during the upcoming 1940 season. Westinghouse Electric and Manufacturing would install the lighting equipment "and it will be the most perfect system of illuminations ever designed at any ballpark or institution of the kind in the world," the *Post-Gazette's* Edward F. Balinger wrote. Benswanger said the club had been considering night baseball for about three years, but held off until developments in the lighting industry convinced him that Pirates fans would get the same enjoyment—visibility-wise—as they would at a day game. The ballpark would feature eight steel towers, each weighing 160 tons, that would hold 864 floodlights equal to 1.5 million watts of electrical power. It was said that the towers would produce sufficient light to illuminate all the homes in a city of 25,000 people.[50]

While the local press was busy reporting on the Pirates, Vaughan was busy working on and around his Potter Valley ranch, which he had converted from sheep to cattle. The work was difficult, but Vaughan enjoyed the rancher's life. In late February, the *Post-Gazette* ran a photograph of Vaughan on his ranch, decked out in a cowboy hat, next to a horse with four hunting dogs. "Arky devotes much time during the winter season to chasing coyotes and bobcats on his ranch," the photo caption read. "A bobcat is tied to his saddle and Arky's trusty rifle is in a carrier on the side of the saddle. Vaughan is one of four unsigned Pirates, but he is expected to attend to that business when the Pirates arrive at the San Bernardino camp."[51]

Vaughan made it to camp the first week of March and signed his contract on March 5 after a short talk with Benswanger. He was also appointed team captain by Frisch, succeeding Gus Suhr, who had served in that position until he was traded to the Phillies during the 1939 season.[52] Frisch said naming Vaughan, who was about to enter his ninth season with the Pirates, the Bucs' captain made perfect sense, given his track record—and the fact that plenty of good days remained. In fact, Frisch estimated that the 28-year-old Vaughan had seven or eight quality seasons left. "I've always rated him among the best all-round baseball players in the game," Frisch said of Vaughan. "He can hit, run, throw and field.... Even though he doesn't make a lot of noise out there, he's always hustling."[53]

Frisch said he believed that naming Vaughan captain would prompt the player to show a little more aggressiveness on the field. He said a similar thing happened when he named Leo Durocher captain of the Cardinals after he came over from Cincinnati. "I want Vaughan sticking up for his rights and for the rights of the entire team out on that field and I have a hunch you're going to see a talkative fellow at shortstop for the Pirates." No contract terms were released, but the *Press*' Biederman speculated Vaughan's deal likely was in the $17,500 range, including $500 for the team captaincy.[54]

Boyle wrote that naming Vaughan captain was a good move: "While the position carries no great weight, in the larger scheme of things, it has a tendency to spur on a fellow thus nominated. The captain has a few extra privileges in thumbing his nose at the umpire and he delivers the batting order to the man in blue. It is a post that the big leaguers like to get. No one, incidentally, not even Traynor, took the losing of the 1938 pennant harder than Vaughan, and it was as much his amateur spirit as his professional pay that brought about his disappointment."[55]

Bob Ray of the *Los Angeles Times* described Vaughan as "the Bucs' gifted but sometimes lethargic shortstop" and added that Frisch is hoping the added responsibility of serving as captain "will make Arky take a lot more interest in the ball games. Vaughan will realize it's up to him to set an example for his mates by hustling at all times, and a team that hustles is going to win a lot of ball games, all other things being fairly even."[56] Some local writers, though, said Vaughan didn't need the captain's mantle to spur him on to greater spirit. "A Boston scribe's recent crack that it's one thing for Frankie Frisch to instill spirit into a guy like Pepper Martin, and another thing to try to inject a bit of the same into a fellow like Arky Vaughan, is a lot of tommy-rot," wrote Abrams. "There isn't a faster-moving or better hustling type of player than Arky."[57]

Vaughan got off to a hot start in spring training, hitting .429 in the first 18 games, with 13 of his 24 hits going for extra bases.[58] Once the regular season got under way, Vaughan was hampered by a painful heel bruise on his right foot that limited his effectiveness in the field. But he "didn't feel at home sitting on the bench" and wouldn't come out of the lineup.[59] The *Post-Gazette's* Edward F. Balinger reported that team doctor Charles Jorgensen had been applying frequent treatments of healing balm and electric heat to alleviate the pain in Vaughan's heel but added that Vaughan would remain in the lineup, injury or no injury.[60]

By mid–May, though, with the Pirates in a tailspin that had seen the club lose 13 of its previous 15 games, Frisch was talking of moving Vaughan from shortstop permanently; he'd already played him at third base on May 6 against Brooklyn. Biederman wrote that while Frisch had deep respect for Vaughan's ability as a player in that he "hustles every minute, is fast, and can really lather that ball," Vaughan was not the "streamlined-type" of shortstop that Frisch needed. Biederman wrote that Frisch was contemplating moving Vaughan to either third base or right field. He also wrote that Vaughan might have saved two games lost in Chicago the previous week "with a faster jump on some infield taps." Biederman wrote that Frisch had nothing but praise for Vaughan's spirit and hustle and had no interest in dealing him. "However, the Old Flash realizes a shortstop with the accent on fielding and a trifle less potent at bat could make a big difference in the Bucs," Biederman added. "But unless Frisch can maneuver these changes, it may be one of the longest summers Pittsburgh fans have had in many a season."[61]

On May 8, Frisch pulled the trigger on one major change, sending slugger Johnny Rizzo to the Cincinnati Reds for fellow outfielder Vince DiMaggio.[62] A week or so later, talk of a mutiny within the Pirates surfaced via a couple of New York newspapers. One such story appeared on May 10 in the *Brooklyn Daily Eagle* after the Pirates headed out of town "leaving behind a batch of rumors that hung heavy as factory smoke." Nine straight losses— some of them lopsided— had some saying that the Pirates were not giving Frisch their best effort. "The Pirates always have been a clique team, and

Arky Vaughan, shown during one of his later years with the Pirates (courtesy Pittsburgh Pirates).

it is the belief in some uniformed quarters here that there is an under-cover drive on to get Paul Waner in as manager," the *Daily Eagle* reported, adding that veteran outfielders Paul and Lloyd Waner were upset at being replaced by young Bob Elliott and Maurice Van Robays.[63] Frisch shrugged off the rumors, and Waner openly refuted them. Biederman wrote that Vaughan, speaking for the team, told reporters that Frisch "plays the best baseball of any manager in the league and there's no manager for whom I'd rather work than Frisch. Does that cover the situation?" In the same column, team president Benswanger defended Frisch, saying that he would be the manager through 1941 when his contract expired. "I think we got one of the best baseball men in the business when we signed Frank Frisch and I was 100 percent for him when I negotiated for his services and am more in his corner now than ever. ... Our players are for Frisch all the way and I know he's getting 100 percent out of each man on our roster."[64]

By the end of May, the Pirates occupied the National League basement with a 9–21 record and already trailed first-place Cincinnati by 13½ games. Vaughan was doing his part, scoring 21 runs and driving in 23 while batting .319 in the first 30 games. Things went south in June for Vaughan, though, as he endured one of the roughest stretches of his big-league career. In 112 at-bats that month, he hit just .205 to drop his average on the season to .263. Vaughan did manage to score 16 runs and drive in 16 as the Pirates went 15–14 to move to fifth place in the NL chase, but the club still trailed Cincinnati by 15 games.

One of the highlights of an otherwise forgettable month of June was the Pirates' first foray into night baseball at Forbes Field. That came on June 4 when the Bucs hosted the Boston Bees. A crowd of 25,000 was expected for the game; gates were to open at 6:30 p.m. but the game would not start until darkness arrived, and that was anticipated to be about 8:45 p.m. Forbes Field, with its $125,000 lighting system, would be the seventh major-league ball-park to embrace night baseball, and its maiden outing would come five years after Crosley Field in Cincinnati hosted the big leagues' first night game. On the same day, Hitler ordered some 675,000 troops into battle against France, threatened the early "annihilation of our enemies in London" and warned neutral Switzerland about attacking German aircraft. In his homeland, Hitler was being praised as a military genius for orchestrating successful battles; a spokesman said Hitler was "solely responsible for the blitzkrieg that smoth-ered Poland in 18 days and that he worked out the strategy that sent German armies sweeping through the Netherlands, Belgium and northern France to the English Channel in three weeks."[65]

The Pirates' first home night game proved successful, as they came away with a 14–2 victory. Young Frankie Gustine slugged two doubles and a single and drove in three runs to lead the attack. A turnout of 20,319, including the commissioner of baseball, Judge Kenesaw Mountain Landis, took in the contest. Some of the outfielders complained about the lighting conditions, saying that it was tough to follow low liners, and some spectators said it was difficult to track some balls hit to the outfield. "There were distinct patches of darkness around the edges of the fences," Biederman noted. "The scoreboard was hardly visible from the press box and some of the patrons on the first base side found the same difficulties." Biederman said that outfielders learned not to take their eyes off a ball for a second because if they did, and then tried to find it again, they were out of luck. Players took batting practice early, long before twilight, and then had to sit around in their respective dugouts from 8:30 p.m. until 9 p.m. waiting for darkness, and the game didn't start until 9:28 p.m., finishing at midnight. Honus Wagner, the Pirates' venerable coach, joked that it would be another two hours before he made it home to Carnegie. "That's the only thing I don't like about night ball," Wagner said. "I get home in time to meet the milkman!"[66]

Despite his subpar month of June, Vaughan was named to the National League All-Star team for the seventh time, with the game slated for July 9 in St. Louis. Not everyone was on board with the selection, though. The *Pitsburgh Press*' Chet Smith questioned it, saying that if someone had to represent the Pirates it should be Gustine—not Vaughan. "Gustine has been one of the reasons why the Buccaneers still aren't in eighth place," Smith wrote. "His hitting and all-around deportment in the field put him well up among the recruit finds of the year."[67] Biederman wrote that Vaughan didn't care much for the All-Star honor. "Secretly, he would gladly exchange places with Frankie Gustine. He would like to see the kid get his chance. Arky has been there before and the thrill is gone for him."[68]

Vaughan began picking up the pace the first week of July and went on a hot streak sandwiched around the All-Star Game that saw him pound out 14 hits—including two home runs and two doubles—in 31 at-bats from July 5–14, a .452 streak that picked his average up to .287. At the annual mid-summer classic, Vaughan collected the game's first hit and scored its first run when he singled off Red Ruffing and came home on Max West's three-run homer as the National League claimed a 4–0 victory. He handled his only attempt in the field—a slow grounder hit by Jimmy Foxx—without incident.[69] When play resumed, Vaughan's hitting continued, and he finished the month of July at .287 overall after going 36 for 107 (.336) with 30 runs scored, 18 RBIs, and an OPS of .955. The Pirates, though, remained buried in the second division with a 42–46 record, 18 games in back of Cincinnati, through the month of July. But Frisch had plenty of compliments for his standout shortstop. "A great fellow to have on a ball club," he said of Vaughan. "He plays so easily that sometimes it doesn't look as if he's hustling. But don't make that mistake, he's hustling every minute he's on the field."[70]

But Smith wasn't as high on Vaughan's play, saying that his subpar offensive production overall on the season made him a liability instead of an asset because of what he saw as shortcomings on defense. "Just as a guess, it may be said that he has lost more games by his deficiencies in the field this year than he has won at the plate," Smith wrote.[71]

Vaughan punctuated his hot month of July at the plate by getting into an on-field scrap with Brooklyn catcher Babe Phelps in a night game at Ebbets Field on July 29. The fisticuffs occurred in the ninth inning when Phelps grounded back to Pittsburgh pitcher Mace Brown, who tossed to first baseman Elbie Fletcher to retire him. The Pirates thought Phelps spiked Fletcher in crossing the first base bag. Tempers were already rising after an incident in the top of the ninth that ended in a disputed out call at home plate.

After the play at first base involving Phelps and Fletcher, while the Pirates were tossing the ball around the infield, Phelps and Vaughan "exchanged remarks which did not seem to appeal to the Corsair captain," wrote Balinger. He added: "The usually placid Arky instantly rushed to the first base line and Phelps leaped toward him. They walloped each other several times as Umpire Sears sprang between them. Phelps led to the neck and Arky came back with a punch that seemed to reach Babe's jaw. By this time, the other umpires and the coaches were tearing the belligerents apart."[72]

Both players were ejected and both were fined $25. Later in the same story, Balinger revisited the battle between Vaughan and Phelps:

> According to the Buccos, Babe had to go out of his way in order to tread upon Elbie's toes and it was this which inspired Vaughan to scamper across the diamond and accuse the big catcher of dirty baseball. Vaughan then found himself hailed as a fellow whose word was false and when Phelps lurched closer, Arky seemed willing to put away a little matter of more than 50 pounds and he sailed right into Phelps like a sparrow attacking a dirigible balloon. Arky delivered at least two pokes that must have stung and he also took one which had power behind it.[73]

The *Brooklyn Daily Eagle*—not surprisingly—saw things a little differently. Holmes wrote that Fletcher "looked at Phelps with the eyes of a wounded fawn and said that Babe had stepped on his foot—intentionally, too—at first base. Babe said that he didn't, and made what seemed to be suitable apologies. Then Mr. Vaughan, who had walked over to the pitcher's box, said something to Phelps, who replied in kind." Holmes added that Vaughan had "struck an attitude" similar to that of an old prizefighter named Peter Maher, and that prompted Phelps to throw his cap to the ground and charged Vaughan. "Several missed punches were followed by a clinch," Holmes wrote. "As the umpires separated the men, Phelps did land a heavy punch to Vaughan's face." Holmes ran into Pirates coach Mike Kelly afterward and Kelly told him that "Phelps got red-headed because Brown threw one close to him and took it out on Fletcher." When Holmes told Kelly that Phelps wasn't the fighting type,

Kelly responded, "But you know that Vaughan isn't a tough guy, either, unless he has reason to be riled."[74]

Gustine remembered the play well when he spoke with Patricia Vaughan Johnson 50 years later. "Your dad, as quiet as he was, runs over and pushes Fletcher aside to fight [Phelps]. He was the last guy in the world who would want to fight, but he was a very powerful, barrel-chested man. We were all in awe to see Arky running over there to give protection to his teammate."[75]

The rhubarb reminded Biederman of some of Vaughan's previous battles. "Those who have been mixed up with Vaughan, or have seen him riled, always keep their distance," he wrote. "Though he isn't Joe Pep personified on the field, the Californian can handle his dukes and he seldom comes out second best." Biederman recalled the time when Alex Kampouris arrived at second base with his cleats high at Forbes Field in a game during the 1938 season and "then gave Vaughan some words that Arky didn't think were appropriate. Remember how Vaughan picked Kampouris up with his right hand and was ready to cart him away when the other boys stepped in?" Biederman also mentioned the harsh words that Vaughan and Dizzy Dean exchanged in Chicago during that same season. Dean had hit a double and when he got to second base, he began riding Vaughan, who threw down his glove and was ready to have a go at Dean. "Dean drew back when he saw Vaughan really meant business and cracked, 'You wouldn't dare touch me with all my friends here in the stands?' Arky laughed right in his face and went back to shortstop. He knew the Diz never would fight and, if he did, wouldn't last long."[76]

Abrams, in a column that ran on July 31, wrote that the Vaughan-Phelps fight reminded him of a conversation he once had with a National League umpire whom he wouldn't name. The two were talking about fighting, and the umpire told him that the rowdy, loud-mouth types weren't the most dangerous fighters. Instead, it was the easy-going type—and he named Vaughan as the No. 2 example behind Ethan Allen, an outfielder with the Phillies at the time. "Arky is one of those nice, pleasant chaps everyone likes, but cross him up or do something he doesn't like and he'll fight at the drop of a hat. There are few men in this league, or any other league for that matter, who can give Arky an argument with their fists."[77] The fight on the field in Brooklyn was overshadowed by news of different kind of fight in Pittsburgh, as Conn—the hometown light heavyweight champ and a close friend of Vaughan's—had reached agreement to battle reigning heavyweight champion Joe Louis. There was a catch—Conn had to defeat heavyweight Bob Pastor in a match at the Polo Grounds on August 13. If Conn could get past Pastor, he would earn the right to meet Louis at Forbes Field.

With the season entering the dog days of August, the baseball world was rocked by the suicide of a player who had close ties to Vaughan— Cincinnati Reds catcher Willard Hershberger. Hershberger grew up in

Southern California and graduated from Fullerton High School a year ahead of Vaughan, and the two were teammates for several years on the Indians' football and baseball teams. Legend had it that Hershberger was actually the player that scout Art Griggs was most interested in when he went to watch the Cypress Merchants play in the winter of 1930–31, but that he became enamored of Vaughan and wound up signing him instead. Legend also had it that Yankees scout Bill Essick chose to go see Hershberger play on another team that same weekend instead of going to check out Vaughan—and missed his chance to sign the standout shortstop. Essick eventually signed Hershberger, who was stuck in the minor leagues behind Hall of Fame catcher Bill Dickey for years before he reached the big leagues with Cincinnati. Hershberger then had to back up another standout catcher, Ernie Lombardi, but eventually earned some playing time, and in his second season he batted .349 in 63 games for the league champion Reds. In his third season with Cincinnati, he began solidifying his reputation as a fine hitter and an excellent receiver. He was hitting a solid .309 in 48 games with the Reds during the 1940 season and was well-liked by his teammates, several of whom said he could have started for most teams in the big leagues but apparently was happy just backing up Lombardi. Reds pitcher Gene Thompson said he didn't think Hershberger realized how good he was. "We pitchers just thought he was outstanding," Thompson said. "Most guys with Hershie's ability would say, 'Trade me. I want to go to a place where I can catch every day.' He had no confidence. He was satisfied."[78] Hershberger was pressed into regular duty in July when Lombardi was injured, and he blamed himself for a rough patch that saw the league-leading Reds lose five out of 11 games. After a doubleheader loss to the Boston Bees, a game in which Hershberger failed to pursue a topped ball hit in front of home plate, he had a long talk with manager Bill McKechnie at the team's hotel in Boston. At that time, Hershberger told McKechnie that he was contemplating suicide, so McKechnie went to dinner with him and stayed with him for several hours. The next morning, Hershberger—whose father committed suicide when the younger Hershberger was in high school—failed to make it to the ballpark for batting practice, and the team became concerned and reached him by phone at his hotel room. Hershberger told a team official he was sick but would come to watch the game. When the catcher never showed up, McKechnie sent someone to the hotel to check on him, and when a hotel employee opened the locked door, Hershberger's body was found in the bathroom. He had found a safety razor in his teammate's bag and slit his throat, bleeding to death in the bathtub.[79]

Hershberger's suicide reverberated throughout baseball, and Pittsburgh was no exception, as the Pirates had tried to acquire the young catcher several times over the years when he was property of the Yankees. Pittsburgh also had offered the Reds Johnny Rizzo for Hershberger but was turned down.[80] Boyle recalled sitting with Frisch during the 1939 World Series and hearing Frisch talking about Hershberger in glowing terms. "Look at him challenging the pitcher," Frisch said when Hershberger went up to pinch hit in one of the games. "He's a good one. How I wish I had him for the Pirates."[81]

Vaughan continued to raise his average during the month of August as he batted .303 for the month with 21 runs scored and 18 RBIs, and he took an overall mark of .291 into the final month of the season. Although the Pirates were out of the race, Vaughan continued to play hard, as evidenced by a play that occurred on August 7 against St. Louis when Vaughan tagged up on a long fly ball off the bat of Maurice Van Robays and scored all the way from second base. It was a rare two-run sacrifice fly, as Debs Garms also scored from third. As a team, the Pirates showed some life, putting together a 20–12 record to improve to 62–58 and climb to fifth place, 14 games behind the Reds. The club would continue to play nearly .500 ball the rest of the way and wound up the season in fourth place at 78–76, 22½ games behind the pennant-winning Reds, who went on to defeat Detroit in the World Series, four games to three, and sent Hershberger's mother a check for the winner's share—$5,083.62.[82]

Vaughan used a hot September, when he batted .331 and had an OPS of .989 with 23 RBIs and 25 runs scored, to finish the season at an even .300 with an OPS of .846. He led the major leagues in both runs scored (113) and triples (15)—marking the third time he had paced the majors in triples in his career—and combined with his solid defense, Vaughan posted the No. 2 WAR for position players in the major leagues at 6.3, behind only Johnny Mize's 7.4. He also topped the big leagues in games played at 156 and plate appearances with 689, tied for first in times on base with 269, was fourth in the majors in hits with 178, fourth in walks with 88, fifth in total bases at 269, seventh in on-base percentage at .393, eighth in RBIs at 95 and tied for eighth in stolen bases with 12. If it weren't for his slow start, Vaughan's final numbers would have been even more impressive, as he batted .323 from the Fourth of July to the end of the season.

As usual, Arky headed back to California for the off-season, bringing a friend—Doc Wilson—with him. On the way, they stopped in Oklahoma City to see teammate Debs Garms, who had won the National League batting title that year with a .355 average. Vaughan also sent postcards to Tom and Helen Smith, including one dated October 2 from Grants Pass, New Mexico. "Still going strong," Arky wrote. "Will be in Phoenix this evening. We're getting 400 miles to a quart. Regards, 'Arky.'" The "quart" referred to a bottle of "Old Grand-Dad" whiskey—Arky's liquor of choice. A few days later, Wilson sent another postcard to the Smiths: "We arrived right side up in Potter Valley— nice trip. Arky is out in hay field—pitching."[83]

As the fall wore on, talk inevitably turned to trades and a potential makeover for the Pirates. Once again, rumors surfaced regarding Brooklyn's Branch Rickey's desire to obtain Vaughan, but it appeared as though Vaughan "would be about the last man the Pirates would consider using in a trade," Boyle speculated.[84] Frisch had already been busy, as just about the entire lineup—aside from the pitching staff—had turned over from Traynor's final year as manager in 1939. Only Vaughan—a fixture at shortstop since 1932—and Elbie Fletcher, who had come over part-way through the 1939 season—had held on to their positions through Frisch's first year at the helm.

In late November, Biederman reported that Frisch and team president Benswanger could have made a trade with the Cardinals "two minutes after they took off their hats and coats, pulled up chairs and went into a conference with Branch Rickey in Columbus the other day." He then caught himself: "Two minutes? It wouldn't have required that much time. The trio would have established a new Olympic record for manufacturing a trade had Messrs. Frisch and Benswanger merely nodded when the name of Arky Vaughan came up, as it always does when rival owners and managers sit down to talk with the Pirate bosses. It seems like every team in the league would like to acquire Vaughan, and the Bucco shortstop's name invariably bobs up as soon as discussions begin."[85] Biederman quoted Frisch as saying, "I've been manager of the Pirates a little over a year now, and I'd like to have $1 for every time Vaughan's name has come up in a proposed trade."[86]

In December, at the winter meetings in Chicago, Frisch and Benswanger once again spiked rumors of a Vaughan deal, as the club issued a statement that read: "Arky Vaughan remains with the Pirates. He will not be traded."[87] The *Pittsburgh Press*' Chet Smith, though, wrote that the team could afford to part with Vaughan, adding that he wasn't so valuable that his departure would ruin the team even if the return wasn't equal to his worth as a shortstop. Smith acknowledged Vaughan's hitting prowess—he hit at least .300 every season up to that point in his career—but said he lacked aggressiveness on defense and couldn't hold a candle to some other shortstops in the league. "Vaughan has not won a pennant for the Pirates," Smith wrote. "To put it another way, for convenience sake, the Pirates haven't won a pennant since Vaughan arrived on the scene. By this token it would appear he is not indispensable." Smith said that while it would make sense for the Indians to turn down all offers for Bob Feller and for the Yankees to do the same with Joe DiMaggio, "it is questionable whether [Vaughan] should be classed with any of these gentlemen."[88]

♦♦ 7 ♦♦

Walking the Plank

The winter of 1940–41 saw world tension heightened to an unprecedented point as President Franklin Roosevelt began his third term in office in late January. The war in Europe raged, and famed U.S. aviator Charles Lindbergh urged Congress and Roosevelt to negotiate a neutrality agreement with Hitler. Meanwhile, in late January, Joseph Grew, the U.S. ambassador to Japan, contacted officials in Washington to pass along rumors that Japan was preparing a surprise attack on a U.S. Navy base at Pearl Harbor, in Hawaii. Less than a year later, those rumors would become a horrific and deadly reality.

In the world of sports, the Hot Stove League had its usual rumor kettles simmering. Talk in Pittsburgh focused on whether the Pirates might move Vaughan—their perennial All-Star shortstop—to third base or perhaps the outfield. Manager Frankie Frisch had said prior to his first season as the Pirates' skipper that it wouldn't make sense to move Vaughan, even if he wasn't the best defensive shortstop, because he had no one capable of replacing him. But a year later, the club had its eyes on a possible successor—a 26-year-old Georgian named Alf Anderson, who was acquired from Atlanta in the Southern Association in exchange for Pep Young the previous September. Anderson batted .351 with Atlanta, slugging 41 doubles and 11 triples. *Pittsburgh Press* columnist Chet Smith opined that Vaughan's primary defensive shortcomings—a tendency to overplay balls hit right at him and a need to wind up before getting rid of the ball—might not hurt him as much at third base, where the ball tends to reach the fielder much quicker. Some, Smith noted, had suggested that Vaughan would be more at home on third "where he could knock down hits and still have plenty of time to toss out the runner."[1]

Other media members, though, said it would be foolish to move one of the best in the game at his position. Paul Scheffels, a United Press staff writer based in New York, wrote that a check of the National League records over the previous nine years would show there was virtually no basis for moving Vaughan "and little room for improvement. Arkie, only 28 years old, lacks only the color and ash of a Babe Ruth to be one of baseball's greats. Chin tucked in, he resembles a West Point cadet or heavyweight fighter in action when he takes his cut at the plate. He has powerful legs and tremendous speed in getting down to first and seldom hits into a double play." Scheffels then rattled off a few facts that made the "'shift Vaughan for Anderson'" movement look absurd, noting that Vaughan had batted at least .300 for nine straight seasons, he played in every game the previous year and was the ninth-hardest player to strike out, sixth in walks and seventh-toughest to double up, as he grounded into only five double plays in 1939. "That's all Anderson has to equal to stick with Pittsburgh," Scheffels concluded.[2] Even Frisch admitted it was a longshot, saying, "Anderson would have to be a hell of a shortstop to force Vaughan out of a position he's held down for nine years."[3]

As the time to report to spring training grew closer, talk of a new contract for Vaughan reached the papers. Biederman of the *Pittsburgh Press* reported that Vaughan had written the Pirates and said he would be in San Bernardino, the team's spring training home, on February 24. He kept his word despite having to take care of some very important business first. On February 22, Vaughan and his wife welcomed their third child—and third girl—six-pound, seven-ounce Judith Margaret. The family had left Potter Valley a little earlier than usual so Margaret could deliver their newest addition in Fullerton, where most of her and her husband's families still resided. Vaughan made it to camp two days later, but his contract discussions with club president Benswanger would have to wait, as Benswanger received news of his mother's passing and had to head back east. Despite being unsigned, Vaughan received permission to work out with the team—breaking a long-standing Pirate precedent that held that no player would be able to work out until signing a contract or at least agreeing to terms. Benswanger eventually returned to camp and Vaughan signed his contract for a reported $17,000—highest on the club.[4] Benswanger said the two didn't need much time to reach agreement. "I asked him how much he wanted," Benswanger told the *Pittsburgh Press*' Les Biederman. "He told me. I said okay. I brought out the contract, filled in the terms and Vaughan signed it. He thanked me, shook hands again and said goodbye. It didn't take more than four or five minutes."[5]

The day before, Biederman wrote that when you mentioned Vaughan's name in Frisch's presence, the manager's face would light up "and he goes into raptures." Biederman wrote that Vaughan was something of a hero to Frisch and quoted the manager:

> That's my kind of ball player, that Vaughan. If he only had the fire of a Pepper Martin, he'd be the best in my book. That's all he lacks. But don't think for a minute that because he isn't fighting and fuming and swearing at everything and everybody, he isn't an A-1 hustler. He sure is. I've never seen him loaf going down to first base, no matter whether he hit an infield fly, a grounder to the pitcher or missed a third strike

that got by the catcher. And I'm not just speaking from the time I took this club last year. I've watched that fellow ever since he broke into the big leagues and I've always admired him.[6]

Biederman characterized Vaughan as "a very peculiar fellow. He doesn't make friends easily, yet when he does warm up to you, he's on your side and you can bet on that. He's the most popular of the Pirates and one of the most popular in the league."[7]

Spring training was mostly uneventful for Vaughan and the Pirates; two days after he signed his contract, he collected three hits in an intrasquad game. Three weeks later, his ninth-inning home run ignited a comeback that resulted in an 8–7 win over the White Sox in Los Angeles. Vaughan singled and doubled as well, appearing ready to head into the season.[8] Vaughan, who led the NL in triples in 1940 with 15, banged out two three-baggers on Opening Day, driving in a pair of runs in a 7–4 loss to Chicago before a crowd of just 17,008 at Wrigley Field. After those heroics, Vaughan stumbled briefly, thanks in part to a chipped bone in his right index finger that kept him out of the lineup for several games and limited his effectiveness when he returned. He sat out the next day's game—the first game he'd missed with an injury since 1938. The previous year, in fact, Vaughan played 156 games in a 154-game schedule, as the Pirates had to play off two ties. The *Pittsburgh Post-Gazette* reported on April 25 that Vaughan would be unable to handle a baseball for at least two more weeks due to the injury.[9] But after pinch hitting twice in three days, he was back in the lineup on April 29, starting a mini-tear that saw him go 12 for 24 and raise his average more than 100 points to .362 at the end of the first week in May. So much for a two-week break for Vaughan, who told Frisch on the train from Cincinnati to Philadelphia that he was ready to go. Vaughan believed that the chipped bone had already "knitted back where it belongs" and that he was ready to return to the starting lineup. Vaughan, *Post-Gazette* reporter Edward F. Balinger wrote, "has the hardihood of the typical westerner. He takes his bruises, bumps and even broken bones without whimpering."[10]

Concern about a different type of injury prompted Major League Baseball to begin experimenting with a new piece of equipment in 1941—the batting helmet. The Brooklyn Dodgers announced that their players would begin wearing helmets that season, and several other teams joined the ranks before the season ended. The Pirates had four of the new helmets—referred to as "protective caps with the cork-lined interior"—available for the 1941 season, but none of them had been worn during the first 10 days of the season, as Frisch made them optional equipment. Biederman noted that Vaughan inspected one and said, "If I can't get out of the way of a pitched ball and need a helmet for protection, I'll be ready to quit the game."[11] Ironically, Vaughan would indeed be hit in the head with a pitch later that season—in an exhibition game, of all places—and the concussion that came with the beaning wiped out most of his final month of the season.

The Pirates, without several familiar faces including the Waner Brothers, Paul and Lloyd, Pep Young, Wilbur Brubaker and Mace Brown—one of Vaughan's closest friends on the team—got off to a slow start, going just 14–21 in April and May and trailed pace-setting St. Louis by 13½ games. Vaughan continued to hit in May, finishing the month with a .346 average with 15 runs scored and 10 RBIs. One of the highlights of Vaughan's month came off the field, when he dropped in to watch his pal, Conn, prepare for what would be—at least at temporarily—the biggest fight of his career. Conn, the light-heavyweight champ, was getting ready to take on Buddy Knox at Forbes Field later in the month in what would be a stepping stone fight for the big one—a match against reigning heavyweight champion Joe Louis. Conn stopped Knox in the eighth round of their match and promptly set his sights on Louis. When the Pirates made a trip to New York to play the Giants the first week of June, Vaughan took a few of his Pirates teammates to Pompton Lakes, New Jersey, where Conn began training for his shot at the heavyweight crown, which would come on June 18 in New York's Polo Grounds. A week or so later, in a bylined article that appeared in the June 12, 1941, edition of the *Pittsburgh Post-Gazette*, Conn wrote:

> One of my most distinguished training camp visitors to date, and my favorite sports hero any time, spent today with me here. Arky Vaughan of the Pirates had a day off because Pittsburgh was playing the Dodgers at Ebbets Field tonight, so he drove over here to watch me work. There's been many a day I've gone out to Forbes Field to watch Arky work, so he figured he'd return the call. If I could fight like Arky Vaughan can play ball, Joe Louis would really have two strikes on him. I wanted to go back to Brooklyn with Arky to see the Pirates-Dodgers game tonight, but my keepers would not let me.[12]

Prior to the Louis-Conn heavyweight bout, reporters asked a number of Pittsburgh residents—judges, politicians, sports figures, businessmen and even a mortician—how they saw the fight going. Vaughan responded, "Nothing to it. Conn by a decision. Billy is a personal friend of mine and he's been waiting for this chance too long to throw it away. Louis has slipped and Conn is still coming."[13] On the afternoon of the fight, the weigh-in results earned top billing among the front-page headlines in the *Pittsburgh Press*; the other main headline read, "British Drive in Libya Halted; Ruhr Battered for 7th Night." Below that, a headline read "Hitler Can't Win, High-Ranking Nazis Admit in Private" and another read, "Axis Reports Big Victory in North Africa."

But perhaps the most interesting of all the Page 1 headlines that day declared, "Conn Battles Louis, Cupid and Irate Father of Girl, 18." The "irate father" in question was "Greenfield" Jimmy Smith—the brother of Vaughan's close personal friend, Tom Smith—and the "girl" was his daughter, Mary

Louise. Conn was head over heels over Mary Louise and wanted to marry her, but her father would have none of it, saying, "I'll punch the hell out of that fellow. I'm trying to raise a decent family ... and I don't want any of my children mixed up with prize fighters. My daughter has just turned 18, and at her age I wouldn't want her to have anything to do with the greatest fellow in the world."[14] The *Pittsburgh Press* story also noted that a month earlier, Conn and Mary Louise had driven to Brookville, about 60 miles northeast of Pittsburgh, and applied for a marriage license, accompanied by a priest and a physician. However, Conn asked that the application not be filed until June 16, which would result in the license being issued June 19 due to a three-day waiting period. Smith said the application was not valid because it gave his daughter's age as 21—the minimum age that a woman could marry in Pennsylvania without parental consent. But a Jefferson County judge said there was nothing in the law that could prevent the license from being issued unless Smith filed a formal appeal in court.[15]

Smith had introduced Conn to his daughter before Conn began moving up the ranks as a fighter, but what started out as a harmless friendship blossomed into love—and that's when Smith "soured" on Conn because he didn't think boxers made the best husbands. "Win or lose," Smith said, "I know where those fellows end up." Smith banned Conn from the Smith home, but the couple began sneaking around. As a result, Smith sent his daughter to a boarding school near Philadelphia, but she returned during the winter of 1940–41. Smith finally gave Conn permission to see Mary Louise at the Smith home, "but they won't get married," Smith said. "I'll see to that. I'll beat the hell out of him, and he'd probably be the first one to say I could do it." Despite the bad blood between Conn and Smith, it hadn't reached the point where Smith was pulling for Louis. "I hope that fellow wins," said Smith, who never referred to Conn by name in the story—only as "that fellow." "But I want him to stay away from my family."[16]

Later that night, before 55,000 people at the Polo Grounds, Conn had Louis on the ropes and appeared to be on the way to dethroning the champion. In the 13th round, though, the champ caught Conn with a short right to the jaw and then followed up with a half-dozen or so more blows, and Conn was counted out with only two seconds remaining in the round. After the fight, some ringside observers wrote that Conn had the fight won after 12 rounds, and that all he needed to do was play things conservatively over the final three rounds to take the crown from Louis. "We had him definitely ahead on points and the assembled thousands who had refused to believe their eyes at first were beginning to relax in preparation of a thunderous ovation to a modern giant killer," wrote Joe Williams in the *Pittsburgh Press*. "They were sitting in on an epic thing—the dethronement of the greatest champion since Dempsey's day."[17] Harry Ferguson, a United Press sports editor, wrote that despite being outweighed and outgunned, Conn gave the crowd "something to carry down the years. He gave them the memory of a frail stripling who came within a whisper of winning the heavyweight championship of the world, the memory of a gallant kid who lasted almost 39 minutes against the most destructive puncher in the business and carried the battle to him a good part of the way."[18] Conn told reporters, "I guess maybe I just had too much guts—and not enough common sense. But I made a good fight of it, didn't I?" Louis expressed neither joy nor disappointment in the outcome: "I figured it would end just as it did. I felt sure that sooner or later he would be very wide with one of those lefts and that I would nail him with a right. That's just what happened. ... That one punch got him, although it took another seven or eight to finish him off. He was a pretty tough boy up to then, you know."[19]

The trip to New York was hardly a total loss for Conn, however. The morning after the fight, Conn "gave everyone the slip—even his manager, Johnny Ray—and left the hotel in New York," according to a story in the *Pittsburgh Press*. Mary Louise, meanwhile, had gone to New York with her mother the previous night to watch the fight while her father headed to the Smiths' summer home at Ocean Beach, New Jersey. And the marriage license that the couple had applied for in Brookville had been picked up by a "special messenger"—an unnamed attorney—and taken to Brockway, Pennsylvania, then delivered to Dr. J.J. Menegas, who also attended the Conn-Louis fight in New York. The elder Smith had failed to file a protest with the court in a timely manner, so the license remained valid.[20] The next day, though, a headline in the *Pittsburgh Press* declared, "I Can't Be Married Today, Billy Says as Crowd Waits." Below the headline and above the main story, a bulletin conveyed that the marriage of Billy and Mary Louise was called off "because of the continued objection of James L. [Greenfield Jimmy] Smith, father of Mary Louise. Conn, after an hour-and-a-half's conference with Mr. and Mrs. Smith with Mary Louise and a priest said he would not marry against Mr. Smith's wishes." The story noted that the postponement was "just about as big an upset as the East Liberty Flash almost scored over Joe Louis two days ago," and that hundreds of children had gathered at St. Philomena's Church, where the wedding ceremony was to have taken place before noon on June 20. "But there was no wedding."[21] That would all change before too long, as Billy and Mary Louise were secretly married in Philadelphia on July 1—just 40 miles or so from "Greenfield" Jimmy. Conn told the *Pittsburgh Press* that he called his father-in-law to tell him the news and the former big-league ball player exclaimed, "As soon as I get my hands on you, I'll—well, use your imagination." Conn said he wanted to smooth things over with his father-in-law. "I never hurt anybody and I don't think this will hurt him or Mary Lou," Conn said. "But what can you do with a wild man?"[22] Conn was not exaggerating;

a year later, on May 12, Smith and Conn would get into a full-scale brawl at a christening party for Billy and Mary Louise's first child, Timmy—a fight that would result in Conn breaking his left hand and losing a shot at a rematch with Louis—and an estimated take of $150,000.[23] The fight, scheduled for June 25, 1942, had to be postponed due to Conn's injury, and the two would not meet again until June 1946.

While Conn and his father-in-law spent weeks battling, that was not the only heavyweight struggle reported on the front page during the months of June and July. "Yield or Face Invasion, Nazi Threat to Russia," the headline atop the front page of the *Pittsburgh Press* on June 19 read, as the alliance between the two Axis powers was crumbling. A pro–Axis diplomat reported that "Der Fuehrer is anxious to complete his new order in Europe, and he must know where Russia stands."[24] By early July, the two one-time cohorts were deep in the throes of a major battle some 285 miles from Moscow.[25]

Back in Pittsburgh, the Pirates continued to scuffle, as they fell a game further off the pace in June, finishing the month at 28–33 in fifth place, 14½ games in back of Brooklyn and St. Louis, which were tied for first. Vaughan, who started the month with a .346 batting average, saw that mark dip to .300 after hitting just .229 for the month with 10 RBIs. Frisch, seeking to spark a change in his team's fortunes, said he would move Vaughan to third base before a game with the Cubs on June 27, but it turned out Vaughan was relegated to pinch-hit duty. He delivered an infield single in the ninth inning that proved to be the game-winner in a 4–2 victory over the Cubs.[26] But he did not start the next game, appearing again as a pinch hitter, and he did not play again until yet another pinch-hitting appearance on July 6 against the Cubs. Ironically, while Vaughan couldn't crack the Pirates' lineup, he had been named to yet another National League All-Star team for the game that would be played on July 8 in Detroit's Briggs Stadium. "There are no records to prove it, but we wonder if Arky Vaughan's case isn't unique in baseball history," Smith wrote on July 2. "The Pirate captain had the odd experience of being benched and named on the National League all-star team with in the space of less than a week. And, come to think of it, there has been no explanation why Arky was thumbed into the dugout."[27] The word was that Vaughan would be moved to third and Anderson would take over at short. Anderson did assume the shortstop position, but there was no sign of Vaughan. Biederman, though, reported on July 1 that Vaughan was held out of the lineup to rest an injured heel.[28]

Somehow, the Pirates got hot during Vaughan's absence, putting together a 9–3 stretch going into the All-Star break. The hot streak boosted the Pirates to within two games of the .500 mark at 33–35, but they still trailed first-place Brooklyn by 14 games. Despite not starting the last 12 games prior to the break, Vaughan did get the start in the All-Star Game—and very nearly became the star of stars that afternoon. Vaughan popped out to left field in his first at-bat, which came off Bob Feller—the same Feller who induced Vaughan to hit into a key double play in the 1939 midsummer classic. In the fifth, Vaughan singled off Thornton Lee, and then in the seventh, with the National League trailing 2–1, Vaughan followed Enos Slaughter's base hit off Sid Hudson with a two-run homer, giving the NL a 3–2 lead. An inning later, Johnny Mize stroked a one-out double off Eddie Smith and with two outs, Vaughan delivered again—this time clubbing a two-run homer off Smith to widen the NL's lead to 5–2 with just six outs remaining.

The American League scratched out a run in the bottom of the eighth to make it 5–3, and that left the AL with just three outs to either tie or win the game. Claude Passeau, pitching for the NL team on just one day's rest after an eight-inning outing against the Pirates in Pittsburgh, retired the first hitter, then surrendered back-to-back base hits before walking Cecil Travis to load the bases. That brought up Yankees star Joe DiMaggio, who took a 48-game hitting streak into the All-Star break, shattering the previous mark of 44 consecutive games set in 1897 by Wee Willie Keeler. Passeau induced DiMaggio to hit what appeared to be a perfect double-play ball to shortstop Eddie Miller, who threw to second baseman Billy Herman to force Travis for the second out. But Herman hurried his would-be game-ending throw to first, and that forced Frank McCormick to come off the bag, allowing a run to score and bringing up Ted Williams with two runners aboard. Passeau struck out Williams the previous inning and chose to pitch to him again rather than walk him with second base open. Williams, who was batting .405 at the break and would go on to hit .401 that season, got ahead in the count 2–1 and made Passeau—and the NL—pay dearly, as he blasted a three-run homer to the right field pavilion to give the AL a 7–5 victory.[29] "I had a feeling I might do it," Williams told the press later. "I just let go on an inside slider. Wasn't it a pip?"[30] The National League clubhouse, meanwhile, was a different story. The only player who could be seen sporting a grin was Bill Nicholson of the Cubs. "After all," he said, "it's just another ball game."[31] Eleven records were set in the game, and Vaughan figured in five of them—most RBIs in a game (four), most homers in a game (two), homers in consecutive innings, homers in consecutive times at bat (two) and most successive hits (three).

Back in Pittsburgh's Squirrel Hill neighborhood, Vaughan's wife, Margaret, took in the game via radio with her three daughters nearby. Young Patricia, eight, was outside playing ball in the yard while Mikie, three and a half, was "sitting on the steps, listening to the radio but declined to get excited," according to Biederman. "When Arky hit his first homer about 4 o'clock, with a man on base, to put his side ahead 3 to 2, Patricia burst into the room, threw her hands in the air and let out a wild yell," Biederman wrote. He also wrote that when Vaughan followed with his second homer to make it 5–2, Patricia was "about ready to ditch her ball game in the yard in favor of listening to the final reports," but she likes baseball and tried to combine the two adventures. When Williams delivered his game-winning blow, Patricia walked into the house and threw down the ball before going upstairs. "Mrs. Vaughan says she thinks she heard the oldest Vaughan daughter say something close to 'darn that Williams.'" Biederman surmised that Vaughan's All-Star Game performance would be enough to give him back his spot in the Pirates' starting lineup when play resumed. "Frankie Frisch was about set to return Vaughan to shortstop anyway but wanted to give his injured heel as much rest as possible as long as the Pirates were winning with rookie Alf Anderson at short."[32]

But Smith wrote that the fact that the Pirates went on a win streak with Vaughan on the bench should make the team management reconsider its long-term plans for Vaughan. "Another 10 days or two weeks of this and it is almost certain the front office will wonder if the veteran wouldn't be good bait for big fish in the market next winter," Smith wrote.[33] When play resumed after the break, Vaughan still wasn't starting, although he did pinch hit for Rip Sewell and delivered a hit and scored the tying run in a 6–3 win over the Phillies on July 10. Two days later, after the latest win by the streaking Pirates, Frisch defended his lineup decision, saying he didn't want to break up his winning combination, even for the player who slammed two home

Arky Vaughan and his wife, Margaret, are shown with their oldest daughter, Patricia Ann (far left) and second-oldest Michaela Elizabeth around 1940 (courtesy Pittsburgh Pirates).

runs in the All-Star Game. "I put Anderson in at short, and he is going great guns," Frisch said. "I don't want to break up the combination. Arky's bat is still valuable, as he has proved in pinch-hitting roles."[34] Vaughan seemed to understand the situation. "Naturally Frisch doesn't want to break up a winning combination," he told an Associated Press reporter in Philadelphia. "I'd like to play, but as long as the team wins I'm satisfied to sit on the bench."[35]

Frisch's handling of Vaughan was the talk of the town. F.A. Jarvis, in a letter to *Post-Gazette* columnist Havey Boyle, wrote that Vaughan had no peer as a hitting shortstop and that over the long haul was better on defense than the Braves' Eddie "Eppie" Miller, who had been slated to start ahead of Vaughan in the NL lineup until a last-minute switch was made. Added Jarvis: "Over a period of years, no one can come close to Arky's achievements. Apparently many of Pittsburgh's fickle fans lose sight of Arky's consistent good playing. ... Is it not about time that Arky was given his due by some of our local papers? John Kieran of *The New York Times* is far ahead of you in his observation of Arky Vaughan, for only a few weeks ago Kieran classed Arky as one of the most, if not the most, underrated players in the National League."[36]

Three days later, Smith wrote that there had been no hotter topic in town in years than the benching of Vaughan, at least based on letters Smith had received. He noted: "The pro–Vaughans are accusing Frisch of sabotaging the Captain; the anti–Vaughans are saying they knew it all along. Frisch wouldn't have been on the hot seat had it not been for the way Arky mistreated American League pitching in Detroit last week, but to one and all there will be no change until the Buccos begin losing more games than they win. Simply an ancient baseball custom. If the man's name were Honus Wagner, he'd still be out of the lineup."[37] However, after the Pirates dropped consecutive games to New York, Vaughan did return to the lineup on July 15 in a 5–1 loss to the Giants, going one for five, and remained there for most of the next two weeks.

While debate raged in Pittsburgh regarding Vaughan's playing status, New York's Joe DiMaggio continued hitting up a storm. He stretched his consecutive-game hitting streak to 56 on July 16 at Cleveland by going one for five, but the streak ended the following day when he went hitless in three at-bats in a 4–3 win over the Indians. In his final time at bat, DiMaggio faced Jim Bagby, who induced him to hit into a double play in the eighth inning. DiMaggio's streak started on May 15, and he shattered two consecutive-game hitting streaks along the way—George Sisler's modern mark of 41, which was set in 1922, and Willie Keeler's 44-game stretch, which he established in 1897.[38]

One of New York's other big-league teams—the Brooklyn Dodgers—would be hosting the Pirates in their next series following their split of a four-game series with Boston in which Vaughan started all four games and went five for 16 with three runs scored and two RBIs. The *Brooklyn Daily Eagle* put forth the premise that Vaughan and Frisch might be feuding, and noted that Pittsburgh's acquisition of a young infielder from Harrisburg named Bill Cox was proof that the Pirates were planning to unload Vaughan after the season in exchange for some pitching "to bolster a feeble staff." *Daily Eagle* reporter James J. Murphy wrote that Vaughan had resented being removed from the lineup earlier that month "in view of his record with the club."[39]

In the midst of all the trade/benching talk, a story appeared in the July 24 issue of *The Sporting News* that gave a glimpse into Vaughan's family life. The story was an installment of a series known as "Meet the Missus," and it focused on Vaughan's wife, Margaret, and the fact that the Vaughan household had no little boys running around—only little girls. The unnamed writer noted: "But one would never believe it when Pittsburgh's hard-hitting shortstop is at home. ... For it's Pat, or Pattie this, Mikie that, and.... Mrs. Vaughan smiles pleasantly and knowingly as she surveys her boyless little group. ... She remembers how badly Arky wanted a boy; how he would name them before their arrival and then happily accept the decision of the stork, but would insist on names from which a boyish cognomen could be derived."[40]

But when Margaret delivered the couple's third child, on February 22 of that year, "Arky and Mrs. Vaughan decided it was about time they surrendered, so she was christened Judith Margaret. ... And the Pittsburgh shortstop forgot about such nicknames as Bucky and Sparky."[41] The story went on to note that Margaret did not like Pittsburgh at first, but grew to look forward to spending the seasons there. "A group of Pirate 'baseball widows' formed a badminton club and she became enthusiastic about the sport," the story noted. "Another sport which the shortstop's wife enjoys is hunting. ... During the off-season in Potter Valley, she likes to go after quail. ... She uses a lightweight .410 shotgun which Arky bought for her."[42]

Vaughan continued in the starting lineup until he was spiked in the foot in a game on July 27 against the Dodgers. He returned on July 30 after missing two games and then sat out two more. The Pirates won all five games that he missed during that stretch, and on August 1, the Pirates stood 51–42 and in fourth place, nine games behind St. Louis. Although Vaughan returned to the lineup on August 2, he was not completely healthy, but that didn't stop some of the fans from letting him have it when he booted a first-inning ground ball in a game the Pirates went on to win, 5–4, over the Giants. His misplay opened the gates for a four-running inning for New York. The booing, Biederman wrote later, "was a bad gesture because Vaughan is playing with an injured foot these days and if ever there was a hustler in baseball, Vaughan fully answers that description."[43]

Near the end of July, relations between Vaughan and Frisch appeared to be worsening, even though Frisch claimed he genuinely appreciated Vaughan's talents and was a longtime admirer.

Vaughan's daughter, Patricia, wrote years later that the Vaughan house was the site of frequent parties and during one of these gatherings, "after several rounds of drinks had been consumed, a conga line was formed which wound through Arky's home singing, 'Down with Frisch, Down with Frisch!'"[44]

In mid–August, with the Pirates in third place at 58–46, nine and a half games behind Brooklyn and St. Louis, which were tied for first, a play occurred that some say was the final straw for Frisch when it came to his opinion of Vaughan. With the bases loaded in the eighth inning of the first game of doubleheader against St. Louis on August 10, the Pirates were locked in a 2–2 tie. According to Biederman, the Cardinals' Terry Moore "slashed a ball a trifle to the right of Vaughan. Arky should have broken it down to hold it in the infield. It skipped into left field for a single and two runs came over."[45] Pirates second baseman Frankie Gustine recounted the play to Patricia Vaughan Johnson in an interview in November 1989. Gustine said that Moore's grounder to the hole between short and third "took a little hop" and went over Vaughan's shoulder. Frisch, Gustine said, never said much to Vaughan. But this time, Gustine said, Frisch told Vaughan: "'You should have gotten in front of the ball and knocked the ball down.' Your dad never said much, but he let, uh, well, he let him have it just a little bit. My god, we were all in awe that Arky Vaughan would say something to Frisch. We all felt that was *the* play. That off-season they made the deal. But they should have never traded your dad in a million years."[46]

The ironic part, Gustine said, was that Frisch was genuinely fond of Vaughan. "Frisch loved Arky," Gustine said of the manager, who fancied himself as a protégé of the gruff John McGraw and in fact served as a team captain under McGraw when Frisch played on back-to-back World Series champions with the Giants in the early 1920s. "You had to love a guy like Arky. But Frisch was from the old school. He was a great ballplayer, but he didn't know how to handle men at all. He wanted to manage like McGraw, but you gotta know how to handle people when you're a manager. He just couldn't handle people."[47]

Despite his issues with Frisch, Vaughan put together a solid month of July, batting .377 in 61 at-bats while scoring 14 runs, but he drove in just seven. He dropped off a bit in August but still hit .307 in 88 at-bats. While tensions were high between the manager and his star shortstop, now and then a little levity would enter the picture. One such incident occurred on August 19 when Pirates pitcher Joe Sullivan showed up for the first game of a doubleheader at Brooklyn's Ebbets Field "in no condition to work," as Frisch put it. Sullivan, who was hung over, crawled inside a tarpaulin tube, where Frisch discovered him sleeping. He was suspended for 30 days, fined $200 and sent back to Pittsburgh. After the game, which the Pirates lost 9–0, Pirates players were in the clubhouse and the mood was a somber one. "Next thing I knew,

Arky was in his locker next to me kind of grinning and giggling in a very quiet way," catcher Al Lopez recounted to Vaughan's daughter in an interview several decades later. "I finally looked over and said, 'Arky, what the hell are you laughing about?' He says, 'I was just thinking: if it had started raining, Joe Sullivan had been inside that cylinder and they'd have rolled him out there with the tarp in the middle of the infield.' I busted out laughing. And then [Frisch] turned around and looked."[48] A few days later, Vaughan—who displayed a dry, quiet wit to those who knew him—motioned for *Pittsburgh Sun-Telegraph* reporter Chilly Doyle to join him in the dugout before a game. Vaughan, who never once complained about an official scorer's ruling that might have cost him a hit or an error, had been charged the previous day with an error that should have been charged to his teammate. "I figured that he was about to register his first squawk in 10 years, and I was just about to tell him that he had been victimized when he remarked with a smile: 'You know after what happened to Sullivan last night I'm afraid to get an alcohol rub.'"[49]

The month of August featured a major high note and a devastating low

Arky Vaughan, during spring training in San Bernardino, California, in 1937, takes a look at the lumber that helped put him among the league leaders in hitting virtually every year of his Hall of Fame career (courtesy Pittsburgh Pirates).

note in the space of two days. In a game against Philadelphia on August 27, Vaughan rapped out five hits—three doubles and two singles—and scored four runs. Two days later, he was hit in the head by a pitch in an exhibition game against the London Pirates—one of Pittsburgh's minor-league affiliates—in a game played in Ontario. The pitch from London's George Carlonas was described as a "slow ball that caught Vaughan on the back of the head" and he wasn't expected to be out of the lineup when the Pirates resumed play the following day against the Cubs.[50] But Vaughan did not start that day—he replaced Alf Anderson in the eighth inning but did not bat—and he complained of dizziness the following day and was held out of the starting lineup against the Cubs. For the rest of the trip to Chicago, Vaughan remained sidelined, resting on a table in the clubhouse until game time. When the team took a train to St. Louis, Vaughan "sat by himself, read a little or merely looked out the window," wrote Biederman. "He had no pep and said he would have an X-ray taken when he gets back home." But when his sub—Anderson—was hit in the knee with a pitched ball late in the game, Vaughan took his place and then played the second game of a doubleheader against St. Louis on September 1. But he still wasn't feeling right.[51] On September 4, the Post-Gazette reported that Vaughan had been bothered by headaches every time he ran "above ordinary speed," and team doctor Charles Jorgensen advised Vaughan to stay off the field for a couple of days and "take complete rest in his home."[52]

When Vaughan recovered from the dizziness and headaches that followed his beaning, he suffered an attack of grippe and was expected to miss a few more games. As it turned out, Vaughan would start only four games in the season's final month, and all the while rumors of a potential move—to third base or the outfield, or even out of town—began swirling. "There is a recurring story which, by the way, does not emanate from the powers, that Arky Vaughan will be among the chattels the Pirates may offer," Boyle wrote on September 25. "As an 18-karat star, he should bring sparkling talent in return. In nearly every trade the Pirates have broached in recent years, Vaughan was the first fellow the rival clubs asked for." Boyle noted that a fourth-place finish left the fans "in a dangerously indifferent mood and the obvious thing to do is start a rebuilding process."[53] Over at the *Pittsburgh Press*, a headline on Smith's column flatly declared "Vaughan's Days as Buc Shortstop Are Over." Smith wrote that Frisch, whom he often referred to as Onkel Franz, had made up his mind that a change was needed, particularly in the infield. "It may be for better or worse, but Onkel Franz doesn't want to stagger through another summer with a humdrum fourth-place club that had to have a white-hot month to make its escape from the second division," Smith wrote.[54] Smith said the belief was that Vaughan would either play third base or he would be dealt in the winter. However, Smith also wrote that Frisch would need to do a major selling job in the front office, seeing as how every time Vaughan's name came up in trade talks in previous off-seasons, Pirates management would end the conversation. "The same thing held good for the Waner boys when they were in their prime," Smith wrote, "but they came to the end eventually and now there are indications that Arky is no longer the team's sacred cow."[55]

Vaughan's final game in a Pittsburgh uniform came in the season's penultimate game against Cincinnati on September 27 at Forbes Field. Batting fifth and playing third base, he went one for two, scored a run and was credited with a sacrifice in a 15–9 loss to the Reds. He singled to right off Elmer Riddle in the second inning and scored on Ripper Collins' double, sacrificed in the third inning and in his final at-bat as a Pirate, he was retired on a fly ball to right field in the sixth inning. Vaughan was slated to bat in the seventh, but Frankie Gustine pinch hit for him. There's no telling how many Pirate fans were on hand to witness Vaughan's final appearance as a Pirate; just 1,695 fans made their way into Forbes Field for the game.

Playing shortstop that day was young Billy Cox, who figured to be Vaughan's successor. Vaughan finished the season with a more than respectable .316 batting average, scored 69 runs and drove in just 38 in 374 at-bats to finish with an .855 OPS. The Pirates wound up 81–73, good for fourth place in the NL, 19 games behind pennant-winning Brooklyn.

Fourth place was not good enough, though, and it didn't take long for talk to turn to trade. Frisch was quoted in the Post-Gazette as saying, "I'll swap anyone on the Pittsburgh club, including Arky Vaughan, if I can get some help in the pitching line. I would like to talk turkey with the Phillies. Ike Pearson, Tom Hughes, Johnny Podgajny or Frank Hoerst. I'll take any of them."[56] A few days later, rumor had it that the Pirates were willing to trade Vaughan to the Dodgers for pitcher Luke Hamlin and infielder Cookie Lavagetto. Boyle wrote that fans would not readily accept such as scenario, but several of Vaughan's teammates indicated the longtime star would not be averse to being dealt to a first-division club. Boyle added:

> They say and perhaps they are reflecting Vaughan's mood that Arky was kept idle last season even after he had recovered from injuries that bothered him. Vaughan is the type that would never publicly complain about anything. In his long service here he has been the perfect team worker, doing his best at any assignment offered him. That he is not the ideal shortstop defensively is not to say that he hasn't always put out. Sometimes a change helps both the player and the club and while previous talk of a Vaughan trade here has brought a letter or two threatening dire revenge on the management if Arky is sent away the great majority would want to see what the locals got in return before entering any loud beef. Manager Frisch has never criticized his shortstop, but there is so much undercurrent talk about a dicker that the winter undoubtedly will see negotiations mulled over, at least. But Hamlin and Lavagetto will not be enough to replace the speedy Corsair veteran.[57]

A few weeks later, Smith quipped in his column, "Did Frankie Frisch have his tonsils out so he could root louder for Fordham or talk trade for Arky Vaughan? ... We'll know when Onkel Franz heaves into town with his beloved Rams early next month.... The Brooklyns want Vaughan, but haven't too much to give for him, and what the Pirates want is talent, not cash.... So the Phils or Braves may be called in to see what they have to offer."[58] In Brooklyn, Dodgers general manager Larry MacPhail made no secret of his desire to acquire Vaughan, who would be installed at third base for the reigning NL champs.[59] However, in November, Frisch claimed that he hadn't "talked any deals in which Vaughan's name was mentioned," although at the time he was still recovering from his tonsillectomy.[60] A little less than two weeks later, Frisch changed his tune somewhat, telling an unnamed Associated Press reporter, "If any club gets Vaughan it will have to go high. I've been hearing a lot about how we're trying to peddle Arky, but the truth is we're not anxious to let him go at all. If we do, somebody will have to give up something—something good."[61] Frisch specifically referenced a top-of-the-line starting pitcher. Frisch added: "The kind of deal I would like to make is a star for a star. I don't care much for the sort of trades they make in the majors any more—you know, where a club gives up one good man for three or four run-of-the-mine players. I want to get somebody who will help us, and I'd like to make a deal that would help the other fellow, too. I'm not out to trim anybody. But when you try to get a club to give you a real good ball player for a real good player, you're up against a stone wall. It's almost impossible for us to make that kind of a deal these days."[62]

One week later, the *Pittsburgh Press'* Lester Biederman said fans and even some baseball folks might have jumped to the wrong conclusion regarding Vaughan's availability in a trade—and the Pirates' desire to ship him out of town. "Frisch may be playing Vaughan as a pawn," Biederman wrote. "He might get some other clubs interested in a trade, find out what they have to offer, then try to palm off somebody else on the clubs and still keep Vaughan."[63] He also noted that Billy Cox and Frankie Gustine, both of whom had been mentioned as potential successors to Vaughn at shortstop, might end up being prime draft bait as the war in Europe and the Far East was escalating.[64]

On December 2, Frisch reiterated to Tommy Holmes of the *Brooklyn Daily Eagle* Pittsburgh's desire for pitching: "The Dodgers can have Vaughan if they can give us something that will help the Pirates as much as Arky will help Brooklyn. I realize that it won't be an easy deal to make. For example, I want good pitchers. And I know before we start that I'm not going to get [Whit] Wyatt or [Kirby] Higbe. But as a matter of fact, I'm fairly hopeful that we can get together on a proposition when we sit down and talk things over."[65] The *Pittsburgh Press* reported the next day that Frisch offered Vaughan to the Reds for pitcher Elmer Riddle but was turned down, and that he also offered Vaughan to the Dodgers for either Wyatt or Higbe but was again re-buffed.[66] Dozens of names were swirling the first week of December at the minor league meetings held in Jacksonville, Florida. Those talks gave way to the major league meetings in Chicago, as club representatives began filtering into the Windy City on December 7.

But an event that took place thousands of miles from Chicago would turn those winter meetings—and life in the United States—upside down. The *Pittsburgh Press* reported on December 7 that additional Japanese troops were headed to "Indo-China" and that all of the Far East was getting ready for war as the world crisis intensified. United Press reporter Harrison Salisbury wrote: "The long-threatened Pacific war appeared very close last night. President Roosevelt has sent a message directly to Emperor Hirohito of Japan. Authoritative sources said the message was an appeal to the Emperor, over the heads of Japanese political leaders, to prevent an explosion in the Far East."[67]

The message fell upon deaf ears, however; at just about 8 a.m. Hawaii time on December 7, hundreds of Japanese war planes began attacking the United States naval base at Pearl Harbor and ultimately destroyed much of America's Pacific fleet while killing some 2,400 Americans. Later that day, the United States declared war on Japan. "No matter how long it may take us to overcome this premeditated invasion, the American people in their righteous might will win through to absolute victory," Roosevelt said in his war message to Congress.[68]

For the Vaughan family, that Sunday started like many others during the off-season. Arky, Margaret and their children had attended Mass at the Catholic church in Ukiah—Potter Valley had only a community church—and they settled in to begin reading the Sunday paper.

Arky Vaughan, shown with a textbook follow-through on a swing that produced a career .318 batting average and a spot in the Baseball Hall of Fame (courtesy Pittsburgh Pirates).

Patricia Vaughan Johnson recalled that the children went for the comics while Arky grabbed the sports section. He was also listening to the Mutual Broadcasting System's radio call of a National Football League game between the New York Giants and the Brooklyn Dodgers being played at the Polo Grounds in New York when a bulletin announcing the attack interrupted the broadcast.[69]

The Japanese attack, at least temporarily, silenced all talk of trades in Chicago—and specifically the Palmer House hotel, site of the annual winter baseball meetings. Biederman wrote that Frisch and team president Benswanger were too shocked by what happened in Hawaii "to devote any enthusiasm to baseball." Said Benswanger: "Frankly, we don't know what to do. Up to this point, our chief worry was the army draft. Now it's war. I'm afraid this meeting may be a washout as far as trades are concerned. Everybody's going to be afraid to deal. That's only natural, too. Nobody wants to talk baseball with this war situation as serious as it is. We don't even know if we'll open the season."[70] Biederman also wrote that Vaughan's status as a Pirate "appears more secure than ever" given the war situation and the draft status of both Cox and Gustine. However, he also wrote that both young players had issues that might result in deferments. "In the meantime, Frisch says he must wait for the final status on Gustine and Cox, but probably Arky will be back in a Pittsburgh uniform for the 11th year next April."[71]

War would figure to have a profound impact on baseball and the men who played it, Balinger wrote, adding: "Veteran players now are visioning a new lease on life. Old boys who have been hanging on once more can dope out how they may not yet outlived their period of usefulness. The younger generation is joining the fighting forces and it is to be expected that the army draft will be speeded up and possibly revised to include men above the age of 28. In such an event every club in the business would be required to bring back a number of discards."[72]

Baseball industry officials speculated on whether there would even be a 1942 season. Commissioner Kenesaw M. Landis said it was too early to make any decisions but American League president William Harridge said that while "the nation's welfare is our first consideration, I am sure baseball will carry on as it always has and complete its schedule in 1942 and for years to come."[73]

◆◆ 8 ◆◆

A New Home
in Brooklyn

Two days after Pearl Harbor, more trade rumors involving Vaughan found their way into print. One had Brooklyn offering Babe Phelps, Luke Hamlin and $25,000 for Vaughan, but Frisch would not bite. The Reds, meanwhile, offered Ernie Lombardi, Jim Gleeson and cash, but again the Pittsburgh rejected that deal.[1] But rumors became reality late on the night of December 12, as the stellar shortstop finally was dealt to Brooklyn. In return, the Pirates received infielders Pete Coscarart and Jimmy Wasdell and two players whose names were mentioned earlier in connection with Vaughan—pitcher Luke Hamlin and catcher Babe Phelps.

The *Post-Gazette*'s Edward Balinger wrote after the trade that Frisch believed he had added strength to his infield and to his pitching staff. Wasdell had the ability to play all over the infield, while Coscarart was equally comfortable at second and third. Vaughan, Balinger wrote, "ranks as one of the best in the business, but Frisch reached the conclusion to part with almost anybody in the event he found a deal which promised to bolster several other positions at the same time."[2]

The *Press*' Les Biederman described Wasdell as a "cracker-jack man … who can play either first base or the outfield and can hit that ball." The left-handed hitting Phelps, Biederman said, was "best known for his slugging, especially his long hits." Hamlin was a 20-game winner for the Dodgers as recently as 1939 and Coscarart was "as good a fielding second baseman as there is in the league" although his bat was suspect. Vaughan, Biederman wrote, "never has been a troublemaker, always a model athlete. He's been a hustler right from the start, a capable fielder, a Grade A base runner and a mighty dangerous batsman. Never in his 10 years has he failed to hit .300." Frisch wished Vaughan "all the luck in the world, except in 22 games next season—when he's playing the Pirates. It was a question of plugging some gaps on the Pirates and in order to get what I wanted, I had to give something up." Benswanger, who watched Vaughan compile a .324 career batting average with 1,709 hits, 116 triples, 764 RBIs and 936 runs in 10 seasons, said he was both happy and sad to see the trade consummated: "Arky's been here a long time and I'm genuinely sorry to see him go. But baseball is baseball. We didn't set out to get rid of Vaughan. And as long as Arky is going, he can't kick about the team he's headed for. Due to the uncertainty of war conditions, we felt we had to strengthen certain positions on the team and we had to pay to do that. We feel we're getting some good players who will help us and I wish Arky all the luck in the world."[3]

Although the trade of Vaughan certainly was big news in Pittsburgh, it could not move the war off Page 1. There, the main headline of The *Pittsburgh Press* on December 13 declared, "Russia Wins Great Victory" and Henry Shapiro, a United Press staff writer, started his story like this: "Russia claimed one of the greatest military victories in modern history today." Shapiro wrote that the Russians said they had "definitely smashed an offensive on Moscow by 51 German divisions, upwards of 750,000 men, and said the Germans were fleeing."[4]

As time passed, various Pirates officials continued to comment on the trade that sent Vaughan to Brooklyn. Frisch said he wasn't worried about losing Vaughan and he thought both teams would benefit from the trade. "I believe I got all I could for Arky," Frisch said, "and the fellows we receive will help us where we need it most." Benswanger, noting that Vaughan was the first player he'd signed after becoming team president, had the unenviable task of writing Vaughan and telling him of the deal. "I've watched him grow up in baseball and always have had a lot of respect and admiration for him," Benswanger said. "This isn't an easy thing to do. I sent him notification of the trade and also wrote that I was sorry to part with him, but he could be thankful he's going to a good team." Benswanger's son, 14-year-old Billy Jr., was not a fan of the trade. When his father asked why, the younger Benswanger responded, "Well, I kept telling all the kids in the neighborhood Arky wouldn't be traded and now I'll have to go around and make explanations!"[5]

Some members of the local media were sorry to see Vaughan headed out of town. "Quiet and reserved, Arky always has been popular here," wrote Harry Keck, the *Pittsburgh Sun-Telegraph*'s sports editor. "His heavy hitting overcame some fielding defects and he was held in high esteem by all major league managers and players."[6] But Chet Smith, the *Pittsburgh Press* columnist, wrote that the Vaughan trade should benefit the Pirates because the incoming players would serve as insurance in case some of the club's younger players—specifically Cox and Gustine—were lost to the war effort. "Viewed from this angle," Smith wrote, "the Buccaneers made a good deal. Moreover, they weren't winning any flags with Vaughan, and weren't likely to."[7] Smith wrote that Frisch "was convinced by mid-summer that Vaughan's power at the plate was not enough to offset his defensive lapses and his inability to fit into the kind of infield Frisch knew he needed to make up for weaknesses in other departments." Smith wrote that ever since Vaughan joined the club in 1932, he had been a "controversial figure." To some, he was a shortstop to be mentioned in the same breath with Honus Wagner, Rabbit Maranville and Glenn Wright. To another faction, he was a good hitter who couldn't play shortstop at all."[8]

Out-of-town writers, though, said Vaughan's failure to see eye-to-eye with Frisch essentially paved Vaughan's way out of Pittsburgh. "That the Dodgers were able to get him appears to have been due to some clash of temperament between Vaughan and Frank Frisch," wrote Tommy Holmes of the *Brooklyn Daily Eagle*, who surmised that Vaughan might be shifted to third base in Brooklyn because the Dodgers already had a solid shortstop in Pee Wee Reese. Holmes also noted that Frisch had Vaughan on the bench before the most recent All-Star Game and kept him there afterward despite his two home-run game in the Midsummer Classic.[9] The next day, Holmes wrote that Dodgers GM Larry MacPhail had his sights set on Vaughan above all others and he was able to get him for four players the club "was not counting on."[10] Elsewhere, some writers panned the return the Pirates received for the all-star shortstop. George Wright of the *Daily Press* in Newport News, Virginia, referred to the four Dodgers-turned-Pirates as "just deadwood" but noting that the Dodgers already had Reese, speculated that Brooklyn might flip Vaughan for some pitching. "The developments on the heels of this Vaughan-Deadwood deal probably will be interesting," Wright wrote. "They bear watching."[11]

In Uniontown, Pennsylvania, 45 miles southeast of Pittsburgh, *Evening Standard* sports editor J.S. (Dad) Albright wrote that the Pirates' return on Vaughan was rather underwhelming:

> Vaughan's worth has been proved. In 10 years he has remained about the .300 hitting mark. And he has covered his bailiwick in fine fashion. There were times during the 1941 season that he appeared to be the "goat" of the Pittsburgh management. He was lifted from the lineup for reasons and causes which did not seem at all justified. Even then there were rumors that the plank-walking performance was only a matter of time. And it came, although a little behind schedule. For one of the best all-around infielders in the big show, what did the Bucs get in return, except the best wishes of Larry MacPhail?[12]

Harold Parrott of the *Brooklyn Daily Eagle* noted that Vaughan looked good at Ebbets Field in 1941, as he managed to hit .333, but the previous season, Vaughan had only seven hits in 50 at-bats—a .140 batting average. The year before that, however, Vaughan batted .400, going 17 for 43. Parrot claimed that Vaughan and another new acquisition, Don Padgett, both "can hit a baseball a country mile. They should like Ebbets Field's handy right field fence, with the artillery they carry."[13]

In Brooklyn, Tommy Holmes wrote about the behind-the-scenes machinations related to the Vaughan trade. Dodgers general manager Larry MacPhail told Holmes that Vaughan was his primary target "and prying him away from Pittsburgh was work. Frisch had me nuts." MacPhail also said Benswanger wanted Claude Corbitt instead of Pete Coscarart "and that one almost floored me, because Corbitt is almost a cinch to be drafted, and probably won't play any ball next year. I explained this to Benswanger and then asked him what he wanted to do and he finally agreed to take Coscarart and call it a deal." MacPhail noted that Vaughan not only would be an upgrade at third base for Brooklyn but also would serve as shortstop insurance in case the club lost Reese to the service.[14]

Chilly Doyle of the *Pittsburgh Sun-Telegraph*, writing for *The Sporting News*, surmised that MacPhail and Dodger manager Leo Durocher got the better of Benswanger and Frisch, "especially when the terms of the deal revealed that no money changed hands. ... although I realize that Jimmy Wasdell, Luke Hamlin, Babe Phelps and Pete Coscarart might merge their diamond talents to justify the exchange."[15] In the St. Cloud, Minnesota, *Times*, a columnist known as "Pap" wrote that it was an open secret that Vaughan wanted out of Pittsburgh because of his dissatisfaction with Frisch, who kept him on the bench for long stretches. Even Vaughan's record-breaking performance at the All-Star Game didn't immediately guarantee him a spot in the Pirates' starting lineup. "It was not that Frisch figured that Vaughan was no longer a top-flight fielder and hitter that prompted him to put the star on the auction block," the column read. "Rather, it was his feeling that Arky had outlived his usefulness in Pittsburgh."[16] The Pirates also might have been affected by watching Paul Waner grow old before their eyes and not be able to get anything in return for him when he finally moved on. "They didn't want the same thing to happen to their veteran shortstop," *The Press*' Chet Smith wrote.[17]

Biederman received telegrams from all of the players involved in the trade, voicing their thoughts. Wasdell acknowledged that Vaughan was a great player but added that Pittsburgh made a fine trade. "Any one of us four ... may overshadow Arky this coming season," Wasdell wrote. Vaughan, meanwhile, wrote that he was not surprised at the trade and was "very happy to be going to Brooklyn. Think it a great break. Will seem strange after 10 years with Pirates. Pittsburgh has been so good to me. So I leave with no kicks and no regrets. Tell Happy [Frisch] I'm happy. Regards—Arky."[18]

A few days after the deal, Biederman recalled the 1938 pennant chase, in which the Bucs fell victim to a late Chicago Cubs charge and gave up the National League lead in the waning days of the season. Biederman noted that

Vaughan's one ambition from the time he joined the Pirates in 1932 was to play for a pennant winner:

> To come so close and then lose out almost broke Arky's heart. He has never been much of an emotional fellow and outwardly he displayed none of his disappointment. But his teammates knew how he felt and he confided to intimates that he believed he'd never get that near to a pennant again. "Those chances don't come often," [Vaughan] said at the time with a shake of his head, "and I'm afraid I missed the boat."[19]

Biederman wrote that Vaughan "is the kind of boy you'd feel sure would be an All-American soldier in the front-line trenches. He always has had a world of courage. He's absolutely fearless. He lived a full baseball life here in Pittsburgh." Biederman commented on Vaughan's style of play, saying that he "plays baseball to the hilt. He asks for no favors and gives none. He was a hustler from the first time he pulled on a pair of spikes." Teammates, Biederman wrote, would always seek out Vaughan if they had a good joke. "Arky is a good listener and owns a peculiar laugh, implying a good audience." Biederman also related that in Vaughan's 10 years as a Pirate, he never once complained about being charged with an error or having a hit taken away through "faulty" scoring. "He just isn't built that way," Biederman said. "And never did he ever give out any inkling that he knew what his batting average was at any particular moment. Some players carry their averages 'on their sleeves.' But not Vaughan. There isn't one bit of ego in the fellow."[20]

Still, some local reporters said that community sentiment was divided over the trade. Chet Smith said despite the fact that some had questioned Frisch's judgment in trading Vaughan, the Bucs' manager didn't seem worried about the prospect of young Alfie Anderson replacing Vaughan at shortstop. Smith wrote that Anderson could do what Vaughan couldn't do defensively— but he also couldn't do what Vaughan could do offensively. On the plus side, Smith said, Anderson was better at turning the double play. "When you add them all together," Smith wrote, "the conclusion must be that Anderson will be worth more than Vaughan defensively but will take much away from the attack."[21]

Havey Boyle, the *Post-Gazette* columnist, wrote:

> If you had nine Vaughans on a team you'd win a pennant—several pennants in a row. Even with his sub-par fielding he could carry his own load. There was, however, a feeling, whether sound or unsound, that Arky didn't have a communal spirit. After 1938, while giving everything he had, he grew complacent in defeat. This might have been a natural reaction after the flop the club took in 1938 when Vaughan was playing his heart out to help win a pennant.[22]

As the off-season progressed and spring training grew near, the conversation turned to whether Vaughan would move to third base for Brooklyn—and how he might adapt to the switch. Cookie Lavagetto, the former Pirate who ended up in Brooklyn, enlisted in the service in February 1942, and in an interview from his hometown of Oakland, California, said he had doubts about Vaughan cutting it at third base. But he acknowledged that it wouldn't make sense to keep Vaughan's bat out of the lineup. Lavagetto intimated that Vaughan had trouble throwing on the run and that hitters would "bunt him to death."[23]

But Vaughan, preparing for spring training in Florida, said he had no fears about moving to third. "I just hope they try me on bunts," Vaughan said. "I think third base is a lot easier than shortstop. At first it'll be strange, but it won't be long before I'll get set and get used to it." After all, Vaughan did play some third base back in his first season of professional baseball—1931 with Wichita of the Western League. Vaughan said he held no grudges regarding the trade that sent him packing. "You can't blame Frankie Frisch for making a deal. We never had a bit of trouble. I think he's a great manager. But I've been around a long time with one club and look at all the others who have gone before me. If Brooklyn can't win the pennant, I hope the Pirates do."[24]

Although some criticized the trade, Smith wrote in late February that Benswanger hadn't received a single "abusive note" or "nasty letter of complaint" from a fan regarding the trade. "I have been buttonholed now and then by fans who tell me they do not like the deal, but they have been mild about it," Benswanger was quoted as saying. "Both Frisch and I were ready to take a panning. We may get it yet, but so far they're giving us the benefit of the doubt."[25]

Durocher said his club overpaid for Vaughan, putting his value at $50,000 while the dollar value he placed on the four players the Dodgers shipped to Pittsburgh was around $70,000. "Sure, I gave too much for Vaughan," he said. "But I wanted Vaughan that badly."[26] Durocher said he had Vaughan penciled in at third base for Brooklyn unless Pee Wee Reese was lost to the draft, in which case Vaughan would shift to shortstop, and Lew Riggs—Lavagetto's backup in 1941—would move into the hot corner. Either way, Durocher expected big things. "Arky Vaughan, of course, was the fellow we wanted most," Durocher said of his off-season targets. "He has been a real good ball player and a whale of a hitter for ten years and he's still only 30 years old. He'd be bound to help any club." As for where Vaughan might hit in the batting order, Durocher wasn't sure. He acknowledged that Vaughan had the speed and patience to hit leadoff but said he didn't think he'd use him in that slot in Brooklyn. "He has too much power for that," he said. "He'll probably be second, fourth or fifth depending on what else happens in spring training."[27]

Vaughan, who spent the off-season working on his ranch and taking the occasional hunting trip—including one during which he bagged a 400-pound bear—was optimistic about the Dodgers' chances in 1942—and for good reason. The club finished 100–54 and won the 1941 National League pennant before losing to the Yankees four games to one in the World Series. Adding a big bat like Vaughan's only figured to strengthen the roster. Vaughan told a writer in his hometown of Fullerton that getting dealt to Brooklyn was the "biggest break" in his career.[28] In a letter to the Dodgers, Vaughan said that "he was delighted to join the Brooklyn club, predicted the Dodgers would win another pennant and was positive that he'd have no difficulty on salary when Ebbets Field finally sends out contracts."[29]

Vaughan headed for spring training a little earlier than usual, as he left California on February 2 via train for Sarasota, Florida. There, he planned to take part in an early conditioning program with several other major-leaguers before the official start of spring training on February 19. Vaughan's change of scenery—it was his first time training in Florida, as the Pirates had always held their spring camps on the West Coast during Vaughan's time there— didn't seem to affect his ability to hit, as he had great results on an early swing through Havana, Cuba. "Always a redoubtable lefthanded hitter, the broad-shouldered fellow has been cutting and slashing away in practice at a great rate," Holmes wrote from the Dodgers' spring-training camp. Holmes tried to describe Vaughan's approach to the Brooklyn fans who might not have been familiar:

> He bats from darned near behind the plate. A lefthand hitter, he plants his left dog in the extreme corner of the box nearest the plate, while his right foot, in his wide-open stance, is pointed for the general direction of the first base dugout. A semi-squat adds to the weirdness of the operation. But this fellow makes an awkward looking system click. Part of it, I suspect, is the extra clear vision he has with both eyes directly focused on the ball. Arky goes "down the line" with a pitcher farther than any good hitter I ever saw, and is deadly at a three-and-two count if the next pitch comes in there. Note that he's way up there in the base on balls department, that he rarely strikes out. He does pick good balls to hit and his lifetime batting average of .322 shows how often he hits 'em.[30]

Some debated whether Vaughan would be able to make the transition to third base, but Durocher had no complaints with Vaughan's work at the position during the three weeks of camp in Havana. He certainly was putting the time in. "He's at it every day for what seems hours," Holmes wrote of Vaughan. "It's move to the right, get down, grab a grounder from Chuck Dressen's fungo stick, straighten, throw to first, then to the left for the same operation. Then in for an attempt to field a rolling imitation of a bunt. 'Is it any wonder,' gasps the stocky, curly-haired athlete, 'that I'm sleeping ten hours every night?'"[31] Dodgers coach Red Corriden, so impressed with Vaughan's glove work at his new position, pinned a new nickname on the veteran infielder: Arky the Octopus. "He's been getting them all over the field," said Corriden, "so we gave him a new name."[32]

Vaughan would also have to make a transition of sorts in the batting order for Brooklyn. After hitting mostly third and fourth as a Pirate, Vaughan figured to move either up or down due to the makeup of the Dodgers' lineup. Back in Pittsburgh, Boyle suggested that Durocher take advantage of Vaughan's elite speed and keen batting eye and have him lead off. "With the Dodger lineup able to show Camilli and Medwick and Reiser for heavy service, Vaughan's spot may prove to be the top of the order," Boyle wrote.[33] Ultimately, though, Vaughan was slotted in at No. 2 in the Brooklyn order.

Expectations were high as the start of the 1942 regular season drew closer. The "Arky the Octopus" or "Oscar the Octopus" nicknames seemed to fit from the way he was fielding his position at third base during exhibition play. As Keck put it, Vaughan was "gradually mastering the art of playing third base," despite a few hiccups along the way. Keck wrote that Dodgers

coach Charlie Dressen was "amazed" to learn that Vaughan—a 10-year veteran—knew so little about playing the position.[34]

The fact that Vaughan was picking up the new position hardly came as a surprise to Larry MacPhail, the Dodgers' general manager, who had said flat out a year earlier that "Arky Vaughan is the best third baseman in the National League"—and that was while Vaughan was getting ready to start at shortstop for Pittsburgh the 10th straight season. Durocher echoed that same sentiment after having seen Arky play the hot corner in 19 Dodgers exhibition games, during which he batted .354 and made only one error in 70 chances. "Don't worry about Vaughan," Durocher said. "He will be with us this year what Herman was when we got him from the Cubs last summer.

The veteran Arky Vaughan follows the flight of one of his patented line drives during a spring training game with the Brooklyn Dodgers prior to the 1943 season. Despite being limited by injuries and health issues, Vaughan remained a highly productive player well into his 30s; in his next-to-last season with Brooklyn in 1947, at age 35, he finished with a .325 batting average and an OPS of .889 (courtesy National Baseball Hall of Fame Library, Cooperstown, New York).

Herman made the team then and Vaughan will make it this season."[35] Durocher said his club had the best infield in the National League, and Vaughan was no weak link. "If you don't think he can field, just take a look at the records. He's always up there in chances accepted and is one of the leading players when it comes to engineering double plays." At the plate, Durocher said, "He'll do plenty of hitting for us. That short wall at Ebbets Field is a perfect target for us. He's a cinch to clout many a ball out of the park."[36]

Vaughan's defensive transition was considered "the most gratifying development" of Dodger spring training, according to Holmes. "In February, whether Vaughan could or could not play third base was a burning question. Today, the conundrum is why in the world Arkie spent ten years of his life at shortstop. He had speed, good strong hands and a powerful throwing arm." Holmes wrote that Vaughan's need to straighten and cock his arm before releasing his throw to first base would not hurt him at third base. "As a rule, he has a shorter throw to first, on sharp hit balls, he can turn a somersault if he likes and still cock his arm in time to shoot the runner out. He charges bunts and rollers, and because he isn't playing as deep as he did at short, can reach them, straighten up and let 'er go." Holmes also said that Vaughan's range to his left likely would make Reese a better shortstop.[37]

Although Vaughan appeared to be settling in on the field, he remained somewhat of a mystery to the beat writers covering the team. Tom Meany of the New York PM wrote:

Vaughan is a loner. Writers have been trying to interview him since the Dodgers arrived, but they've had no success. Arky is polite, but not garrulous. Ask him a leading question and a veil appears to cover his eyes. He doesn't barber with the players, either. Arky's idea of a good time is to sit in a comfortable chair in a hotel lobby and stare into space. Dodger fans aren't likely to go into any raves over Vaughan. He has no more color than the guy behind the cage in a loan agency, but his bat speaks with authority. Over and above all other factors, I would say Vaughan is the reason for the superabundance of confidence on the team.[38]

Vaughan continued to hit as spring training progressed; he collected a home run, a double and three singles in going five for five in a 13–9 win over the New York Yankees on April 8 in a rematch of the 1941 World Series combatants.[39] His regular-season debut, though, was quite forgettable, as he went zero for four and after fielding a ground ball off the bat of Harry Danning, fired the ball over first baseman Dolph Camilli's head. Holmes, after doing his post-game interviews, wrote that "Vaughan, never a chatterbox, is the quietest guy in the locker room. He was positively embarrassed. He hit like a machine through the South, committed one error on the training trip, and here on opening day, he went hitless and unloaded a heave that might have cost the game."[40] Brooklyn got out of the gate blazing hot, winning 14 of its first 17 games to finish the month of April in first place with a four-game lead over second-place Pittsburgh. Vaughan missed part of the fun, though, as he pulled a tendon in his left ankle in a 9–5 win over Boston on April 23 and had to miss the next four games. Vaughan, also bothered by a charley horse in his left thigh, finished the month with a three-for-six effort in an 11–8 win over Cincinnati, scoring three runs in the process. In the 13 games in which he played, the Dodgers went 11–2 but Vaughan batted just .241 with three RBIs, although he did score 10 runs.

Brooklyn continued to roll through the month of May, compiling an 18–10 record to boost its overall mark to 32–13, good for a six-game edge over second-place St. Louis. Vaughan's old team, Pittsburgh, got off to a good start at 14–9 but then went 5–18 to drop to 19–27, 13½ games in back of the Dodgers. Vaughan, aided by extra batting practice before home games at Ebbets Field, heated up in May, as he collected 10 multi-hit games, including two four-hit efforts, and compiled a .281 mark during the 28 games to boost his overall mark to .268. One of the month's highlights was Vaughan's May 1 return to Pittsburgh for the first time in an enemy uniform after 10 splendid years with the Pirates. The former All-Star "got a big round of applause when he stepped up to the plate the first time," Al Abrams of the *Pittsburgh Post-Gazette* reported after the Bucs' thrilling 7–6 victory.[41] Vaughan had three hits, including an RBI double that plated Billy Herman with the go-ahead run in the top of the eighth inning, but saw Vince DiMaggio's hard grounder skip through his legs in the bottom half of the frame to allow the Bucs to push home the winning run. The Pirates finished off their two-game sweep with a 10–5 victory the next day, despite two hits, an RBI and two runs scored from Vaughan. The former Bucco had a scare during pregame batting practice as he was struck in the stomach by a ball thrown by catcher Mickey Owen. Vaughan was standing on third base, looking toward first, when Owen threw the ball to Vaughan. "Arky went down on his knees, held his head in his hands, then toppled over," the *Pittsburgh Press* reported. "His teammates rushed to his side, but he recovered quickly, just had the wind knocked out." The *Press* also reported that Vaughan and teammate Johnny Rizzo—another former Pirate—spent their first night in town as the guests of boxing great Billy Conn and his family. The two reported "the Conn baby is a handsome young chap."[42] Syndicated columnist Grantland Rice, writing in the *Pittsburgh Post-Gazette*, recalled Dodgers general manager Larry MacPhail's prophecy that "Arky Vaughan had more than made our team a pennant winner." "We recalled this prophecy," Rice wrote. "But Larry tells you so many things that only a magic memory can remember all he says. In spite of this MacPhail, in a baseball way, is right more often than he is wrong. [Yet] there are still doubters who believe that Vaughan won't be so hot after summer heat arrives."[43] The Brooklyn faithful, though, seemed to have taken to Vaughan. "He's one of the best 'Bums' we got," a Dodger fan was overheard saying at Forbes Field during Vaughan's first visit to Pittsburgh.[44] Frisch wasn't surprised that the Brooklyn fans appreciated Vaughan, nor was he surprised his former short-stop was playing well. Frisch said he knew Vaughan would help the Dodgers, but his goal wasn't to hurt his trading partner—it was to help his own ball club. A New York sportswriter who used the byline "The Old Scout" wrote that Frisch dismissed rumors that he and Vaughan were quarreling, and that precipitated the trade. Said Frisch:

> There wasn't any truth to that. Vaughan is a fine boy, and he will help the Dodgers. He is fast and he has moxie. He's a quiet fellow, but don't think he doesn't fight. I traded him only because I thought he needed a change of environment. We wanted an extra catcher to help Lopez, who is the best in the business with a mitt. So we got Phelps. We wanted a second baseman because we thought we might lose Gustine. So we got Coscarart. We wanted a left-handed hitting outfielder because our regular outfield in 1942 was all right-handed. So we got Jimmy Wasdell. And we took Luke Hamlin because we never have enough pitchers.[45]

Not everyone, though, was high on Vaughan. Eddie Brannick, the New York Giants team secretary and an avowed Dodger hater, said point blank that Vaughan "cannot play third base" and also called the Dodgers outfield "a fraud and a delusion."[46] Bill Terry, the Hall of Fame first baseman who went on to manage the New York Giants from 1932 through 1941, said Vaughan "always hits a ball one way. Give me a pitcher with good control and I can put a man right where Arky will hit that ball. We have always had good luck pitching him." Terry pointed out that in 1935—the season that Vaughan won the NL batting crown and hit over .400 much of the year before finishing at .385—Vaughan batted just .240 against the Giants. "He is such a good hitter that if he shifted a bit on us, he could make us change pitching to him instantly. But he does not do it."[47]

Brooklyn continued to set a fast pace through the month of June, going 16–7 to keep a comfortable eight-and-a-half-game edge over second-place St. Louis. Vaughan, though, had a challenging month as he appeared in only 13 games and batted just .255 with 11 runs scored and seven driven in. He came down with a stiff neck while en route to St. Louis aboard an air-cooled sleeper car and missed several games.[48] Vaughan returned to play for the first time in nine days on June 17 and promptly launched a two-run triple to help key a 5–1 victory over the Cubs. But he was able to play only the next six games, during which he went five for 24 before missing the next seven games with a case of intestinal flu that required a trip to Long Island College Hospital.[49] Despite Vaughan's relatively unproductive first half—he was batting just .265—he was one of seven Dodger players named to the National League team in the annual All-Star Game, set for July 6 at the Polo Grounds in New York. Although operating at less than 100 percent, Vaughan started for the NL team and went zero for two with a walk in a 3–1 loss to the American League.

Later that summer, the issue of race and baseball's color barrier perco-
lated to the surface, as writers began questioning why no blacks were playing
in the American or National leagues. Several noted some of the outstanding
players performing in the Negro League, including catcher Josh Gibson, then
playing with the Homestead Grays in Pittsburgh. Gibson hit 73 home runs in
1940 and was the only player besides Hank Greenberg ever to hit a home run
into the left field bleachers at Yankee Stadium. While some writers said the
time had come to integrate the game, others such as *The Sporting News*—the
so-called "Bible of the Baseball World"—wanted no part of it. An editorial
with the headline "No Good from Raising Race Issue," which appeared in the
August 6, 1942, issue, read:

> It is not difficult to imagine what would happen if a player on a mixed team, per-
> forming before a crowd of the opposite color, should throw a bean ball, strike out
> with the bases full or spike a rival. Clear-minded men of tolerance of both races real-
> ize the tragic possibilities and have steered clear of such complications, because they
> realize it is to the benefit of each and also of the game. However, there are agitators,
> ever ready to seize an issue that will redound to their profit or self-aggrandizement,
> who have sought to force Negro players on the big leagues, not because it would help
> the game, but because it gives them a chance to thrust themselves into the limelight
> as great crusaders in the guise of democracy. There would be as much point in the
> reverse being tried and an attempt made by Negro teams to bolster their lineups with
> white stars. It is not difficult to visualize what would happen in the latter case.[50]

If the Negro League was "raided" by the Major Leagues, the editorial went
on, it would have fewer stars and the caliber of ball would be lowered and
ultimately it would sink to the status of an "inferior minor circuit." The
Negro League, the writer claimed, was just beginning to make a profit and
losing its players would be a "staggering blow." It would be doubtful the
league could survive. "Instead of gaining anything, Negro baseball would
lose everything and without a medium for developing talent there would
be no players, in a short time, who could make the grade, even if given the
opportunity, in the American or National, not to mention the minors."[51]

In less than five years, though, the entire picture of baseball and race
would change forever with the arrival of Jackie Robinson in Brooklyn.

The Dodgers finished the month of July with a 70–29 mark and an
eight-and-a-half-game edge over second-place St. Louis. After being limited
to 13 games in June, Vaughan appeared in 27 games in July and batted .278
with 16 runs scored and eight RBIs. Vaughan tortured his former mates in
one of those games, as he stole home in the first inning of a 6–4 victory over
Pittsburgh at Ebbets Field on July 24, singled to drive home two more runs
in the fourth, stole second in the seventh inning and shifted over from third
base to shortstop in the sixth inning after Pee Wee Reese sustained an injury.[52] Up to that point in the season, Pittsburgh and Brooklyn had played 15

times, with the Dodgers winning 11 of them. "In nearly every clash between the natural rivals, Vaughan has been a rich contributor, the self-effacing Arky apparently feeling a big thrill in rubbing it in on Frank Frisch and his office associates in his own pleasant, yet determined, manner," Doyle wrote for *The Sporting News.* Doyle noted that Vaughan's steal of home helped defeat the Pirates on July 24 and he played a key role in a doubleheader sweep two days later. "Inasmuch as the two clubs have only seven more meetings, fans here are ready to admit Durocher and MacPhail won a decision when last winter's snows were on the ground in annexing the fleet Vaughan for four Brooklyn players," Doyle wrote. He added that thousands of Pittsburgh fans "would be delighted to see Arky in a World's Series, now that the Pirates are definitely out of all flag reckoning."[53]

Vaughan picked it up in August with a .295 mark but appeared less frequently than he did the previous month. Durocher held Vaughan out of six games in a seven-game stretch, instead playing young Lew Riggs, despite the fact that Vaughan was not injured—and the fact that Riggs, like Vaughan, hit left-handed. With the Dodgers in a funk and scoring just three runs in 33 innings, Durocher benched shortstop Pee Wee Reese for a night and inserted Vaughan at his old position, but it wasn't enough to prevent a 2–1 10-inning loss to St. Louis—a loss that sliced Brooklyn's lead to 4½ games over St. Louis. Vaughan went two for five and scored the Dodgers' only run.[54]

The Dodgers by no means hit the skids in August, compiling an 18–11 record, but the second-place Cardinals would not go away. St. Louis ended the month at 85–44 and trailed Brooklyn (88–40) by just three and a half games going into the final month of the season. Vaughan saw regular playing time down the stretch, batting .287 for the month to finish with an overall batting average of .277—the first time in 11 major league seasons that he failed to hit at least .300. He was particularly effective in the latter half of the month, as he put together a 13-for-35 stretch over a nine-game stretch. Vaughan's new club got red-hot in the season's final weeks, winning the final eight games in a row and taking nine out of the last 10 to finish 104–50–1 on the season. Somehow, though, the Dodgers failed to close the deal and finished second to surging St. Louis, which won 16 of its last 18 games to vault over Brooklyn and capture the pennant with a two-game cushion.

From the final week of August to the end of the season, the two contenders went head to head six times, and the Cardinals won five of them. The Dodgers, who at one point held a 10-game lead and tied a major-league record for most victories in a season by a second-place team, won four more games than they did during their pennant-winning season the previous year. They were mortally wounded by a sub-par streak that began the second week of September during which they lost five straight and eight of 11 games. During that same stretch, which began September 10 and ended

September 20, the Cardinals won nine of 10. By that time, St. Louis owned a two-and-a-half-game cushion, and Brooklyn could not get closer than one and a half games the rest of the way.

Back in Pittsburgh, the writers couldn't help but recall 1938, when the Pirates were overtaken in the final week of the season by the Cubs and lost the NL pennant. John P. McFarlane of the *Pittsburgh Post-Gazette* wrote:

> Two fellows whom the Dodgers' late season foldup probably hit a bit harder than some of their teammates were Arky Vaughan and Johnny Rizzo, ex-Pirates. Both were members of the 1938 Pirates who blew the flag in almost as tragic fashion as the men of Flatbush, allowing Chicago to dip into the world series gravy bowl as a result of Gabby Hartnett's home run off Mace Brown. There is no use in anyone kidding themselves that the "Bums" were sold a long time ago that they'd get into the series, for, believe it or not they are only human, even though they weren't talking out loud about what they'd do with the extra currency.[55]

If the drama of the pennant race wasn't enough, Brooklyn general manager Larry MacPhail announced during the season's final week that he would be stepping away after five years with the club so he could join the U.S. Army, where he figured to serve as either a major or a lieutenant colonel, effective at the end of the season. Club directors said the resignation had nothing to do with the team's collapse and also said there was nothing to the rumors that either Branch Rickey or Bill Terry might be in line to succeed MacPhail.[56]

Holmes described the scene when Dodger players returned home from the final series of the season in Philadelphia:

> [They] wore dazed expressions when the porter dusted them off at Pennsylvania Station. You could write all the intelligent conversation that took place on that train ride on the back of a postage stamp. Probably the only remark worth recording was that of one of the lads who recommended that every one inhale a large Mickey Finn, fall into bed and pretend the 1942 season never happened. Durocher said it all in the telegram he sent to [Cardinals manager] Billy Southworth from the North Philadelphia Station. It read: "Congratulations. We have been beaten by a great ball club and we'll all be pulling for you in the World Series." Dodger players held their heads up. "You've got to give the Cardinals credit for a drive like that," said Dixie Walker. "There isn't anything you can take away from a bunch that can come far from behind when they should have known they were beaten. Remember—they won it. We didn't lose it." Billy Herman recalled a few tough pennant races that his Cubs teams did not win. "But this is the hardest thing I've ever gone through," he said. "When you win 104 games and finish second there isn't anything to say."[57]

Some blamed the loose atmosphere in the clubhouse, where high-stakes card games were the norm. But Dick McCann, writing in *The Sporting News*, said it was the Cards—St. Louis—not the "cards" that did in the Dodgers. "We've maintained all along that the Dodgers didn't slump ... the Cards just kept on winning." Still, McCann noted that there was considerable gambling going on, noting that "at times their Pullman car or dressing room would look like something out of Monte Carlo." The game of choice was seven-card stud and McCann said it wasn't unusual to see a player put a $100 bill into the pot and "take back only a few singles in change."[58]

In mid–October, Holmes did a more thorough post-mortem on the Dodgers' season and noted that of the eight regular players in the lineup, only two of them had better batting averages than they did the year before, and the pitching staff, which boasted two 22-game winners in 1941, did not have a single 20-game winner in 1942. Outfielders Pete Reiser and Dixie Walker saw their averages drop 20 points or more, and Joe Medwick's power numbers declined precipitously from 18 home runs in '41 to four in '42. Vaughan, the Dodgers' biggest off-season acquisition was "probably ... the biggest disappointment of the lot," wrote Holmes. He noted that in 10 years in Pittsburgh, he never hit less than .300 and the previous year batted .316. Then, during spring training, Vaughan "literally sprayed line drives over the landscape," Holmes wrote. "Then he went down with the flu and never did become himself. Arky was still searching for ten lost pounds when the season ended. He hit .277."[59] Vaughan also finished with just 48 RBIs and 51 walks in 558 plate appearances.

The Dodgers came under criticism elsewhere, even from other National League club officials. Branch Rickey, who spent nearly 20 years with the St. Louis Cardinals' organization, said during a visit to Denver that Brooklyn "will be a burial ground for the 1943 manager of the Dodgers." Rickey also said former Dodgers general manager Larry MacPhail "spent a million dollars building a one-season club. The Dodgers were ahead by 10½ games on Aug. 4 and finished two games behind the Cards. A club must be disintegrating to do that."[60]

Within two weeks, though, that very same Rickey was named to take over for MacPhail as Brooklyn's new boss, assuming the title of team president and general manager. Rickey, described as a "religious, non-drinking, non-cussing crusader ... up to his armpits in a War Bond drive," was credited with multiple innovations during his lengthy stay with St. Louis, including devising baseball's farm system, which relied on minor-league clubs to supply the big league team with talent, and creating the first Knothole Gang, which allowed children to watch games for free. Rickey had some concerns about his new team's chances of winning the pennant in 1943, given the average age of the players. "There are an amazing number of 10-year veterans on the Brooklyn club," he said, "and the rate of disintegration, or, fall, which set in last September and enabled my Cardinals to win, must be checked. I do not think, however, the Dodgers could finish worse than second."[61]

One of those 10-year veterans—Vaughan—dropped his own bomb-

shell on the Dodgers two weeks later when he admitted in a telephone conversation with an Associated Press writer that he was uncertain whether he
would report to the Brooklyn club in the spring and he was seriously considering remaining at home. He noted the difficulty of running his ranch,
pointing out that the war effort made it difficult for him to find able-bodied
ranch hands. He also mentioned the challenges associated with transporting
his wife and three children from California to Brooklyn and back each year
while playing for the Dodgers. "And I wouldn't want to leave the family here
while I played baseball," he added.[62] One rumor that made the rounds—and
proved to be unfounded—was that Vaughan was quitting baseball to work
in a bomber factory. "Vaughan may not return to the Dodgers, but it will
not be war work that will prevent [it]," reported the *Ukiah Daily Journal*
on November 19. Instead, the paper noted the added acreage that Vaughan
was eyeing and the difficulty in securing labor for his ranching operation as
two likely reasons for Vaughan to give up the game—if he indeed planned
to do so.[63]

Any questions regarding the Dodgers' leadership were answered on November 19 when the club announced that Durocher was hired for a fifth term
as manager—this time on a one-year deal that allowed Rickey to fire him
at any time with 10 days' notice.[64] Rickey admitted that he had more than
a few challenges ahead of him when it came to player procurement, given
the retirement rumors swirling around Vaughan and first baseman Dolph
Camilli. "I hope that Dolph Camilli will have a change of heart and decide
not to retire," he said. "Meanwhile we must look for a first baseman to replace
him."[65] Some reporters felt that ultimately both Camilli and Vaughan would
relent and return for the 1943 season, if for no other reason than they were
needed to help the game survive in the wake of the war. Back in Pittsburgh,
Chet Smith weighed in:

> There is a hunch here that Arky Vaughan and Dolph Camilli both mean it when
> they say they are retiring from the Dodgers—but that circumstances beyond their
> control may fetch them back to Flatbush, come next winter. The 'circumstances' will,
> of course, be the debt they owe to baseball. They will be reminded of it frequently
> during the next few months when there will be a drive by the major leagues to keep
> all the available old-man power and bring back not a few of the veterans who have
> faded in the last season or two but will be welcome timber while the younger players
> are away.[66]

In addition to retirement talk focusing on Camilli and Vaughan, Dixie
Walker also was said to be considering stepping away from the game. He
first brought up that possibility during a talk at the Montauk Club and later
during a visit to the Holy Name Society of St. Francis Xavier church. Walker
told the crowd this was no attempt to secure a raise from the Dodgers but
rather that at 32, he'd reached a point in his career when a player begins to

realize he is on the decline and it was time to "prepare for the inevitable." Walker noted that he had a good job away from baseball and while acknowledging the great support he'd received from the fans in Brooklyn over the years, "I have got to prepare for the future in view of the fact that I have a family to support."[67]

♦♦ 9 ♦♦

Mutiny in Flatbush

Up to this point in the evolution of baseball, most off-seasons were reserved for player movement, and the 1942–43 off-season was no exception. But this time, instead of that movement being precipitated by player trades, Uncle Sam was responsible for players coming and going. According to *The Sporting News*, nearly 200 major-league players—or close to half of the players in the big leagues—were in the armed forces by early January 1943. And it was anticipated that many more players would trade their baseball uniforms for military togs before the 1943 season opened. Not one club had a full 40-man off-season roster. The Phillies, for example, had lost 14 players to the armed forces and had just 23 players on their roster. The Washington Senators, with a 30-man roster, had seen 15 players leave for the war effort.[1]

The Brooklyn club was not immune; manager Leo Durocher was summoned to his St. Louis draft board for a physical, and other players were getting jobs in the defense industry. When team president Branch Rickey heard the news regarding Durocher's draft status, he wouldn't say who might replace him as manager if Uncle Sam came calling. He did talk up Dolph Camilli but denied he was the chosen successor. "Why I hadn't even thought about it," Rickey said. The Dodgers boss had bigger worries—the overall manpower picture itself in the big leagues. "If the armed services continue to take our men at the rate they've done so for the last two months, it will be acute by the time the season starts," he said. Rickey was worried that the Dodgers would have a smaller roster than everyone but the Phillies by the time spring training started "and that's a terrible thing. Right now, four outfielders are all we can count on and we face the possibility of starting training with only Herman, Kampouris and Vaughan as infielders."[2] In late January 1943, shortstop Pee Wee Reese became the latest Dodger to heed the draft call. He had been classified III-A, which meant he was deferred for dependency reasons, as he supported his widowed mother and younger sister and had gotten married the previous year. Rickey said it would be up to Durocher to figure out how to replace Reese at shortstop if the latter was called to serve. "However, I don't

146

see what he can do except count on Vaughan to play the position," Rickey said. "The problem then arises: Who will we use at third base? I don't know now. But I do know that we need infielders badly and I'm out to grab any of them I can find lying around loose."[3]

Of course, not all the off-season talk revolved around baseball. A note in the January 8 edition of The *Pittsburgh Press* noted that Vaughan had seen both his ranch and his family grow. He purchased an additional 1,100 acres for his Potter Valley cattle ranch, and the *Press* noted that the purchase "was in the nature of a celebration of the birth of his first son, Timothy," who was "born just 30 minutes after midnight on New Year's Day at Ukiah General Hospital in Ukiah. Timothy's arrival expanded the roster of Vaughan children to four."[4]

With spring training just around the corner, Rickey traveled to California to meet with several players, including Camilli, but the slugger said after speaking with Rickey that he was still not sure if he would play in 1943 because he'd been unable to find a suitable operator for his cattle ranch in Laytonville, about 50 miles north of Vaughan's Potter Valley spread. Camilli said many Dodger fans had mailed him with offers to run his ranch while he suited up for Brooklyn, but added, "I can't hire a ranch manager by mail." Rickey said he had not imposed a deadline on Camilli to sign a contract, adding that Dolph was the type of player to keep in shape year-round. "We would be glad to have him whenever he could report."[5] Rickey also connected with Vaughan by telephone before he returned to Brooklyn and said that given Vaughan's family situation and the fact that he had just added some acreage to his ranch, he might want to stay put on the West Coast. However, Rickey said that Vaughan didn't appear to be as "serious" about his intentions to remain there as Camilli was.[6]

The Dodgers got a shot of good news in early March when the U.S. Army rejected the 37-year-old Durocher due to a punctured right eardrum. "Leo Durocher was called 'out' today—and for the first time in his life he didn't protest the decision," is the way that *Brooklyn Daily Eagle* writer Harold Parrott put it. Rickey said that from a patriotic viewpoint, he was sorry to see Durocher rejected. "But from the team standpoint I'm very happy to have him remain. I've always considered him a very worthwhile pilot and that's why I was prepared to wait until the last moment before naming a new man." Durocher, meanwhile, said he was disappointed at the rejection and that he protested it. "I feel terrible about it," Durocher said, "because I am in the best physical condition of my life." Had he been accepted, Durocher would have been the first big league skipper to enter the armed services.[7]

Two days later, the case of a New York Giants player caused Dodger followers to wonder if the same fate might befall a couple of key Brooklyn players—Camilli and Vaughan. Bill McGee, a right-handed pitcher, was essentially ordered to remain on his Illinois farm or lose his Class III-C exemption, which meant he was deferred from the armed services by both reasons of dependency and agricultural occupation. But McGee's situation differed from that of Camilli and Vaughan because while McGee was married, he had no children and therefore his deferment was largely based on his farm work. Both Vaughan and Camilli had children and were classified III-A—deferred for dependency reasons. Regardless, the situation was confusing to all. Tommy Holmes of the *Brooklyn Daily Eagle* wrote that while in years prior to the war, teams had the advantage over the players due to the reserve clause, which restricted player movement. "That's not so today," Holmes wrote. "In many instances, the clubs need the players more than the players need the clubs." Holmes wrote that many veteran players in twilight of their careers were wondering if it would even be worth it to try to play another season, especially if they had jobs promised them outside of baseball or—like Camilli and Vaughan—had a farm or ranch to tend to. "Practically every day brings additional news that causes this club owner or that to reach for the aspirin," Holmes wrote.[8]

Vaughan celebrated his 31st birthday on March 9 but remained unsigned with the regular season a little less than six weeks away. Rickey received good news, though, when Camilli notified him by wire that he had found help for his California ranch and would be heading east on April 2, with the goal of arriving by April 5. That would give him more than two weeks to prepare for the season opener on April 22.[9]

On March 14, Vaughan joined Camilli and decided to come back to Brooklyn for the 1943 season. He planned to report to the club's new spring training home in Bear Mountain, New York, the first week in April.[10] Now the question became, would Vaughan be asked to slide over to his old shortstop position, given Reese's pending absence and Durocher's age? Early in camp it appeared Durocher—who would turn 38 in July—was intent on taking up the shortstop slack, but even he admitted that it was a "young man's game."[11] Durocher didn't play at all in 1942 and appeared in only 18 games in 1941.

Camilli and Vaughan finally arrived in Brooklyn on April 5, took a subway to Ebbets Field and staged their own workout. Camilli said he'd certainly be able to go on Opening Day and figured to be ready much sooner. Vaughan estimated he'd need a week to get into baseball shape, despite Durocher's contention that it would take the California rancher three weeks to work out the kinks. Camilli told reporters he "never did need much Spring training, you know. I did some throwing in California, fooling around on the ranch in the late afternoon when the work was done." When a reporter sarcastically asked Camilli if his ear was "cut and bleeding" after a cross-country train trip with the quiet Vaughan, the slugging first baseman laughed and replied, "We barbered a bit and played a lot of gin rummy." Holmes wrote: "Our Mr. Vaughan is noted as one of the most inarticulate of athletes. He probably knows the words but they come out slowly and sparsely. It was a rare stroke of genius when somebody in the Treasury Department paired Arky up with Leo Durocher for the bond-selling campaign upon which the Dodgers embark today. The Skipper can talk enough for two or three or six if necessary."[12] Holmes surmised that Vaughan probably would move in at shortstop, with Billy Herman moving from second to third. Holmes added that Vaughan could be primed for a strong comeback after a rough 1942 season, in which he failed to hit .300 for the first time in his 11-year big league career. "Arky had a tough battle with influenza early in the campaign. He dropped far below his normal weight and never did fully regain his strength."[13]

Vaughan expressed no hesitation about taking on the shortstop role if it was given to him, reminding writers that he had more than a little experience at the position. They hadn't forgotten. "For more than 10 years Arky played that position for the Pirates and he was rated a good one," Lee Scott of the *Brooklyn Citizen* wrote.[14] It didn't take long for those around the ball club to be impressed with Vaughan's performance at his old position. "So far, Arky Vaughan is the star afield," the *Brooklyn Citizen* wrote on April 27. "Vaughan has come up with several smart plays at short. He robbed opposing players of base hits. Those who were in doubt as to whether Vaughan could take Pee Wee Reese's place now realize that he can."[15]

The Dodgers got off to a fine start, winning five of their first six contests, and Vaughan went seven for 23 with three runs scored and four RBIs while playing shortstop. On May 1, he clubbed Brooklyn's first home run of the season, a three-run shot that propelled the Dodgers to a 9–2 win over the Giants. Over the next month, Brooklyn compiled a 20–12 mark and built a one-and-a-half-game lead over St. Louis in the National League by Memorial Day. Vaughan, looking more like the old Pirate, batted .295 for the month, scoring 22 runs and driving in 12 while drawing 16 walks for a .377 on-base percentage. He seemed to regain some of his old on-field fire as well; in a game against St. Louis, young Cardinals infielder Eddie Stanky went out of his way on a slide into second base to break up a double play that Vaughan had no chance of turning. Stanky's "cap flew off and Vaughan kicked it into left field, then told Stanky what a busher he was."[16] That was one side of the story, at least. In an article that appeared in the June 24 issue of *The Sporting News*, John P. Carmichael, sports editor of the *Chicago Daily News*, reported that after Vaughan kicked Stanky's cap toward the outfield, Stanky retrieved the cap and approached Vaughan, saying, "If you want to kick anything, kick me, not my cap, if you have any guts." Nothing came of it at the time, and an inning or so later, Vaughan roped a double and pulled up at second. Stanky, still upset after being "shown up" by Vaughan, ranged alongside the veteran and asked, "What's the matter, didn't anybody ever slide into you before?

Can't you take it? I'm an infielder myself and I'll be playing out here every day, so you can take your turn whenever you want to. Vaughan spoke up, 'Aw, forget it, Stanky.... I was a little red. I'm sorry.'"[17]

Vaughan got even hotter as the season reached the halfway mark, pounding the ball at a .352 clip and slugging .565 for the month of July to raise his season's batting average to .311—all despite battling severe stomach problems. He had seven games of at least three hits that month alone—including a four-hit game with five RBIs in a 10–9 loss to Cincinnati on July 1—but the Dodgers slumped badly. The club went 10–19 to fall to third place, 11½ games in back of the red-hot Cardinals and a half-game behind Pittsburgh. Vaughan's hitting heroics did not translate to All-Star recognition, despite the fact that he led the league in runs, hits and stolen bases at the midway point. But Vaughan's actions in the clubhouse on July 10 certainly attracted national attention, as he staged a one-man revolt before a game against his old team, the Pittsburgh Pirates, at Ebbets Field. Numerous accounts of the incident exist, from newspaper articles of that time to recollections by former players in books and magazine articles published in the months and years that followed. The details vary, according to the source, but essentially it boiled down to Vaughan's reaction to Durocher's suspension of teammate Bobo Newsom, who was the club's best pitcher at the time.

The incident began on the night of July 9, when Newsom uncorked a pitch that backup catcher Bobby Bragan could not handle, a miscue that eventually cost Newsom his 10th victory of the season. Durocher accused Newsom of trying to make Bragan look bad by throwing a spitball, which caught Bragan off-guard. A New York writer named Tim Cohane of the *World-Telegram* happened to be in Durocher's office when the manager related the spitball story to Hugh Casey, a former Dodger who was home on leave from the armed forces. Durocher told Casey that he suspended Newsom on the spot and said he would try to make the suspension effective for the rest of the season.

Teammate Billy Herman told baseball historian Donald Honig in his book *Baseball When the Grass Was Real* that he was having breakfast the next morning with Vaughan and another teammate, Augie Galan, at the New Yorker Hotel, where they were staying. Herman recalled:

> Vaughan, you know, was a guy who always had everybody's respect, as a ballplayer and as a man. He never said too much, but everybody admired and respected him. Arky's reading the newspaper. Durocher had given an interview saying that Newsom had crossed Bragan up, giving him a spitball, and that was why Bobo was suspended. But it had been building up, you see. Newsom had been getting to Durocher for weeks, throwing cutting little remarks at him. Bobo didn't mean any harm, but Leo was getting madder and madder. So finally he had a chance to stick it to Bobo, and he did. So Vaughan's reading this, and he's very quiet, not saying anything to anybody. But something's bothering him, we could tell.[18]

Herman told Honig that the players went to the ballpark, put on their uniforms and went out to warm up. After batting practice, they went back to the clubhouse, where Durocher was in his office. Vaughan, Herman said, had been waiting to ask Durocher if he had been quoted correctly in the story Vaughan had read in the paper during breakfast. Vaughan walked into Durocher's office with the newspaper in hand.

"'Leo,'" he said, "'did you tell this to the writers?'"

"'Yeah,'" Durocher said, "'I told them that.'"

"Arky didn't say another word," Herman said. "He went back to his locker and took off his uniform—pants, blouse, socks, cap—made a big bundle out of it and went back to the office.

'Take this uniform,' he said, 'and shove it right up your ass.' And he threw it in Durocher's face. 'If you would lie about Bobo,' he said, 'then you would lie about me and everybody else. I'm not playing for you.'"[19]

Other reporters had slightly different accounts. An unnamed Associated Press reporter wrote that Vaughan was incensed over Newsom's suspension and handed Durocher his uniform, saying, "Well, here's my uniform. You can do what you want."[20] Some were more similar to Herman's in noting that Vaughan used a bit more colorful—and pointed—language in handing Durocher his uniform. Holmes wrote that the tension in the meeting room was so great "it literally crackled." Holmes said that Vaughan followed his remark of "'Here's another uniform you can have' with a suggestion to Durocher not only unprintable but virtually impossible."[21] At one point during the meeting, Holmes wrote, Vaughan snapped at a reporter, "Why don't you ask Leo why he suspended Newsom? He won't tell you. It wouldn't make him look good. And there are a lot of men in this room who think that the reason was insufficient."[22]

According to Arthur Patterson of the *New York Herald Tribune*—in a story published by the *Dayton Daily News*—Durocher responded to Vaughan by saying, "I don't know what it's all about, but if that's the way you feel about it, you're suspended, too." To which Vaughan replied, "You can't suspend me. I've quit."[23] When Dixie Walker backed up Vaughan and told Durocher he could have his uniform as well, it appeared a full-scale mutiny might be at hand, but it turned out that Vaughan was the only player who chose not to play. According to Patterson's story, Vaughan told Durocher that his grounds for suspending Newsom were "silly" and said Newsom and Durocher simply disagreed with one another and that no suspension was warranted. "He thought he was right, you thought you were right," Vaughan was quoted as saying. "He had a right to say what he did. And he didn't cuss you. And what's more, you tried to suspend him for the rest of the season. You said you would if you could make it stick." Durocher responded: "I suspended him for insubordination. Maybe they should have asked you to manage this ball club." To which Vaughan replied, "I wouldn't take it if they did."[24] Ultimately, Vaughan sat in the stands for part of the game before Rickey talked him into changing into his uniform and joining his teammates for the last part of the Dodgers' 23–6 beating of the Pirates. It was the first game that season that Vaughan had missed.[25]

Camilli, years later in an interview with Patricia Vaughan Johnson, said he thought Vaughan's outburst stemmed from Durocher's habit of constantly riding players. Camilli said he didn't think Vaughan "had any real love" for Durocher and that Vaughan disagreed with Durocher's treatment of Newsom that day—"and, boy, did he let Leo know." Camilli was not surprised to see Vaughan's reaction, even though he called Vaughan one of the easiest guys in the world to get along with. "He played against Leo when Leo was a player," Camilli said of Vaughan. "Leo was a guy you could take a disliking to when you played against him. He was one of these yappy guys, hollering all the time and getting on players." Camilli said he could understand why Vaughan might not be enamored with Durocher, given their two personalities. "Leo was a funny guy—if he liked you, he would bend over backwards for you," Camilli said. "If he didn't, he'd cut your throat. He liked me. I could do anything I wanted."[26]

Holmes had a bit more detail in his story of the rebellion, saying that at one point during the players meeting, Durocher claimed he was misquoted in the story that set Vaughan off. Durocher maintained throughout the meeting that the Newsom suspension had nothing to do with Newsom crossing up Bragan, but Cohane—the reporter who wrote the story—said indeed that Durocher had gone into details of that incident with Hugh Casey.[27]

Cohane believed his reputation as a journalist—and his dignity—was damaged when Durocher denied telling Casey and Cohane that Newsom had tried to "show up" Bragan in the Friday night game. Cohane demanded an opportunity to confront Durocher in front of the players and other reporters, and that chance came in a clubhouse meeting prior to the next day's game, on Sunday, July 12. According to Parrott, Newsom was there, and he asked Cohane if Durocher had told Hugh Casey that Newsom was trying to "show up" Bragan. Cohane said that Durocher indeed said as much and that in fact Durocher told Cohane to tell the other reporters about it. Newsom then turned to Durocher and asked, "Why did you do that and then on Saturday tell all your players you never did that?"

"'Well,'" Leo said weakly. "'You know how you talk to a ballplayer.... I said I was going to suspend you for the full season, didn't I? ... And you got only three games, didn't you?' You could see the surprised looks around the room." Parrott asked Vaughan why he got so angry over the whole incident and Vaughan responded, "I boiled over because I thought Newsom was wrongly treated, and I thought to myself 'the same thing could just as well happen to me. I could be the next victim.'" Parrott wrote that it was nothing new for Durocher—referred to as Leo the Lip or Lippy by some members of the media—to deny making statements that he had indeed made. "Lippy's behavior is based almost entirely on convenience. If it becomes inconvenient to have said something, Leo just decides he never did say it. Veteran newspapermen have known this for years, but, apparently, Lippy's players have just discovered it."[28]

A number of writers in New York and elsewhere saw the Vaughan rebellion as the first step toward Durocher's dismissal. Parrott wrote that the Dodgers players—the "flannel-suited jury," as he referred to them, would determine Durocher's fate. "Leo the Lip is at the fork in the road," Parrott wrote. "He won't last the season out if the team starts just going through the motions. But he could re-establish himself with his men, perhaps. He always was the orator, always the salesman." Parrott said that Durocher needed to take stock of things during the All-Star break. "He should add things up," he wrote. "He must get a grip on himself—and on his players!"[29] Some were more succinct. "So, summing up, the Dodgers seem to be sure-fire also-rans," wrote Havey Boyle of the *Pittsburgh Post-Gazette*, "and Durocher's goose is cooked."[30] J. Roy Stockton of the *St. Louis Post Dispatch*, writing in *The Sporting News*, noted that it wasn't the Newsom suspension that caused the rebellion. "It was an accumulation of explosive resentment and the Newsom case merely touched off the fuse," he said. "The big surprise was that Arky Vaughan figured so prominently. Arky is a gamecock, but unobtrusive and never in trouble. ... When he mounted the soap box, the boys knew the situation was serious and the fire had been burning for a long time."[31]

In a story that appeared in the *Pittsburgh Post-Gazette* on July 13, United Press writer Jack Cuddy wrote that the Dodgers appeared on the brink of a full-scale collapse:

> Despair spun a halo of gloom over the Borough of Brooklyn today. Not only were the beloved Dodgers a full 5½ games behind in the National League chase but internal dissension seemed about to burst the club wide open. ... We have no intention of sticking our already well-bruised nose into the affairs politic of any baseball team, but even from a distant point of vantage, it wouldn't be too risky to predict that a shakeup in the Dodgers is due—perhaps overdue. Rickey is too intelligent a baseball strategist to let an occurrence like this slip by like water under the bridge and the ax right now may be swinging into position. Whose head will fall, we have no way of knowing, but it wouldn't be too hard to guess—would it?[32]

Two days later, Newsom was sent packing to the St. Louis Browns for two veteran left-handed pitchers, Archie McKain and Fred Ostermueller. In doing so, Rickey clearly was sending a message of support for his embattled manager. "A manager must be fired or supported," Rickey told reporters after the trade. "There is no middle ground." Rickey also told reporters that he did

not consider Vaughan to be a disturbing influence on the team. "You've got
to understand impulses," Rickey said. "Vaughan is a fine fellow and a loyal
player and, incidentally, I think that Leo used good judgment in his handling
of that phase of the situation." Some critics had said Durocher should have
suspended Vaughan for his actions, but Rickey disagreed, saying that would
have helped no one. Durocher, meanwhile, defended his actions, saying he
felt he did nothing wrong. "I'll make a million mistakes; I've made plenty of
them in the past, but I don't think I made one here," he said.[33]

That Durocher and Newsom would clash was inevitable, based on the
history of the two men. Dan Desmond of the *Chicago Herald-American* put
together a chronological rundown of the various incidents that each was involved in over the years. For Newsom, the list went back to early 1932 and
included incidents where he refused a minor-league assignment and said of
Cleveland manager Oscar Vitt that Newsom "could have managed Cleveland
by telephone from St. Louis better than Vitt did last year." Durocher, meanwhile, had incurred multiple fines for arguments, using profane language and
fisticuffs with players and even an opposing manager—Casey Stengel, then
with the Dodgers, when Durocher played for St. Louis. That brouhaha occurred on May 12, 1936. Durocher claimed Stengel "hit him with a bat when
they carried an argument from the playing field to a spot under the grandstand. Stengel said it was a case of mistaken identity, accusing Leo of not
being able to distinguish between a bat and his fist."[34]

The brief rebellion didn't seem to have a sizable impact on the club's
on-field performance, as the Dodgers won four of their next six, including
a series in Boston where they took two of three games. Vaughan certainly
didn't appear to be bothered, as he banged out eight hits, including two home
runs, in a four-game stretch and went 11 for 25 in the six games that followed
his "strike." One player, who did not want to be quoted by name, said a week
or so after the flare-up:

> Things are all right again. In that Boston series Durocher was really a good manager
> and we were a good ball club. I think I can say that all of the fellows feel the same
> way about it. We'll do our best to win this year. If we don't make it we'll fail because
> we're not good enough. It won't be because of what you guys call internal dissension.
> Durocher always was a good manager. He was one last season and the year before. I
> don't know what got into him a while back. He was nervous, irritable and edgy. When
> we lost one he'd eat our ears off. To be frank about it, I don't think he realized the
> resentment he was creating among the players until that big blow-off came last week.
> But once he did realize what happened, he snapped right out of it.[35]

As of July 18, Vaughan was hitting at a .307 clip with 107 hits and was battling teammate Billy Herman and St. Louis' Stan Musial for the league lead in
that category. He also led the NL in runs scored with 70, and his 12 steals also
led the league. In 84 games he had struck out only six times. Still, not all was

right with him. He left the club after the Boston series to undergo treatments for stomach ulcers at Memorial Hospital in New York, yet still managed to put a 12-game hit streak together.[36] Vaughan was placed on a strict diet of milk and eggs and told by his doctor to give up his occasional smoke and limited him to one game on doubleheader days in an effort to preserve his strength.[37] Three days later, putting his physical woes aside and playing at his old home ballpark in Pittsburgh, Vaughan collected three hits and unloaded an inside-the-park grand slam in the top of the 10th inning to give Brooklyn a 10–6 victory. When the Dodgers left Pittsburgh after that series ended, Vaughan stayed put to await a report on some X-rays that he had taken on July 25. In a story published by the *Pittsburgh Press* on July 27, a writer named Dick Fortune wrote, "Vaughan hasn't been feeling right all year and goes to his room immediately after each day's game and rests. If the X-rays show definitely that he has ulcers, this probably will be Vaughan's last season in baseball."[38] Holmes concurred that the '43 season might be Vaughan's last. "Vaughan is having what the trade calls a good season," he wrote. "But he isn't having any fun, playing ball with a serious case of stomach ulcers and on a strict diet of eggs and milk. You can bet your ration book that Arky won't be back for more next Spring, unless he feels a lot better than he does right now."[39]

Teammates who knew Vaughan were not surprised that he had stomach issues. "He was a very quiet man and it always looked like nothing ever bothered him," said Al Lopez, a longtime major leaguer who played with Vaughan in Pittsburgh. "He kept everything inside—he never showed his feelings. He could have hit a home run and won the game and he'd show no emotions."[40]

The '43 season marked the first time that Vaughan's family did not accompany him to the East Coast during the baseball season, and some felt that was weighing on him. Dolph Camilli's wife, Ruth, in a phone conversation with Parrott on August 1—the day after Camilli was traded to the New York Giants—said her husband was ready to return to California and that he never wanted to play that season. Added Ruth Camilli: "Mr. Rickey talked us into playing again, and we've been happy here, and we like Mr. Rickey. But it's just been a hard-luck year. Look at Arky Vaughan; he didn't want to come East, either. Finally he came and then his family was supposed to come, and then couldn't, because his little girl was kicked in the face by a horse, and here he is playing the string out on his nerve, although he's a sick man. Yes, really sick. In pain—he's in bed when he's not on the ball field."[41]

Two days later, Holmes reported that Dr. Robert Hyland examined Vaughan on August 3 and found no trace of any stomach ulcers. "The St. Louis medical man says that Vaughan suffers from low blood pressure and hyper myelitis. Trying to make us understand what that meant, the Doc says that Arky's digestive action works so fast that the food he eats does him little good."[42] Despite his ailment, Vaughan continued to hit, as he appeared in 25 games in August and batted .324 with 14 RBIs and 20 runs scored. The Dodgers, though, were nowhere near contenders in the National League, as they were battling Pittsburgh for third place heading into the final full month of the season, 16 games in back of pace-setting St. Louis. Conflicting reports about Vaughan's willingness to play again in 1944 began filtering out in mid–August. Al Abrams, a writer with the *Pittsburgh Post-Gazette*, reported on August 14 that Vaughan told friends in Pittsburgh that the current season would be his last, despite Abrams' contention that Vaughan had three or four good years remaining.[43] But four days later, Branch Rickey announced that Vaughan had been "undergoing a medical overhaul" with the idea of returning to Brooklyn in 1944. "He wants to play, and he is the kind we need to win," Rickey said of Vaughan.[44] Vaughan reached a personal statistical milestone on August 29 against Philadelphia when he banged out three hits in a double-header sweep, the last of which put him in the 2,000-hit club.[45]

Despite his physical woes, Arky saw action in 26 September games and three more in October as the Dodgers wrapped up their season with an 81–72 record, good for third place in the National League behind the pennant-winning Cardinals, who finished with an 18-game bulge over the runner-up Reds and a 23½-game margin over Brooklyn. As the season wound down, Rickey gave Durocher his release and said he wanted to start from scratch in contract talks for the 1944 season. Rickey said he wanted to give Durocher a chance to explore other options, perhaps elsewhere in baseball or radio or even Hollywood. Rickey also said he figured to finalize his managerial decision shortly after the World Series concluded. He did not close the door on Durocher returning and in fact said he would welcome him back if Durocher wanted the job "badly enough."[46]

Vaughan finished the season with a .305 batting average—good for eighth in the league—and a .370 on-base percentage. He finished sixth in the league in WAR among position players, was fourth in offensive WAR, was sixth in at-bats with 610, fifth in hits with 186, tied for fifth in total bases with 252, fifth in the league in extra base hits with 50, fifth in times on base with 249, fourth in doubles with 39 and led the league in stolen bases with 20. He was also the toughest man to strike out in the National League, as he went down on strikes just once every 47 at-bats. The next closest was Stan Musial at one in every 34.3 at-bats.

In late October, Rickey and Durocher met to discuss the Dodgers' managerial post for 1944, and on October 26, Rickey announced that Durocher indeed would return to skipper the club the following season—despite the upheaval surrounding the Vaughan mutiny the previous July and the club's third-place finish. At a press conference announcing Durocher's return, Durocher was asked if he could regain the confidence of all the members of his

25-player roster. "I like all the players but one," Durocher responded, much to Rickey's chagrin.[47] Immediately, the press began to speculate on the 25th player, and reporters questioned Durocher if it was Billy Herman, who some had speculated might succeed Durocher as manager. "No, Herman is a great guy," Durocher said of the club's second baseman. "It isn't Arky Vaughan, is it?" a writer asked. "It is not Herman or Vaughan," Durocher said. "But I don't want to go into personalities." Rickey said it was unlikely that the player in question would be traded. "I don't think Leo has such a feeling against the man that he can't tolerate him," Rickey said.[48]

Rickey said he hoped that Durocher would be able to control his players and added: "I've discussed it with every member of the team—except one. Nobody claims that Durocher is perfection. But the boy wants to do a good job. He was hurt when some of the players flared up over the Newsom interlude last [July]. He likes ball players. It isn't in his nature to apologize to any one. But he never whines. Not once did he ask me to rehire him. But if he's only 10 percent right he sticks to it. He's emotional under stress and is prone to exaggerate."[49]

Talk continued to focus on the mystery 25th player—the one that Durocher said he didn't like. Dixie Walker, a popular veteran Dodger, told a United Press reporter after returning from a fishing trip in Birmingham, Alabama, that he didn't think the player in question was him: "Only Leo knows and he isn't going to say. It wouldn't be smart. He wouldn't go around saying: 'I don't like Walker, or, I don't like Herman, or, I don't like Vaughan.' I've always gotten along with Leo. More power to him. You've got to hand it to a guy who is fired and then wins back his job. And that's what Durocher did. You have to admire fellows like him."[50]

Walker also said he didn't believe Vaughan was the mystery man. "I believe Leo admires Arky for his courage in getting right up and backing a teammate," Walker continued. "Besides, Vaughan showed more courage than anybody I know last summer. Hustling like he did when he wasn't well."[51] Speculation went on for months about the identity of that player. On November 13, the *New York Daily News* devoted a column to the question: Who do you think is the player that Durocher doesn't like? Half of the six respondents tabbed Dixie Walker while others cast a vote for Vaughan, Billy Herman and Durocher himself.[52] The question wasn't put to rest for good until the publication of Durocher's autobiography, *The Dodgers and Me: The Inside Story*, in 1948. "Although his name has never been revealed in this connection, I can now say that it was Dixie Walker," Durocher wrote. "I was bitter at Walker for the way he had sided with Newsom and Vaughan. He hadn't bothered to find out the facts or to think them through. I was also peeved at Dixie because of other, if minor, incidents."[53] However, Durocher conceded that Walker was a fine player and did not lobby for Rickey to trade him. It's a good thing; Walker hit .357 in 1944 and won the National League batting title, although the Dodgers finished in seventh place at 63–91, 42 games behind the first-place Cardinals.[54]

After Durocher was rehired to manage the club in 1944, he traveled to the West Coast, where he met with several players—including Vaughan, whom he visited on his Potter Valley ranch. He told Parrott that Vaughan wanted to play with the Dodgers the following season if his health was up to it. He also described Vaughan's ranch for Parrott, who was writing for *The Sporting News*: "What a place Arky has out there. They call it Potter Valley, and there's no train runs anywhere near it. You take a bus and it leaves you 60 miles short. They tell you: 'Keep goin' up the valley, turn left at a puff of smoke, right at the second general store.' Well, finally I found it. The guy owns a whole mountain and what's on the other side of it too."[55]

As the year wound to a close, Rickey held a press conference to announce the acquisition of a pitcher named Clay Smith, and he also made public a letter that Vaughan had written from his ranch. The letter referenced Durocher's visit and reiterated that he wanted to play next season for Brooklyn if his health permitted—and if he was able to find enough help to get his cattle to market. "I have always considered Brooklyn the best town in baseball," Vaughan wrote, "and I still think it is. The trouble we had last Summer is forgiven and forgotten so far as I'm concerned and I'm sure Leo feels the same way."[56]

As 1944 dawned, Brooklyn club officials were doing their best to put together a representative club given the constraints of the war. On a lighter note, a new Hollywood movie titled *Whistling in Brooklyn* began gaining some attention. The film starred comedian Red Skelton as a radio detective known as "The Fox" and also featured several members of the Dodgers cast for a scene that called for an exhibition baseball game between the mythical Battling Beavers and several members of the Dodgers, including Vaughan and Durocher. But the magic of Hollywood couldn't outweigh the gravity of the roster situation on the "real" Dodger ball club. Fifteen players were classified as III-A, meaning they were deferred from the service because of dependency reasons. But, as Holmes noted, "Even though they're veterans the Dodgers can do no more than count on them month to month or maybe from week to week." The veterans in the III-A category included Billy Herman, Dixie Walker and Bobby Bragan.[57] Both Rickey and Durocher were concerned about Vaughan's availability; Durocher said several times during the winter that Vaughan held the key to the club's pennant chances. As *Daily Eagle* writer Harold C. Burr put it:

> Out in California stands a young man with a monkey wrench poised in his uplifted right arm, undecided whether or not to toss it into the 1944 Dodger infield. Should Arky Vaughan stick to his threat to stay on his ranch with his lowing kine and nurse

his set of troublesome ulcers in retirement, Manager Leo Durocher will have to come up with another high-grade shortstop some place, and in these days of manpower shortage in baseball, it's going to take some doing. Something will likely break in the Vaughan case when the Dodgers put their contracts in the mail, presumably this week. Nothing has been heard from Arky since the last pessimistic letter in which he said that he hadn't made up his mind. He mentioned that he had some cattle he wanted to sell in June and said that new X-ray pictures showed that his ulcers hadn't cleared up. ... Outwardly, at least, the Dodgers are not taking Arky seriously. But it could well be that they are just whistling in the dark before getting ready to duck that monkey wrench.[58]

A month passed and still the Dodgers hadn't heard from Vaughan, yet the club—and the media—remained optimistic. "Arky will probably play ball for the Dodgers again," Burr wrote. "The hitch is that he can't hire any hands to work his ranch, what with the war shortage of cowboys worth their weight in gold on the hoof. Arky's ulcers should excuse him from military service. His stomach trouble might even prevent him from being a playing-through infielder."[59] By mid–March, Vaughan had yet to inform the club of his definitive plans for the upcoming season, but the Dodgers still held out hope. Rickey said he had heard nothing from Vaughan other than a letter that Vaughan had sent earlier, expressing that he remained undecided about playing in 1944. Still, Rickey said he was "inclined to believe he will play."[60]

Durocher certainly hoped that would be the case. "Lippy never wanted anything more in his life as he wants the Brooklyn shortstop," Lee Scott of the *Brooklyn Citizen* wrote. "As the days go by Leo realizes more and more the importance of Vaughan's presence." Durocher not only respected Vaughan's ability, but if the veteran star did not return, Durocher himself might have to plug the gap at shortstop, at least temporarily, and Scott noted that Durocher had made it known that he "doesn't particularly care to cavort around the short field. In fact, he wants no part of it. Hence his anxiety to have Vaughan wire President Rickey his acceptance."[61] Vaughan, Scott wrote, was the key man in Durocher's plans. "Without him, the Dodgers are truly in a desperate plight."[62] Durocher didn't mince words. "He's the key to our whole infield setup," the fiery manager said, "and I'd be only kidding myself, and the fans, if I said he wasn't. ... Minus Vaughan, we're a club without a shortstop."[63] Some of the Brooklyn beat writers theorized that Vaughan might have been holding out for more money, but Durocher rejected that idea. "Money would never stand between the Dodgers and Vaughan," Durocher said.[64]

At the end of March, the Rickey and the Dodgers finally received word from Vaughan that he would not be available for at least the first half of the season. "A letter from the missing veteran was read to Rickey over the telephone by the home office while Branch was in the Middle West," wrote Burr. "It wasn't good listening." Rickey indicated that Vaughan was hoping to rejoin the club in July or August. But Burr theorized: "It means, looking at the transmitted communication bluntly, that Arky isn't going to play any baseball for the duration [of the war], if ever again. That word hopeful is the hateful little joker in the letter. Even admitting that Vaughan shows up sometime during the last three months of the National League campaign it would take another 30 days before he would be in physical shape to play regularly."[65] Rickey reiterated that it wasn't money that was keeping Vaughan away—it was his inability to secure labor for his Potter Valley ranch.[66]

The same day the Dodgers got word of Vaughan's plans, they also learned of possible changes to the Selective Service system that could require all men classified as 4-F—ineligible for the draft and therefore eligible to play baseball—to give up the game for a war-related job. Such a change could have had a major impact on major-league rosters and would have given a major advantage to franchises that employed a "farm" system. Rickey said his farm system would allow him to field a team and even suggested the major leagues might consider pooling talent, where clubs with sufficient manpower might loan players to teams that were hurting. Rickey said he would be willing to put 50 of his 80 organizational players into a pool for distribution among the other 15 major league clubs for as long as the war lasted. "I am ready to do anything that would keep baseball going in the major leagues," Rickey said.[67]

Despite the Dodgers' contention that Vaughan might be able to play for the second half of the season, some members of the media feared the standout shortstop might have played his last game for the Dodgers. A story in the *New York World-Telegram* read in part: "A good part of the savings of his big league career has been invested in Vaughan's ranch, and it is unreasonable to feel he will leave it just for three months of baseball, especially in view of the added considerations of an ever-tightening war manpower situation and his own uncertain stomach condition, which made playing ball a painful task through the last three months of last season."[68] Rumors began circulating in mid–April that Vaughan was en route from California to join the club, but they proved to be unfounded. Brooklyn started its season without Vaughan, and the Dodgers took two of their first three at Philadelphia before returning for the home opener against the crosstown rival Giants. A preview of the game was squeezed onto the front page of the *Brooklyn Daily Eagle*, amid stories about Allied bombers dropping 5,040 tons of bombs on Europe the previous night and the German army preparing for a possible Allied invasion on the French side of the English Channel. Another front-page story highlighted five teenage boys who rose early in the morning and made it down to Ebbets Field to be first in line for bleacher seats. "They came, they said, speaking almost all at once, 'because we want to see the Dodgers beat the Giants.'" When the boys were asked who their favorite player was, one replied, "'Mel Ott'" but the others responded, "'We want Vaughan back.'"[69]

Throughout the spring, reports would filter back to Brooklyn that Vaughan was about to lock up his ranch and return to baseball. Burr reported on May 17 that Vaughan might rejoin the club during the Dodgers' long home stand in June. "The club has been using pressure through its California agents to get the strong, silent man of Potter Valley to change his mind about quitting baseball and the shortstop is said to have weakened. The return of Vaughan would add 50 percent more strength to the Brooklyn infield."[70] On May 29, Holmes again stoked Dodgers fans' hopes by saying they shouldn't think that Vaughan's "eventual return is an impossibility. Branch Rickey has had nothing new to say about Vaughan for a long time, but it is a cinch that he has kept as close as possible to the situation in Potter Valley, Cal."[71]

The mystery ended when, on May 30, Rickey announced that Vaughan had been "irrevocably lost" to the club: "I was optimistic about Vaughan right up to the end. Everything that had kept him on the coast, with the exception of his draft status, had been ironed out. Farm labor? We would have been glad to underwrite that added expense. His health is plenty good enough to permit his playing ball. He wants to play with the Dodgers. He has told me repeatedly. His differences with Durocher last year isn't a factor. Now he informs me that he doesn't intend to go to his draft board for reclassification. … Well, that settles it."[72] Vaughan had been classified 2-C, which deferred agricultural workers from serving in the armed forces, but a change in the draft laws exempted those over 30 from serving. Rickey theorized that if Vaughan had sought to be reclassified, he would be free from the specter of the draft and able to continue his baseball career.[73]

A week later, more important news dominated the headlines, as the Allies launched what would come to be known as the D-Day invasion, sending scores of troops to the beaches of France's Normandy region. More than 150,000 troops—many of them American—stormed five beaches and eventually gained a foothold on the continent, setting the stage for the ultimate downfall of Germany's Third Reich a year later. "Invaders Drive 10 Miles Into Nazis' Coastal Wall," screamed the all-caps headline in the June 6 edition of the *Pittsburgh Press*. "11,000 Planes Aid 4000-Ship Fleet," read the sub-head.[74] "Allies Smash 9½ Mi. Beyond French Coast," the *Brooklyn Daily Eagle* head-line read, also in all-caps, with a sub-head: "Battle Rages at Caen; Our Casualties 'Light.'"[75]

Even though he remained away from the game, Vaughan's name continued to appear on the sports pages. According to a news brief that ran in the *Brooklyn Daily Eagle* on June 7, the Dodgers denied a rumor that one reason why Vaughan refused to report to the club was that the shortstop demanded that he be paid a year's salary in full.[76] Three days later, in the *Pittsburgh Post-Gazette*, Durocher was asked if Vaughan did not report to the team because he could not get along with Durocher. "I get along with anybody who can play ball," Durocher responded. "Arky Vaughan was my type of ball player. He wants to win. So do I. He wants to hustle. So do I."[77]

If there was any hope that Vaughan might reconsider and join the club, it was snuffed out for good in late June when Rickey announced that Vaughan was "officially and definitely out of the 1944 baseball picture." Rickey reported that Vaughan had gone on the voluntarily retired list. "In April, the knowledge that I would not be able to call on Vaughan for even half the season would have struck me as being highly deplorable," Rickey said. "Now I regard the blow as a baseball calamity."[78]

Vaughan's daughter Patricia, writing years later, said it was not a difficult choice for Arky to make. His brother Glenn, who had been the main man at the ranch while Arky was back East playing baseball, was in the service, as were just about all of the young men in Potter Valley. "Only the old men, the women and children were available," Patricia Vaughan Johnson wrote. "There was no one he felt competent enough to run the operation and he felt that it was a national service to raise the cattle the armed forces needed." Essentially, she wrote, working the ranch was "more important than playing baseball." In addition, it had become increasingly difficult for Vaughan's wife and children to keep splitting their year between Potter Valley and the East Coast. Travel alone was a challenge during World War II, as most of the preferred railroad accommodations were reserved for the military and defense personnel. Housing in Brooklyn was also difficult to find. "And the blackouts and air raid drills had been frightening to all of them," Johnson wrote. "Arky believed that he and his family were better off at home in Potter Valley."[79]

Vaughan's decision to ask the commissioner to place himself on the voluntarily retired list meant that he would have to remain on that list for a minimum of 60 days, meaning he was effectively lost for the remainder of the season. Rickey said that now that Vaughan was officially retired, he wanted to "make some revelations. It has been hinted that Arky refused to report because I would not meet his terms. It also has been bruited about that the player carried a hate against his manager. Both are downright canards." Rickey then pulled out a file of correspondence that backed up his claims. The letters showed that Rickey had offered a number of inducements, including a substantial pay hike, a bonus to cover the higher cost of living in New York, retroactive to 1943, traveling expenses for the Vaughan family and three experienced cattlemen—their salaries paid—to take care of Vaughan's ranch. "As for that flareup over Newsom last summer, the nonsense strike and things that were said and reported said—Vaughan laughed at the idea that the hangover would keep him from reporting," Rickey said.[80]

At the end of that particular day, Rickey's club would find itself in fifth place with a 28–29 record, 10½ games behind first-place St. Louis. From that point on, however, Brooklyn collapsed, going 35–62 the rest of the way to finish in seventh place, 42 games behind the pennant-winning Cardinals. Without Vaughan, the Dodgers used several players at third base that season, with Frenchy Bordagaray handling the position in 98 games. Overall on the season, Bordagaray batted .281 with six home runs and 51 RBIs.

Despite the seventh-place finish, on September 28 with just a few days remaining in the season, Rickey announced that Durocher would be back to manage the club in 1945. "Naturally I'm tickled to death that Mr. Rickey has seen fit to go along with me for another year," said Durocher. "We understand each other. Next year we'll give the fans—whom I want to thank for standing so staunchly behind a loser—better ball."[81]

That better ball would have to come without one of the club's top players, as it would be years—and not months—before Brooklyn's fans would see Vaughan back in a Dodger uniform.

◆◆ 10 ◆◆

Leaving
and Returning

On New Year's Day 1945, Jim Byrnes, the director of War Mobilization and Reconversion, sent shock waves through professional baseball when he announced his desire to utilize all men classified 4-F—those not qualified for military service—in some ways related to the war effort. This might include putting those men to work in war machinery plants or requiring them to do some sort of limited service. It was just an idea at the time, but it was enough to frighten baseball officials, who counted on the 4-F brigade to populate their rosters. Brooklyn, for example, had 13 of its 31 players classified 4-F. But Byrnes couldn't understand how a man who could play major league baseball or professional football could be declared unfit for military service. "A man may have a trick knee," he told a press conference in Washington on New Year's Day, "but if it doesn't get tricky on the football field, the chances are that it won't get tricky at Verdun or in Belgium. Moreover, color blind athletes could spot an enemy. I haven't seen one of 'em get football sweaters mixed up and they are all colors."[1]

While the fate of the 4-Fs remained in limbo, Vaughan's fate for the 1945 season became known within the first week of the new year. When getting ready for a trip to the West Coast, Rickey wired Vaughan and asked him if he would like to meet in San Francisco. "His answering telegram was cordial enough, but he said that it would be impossible for him to come," Rickey said. "I took it from that there was no chance of getting him to play." In other words, Rickey said, "a period can be put down for that episode."[2]

Vaughan, in fact, would not put on a Dodger uniform until the 1947 season, but he was hardly taking it easy. Patricia Vaughan Johnson recalled her father working "very hard, usually from dawn until dark. There was always something that needed to be done around the ranch. The cattle needed to be tended—branded and marked—and the sick ones given medications." In the spring and summer, Vaughan's cattle were turned out to range for grass

164

but he still had to ride around and check on them, bringing them salt licks and repairing fences when needed. In the fall, the cattle would be rounded up and brought into town. There, the young steers would be sold and the cows that had calves would remain in the valley for the winter. That wasn't all. Johnson said the portion of the ranch that was earmarked for crops had to be plowed, disked and planted with alfalfa, clover and grain. In the summer, those crops would need to be harvested, and much of the work was done by hand. Vaughan's entire family got into the act—his wife, Margaret, his children, father, father-in-law, sisters-in-law and nephews. Margaret's sister, Betty, and her two sons—Fred and Jon—had moved to Potter Valley for the duration, as Betty's husband, John, was in the Navy. She rented a cabin in town and found a job at a café that was part of a complex known as "Hoppers Corner," named after the owners. Margaret and her two oldest daughters—Patricia and Mikie—were thrilled, as the girls considered the two boys more like brothers than cousins. Vaughan's father and mother came up from Fullerton when they could, and Margaret's parents would stay for several months at a time when possible, Patricia recalled. Two of Margaret's other sisters—Nettie and Mary, who worked as secretaries at an air base near Santa Rosa—and her brother Buddy also stayed with the family to help on the ranch. "There was always someone willing to help out with the work," Patricia wrote.[3]

And however willing—or unwilling—the Vaughan children were expected to help with the chores. According to Patricia, her famous father never yelled or scolded his children—or anyone else. "He seemed to command people with his presence," she wrote. "He expected the best of people and somehow because of this, most of those close to him tried to live up to his expectations." Vaughan rarely lost his temper. "The offense had to be very serious in order for him to give a child a spanking, or a friend a cross word," Johnson wrote. However, one aspect of ranching life that would test Vaughan's patience was working on the machinery. Johnson recalled one piece of equipment in particular that got the best of Arky on one specific occasion—his John Deere tractor. "It would die and then not start," she wrote. Vaughan worked on the tractor for days, taking it apart, putting it back together and then trying to start it—with no success. Finally, after three days—and about 50 unsuccessful starts—Vaughan took a tool, slammed it against the tractor's fender with all his might and then tossed the tool as far as he could, out in the alfalfa field. "He stomped into the house and no one said a WORD!" Johnson wrote. When he finally cooled off, he asked Patricia and his nephew, Fred, if they would come out in the field and help him look for the tool. "It was a very quiet search," Johnson recalled.[4]

The rationing of food and other goods was a way of life for most during World War II, and the Vaughans were no exception. However, they were luckier than most, given the products raised and grown on the ranch. Dairy cows meant no shortage of milk, cream or butter. One of the older children's least favorite chores was turning the separator, which would separate the milk from the cream. Later, they would turn a hand churn that helped convert the cream into butter. Johnson recalled her paternal grandfather—affectionately known as Daddy Mike—using his strong arm to make homemade ice cream on Sundays during the summer. The Vaughans also raised chickens, which meant they had plenty of eggs, and the chickens also were used as meat, as were the beef cattle and some pigs. Arky and Margaret also loved to hunt and fish, and they kept the family supplied with game and fish. The menu would feature quail, pheasant, duck and goose as well as deer. Johnson recalled on one occasion her father bringing home bear meat. "This was particularly distasteful to the children," she wrote. In addition, the family also had a good supply of fruit and vegetables, which Margaret's father, Max, grew in a large garden and orchard that he planted. Still, some items were at a premium, as staples such as coffee, sugar and flour were being rationed. Perhaps the one item they all missed the most, Johnson said, was chocolate. Also in somewhat short supply was gasoline. Even though ranchers were entitled to more than many, the Vaughans still needed to conserve. They limited their trips to Ukiah to once a week so Margaret and Betty could do their major shopping, and the children would tag along to attend a Saturday matinee at the Ukiah Theater. Arky also made sure there was enough gas to take the family to Sunday Mass.[5]

Despite the hardships associated with the war, Johnson wrote: "These were probably some of the happiest times of the children's lives. They knew there was a war going on and that it was very serious, but for the first time since they had been born, they had their father with them all of the time. No more months away at Spring Training, no more lengthy road trips, no more what seemed like daily trips to the stadium, no more sharing him with adoring fans. The family had him to themselves."[6]

Vaughan was an active participant, attending school plays and programs as well as sporting events. He took pride in the children's academic accomplishments. He gave the children horses, taught them how to ride, how to herd cattle and how to take care of the animals. "He didn't openly show his affection," Johnson wrote, "but you knew he cared." Rarely did he raise his voice; instead, he would fix the offender "with a stony silence that was louder than words," Johnson wrote.[7]

Arky learned a lot about his children during the three years he was away from baseball, and they learned about him as well. One thing they learned that came as a bit of a surprise to them was that he was an accomplished swimmer. On summer weekends, if the family was caught up on work and if there was enough gas, the whole family would drive out to a swimming hole on the Eel River known as "Billy Dam Hole." They would take picnics or food to barbecue, sometimes with just the family and sometimes with other families. It was there that the Vaughan children first saw their father swimming as well as diving off a large rock at the edge of the river. "They were amazed at how good he could swim," Johnson wrote. "They simply had never thought about it before. They had never seen him engaged in any sport other than baseball."[8]

The Vaughans had a variety of friends in Potter Valley, including some of the old ranching families that Vaughan had known since he was a boy. For example, the Whitaker family was the one that Daddy Mike had stayed with when he first landed in California in the 1890s. Arky would help out a couple of the other ranchers when they needed it, and they returned the favor, whether it was rounding up or branding cattle or other ranching chores. "And when there was no work to be done, they would play together," Johnson wrote. This would consist of hunting, fishing, playing cards—and partying. But Arky took care not to drink in front of his father, who had given up drinking years earlier. He enjoyed the cast of characters that made up Potter Valley—people like Julius Rottluff, who grew prized melons, and a government trapper named Joe Raymond. Vaughan took an interest in hunting dogs and would think nothing of purchasing them from all over the country, including the deep South, and then having them shipped to the valley. He would prepare special food for them, using a big cast iron skillet on the large woodstove that not only was a source of heat in the winter but also came in handy for preparing food. His family hated the smell of that special concoction Vaughan would cook up for the dogs, "but he would sit right there and wait for it to be done," Johnson wrote. Raymond would help Vaughan train the dogs, and they would then use them to hunt predators, including mountain lions and coyotes. On occasion, they would take moonlight hunting trips into the hills; Johnson recalled getting to go on one such trip. "The unusual experience of sitting on the side of a hill, in the moonlight, listening to the baying of the hounds and the sounds of the men following was an exciting memory," she wrote.[9]

Vaughan did not completely forget about his baseball friends. He kept in touch with Camilli, the fellow rancher who lived about 50 miles away in Laytonville. One time, Camilli paid Vaughan a surprise visit and pulled a bit of a fast one on him. Camilli walked up to the front door and knocked and when Arky answered the door, he asked Camilli, "Dolph, where is your car?" Camilli grinned and pointed over to a hayfield across the highway. He had landed a small airplane there. "He got a big surprise," he told Johnson more than 40 years later. Camilli also related a story of how Vaughan came to visit him one day on his ranch in Laytonville. "You know how Arky dressed—he looked like a cowhand," Camilli told Johnson. "Anyway, he came to the house and said to my wife, Ruth, 'Do you know who I am?' She said, 'Yeah, you're one of the cowhands that came up and helped us round up the cattle one year.' 'No,' he says, 'I'm Arky Vaughan.'"[10]

Camilli recalled going on hunting trips with Vaughan after they both retired, trips that often would include other former teammates like Cookie Lavagetto and Augie Galan. "I remember one time about eight of us went up to go duck hunting and we had a ball up there," he told Johnson. "Every morning we'd pick out a duck for ourselves out of what we shot the previous day; we'd bring 'em to this little road house and they'd pluck 'em and clean 'em and we'd have ourselves a duck dinner. We had a lot of fun for a whole week."[11]

Why Vaughan chose to sit out three seasons when he was still one of the top players in baseball was a hot topic during the mid–1940s and remains a conversation piece today, more than 75 years later. Some believed that the falling out between Durocher and Vaughan in July of 1943 prompted the stubborn—and proud—nine-time All-Star to remain at home. But Camilli believed Vaughan simply had no choice—he had to make use of the ranching deferment. Camilli explained to Johnson: "He couldn't have gotten away with [playing baseball]. He would have been in a spot where they could have drafted him, and he would have gone into the service. He was five years younger than me—even with three children they would have taken him. He had the ranch, and it was very legitimate. If you had a ranch and you were producing, you were helping the cause."[12] According to Vaughan's Selective Service records, he was classified three different ways during the course of World War II, but there are no specific dates attached to the various classifications. At

Arky Vaughan, shown on horseback at his Potter Valley ranch in August 1940. Vaughan enjoyed tending to his cattle and hunting with his dogs (courtesy Kathleen Roberts).

one point, he was classified as 1-A, which meant he was available for military service. At some point, he was classified as 2-C, which indicated he had an agricultural deferment, and at another point he was classified as 3-C, which meant he was deferred by reason of dependency and agricultural operation.[13]

Although Vaughan loved ranching—some said he enjoyed it much more than baseball—Camilli said it was dangerous work. For one thing, there was a lots of heavy equipment to contend with. And running the ranch required hours of work on horseback, checking on cattle and young calves—regardless of the weather. "We used to go out in the winter time in those heavy rains, wearing these big rain slickers that would come down to your ankles; they'd cover the whole saddle and half the horse," Camilli recalled. "I had a few falls running them. It was no picnic, but it was enjoyable."[14]

When the weather was too bad for ranch work or outdoor fun, Vaughan would retreat to his ranch home and read—and so would the rest of the family. Vaughan preferred Western novels and detective stories; his wife liked historical novels. "All of the children learned the love of reading and the whole family would gather in the living room in the evenings, each with their particular books," Johnson wrote years later. The family also listened to lots of music, as they owned a modern phonograph and bought the latest music on their Saturday trips to Ukiah. They had scores from many of the musicals they saw in New York, including *Oklahoma!*, and favored records by such artists as Bing Crosby, Perry Como and the Mills Brothers, as well as country western and Irish folk music. Vaughan had taught himself how to play the harmonica and would play for the family. "He would sometimes sit in the kitchen, lean up against the wall and try to play his favorites, such as 'Red River Valley' and other cowboy tunes," Johnson wrote.[15]

In the spring and summer, the family would head outdoors and—when time allowed—they would organize baseball games in the clover field, using dried cow pies for bases. Although family members would try to talk Arky into playing, he preferred umpiring and coaching—for both sides, Johnson recalled. In the spring of 1945, the American public was rocked by the news of the death of President Franklin D. Roosevelt. The nation's commander-in-chief died on April 12 of a massive cerebral hemorrhage "as armies he helped to muster drove momentarily closer to final victory over Nazi Germany," United Press reporter Lyle C. Wilson wrote in a story published in *The Pittsburgh Press*.[16]

In less than a month, Germany surrendered, and it took only a few days before conjecture began in Brooklyn about Vaughan returning to the Dodgers. At the time, the club was off to a fine start and trailed the Giants by just two games. The pitching had been better than expected, but the infield was weak. And that had some fans dreaming on Vaughan, as *Pittsburgh Post-Gazette* columnist Havey Boyle wrote. "Furthermore, the Flatbush fans are hopeful that the smooth-talking Branch Rickey, the headman, may be able to talk Arky Vaughan into coming out of retirement on his California farm."[17]

By the end of April, Durocher was talking openly about the prospect of Vaughan wearing a Dodger uniform again. "The Lip thinks that with the new 30-year-old draft exemptions in effect, there's a chance to reopen the Arky Vaughan case," Brooklyn Daily Eagle reporter Harold C. Burr wrote. "'Give me Vaughan back and we'd win the pennant,' Durocher said all but beside himself with optimism."[18] Rumors of Vaughan's whereabouts surfaced in early June, but this time the story wasn't that he was returning to the Dodgers. Burr reported on June 2 that "it's rumored in Cincinnati that Arky Vaughan, former Dodger infielder, has left his Potter Valley, Cal., ranch to shoulder a gun for Uncle Sam.... The Dodgers doubt the story.... Vaughan is 34 years old and has stomach ulcers."[19] In late July, Durocher again put out a call for Vaughan, saying that the left side of his infield had cost the team at least a dozen games. Durocher said he knew of two people specifically who would make the Dodgers pennant winners—Pee Wee Reese and Vaughan. "With Pee Wee at short and Vaughan at third, we'd have won those dozen games, we'd be out in front and they'd never get close enough to hit us with a rifle," he said.[20] Earlier that month, thousands of miles to the west, the first atomic bomb test was conducted at Alamogordo, New Mexico. When the Japanese refused to surrender to Allied Forces, the United States dropped the first such weapon on the Japanese city of Hiroshima on August 6. The explosion ultimately took some 146,000 lives, and three days later, a second bomb was detonated over the city of Nagasaki, killing another 80,000 people. Less than a week later, Japan surrendered unconditionally, and the formal end to the hostilities came on September 2. By that time, the Dodgers were seven games in back of Chicago with about 30 games to play, and there was no talk in the press about Vaughan's return. During Vaughan's absence, the club had to make do with a platoon of sorts at third base; Frenchy Bordagaray played 57 games there while Augie Galan—Vaughan's hunting partner—played 40 and Bill Hart 39. Bordagaray batted .256 overall with 49 RBIs while Galan—who played 66 games at first base—had a fine season with a .307 average, nine home runs and 92 RBIs. Hart finished at .230 with three homers and 27 RBIs.

Back on the ranch, things were slowly returning to normal for the Vaughans and the other ranching families. But a drop in beef prices for domestic cattle put a major crimp in the Vaughans' finances and that—coupled with the fact that Arky had not collected a baseball salary in 1944 and 1945—meant that the family was facing hard times. As 1945 drew to a close, Vaughan's status as a player again hit the papers—this time in the form of a trade rumor, as it was reported that the Philadelphia Phillies expressed an interest in prying Vaughan from the Dodgers to fill their third base hole. Philadelphia Manager Ben Chapman was reportedly willing to purchase Vaughan or obtain him via trade. "Vaughan, frozen on his western farm during the war, is one of the numerous third basemen on the Brooklyn shelves. They have Cookie Lavagetto and Lew Riggs, among others."[21] Dodger manager Durocher, meanwhile, said just before the end of the year that the club received word that Vaughan had ballooned to over 200 pounds. "He's on our voluntary list and I guess that's where he's going to stay," Durocher told Burr. Burr reported that Branch Rickey thought that with the war coming to an end, Vaughan "might hear the call of the basehit again, which in a ball player's ears is akin to the call of the wild. But evidently the rancher's life suits Arky fine." Burr reported that Vaughan had not been watching his weight or given any thought to returning to baseball. "He hasn't many years left, anyway, and is quite content not to play out the string," Burr wrote. "If he had seen fit to come back, he would have ended his playing days in the third base rocking chair."[22]

In January of 1946, it was clear that the Dodgers had given up on Vaughan coming back, and things hadn't changed over the next month. "Arky Vaughan, of sad memory, has shown no inclination to leave his Pottery Valley ranch," Burr wrote in mid–February.[23] Actually, the previous month, a new development had occurred regarding Vaughan's plans to resume—or not to resume—his baseball career. It was detailed in a hand-written letter that Vaughan sent to Branch Rickey dated January 26, 1946. The letter, part of Rickey's personal files kept at the Library of Congress in Washington, D.C., reads:

Dear Mr. Rickey,

Just a brief note to ask a favor of you. I'm on a deal to get some land down in the bay area, if such comes to pass, I would like to be free to make a deal in the [Pacific] Coast League. I haven't any offers or anything in mind, in fact my plans do not include baseball, but something might come up in the next few years that I would be interested in. So would you please consider giving me my release? Lots of luck to you and all the Dodgers this coming season.

Sincerely,
"Arky" Vaughan[24]

It's unknown how—or if—Rickey responded to Vaughan, but he did not give the former All-Star his release. Every now and then, Vaughan's name would pop up on the sports pages as thoughts turned to the 1946 season. Honus Wagner's daughter, Virginia, was telling stories one day about her father and his protégé—Vaughan—and recalled one in particular. Vaughan and Wagner roomed together on the road during Vaughan's Pirates career and they used to pass the time swapping stories. According to Virginia, Arky once told Honus the story of his "liver" dog: "It seems Arky tied a piece of liver on the tail of his dog when he went fishing," Virginia said. "He placed the dog's tail in the water and when the fish came up to bite, the dog would turn around and smack the fish with his tail and knock the fish silly on the bank."[25]

On March 8—the day before Vaughan's 34th birthday—famed *New York Herald Tribune* columnist Red Smith devoted an entire piece to Vaughan, whom Smith referred to as "baseball's most superbly forgotten man." Writing from Daytona, Florida, Smith opined: "One of the absorbing mysteries of the spring is the strange case of Arky Vaughan, the little man who isn't anywhere, who isn't mentioned, who isn't expected. In the curious philosophy of the Dodgers, Vaughan is neither fish nor fowl nor good fresh trading bait, although it remains unproved that the eldering rancher of Potter Valley, Calif., is too far gone in years to be useful on some National League infield."[26]

Smith reviewed how Vaughan came to the Dodgers and how Vaughan had what Smith termed a "splendid" first year with Brooklyn in 1942. "He was one of the solid men on the team that won more than 100 games and yet finished the race behind the Cardinals," Smith wrote. He noted that Vaughan served as a "trouble-shooter" in 1943, playing at third one day and short the next, attempting to plug holes created by the Selective Service's draft. Smith then recalled Vaughan's one-man rebellion against Durocher in the wake of the manager's suspension of Bobo Newsom, whom Durocher accused of "malfeasance on the pitching mound." Smith characterized the incident as a "putsch" and the argument between Durocher and Newsom "a noisy taffy-pull." The end result, though, had Vaughan stripping off his uniform and presenting it to Durocher "together with a novel proposal regarding its disposition."[27]

Smith noted that several other players came to Vaughan's defense, but ultimately after "frantic arbitration" all but Vaughan agreed to play in that day's game. Smith then brought up the remark that Durocher made after he was rehired following the conclusion of the 1943 season, that there was one player on the club "for whom he had no passionate regard. He did not elaborate, and although there was widespread speculation it never was established that Vaughan was the man he had in mind." Smith wrote that Vaughan did not return to the Dodgers in 1944 or 1945, and "whether he was impelled chiefly by a love for the soil or by some other motive, only he can say."[28]

Smith noted that the Dodgers had not released Vaughan, nor had he made any application for retirement. "If he should wish to come out of his voluntary retirement, the Dodgers would have no right to stand in his way. He would be reinstated by [Commissioner] Happy Chandler, and then it would be up to Brooklyn to use or release him or deal him off to another club." Smith said there was "strong suspicion" that the Dodger management felt Vaughan let the club down during his one-man revolt in 1943 and that they still resented him for it. "The notion is the club authorities will make no overtures, do nothing to encourage his return to baseball."[29] Smith brought up the rumors that Vaughan had let himself go and that his weight had gone over 200 pounds. But he also said a California resident who saw Vaughan recently reported that he "never saw [Vaughan] looking more fit. Asked if Arky planned a return to baseball, this man said, 'I think he'd like to come back.'" Smith suggested that Vaughan might be too old for a comeback. "But there are others older than he in Florida right now who never had Arky's ability and yet believe they have a chance. With a fellow of Vaughan's class you can't just say he's through; you have to prove it."[30]

Patricia Vaughan Johnson wrote years later that her father "must have had a laugh at the rumors of his being fat and out of shape. He had spent the last two years doing the work of several men." She wrote that Smith's reference to Vaughan's love of the soil and ranching "was perfectly true, but he also had a love of his country and his family. All of these factors had combined to compel him to stay home during the war and away from baseball. If now his pride was hurt because the Dodgers did not seem to be interested in him, he would never let it show. He was determined to keep his ranch afloat and do his best for his family."[31]

Vaughan remained out of the sports pages for just about all of the 1946 season as the Dodgers, relying on mostly younger players who were signed in the latter stages of the war, battled to a draw with St. Louis in the National League pennant chase, then lost to the Cardinals in a the first-ever tiebreaking playoff series. Cookie Lavagetto did the bulk of the work at third base for Brooklyn that season, appearing in 67 games at the position and overall

A view of Arky Vaughan's ranch property in Potter Valley, California, in 1938. When Vaughan acquired the property, it was being used as a sheep ranch, but Vaughan quickly lost patience with the sheep and converted the ranch to cattle (courtesy Kathleen Roberts).

Vaughan's former ranch property as it looked in 2017 from approximately the same vantage point. The current property owners have converted much of the acreage to wine grapes (courtesy Frank Garland).

hitting .236 with 27 RBIs. The Cardinals, buoyed by the return of Stan Musial, were heavy favorites to win the NL crown going into the season, but trailed the Dodgers by seven and a half games on July 4. St. Louis then put together a 33–14 run to pull even with Brooklyn in late August. Entering the final day of the regular season, the two teams were tied for first place, but each lost its last game, triggering the need for the best-of-three playoff, which St. Louis swept in two straight.

Nearly two months into the off-season, in late November, word got out that Vaughan had applied for—and received—reinstatement from the voluntarily retired list. Now it was up to Branch Rickey whether the Dodgers would make use of the perennial all-star, who would turn 35 before the 1947 season got under way. Some speculated that Vaughan might not want to return to the active roster as a player, but rather as a coach. Some still believed the dust-up with Durocher in 1943 was the main reason Vaughan walked away from the game. While there was some uncertainty that Durocher would even be back to manage the Dodgers in 1947, that was put to rest before the end of 1946. Despite news of Durocher's involvement with actress Laraine Day, who had been married but fled to Mexico to obtain a one-day divorce in late January of 1947—and married Durocher the same day—Rickey stood behind his manager. "There is not a moment I have not considered him the manager of this club—and I wired him to that effect," Rickey said in mid–February. "I am a Durocher man and he'll get my backing. If he is in trouble I will go to hell and back for him in justifiable circumstances."[32]

As it turned out, Durocher would not manage the Dodgers that season, but it was not Rickey's decision. Instead, Commissioner Happy Chandler, who had interviewed Durocher in late 1946 about a high-stakes dice game that took place in his apartment, suspended Durocher on April 9, citing Durocher's "string of moral shortcomings: gambling debts, associations with known gamblers and nightlife figures, and a scandalous marriage with charges of adultery, bigamy, and contempt of court."[33] As writer Jeffrey Marlett put it, Rickey often said Durocher possessed "the fertile ability to turn a bad situation into something infinitely worse."[34] Durocher's suspension couldn't have come at a more inopportune time for Rickey, who was attempting to take one of the boldest steps any baseball executive had ever taken—he wanted to break the so-called "color barrier" by bringing an African American player named Jackie Robinson to the major leagues. In fact, Vaughan's daughter, Patricia, believed that Rickey's plan to integrate baseball might have been one of the reasons why he wanted to see Vaughan return to the Dodgers.

"Rickey believed that Arky, with his maturity, calmness and experience, would be a stabilizing influence on the team when he brought Robinson up," Johnson wrote years later. "There were many 'Southerners' on the team and it was not known how they would accept Jackie." Johnson believed that Vaughan, although raised in California, had Arkansas roots that might have enabled him to get along better with the players from the South and ease their apprehension about the prospect of Robinson making it to the big-league club.[35] It was clear that some of those players wanted no part of Robinson. Dixie Walker, for example, was quoted the day that Robinson signed with the Brooklyn organization in 1946 as saying of Robinson, "As long as he isn't with the Dodgers, I'm not worried."[36]

The Dodgers also had practical reasons for wanting to see Vaughan return—they needed a third baseman. Rickey had dealt infielder Billy Herman away in 1946, Cookie Lavagetto was trying to return from shoulder surgery, and two younger players—Bob Ramazzotti and Stan Rojek—were unproven. There was a chance Robinson might be installed at third, but he also had the ability to play second and even first base. However, some members of the media said Robinson would have to be far and away the best candidate to win the job.

In early January, Rickey addressed the possible addition of Robinson, saying he definitely would go to spring training as a member of the Montreal Royals—Brooklyn's top farm team. "He never was the property of the Brooklyn ball club," Rickey said. "It's the same situation as several of our players were up against last year. If Robinson can show Durocher and our coaches that he's ready for the National League, as Furillo did last year, we will bring him up." Rickey also talked about the difficulty in housing Robinson in the segregated South during spring training, noting that if any potential road stops had issues with Robinson, Brooklyn's minor league teams would play amongst themselves. "But that situation is rapidly clearing up," said Rickey, who noted that Deland and Savannah—two towns where the Dodgers had problems in the spring of 1946—"are ready to accept Robinson."[37]

In the second week of February, Rickey informed the press that the club had heard from Vaughan and that he had "whittled down" to his playing weight of 185 pounds—and he was "ready and eager to resume at 35 years of age his baseball chores." Rickey said he didn't think the 1943 run-in with Durocher is what kept Vaughan away from the Dodgers, nor did he think it would cause any sort of a hangover. "Vaughan, I'm convinced, wants to play again for the Dodgers," Rickey said. "I wrote to him myself and he wrote back and said he held no grudge against Durocher for what had happened. I had Leo pay him a visit when he was in California and Leo assured me that there was no rancor left between them."[38]

Three days later, Vaughan's signed contract arrived in Brooklyn, sparking title hopes among the faithful. "If he's the old Vaughan of three years ago it could mean the pennant for the Dodgers, third base being a weak link all last year," wrote Burr. He noted that Vaughan hit .305 in 149 games for the Dodgers in 1943 and that he was far better than any third baseman the Dodgers used in 1946. But he also said that .305 mark was a "yellowing old record" and that Vaughan was three years older. "Not every ball player can take on rust for three years and then pick up where he left off."[39] Harry Keck of the *Pittsburgh Sun-Telegraph* recalled Vaughan's days as a former Pirate standout and said it would be interesting to see how successful Vaughan's return would be, considering all of the time he missed. Keck attributed Vaughan's absence at least in part to his disagreement with Durocher in 1943, but said "he has buried the hatchet with Durocher, who recently visited him at his home."[40]

Many observers pointed to Vaughan as being a key to the Dodgers' season. "Much depends on a pair of 34-year-old legs and the return to resilience of a damaged throwing arm, and the righting of some shaking pitching," Burr wrote, with the 34-year-old legs a reference to Vaughan's age. "The old Arky Vaughan and the old Pete Reiser could carry the team to a pennant if Manager Leo Durocher once more is able to jockey his pitchers with the uncanny success of last year. So it's up to the legs of Vaughan and the arm of Reiser." Burr wrote that the third base position shouldn't tax Vaughan's legs all that match. "It's a rockingchair job," he wrote.[41]

Vaughan left California on February 15, headed for Savannah, Georgia, and from there he would continue on to Havana, Cuba, site of the

Dodgers' spring training camp. He arrived in Philadelphia three days later and boarded a train wearing a ten-gallon cowboy hat. Burr wrote that Vaughan "looked as slim as a magazine ad for young men's clothing in his brown suit without an ounce of fat on him." Some reporters joked with Vaughan, asking him what he had done with all that "excess baggage"—the extra weight that Vaughan was purported to be carrying during his years on the ranch. When Vaughan asked who started that story about him being out of shape, someone responded that it was Hank Gowdy, a veteran coach. "I never weighed over 190 in my life," said Vaughan, who noted that riding horseback on his ranch the past three years had kept him trim. He admitted that he hadn't had a bat or ball in his hands since he left the Dodgers in 1943 except to play catch with his kids on the ranch. Vaughan said it would be "silly" for him to say that his legs were as good as ever. "I just don't know how they'll stand up until I start running on 'em," he said. But he was far from pessimistic, noting that he'd never had any trouble with those legs—aside from one knee injury with the Pirates—or his arm.[42]

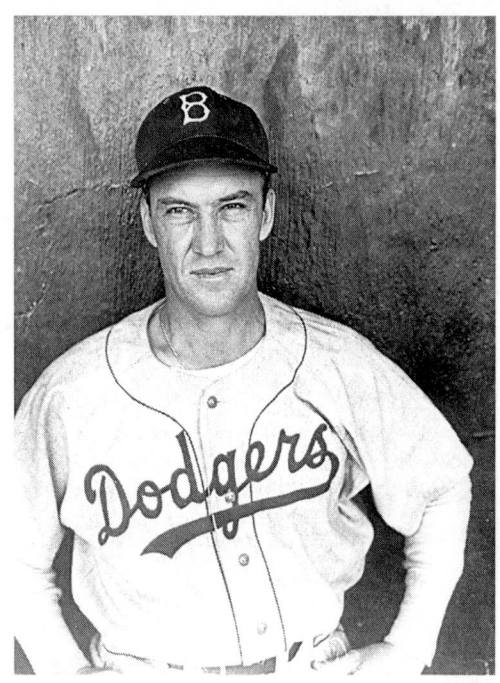

Vaughan also admitted that, although he had filed for reinstatement in November, it took him a while to make up his mind for good to try to come back. He told reporters that he had sold most of his ranch property "but I've kept my boots and saddle and a couple of my favorite horses." For a while, he was thinking about buying another ranch. "But then I got to thinking. I figured I still had some baseball left and I could retire permanently to ranching in my old age. So I got in touch with Mr. Rickey again and he offered me a very fair contract." When pushed for details on that contract, Vaughan would not divulge any numbers, but said it might ulti-

Arky Vaughan, shown here in one of his final two seasons with the Brooklyn Dodgers. Vaughan retired late in the 1948 season after being hit with a gall bladder ailment (courtesy National Baseball Hall of Fame Library, Cooperstown, New York).

mately be worth more than the one he played under in 1943. Vaughan also downplayed his old rift with Durocher, saying that had nothing to do with him walking away from the game after the '43 season. "Oh, I had my run-ins with Leo," he said. "But there isn't any truth in the charge that he chased me off the ball club. I had my ranch demanding a lot of my attention. That was the big reason why I gave up the game."[43] Vaughan told reporters that he never needed much spring training to get ready for the season. "Now, I'll need a little more," he admitted. "Have to go easy for a while."[44]

Vaughan certainly was the center of attention as the Dodgers landed in Havana on February 19—in part for the circuitous route he took to get there. Instead of finding a more direct path from the West Coast to Florida, from where the club would leave for Cuba, Vaughan went from Northern California to Philadelphia by train, and then continued on by rail to Miami. Wrote Bob Cooke of the *New York Herald Tribune*:

> Although cartographers agree that Philadelphia is not on the main line between California and Florida, Vaughan, handling his own navigation, decided to chart his course in that manner. Not since Babe Herman's round-about methods of running bases became famous has an athlete qualified for a Dodger heritage as Vaughan has done. The other day Leo Durocher was worried about Vaughan's speed. He was wondering whether Arky's absenteeism from the big leagues had retarded his running time between bases. Durocher is hopeful that Vaughan will not require navigational charts while en route.[45]

After the first full day of workouts, Durocher said Vaughan looked like the same old Arky—at least at the plate. Vaughan "looks to me as if he swings the same as the day he ended the 1943 season with a .305 average," Durocher wrote in the *Brooklyn Daily Eagle*. "He has been pulling every ball viciously to right. He may be the surprise of this camp."[46] The next day, Durocher was talking up Vaughan's speed after watching him lay down a drag bunt and fly to first base. But seasoned observers pointed to the calendar. "Vaughan's legs have been standing up nobly, but it's still too early to predict that they will be as valuable to the Dodgers as Marlene Dietrich's $1,000,000 props," Burr wrote.[47] At the Dodgers' first intrasquad game later that week, Durocher used the same lineup he used most of 1946 with one exception—Vaughan was given the third base job. While many were focusing on Vaughan's comeback, he was hardly the only story in camp, as the Dodgers were taking a long look at Robinson. Robinson had spent the 1946 season with Montreal, where he batted .349, stole 40 bases, and had a .468 on-base percentage. Robinson said he didn't resent being assigned to the Dodgers' top minor league club. "I can understand that a lot of people might feel my showing in my first year was that of a flash in the pan," he told reporters. While Rickey was hoping that Robinson's on-field performance would win over his potential new teammates, Herbert Goren, a reporter with the *New York Sun* and the

North American Newspaper Alliance, canvassed several of the Dodgers and his assessment was that the team's attitude toward Robinson was "mainly antagonistic. Robinson will have to undo an undercurrent of resentment. Not all the Dodgers feel that way, but a great many do."[48]

One unnamed Dodger, when asked about Robinson, simply replied, "I'm just hoping Arky Vaughan makes a wonderful comeback." Goren wrote that the remark wasn't so much an indication that Vaughan could be any more helpful than Robinson at his best as much as that Vaughan could keep Robinson "from establishing a precedent which, in one man's mind, is regarded with distaste." A few Dodgers, though, were more open-minded. "Robinson's a nice guy," one player said. "If he is able to help our club, I'm all for him." Robinson, Goren wrote, showed an air of confidence that said he expected to do well in spring. "If I don't show well," he says, "I'll continue to play with Montreal and hope for the best."[49]

By mid–March, Vaughan had done nothing to show the Dodger brass that he shouldn't be in the lineup at third base. Durocher even said that, based on early returns, Vaughan would have a prominent place in the Dodger batting order. "Vaughan hit cleanup for the Pirates for years, and No. 5 might very well be where I will use him, if he continues to swish the bat the way he has. Arky has as much or more power than anybody on my roster."[50] Vaughan was also impressing his teammates. Pete Reiser, who missed three years due to his military service but came back to play a full season in 1946, said it hardly looked as though Vaughan had been away from the game for three years. "He's going to help us plenty this year," Reiser said. "He has been hitting and fielding with the best of them."[51]

While Vaughan was readjusting to a life in baseball, back home in California his family had to adjust to some new "old" surroundings. Vaughan's decision to sell his Potter Valley ranch property resulted in his wife and children relocating to Fullerton. There, they stayed with Margaret's parents, who were operating a small hotel, and also spent some time with Arky's parents. With money being tight, the family would not accompany Vaughan back to Brooklyn during the summer, as they had in the past. In addition, Arky was attempting to save as much of his 1947 paycheck as possible, as he had his sights set on another ranch elsewhere in California. That meant the children would stay put in Fullerton for the summer, but his daughter Patricia admitted that wasn't such a hardship, considering all the relatives they had in the area.

While the club was preparing for the '47 season, a front-office feud was simmering behind the scenes. Larry MacPhail, who ran the Dodgers before enlisting to help the U.S. war effort, returned to baseball after the war and became president of the New York Yankees. Prior to the 1947 season, rumors began to surface that MacPhail was interested in prying Durocher away from the Dodgers to manage the Yankees. That didn't happen, but MacPhail did hire away two Brooklyn coaches—Charlie Dressen and Johnny Corriden. Rickey believed MacPhail was guilty of tampering but did not pursue this case with Commissioner Happy Chandler, as Chandler was linked to MacPhail, who had backed Chandler's bid to succeed Kenesaw Landis as commissioner a few years earlier. During the months that preceded the start of spring training, baseball was investigating Durocher's ties with several gambling figures, and this drama continued to unfold while the Dodgers were preparing for the season. Durocher's scandalous involvement with the actress Day didn't help his public persona and in fact in February 1947, the Catholic Youth Organization withdrew from the Dodger Knot-Hole Club, which provided free tickets to Dodger games to youngsters in local schools.

The Rev. Vincent J. Powell, who led the youth group, cited Durocher's behavior as the reason for the withdrawal, saying Durocher was "not the kind of leader we want our youth to idealize and imitate." Powell said his group could not "continue to have our youngsters officially associated with a man who represents to them an example in complete contradiction to our moral teachings." In an apparent reference to Durocher's marriage to Day, Powell said that Durocher "has finally climaxed a long series of events both on and off the field. This had convinced us that the effect of his example will be a powerful force in undermining the moral and spiritual training of our young boys."[52]

The ugliness between MacPhail and the Dodgers escalated, and on March 15, MacPhail formally charged Rickey, Durocher and club secretary Harold Parrott with conduct detrimental to baseball—specifically that the Dodgers had "libeled and slandered" him. Baseball law thus required Chandler to conduct a hearing on the charges.[53] Chandler said there would be two hearings—one in Sarasota and the other in St. Petersburg.

Critics also began turning up the pressure on Rickey regarding his plans for Robinson. *Brooklyn Daily Eagle* reporter Tommy Holmes wrote that Rickey's decision to stash Robinson on the Montreal roster during spring training was "understandable if devious. He seems to feel that as long as Jackie wears that Montreal uniform, no one will notice that he is a Negro. Actually, greater attention has been focused on the International League star. Rickey also seems to hope that Jackie will do so well that the rest of the Brooklyn players will beg him [Rickey] to put Robinson in Dodger livery."[54]

Vaughan, meanwhile, admitted that the rock-hard fields of Panama, Venezuela and Cuba had been taking their toll on his legs and feet. "But it doesn't mean anything," he said. "All of our infielders, young and old, are having the same trouble." Umpire Larry Goetz tried to help, as he gave Vaughan a pair of soft, spongy arch supporters created by Dr. Robert F. Hyland, the St. Louis Cardinals team physician, who had treated Vaughan earlier in his career. "I wish Larry had thought of it sooner," Vaughan said. The veteran said he wasn't sure what else he could do to make sure his wheels were functioning properly. "About all you can do is get out there and start pumping and pray that your legs will take you places."[55]

The next day, in a piece purported to be written by Durocher but actually penned by club secretary Harold Parrott, Durocher said that Vaughan had told him his ankles were bothering him, but he was confident he'd be ready when the regular season bell rang. Vaughan also told Durocher he was having trouble with his timing at the plate, saying he was out in front of everything. He was hoping to see plenty of good pitching the rest of spring training to get him ready for Opening Day on April 15. In the story, Durocher said he asked Vaughan how many games he thought he could play and Vaughan responded, "Why not all of them? I am thin, and ready."[56] When April arrived, writers asked Durocher what his Opening Day starting lineup might be, and he mentioned only three players—and Vaughan wasn't one of them. This surprised the beat writers, given how much Durocher had been praising Vaughan during camp. But on April 5, Durocher added Vaughan and Pete Reiser to the ranks of certain starters.[57] Vaughan also was feeling chipper; after watching a few of the Dodgers' faster players, he told a reporter, "Give me another month and I will run you a race with a lot of these kids. I could walk away from them 10 years ago and I can still beat a lot of them."[58]

By the time the Dodgers returned from Latin America, many questions had been answered, but one huge one remained—whether Jackie Robinson would start the season in Brooklyn or Montreal. Some writers who covered the team in spring training believed Robinson would make the Dodgers roster while others believed he would not. Holmes said both Robinson and Rickey were on the spot as the Dodgers began a two-game exhibition set at Ebbets Field. Robinson, as he had done during the spring, would be wearing the uniform of the Montreal Royals. Holmes wrote:

> [Rickey] has subtly created a strong impression that whatever Robinson accomplishes in this preview performance will determine whether the Negro will be taken off the Montreal roster and set down in the middle of the Dodger clubhouse or whether Jackie will accompany the Royals when they pull up stakes tomorrow night. That puts Mr. Robinson in a well-decorated spot just as it would put any ball player on a spot. Two ball games certainly constitute an extremely brief interlude in which to pass final judgment as to whether or not any athlete is good enough to help a ball club.[59]

The following day, Commissioner Chandler dropped a bomb on Brooklyn, announcing that he had suspended Durocher for the season—the most drastic measure ever taken against a big-league manager—for what he termed "conduct detrimental to baseball." Chandler had warned all parties involved to remain silent but the warning wasn't required, at least as far as the Dodgers brass were concerned. "The Chandler ruling took everyone in the Dodger organization so by surprise that it was a little while before [Rickey] got his breath back," Burr wrote. "The immediate future plans of Durocher are still vague. He has the commissioner's permission to attend any Brooklyn games he sees fit to watch as a spectator." Speculation focused on who would succeed Durocher, and the leading candidates included Dixie Walker, Ray Blades and Clay Hopper. But for the time being, coach Clyde Sukeforth would serve as interim field manager.[60]

Holmes said it appeared as though Chandler wanted to show he was a strong leader by suspending Durocher for the season. Holmes said people had suggested that Chandler was "too gentle a soul" to serve as commissioner, but that proved to be a mistake, adding: "Ultimately this repeated charge had the same effect as repeated dares to a small boy to fire a loaded revolver. In effect, that's what the irritated commissioner did. And he blazed away until the gun was empty—and hit everyone in the room. … A commissioner with a sense of proportion would have spanked all concerned and promised to knock their heads together if any such sort of nursery ranygazoo developed again. But Happy Chandler hit everybody concerned."[61] Chandler went after Durocher, Holmes said, "because he needed a victim to prove his critics were wrong."[62]

Later that same day, Robinson—and the Dodgers—made history when Brooklyn purchased Robinson's contract from the Montreal club, a decision made while Robinson was playing first base for the Royals in an exhibition game against the Dodgers. Robinson had just popped into a double play while attempting to bunt in the fifth inning when a front office assistant to Rickey handed out a brief typed announcement in the press box alerting the writers of the news. The Dodgers boss said the decision to bring Robinson to the club was unanimous, but Rickey said he wasn't 100 percent sold until the middle of the exhibition game. His former manager at Montreal, Clay Hopper, said he didn't think Robinson would have any trouble adapting to the big leagues. "He can adapt himself to any position," he said. "He's been under pressure all Spring. He's a good ballplayer!"[63]

All eyes were on the Dodgers on Opening Day to see how Robinson, penciled in at first base, would do—and some also were interested in seeing whether Vaughan would cap his comeback by earning a spot in the starting lineup. The veteran infielder was given the day off in the final exhibition game due to a slightly pulled right leg muscle, and rookie Johnny "Spider" Jorgensen was given the starting assignment for Opening Day.[64]

The fact that Sukeforth was still on the job as Dodger manager came as a surprise, since Rickey had promised to have a manager in place by the opener. He offered the job to former Yankees skipper Joe McCarthy, but McCarthy turned it down.

Robinson went hitless in his debut but contributed a key sacrifice and his tremendous speed came into play as he reached second on the play as a result of an errant throw in Brooklyn's 5–3 win over Boston. "He bunted with a man on first, then had the presence of mind to be hit by the first baseman's throw," was the way the *Brooklyn Daily Eagle*'s Tommy Holmes described it. That set the stage for Pete Reiser's game-winning two-run double off the wall. Afterward, reporters interviewed Robinson and one asked if Johnny Sain, Boston's pitcher, was the best he'd ever faced. Robinson hesitated, then mentioned that he'd hit against fireballing Bob Feller. When the reporter pointed out Sain's high-quality curveball, Robinson responded, "If that isn't a good curve, I'm going to have a hard time this summer."[65]

Vaughan did not start the game, but did get one plate appearance as a pinch hitter in the seventh inning after Reiser's go-ahead double and grounded out to pitcher Mort Cooper.

Three days later, Rickey found his manager—veteran baseball man Burt Shotton was hired on a one-year contract. Shotton and Rickey went back a long time; during Rickey's managerial tenure in St. Louis, Shotton served as Rickey's "Sunday manager" because the staunchly religious Rickey would not go to the ballpark on Sundays.[66] Shotton had his hands full just a few days later when the Philadelphia Phillies visited Brooklyn, as Philadelphia manager Ben Chapman and several players began berating Robinson with incendiary racial slurs from the dugout. Robinson wrote later that one particular day—Tuesday, April 22—brought him closer to the breaking point than he'd ever been. Chapman denied any wrongdoing, saying that his club treated Robinson "just like anyone else. Baseball is an American game, and there are no nationalities, creeds nor races involved," he said. "Jackie Robinson is an American."[67] Chapman said his players weren't "jockeying Robinson any more than any other boy in the National league. Jackie has been accepted in baseball and we of the Philadelphia organization have no objection to his playing and wish him all the luck we can." National League president Ford Frick wasn't buying Chapman's explanation, however, and he told Chapman and the club that he would not tolerate any abusive language from the bench. "I warned them not to do it anymore," Frick said. "They agreed to abide by my directive."[68]

Philadelphia wasn't the only club upset with the Dodgers' decision to bring Robinson aboard. Word got out that a small group of St. Louis Cardinal players were planning a strike in protest of Robinson's presence on the Brooklyn roster. But when Frick got wind of it, he told the Cardinal players that if they went on strike, the league would suspend them. Said Frick: "You will find that the friends you think you have in the press box will not support you, that you will be outcasts. I do not care if the league strikes. Those who do it will encounter quick retribution. All will be suspended and I don't care if it wrecks the National League for five years. This is the United States of America and one citizen has as much right to play as another."[69]

The managerial change from Sukeforth to Shotton did not alter Vaughan's status, as he did not make another appearance until April 26–27, when he walked in back-to-back pinch-hit appearances against the Giants. He missed another six games before appearing again as a pinch hitter on May 9, and then had two more pinch-hit appearances in both ends of a May 11 doubleheader loss to Philadelphia. He flied out in the first at-bat and was retired on a looping Texas Leaguer in the second. Rumors surfaced that the Dodgers might be interested in making a deal or two to rid themselves of some excess baggage and perhaps open up more playing time for Vaughan. At that point, the club was carrying three third basemen, including Vaughan, but nothing came of it during the first part of May.[70] It was also reported that even though Durocher had been suspended as manager, he would be used by Rickey to provide a full report on his personnel, complete with his recommendations on who to deal and who to keep.[71] On May 7, with the Dodgers getting set to meet the Giants, the trade winds surrounding Vaughan seemed to take more shape. One deal had the Reds sending catcher Al Lakeman to Brooklyn for rookie outfielder Tom Tatum. Another had them exchanging Lakeman for Arky Vaughan, and putting Vaughan at third. But the Reds left town without pulling the trigger on that deal.[72]

Later in May, it was reported that Vaughan might be among those who would be sent packing. Carl Hughes, in the *Pittsburgh Press*, wrote, "Arky Vaughan is to be lopped off the Dodger roster before the May 15 player limit deadline, according to Brooklyn writers."[73] Vaughan, making his first appearance back in his former place of employment since he had left baseball after the 1943 season, received a big hand from the Forbes Field faithful during a mid–May series. "Arky still has plenty of the old stuff," an unnamed writer in the *Pittsburgh Press* wrote.[74]

Nearly a month into the season, Vaughan finally found his way into the starting lineup for the first time on May 12 at home against Boston. Hitless on the season in just four at-bats entering the game, Vaughan ripped a double to drive in a run, walked twice and scored his first run of the season as Brooklyn—tied for second place, a game-and-a-half behind the Cubs—beat the Braves, 8–3, to improve to 12–8. Burr wrote that Vaughan's showing left the Dodgers with a "traffic jam" at third base, as Vaughan was Shotton's third choice to play the position. Jorgensen suffered a knee injury the week before and Stan Rojek went zero for 12 in his place before Shotton turned to Vaughan. "The Hermit of Potter Valley came in fast to field Bob Elliott's slow roller in the second—which proved that his 36-year-old legs are still nimble," Burr wrote. Vaughan walked twice—once intentionally—and doubled to right in a fifth-inning rally "showing that there isn't any mote in the old batting eye," Burr added.[75]

Shotton said he would keep Vaughan at third against right-handed pitching for a few days and then play Cookie Lavagetto against left-handers. He also said he would insert Rojek at third late in games for defensive purposes while Jorgensen rested his ailing knee. "But what if Vaughan continues to hit and field like the old Vaughan and the Dodgers go off on a new winning streak?" Burr wrote. "Then Shotton will have to make a decision to keep the veteran in the lineup or bring back the rookie." Burr noted that the Dodgers tried eight different players at third base in 1946, so Shotton's "headache isn't nearly as severe as was the departed Lip's but Burt is anxious to get his infield set and now a new complication has intruded itself."[76]

The next game, though, Vaughan was out of the starting lineup again, but he did contribute a pinch-hit single in the ninth inning of a 7–5 loss at Cincinnati. Vaughan started the next three games, but managed just three walks in 12 plate appearances and scored two runs. By the end of May, Vaughan had appeared in just 14 of Brooklyn's first 30 games, batting 22 times and managing only three hits for a .136 batting average. It didn't get a whole lot better in June, as he had just 11 at-bats all month, with 10 of them coming as a pinch hitter, and as of June 28, he was batting just .207. He did have a few moments, though; in the first game of a doubleheader against the Giants, his infield single brought home Robinson with the go-ahead run in the sixth inning of the Dodgers' 4–3 win.

On June 30, he received a rare start—and his first start in the outfield all season—and went three for four with a run scored, an RBI and a walk to hike his average to .273. "The Hermit of Potter Valley came out of virtual retirement at Shibe Park last night to become the eighth Dodger left fielder," Burr wrote about Vaughan, erroneously noting that it was his first experience in the outfield; he had played there for 12 games in 1937 with Pittsburgh. "Yet he acquitted himself as if he had spent all his baseball life amid the four-leaf clovers in Brooklyn's 7 to 4 win over the Phillies." Vaughan snagged three line drives, none of which were routine, rapped out three sharp singles, drew a walk and "drove Johnny Wyrostek back against the right field fence to haul down his longest smash for the spoliation of a perfect evening at bat," Burr wrote.[77] Vaughan also stole a base in the win, but it wasn't all positive, as "the strain on his aged legs was too great in the eighth when he tried to go from first to third on Dixie Walker's single to right and was thrown out."[78]

The next day, Vaughan blasted his first home run since 1943 in a loss to the Phillies. He continued to see a little more playing time in July, as he racked up 49 at-bats in 20 games, during which time he batted .327 to raise his average on the season to .301 going into August. But manager Shotton picked his spots, resting the veteran infielder-turned-outfielder when he thought he needed it. One such example was a doubleheader against the Cubs on July 10, when he took him out of the first game in the ninth inning due to a badly bruised right thumb and then held him out of the second game. Shotton explained that he didn't want the Cubs running on Vaughan in the ninth inning of a one-run game. And for the second game? "Well, I rested him up. He isn't so young any more and a doubleheader would have really tired him."[79] As it turned out, he came off the bench in that second game and delivered a game-winning pinch-hit single in the 4–3 victory. "A well aged gentleman named Arky Vaughan who recently came out of retirement, was the direct cause of the breakup of the second argument," is the way Irving Vaughan of the Chicago Tribune Press Service put it.[80] He appeared six times as a pinch hitter that month and all of his other appearances came as a left fielder. During one stretch, which covered five games in a three-day span, Vaughan went eight for 13 with four RBIs and three runs scored.

Vaughan's contributions helped the Dodgers take control in the National League race, as Brooklyn compiled a 63–36 record heading into August, good for a 10-game lead over both the Giants and Cardinals. Over the next month, the Cardinals would trim two games off the lead of the Dodgers, who sat at 82–49 with just over a month remaining. Vaughan made three starts in left field, three starts at third, and appeared as a pinch hitter seven times in August. All told, he had 12 hits in 30 at-bats for a .400 batting average, scored eight runs, and drove in three. That brought his overall mark on the season to a robust .330 with an on-base percentage of .440. Shotton seemed to know when to play Vaughan; he had four or more at-bats in six games that month, and three times he collected three hits and scored a pair of runs—all in Brooklyn victories.

Down the stretch Vaughan made just four starts—all in left field and all in the first week of September. His final five appearances of the regular season came as a pinch hitter. For the month, Vaughan batted .286 and for the season he finished with a .325 batting average in 153 plate appearances, a .444 on-base percentage and an OPS of .889. He was considered by many to be among the top spot players in the game. Al Abrams, sports editor of the *Pittsburgh Post-Gazette*, found it somewhat ironic that Vaughan and Cookie Lavagetto—"two fellows the Dodgers wanted to get rid of in the spring"— were key players down the stretch for Brooklyn.[81]

The Dodgers wound up with a 94–60 mark, finishing with a five-game margin over second-place St. Louis to earn the right to meet the New York Yankees in the 1947 World Series. After 13 seasons in the big leagues in a career that started in 1932, Vaughan would finally fulfill his ultimate goal as a player—winning a pennant and playing in a World Series. He'd come so close before, including the heart-wrenching finish in 1938 when the Cubs roared from behind to snatch the pennant from the Pirates, who had led most of the way.

Cardinals manager Eddie Dyer, who sent a congratulatory telegram to Shotton after the Dodgers officially clinched the pennant on September 22 with a St. Louis loss to Chicago, had no trouble pinpointing the difference between the Dodgers and his club—Brooklyn's reserves. As Dodgers boss Branch Rickey put it, "When the bench is strong enough to threaten the judgment of the manager, that's when you have a potential winner. You don't want men who are substitutes."[82]

Shotton agreed, saying that when Eddie Stanky and Pee Wee Reese were spiked in a game against the Reds, Rojek and Eddie Miksis took over for them "and you could hardly tell the difference," Burr wrote. "Their names might have been Stanky and Reese. Arky Vaughan and Cookie Lavagetto were more than able subs and came through repeatedly in the role of pinch hitters."[83] The national media also took notice of Vaughan's performance in a backup role. Dan Parker noted that when injuries sidelined Pete Reiser and Gene Hermanski, Vaughan and Eddie Miksis "did a most acceptable job of subbing for them in left. Vaughan also was valuable as a third base replacement and his pinch hitting has been exceptionally good."[84]

Vaughan was well aware of what the bench meant to the Dodgers. "It doesn't make much difference what substitutes we throw in—the substitute is generally just as good as the regular," he told syndicated columnist Grantland Rice. "They are all pretty well on a level—but it's a pretty high level."[85]

Looking ahead to the World Series, some observers weren't sure the Dodgers' deep bench would make that much of a difference. In a *Brooklyn Daily Eagle* story previewing the series, an unnamed writer noted, "Reserves, or what Rickey calls a strong bench, have more bearing on a long pennant race than on a short World Series of seven games at most." Still, the story noted that Brooklyn had the better reserve corps than the favored Yankees and pointed out Vaughan's ability to play both the infield and the outfield and to come off the bench to get a hit. "Lavagetto and Vaughan have been the deadliest of pinch hitters," the story noted.[86]

The series certainly had the attention of the nation's biggest city and millions of others, and this was evidenced by the local hotel scene. In a word, virtually no rooms were available. Some hotel guests were reduced to sharing hotel rooms with complete strangers.

The series even brought justice to a halt—at least in Judge Samuel S. Leibowitz's courtroom in Kings County Court. Leibowitz, referred to as a "loyal Dodgerite himself" noticed several jurors sitting on a first-degree rape case against a taxi driver were getting restless as the start of Game 1 approached. Leibowitz decided to call a recess and arranged for a television to be installed in his library so that attorneys and the jury could watch the game "on the promise they would make up the time by resuming the trial after the game ended." The defendant, Peter Girolyne, 27 years old, "heard the game via a portable radio set in the detention pen."[87]

The series—the first to be televised—went the distance, with the Yankees bolting to a 2–0 lead with a pair of wins at home, 5–3 and 10–3, before the Dodgers returned the favor at Ebbets Field, winning 9–8 and 3–2—the latter win coming with just a single hit, Cookie Lavagetto's two-run pinch-hit double with two outs in the bottom of the ninth. New York took a 3–2 lead with a 2–1 win in Game 5 at Brooklyn, but the Dodgers forced a Game 7 by winning 8–6 in Game 6 at Yankee Stadium. It came down to a seventh and deciding game, which the Yankees won, 5–2.

Vaughan's first appearance in a World Series game came in Game 2, when he flied out while pinch hitting for pitcher Hal Gregg with two outs and runners on first and third in the seventh inning. In Game 4, Vaughan pinch hit for Gregg again and this time walked. Vaughan notched his only World Series hit in the seventh inning of Game 5 when—batting for pitcher Hank Behrman—he doubled to right field, putting runners at second and third. A key at-bat occurred right before Vaughan stepped to the plate when Carl Furillo failed to get a sacrifice bunt down to move Bruce Edwards, who had opened the inning with a walk, up to second. Furillo eventually flew out to Joe DiMaggio in center and after Jorgensen flew out to left, Vaughan delivered his double to right. That would have scored Edwards from second had Furillo been successful in his sacrifice attempt, but instead he had to hold at third. After pinch hitter Pete Reiser was intentionally walked to load the bases, Reese was called out on strikes to end the threat. That would be Vaughan's final appearance in his one and only World Series.[88] He didn't exactly go home empty-handed, as the players' shares on the losing side amounted to a little more than $4,000 each—a nice payday considering his annual contract came in at around $18,000.[89]

While Vaughan did not get the playing time he was accustomed to getting prior to his three-year layoff, his experience was appreciated not only by the ball club but by those covering baseball. It was not unusual for reporters to seek out Vaughan's opinions on a variety of things, such as the caliber of baseball being played vs. the caliber of ball played before the war, and even the nature of the baseball itself. Extensive research, however, failed to unearth any of Vaughan's thoughts on Jackie Robinson's color barrier-breaking efforts, and the topic was not broached in his daughter's draft biography, written decades later.

In terms of on-field developments that season, some veteran players, including Vaughan, intimated that the ball in use during the '47 campaign was a bit livelier than it had been in the recent past. Vaughan also told *New York Daily Mirror* reporter Gus Steiger that it would take another year or two before the caliber of play in the major leagues measured up to what it was before the war. Vaughan added:

> The war cut short the career of many players and the boys who ordinarily would have played in the minors preparing to take the places of those who leave the majors also were in the service. So when the war ended there was no crop of proven rookies available to move in for those veterans who failed to return or couldn't make the grade. As a result, there are some players in the National League today who had to be brought up quickly. Some of these fellows are capable players but they could profit by further minor league seasoning. Instead they are gaining their experience in the majors and it will take a year or two for them to really attain the big league level.[90]

Although Vaughan never complained to the press about the way he was used during the World Series and the '47 season in general, his daughter, Patricia, characterized him as a "frustrated player" when he returned home to California after the season. Since he had sold his Potter Valley ranch property the previous year, he was coming home to a different situation—a "normal" home in the town of Ukiah, about 20 miles south of Potter Valley. Although he kept a few of his horses, which he boarded at the local fairgrounds, he did not have his usual array of ranch chores to tend to. He kept his favorite bird dog, a pointer named Lucky, and a cow-herding dog named Jack, but the latter "didn't fit very well into town life and was often in trouble for nipping at people's heels," Patricia wrote later, "trying to herd them when he was bored." Johnson said her mother and siblings had adjusted to living in Ukiah. They missed the ranch in Potter Valley but were fitting in in their new home. Patricia felt more at home among her classmates at Ukiah High School and took a liking to one boy in particular—Kenny Johnson—whom she would later marry and raise a family with. Kenny, an athlete in his own right, admired Vaughan and at first had a hard time understanding Vaughan's reluctance to draw attention to himself and be the town celebrity. For example, he couldn't understand why Vaughan would have taken his beautiful new blue Dodgers jacket and remove the insignia so he could wear the jacket "as you would any other coat," Patricia wrote.[91]

The Vaughans spent hours playing games, including some hotly contested Ping Pong matches. Arky and Margaret's younger sister, Nettie, were the best and would engage one another in marathon games. Vaughan had many friends around Mendocino County, and he spent some of his time with them, hunting and fishing and playing cards. "He loved to play pinochle and gin rummy," Patricia wrote, "and there was usually a card game going on in the back room of the cigar store downtown. Arky would go in and stand quietly in the background watching the men play, until someone would invite him to join in."[92]

He still enjoyed going on hunting trips with his father, brothers, and friends, and they would go at least once a year up to Modoc County in northeastern California. One of Arky's closest friends was a man named George McDermott, who owned a meat processing plant in Berkeley, a little over 100 miles south of Ukiah. Arky, his sights set on buying another ranch, would often accompany McDermott or one of his buyers on their trips to purchase cattle, with an eye toward finding the "perfect ranch," as his daughter put it. That year, the Vaughans decided to take a "real" vacation around the Christmas holidays, so they packed up Arky's new maroon Buick Special and headed south for Fullerton to see the extended family. However, he chose a roundabout route—instead of heading straight south, he looped east over the Sierra Nevada and traveled down what's known as the "eastern slope," past such sights as Mono Lake, Bishop and Mount Whitney. The landscape was beautiful, with plenty of snow, which the Vaughan children were not used to seeing. "It looked like Christmas," Patricia wrote.[93] However, Southern California was a different story—when Arky and his traveling party arrived, the sun was shining brightly and the temperature was hovering around 80 degrees. Still, the Vaughans had a major family reunion—parents, grandparents, aunts, uncles, cousins and in-laws. It was the perfect ending to a most eventful year.

◆◆ 11 ◆◆

Calling It Quits

Rumors regarding Vaughan's willingness—or unwillingness—to come back for a 14th season in 1948 already were making their way into print less than a month after the '47 campaign concluded. In late October, an article that appeared in *The Sporting News* stated that Vaughan had notified Dodgers President Branch Rickey that he was through with baseball and wanted to "live out the rest of his life as the hermit of Potter Valley with his wife and kids on his ranch." However, Vaughan had done no such thing and in fact no longer had his Potter Valley ranch. The writer—Harold C. Burr—surmised that Rickey was skeptical of Vaughan's notification. "He looks upon the Vaughan threat of retirement as just the same old trick used by some players to wheedle more dough out of the boss on a new contract."[1]

As soon as the '47 World Series ended, speculation focused on whether another key piece of the Dodgers would be back—former manager Leo Durocher, who was suspended by Commissioner Happy Chandler for the 1947 season. After all, Burt Shotton had guided the team to a pennant and took it to the brink of a World Series title. But on December 6, Rickey announced he was rehiring Durocher as manager on a one-year contract and said Shotton would oversee the managers of Brooklyn's 26 minor-league clubs.[2] At a press conference a month later, Durocher said he didn't feel he was on the spot, even though his contract allowed Rickey to fire him at any time. He also said he would not change his fiery attitude. "I'll be in there trying to win every game, as I always have done in the past," he said. "If there's any close ones called against the Dodgers I'll be out there battling it out with the umps. I'll just be my natural self."[3]

Back in Ukiah, Vaughan had his doubts about returning to the Dodgers. He did not enjoy the way he was used during the 1947 season, although the numbers say he was used effectively. "He didn't relish the thought of returning to the bench, occasionally being used as a pinch hitter," his daughter, Patricia Vaughan Johnson, wrote years later. "That wasn't his style."[4] Vaughan had always been an everyday player, but even he would admit that age and years of stress—both mentally and physically—had taken their toll on him. He was still fast, but did not possess the speed he had in his younger years. His legs sometimes gave him trouble; in fact, it was a muscle pull that essentially knocked him out of the starting lineup at the end of spring training in 1947 and relegated him to a part-time role, in which he excelled. He spent most of the off-season after the '47 campaign on a bland "baby food" diet, his daughter said, to help with the bleeding ulcers that flared up again during the previous season. He didn't look forward to playing for Durocher again, given their spat in his final season before his self-imposed hiatus. As late as mid–February, it was still unknown if Vaughan would return. "Arky may retire," Rickey told reporters on February 12. "He has more than enough to live on and he doesn't like to come East to play. His contract was returned unsigned."[5] Rickey was disappointed. "I'm sorry about Vaughan," he told the *Brooklyn Daily Eagle*. "We want age on this ball club. Six years ago we had 12 10-year men. Today we may start the race with just one—[Hugh] Casey."[6]

A week later, the Brooklyn paper said Vaughan had asked for his unconditional release so he could sign with a Pacific Coast League team. "It is doubtful whether he will return to the club and will go back into retirement after being out of it for one year during which time he helped win the pennant," James J. Murphy of the *Brooklyn Daily Eagle* wrote. "Rickey hates to part with Arky as he still wields a potent bat and would be valuable as infield insurance and as a pinch hitter. But Arky can no longer stand the strain of being in there day in and day out in a tough flag drive of the type the Flatbushers wage."[7]

But when Rickey reached out one last time and asked Vaughan if he would play in '48, the veteran said yes, thinking he could use the money to help purchase that dream ranch he had in the back of his mind. Reports estimated his contract at about $18,000; the official announcement said the soon-to-be 36-year-old slugger received "a slight raise" over his '47 deal. In an uncredited story that ran in the *New York Sun*, it was reported that Vaughan likely was a bit unhappy with the way he was used in '47 and might have addressed that in his '48 pact. "It is understood that before Vaughan inked his name on a fresh document, he extracted from Branch Rickey two promises: (1) that he would be given an opportunity for more action than last year, (2) that under no circumstances would the Dodgers trade him." The writer surmised that Vaughan's best chance for playing time would be in left field, where he saw some action the previous year, as the Dodgers had dealt veteran outfielder Dixie Walker to Pittsburgh during the off-season. "The position was new to him, but he gave a good account of himself in it. And at bat, the Dodgers saw their best pull hitter step up there when Arky wielded the wood."[8]

Rickey gave Vaughan permission to report a few days late to the Dodgers' spring training site, which that year would be held in Ciudad Trujillo, in the Dominican Republic, as he had some business to conclude in Ukiah. He arrived on March 5 after a 12-hour plane flight from New York with teammate Cookie Lavagetto. Durocher wouldn't say where he planned to use either player. "First let them get in shape," Durocher told reporters. "Then we'll decide."[9] Three days later, the Associated Press ran a photo of Lavagetto presenting a birthday cake to Vaughan, as he turned 36 years old. And by mid–March, the club's plans for Vaughan were clear—he would see time in the Dodgers' crowded outfield—and would hopefully help make up for the power lost when Walker moved on.[10]

The first hint that some trouble might be brewing between Rickey and Durocher surfaced during contract negotiations for infielder Eddie Stanky, who wanted $15,000—a $5,000 raise—for 1948. Rickey was willing to go to $12,500 and called upon Durocher to mediate the disagreement. Durocher sided with Stanky, and it wasn't long before Stanky was sent packing to the Boston Braves. This would clear the way to move Robinson from first to second base—at least in Rickey's mind. Vaughan, meanwhile, seemed to be progressing on schedule in Ciudad Trujillo. "There's an old boy at the batting nets who is attracting lots of favorable attention from the Lip," Burr wrote. "Montreal and Dominican pitchers alike have found it almost impossible to get the old gaffer out in the exhibitions. There's no manner of sense in keeping his identity a secret any longer. He's Arky Vaughan."[11] Following the stint in the Dominican Republic, the Dodgers returned to the states, playing several exhibitions against minor-league teams on their way north to New York. On April 9, they showed up for a game against Class B Asheville of the Tri-State League with just a few hours of sleep after a "wild night in the sky and a bus ride over the Smoky Mountains." Vaughan got the word he was starting from coach Jake Pitler. "I've got bad news for you, Arky. You're going to start," Pitler said. Vaughan, with just four hours of sleep, "never batted an eye. 'That's o.k. by me, Jake,'" he grinned. "'I didn't come down here to go fishing.'"[12]

The Dodgers finally made it back to Brooklyn in mid–April and met the Yankees for an exhibition set, the first game of which drew more than 62,000 people to Yankee Stadium. Vaughan got the start in left field, and he doubled and walked in four trips to the plate while scoring twice. At age 36, he still figured prominently in the Dodgers' plans as a utility man and pinch hitter but some speculated that he might even earn a starting spot somewhere, given the uncertainty of the Dodgers lineup just days before opening day. "Who's the left fielder?" asked Arthur Daley. "It's a mite hard to distinguish him because of his long white beard. By gum, it's Arky Vaughan, who thought he'd retired from baseball five years ago after serving the previous 10 seasons as an infielder."[13]

Unlike the previous year, when Vaughan did not start a game until nearly a month into the season, he was given the start in the season-opener

against the Giants, singling home a run in a four-run seventh-inning rally
that turned a 3–1 deficit into a 5–3 lead in what eventually would be a 7–6
victory. The next day, Vaughan erupted for a pair of solo home runs—the first
one an inside-the-park job—and scored three times, but the Dodgers fell,
9–5, to New York. Vaughan found himself in the starting lineup for the rest
of the month of April and the first game in May, but got off to a slow start,
as his average sat at .216. However, he did draw 10 walks during that stretch,
so his on-base percentage was a respectable .383. A leg muscle pull kept him
out of the lineup for three games, and a sty on his eye also bothered him. But
he recovered enough to torment his old team—the Pirates—when Brooklyn
made its first visit of the season to Forbes Field. In the first two games of the
series—a doubleheader that Brooklyn split—Vaughan went four for nine and
drove in a combined five runs.

Vaughan's medical issues—the pulled leg muscle and the sty—were
compounded by an infection to his lymphatic system that left him with a
104-degree fever—and a seat in the press box.[14] Between May 22 and June 18,
he appeared in left field only twice—in back-to-back games on May 27–28—
and during that stretch he had just 15 total at-bats. He earned a start in left
field on June 19 and another one on June 24 at third base, but those were his
only starts in the month of June. By the end of the month, he was batting
just .229 and he had only four hits the entire month. As a team, the Dodgers
weren't doing much better, as they were limping along in sixth place at 27–33,
eight games in back of first-place Boston, heading into the month of July.

While sidelined, Vaughan was featured prominently in a column on the
life of an official scorer written by Burr, saying:

> I've never questioned the decisions of an official scorer in all my years in baseball.
> Perhaps I should have gotten a hit in the sixth inning. But then I leave the park
> and see some poor little kid waiting at the players' gate all twisted up with infantile
> paralysis, and I ask myself what does it matter? Besides, those things even up in a
> 154-game schedule. Don't get me wrong. At bat, I bear down. I want to make all the
> hits I can and drive in all the runs possible. But as long as the team wins, my individ-
> ual record takes care of itself.[15]

The month of July was no kinder to Vaughan—or the Dodgers. In the
middle of the month, an extraordinary managerial switch occurred that saw
Durocher move from Ebbets Field to the Polo Grounds to manage the rival
Giants, and Burt Shotton—who had guided the Dodgers to the National
League pennant during Durocher's suspension the previous season—come
out of retirement to take over for Durocher in the Dodgers' dugout. Essentially, the Giants accepted former manager Mel Ott's resignation and then
took over Durocher's Brooklyn contract, which called for a base salary of
$45,000 plus bonuses for certain attendance thresholds. Some pundits saw
it coming; Burr called it seven months earlier. "There was no doubt about

Durocher being on the spot," *Daily Eagle* columnist Tommy Holmes wrote. "He knew he had to approximate Shotton's performance or else." When the Dodgers got off to a slow start, Durocher grew increasingly impatient, Holmes wrote. "Leo is a lion and a lion is a big cat and Durocher was wearing out the eighth of his nine lives so far as our town was concerned," he wrote. "When the opportunity to replace Mel Ott at the Polo Grounds opened up, he jumped at it with both feet."[16]

As for Vaughan, he batted just nine times in the month of July and picked up three hits, came to the plate just eight times in August, collecting four hits, and then finished his big-league career with 10 at-bats in September. From June 25 until the end of the season, Vaughan got more than one at-bat just twice—once on July 1 when he went zero for two and the last time on September 15 when he went zero for four. He appeared in just one game after the September 15 start and it came—most fittingly—on September 22 at home against the Pirates. In that game, Vaughan pinch hit for third baseman Tommy Brown in the bottom of the ninth inning and singled off Rip Sewell—the last of his 2,103 hits as a major leaguer.

Although Vaughan's playing time was severely curtailed, he managed to see some humor in various aspects of the game. In late August, Burr devoted a column to Vaughan's "quiet type of humor," which—while not on the level of baseball humorist Lefty Gomez—was most underrated. Burr said that Vaughan had been excused from public appearances by the club because he didn't think he'd make a very successful after-dinner speaker. Burr added: "He prefers the small audience in the Brooklyn dugout, which he frequently sends into stitches by his dry comments. There are laughter wrinkles around his brown eyes, which didn't come from worrying about his batting average. Perhaps that's one of the reasons why he's hung around in the National League for so many years. A sense of humor keeps all of us young."[17]

Vaughan in particular liked telling stories about Honus Wagner, the former Pirate great who took Vaughan under his wing during his playing days in Pittsburgh. Vaughan would tell the story of Wagner's mule, which Wagner used to work at a coal mine outside of Pittsburgh. Wagner, Vaughan would say, swore the mule was so smart that it knew not to show up at the mine on Sundays because the miners had the day off. Then one weekday, the mule was late. "The 7 o'clock whistle and still no mule," Vaughan recalled Wagner saying. "It set Wagner to worrying. He was sure something had happened to the faithful creature. He had visions of it buried under a rock slide, one hoof sticking out pathetically." "Then I remembered," Vaughan—imitating Wagner—said. "It was Washington's Birthday."[18]

After Vaughan's final appearance, he had to be admitted to Swedish Hospital when his groin infection flared up again. When he was discharged, he came out to Ebbets Field on September 28 and cleaned out his locker. He told reporters he was going home to California. "Maybe I'll hook up in the Pacific Coast League next year," he said. "I'd stay in baseball if I could play near home."[19] The next day, the Dodgers announced that Vaughan and veteran relief pitcher Hugh Casey each had been given his unconditional release. The move was triggered by Vaughan, according to his daughter, Patricia. "He was 36 years old and the years had taken a toll on him physically," she wrote.[20] After another personal meeting with Rickey, in which Vaughan expressed his feelings and asked for his unconditional release, Rickey finally obliged.

Vaughan made it back to California, reuniting with his family—most of whom hadn't seen him since he left for spring training; his wife and children remained on the West Coast except for a brief visit that Margaret and daughter Mikie made at one point during the season. He settled into his usual winter routine—playing cards, hunting, fishing and catching up with friends, all the while envisioning his next ranch.

Patricia wrote that her father's physical maladies—his ulcers, most notably, and also his tendency to be hit with migraine headaches—were no longer a problem like they were during his playing days. Migraines ran in his mother's family, and Patricia recalled often seeing him sitting in a chair in the living room in the dark with ice bags on his head. "You would find him there, in the middle of the night, unable to sleep because of the pain." With his ulcer problems waning, he no longer had to rely mostly on pureed foods; Gerber baby food was a staple of his diet during his playing days.[21]

Patricia recalled that her father rarely talked about his baseball career. "He would rather die than brag about himself," she wrote. "He lived by a policy of strict honesty and simple humility, and he taught his family the same code of ethics. He shunned the limelight because he felt that simply because he was a good baseball player it did not necessarily make him better than other people. He thought that the simplest task, done well, made the doer as important as some athlete who had been blessed with physical ability and extra talent. 'Arky' admired those who made good through perseverance and hard work, no matter how simple."[22]

Vaughan made good on his plan to hook up with a Pacific Coast League team closer to his Ukiah home when he signed a contract on February 16, 1949, to play for the San Francisco Seals. A story in the *San Francisco Examiner* the following day, which announced Vaughan's signing, noted that Seals' scout Ted McGrew and H. Roy Hamey, general manager of the Pittsburgh Pirates, recommended that Seals manager Lefty O'Doul try to sign Vaughan. It was believed that Vaughan received a bonus in the neighborhood of $8,500 to sign. "McGrew and Hamey both assure me that Vaughan will be a big help to us," said O'Doul, who indicated Vaughan would be used in left field and as a pinch hitter. "He still can run and he could always hit. He's just what we need for next season while our present crop of kids is developing in the 'B' leagues."[23] Vaughan reported to the Seals' spring training site in Boyes Hot Springs, which was about 80 miles south of his Ukiah home, on February 23 and announced he was ready and willing to play "whatever position Manager Lefty O'Doul wants me in."[24] Given his professional portfolio, Vaughan was an interview target for a number of the San Francisco area reporters who were covering spring training. Bob Stevens, a longtime baseball writer for the *San Francisco Chronicle*, did a tongue-in-cheek column about Vaughan, playing on Vaughan's reticence to talk to reporters. "This Vaughan is a Regular Chatterbox," the column's sub-head stated. Stevens chided Vaughan for his penchant for giving one-word answers to questions—a practice that doesn't exactly endear athletes to sports writers. Stevens reproduced a part of the interview:

"Hello," I said.
"Hello," said "Arky."
"Welcome to the nine."
"Thanks."
"In good condition?"
"Yes."
"Bring your family down?"
"Nope."
"Still own that Potter valley ranch?"
The column omitted Vaughan's "response" and went on to Stevens' next question.
"How come?"
"Sold it."
"When?"
"Two years ago."
"Work out much this winter?"
"Nope."
"Living on your major league savings, huh?"
"Yep."
"Like being a Seal?"
"Wouldn't be here if I didn't."

Stevens concluded by writing that he had other things to do than "listen to 'Arky' dominate a conversation, job or no job, so I left the monologist to bend somebody else's ear."[25] Vaughan had more to say to an unnamed United Press reporter who spoke with him at spring training camp. Vaughan would not reveal what his salary would be but indicated he would net more than he would have if he had returned for another season in the big leagues. Vaughan also said he didn't feel like he was "stepping down, as the saying goes," in going from the National League to the Pacific Coast League, and also said that he could have returned for a 15th major-league season, as Leo Durocher had offered him a roster spot with the Giants. "But I've been up there ever since I checked in with the Pittsburgh Pirates at the age of 20," Vaughan said, referring to the major leagues. "Last year I was away from home for seven months and the thrill of playing with a big league team loses its appeal to me when I don't get to see my wife and kids any oftener than that." While O'Doul said he thought Vaughan could hit as high as .350 in the Coast League, Vaughan wouldn't hazard a guess. "All I can say is that I believe I'm just about as fast now as I was before the war, and I've still got a good batting eye."[26]

On the day that Vaughan turned 37—March 9—a legal notice appeared in the *Ukiah Republican Press*. It was an "order to show cause" in the matter of Vaughan's application to change his name from Floyd Vaughan to Joseph Floyd Vaughan. A brief article regarding the name change appeared in the March 23 edition of *The Sporting News*, which noted that Vaughan was always listed as "Floyd Ellis Vaughan" while playing in the National League. "'Where did you get that Floyd Ellis stuff?'" Arky recently asked a 'Frisco scribe. "'My given name is Joseph and my middle name is Floyd, which an aunt of mine pinned on me. Where the Ellis came from, I'll never know." Vaughan said there had always been a great deal of confusion over his name, and some of his legal papers would have to be changed. "I signed some of them 'Arky' instead of J. Floyd Vaughan or Joseph F. Vaughan," he said. "I never was consistent. Now, I'm going to have to be or there'll be legal battles in my family for years to come."[27] In his high school yearbook, though, Vaughan was always referred to as either "Floyd" or "Arkie" but never "Joseph." Some friends and family members believe that he began to refer to himself as "Joseph" 10 years earlier when he was baptized into the Roman Catholic Church in Pittsburgh.

As spring training progressed, Vaughan continued to be an attraction in Seals camp. On March 13, he was featured in an "as told to" piece in the *San Francisco Examiner*. There, Vaughan recalled the day he sustained an injury that somehow sparked what he called "one of the greatest hitting streaks of my career." It occurred during Frankie Frisch's first season managing the Pirates, in 1940. The fiery Frisch didn't like what he was seeing during infield practice one day and ordered his infielders to show some life. "'Grab that ball and fire it!'" Vaughan remembered Frisch saying. "'Turn it loose! Show a little fire— or else!'" When the infielders went to throw the ball around, rookie Frankie Gustine "opened fire on me at about thirty feet," Vaughan said. "He threw that thing with all he had." Vaughan caught the ball with his bare hand and ended up breaking the index finger of his right hand. But the trainer didn't put it in a splint—he just taped it up. So when Vaughan went to hit, his first finger was sticking straight out. He had a difficult time throwing, but not hitting. "I had one of the greatest hitting streaks of my career," said Vaughan, who had been in a batting slump prior to the injury. "They just couldn't get me out. I hit line drives to all fields." Eventually, his finger healed to the point where he could curl it around the bat—and he promptly went back into a slump. "It was two or three weeks before I could fight my way out of it," he said.[28] In an interview later that month with Will Connolly of the *San Francisco Chronicle*, Vaughan covered lots of ground—at least for him—noting that he didn't think he'd play any longer than one or two years and that he had no desire to manage. "Had a couple a chances this winter, but turned 'em down," he told Connolly. "When I'm through I'll buy a cattle ranch again. My four kids like ranching, for the horses. I do, too." He said he remembered playing in San Francisco when the Pirates used to visit during their spring training schedule and he always felt welcome there:

> "That's one of the reasons I'm glad to finish up here. Not many baseball towns are that way. This will surprise you—Brooklyn is one. Brooklyn is the most generous stopover in the majors for visiting clubs. You hear a lot about how the fans love the Dodgers. But they applaud the opposition just as much. That's right. Pittsburgh is really rough on the home nine and the visitors alike. If a Pirate has rabbit ears and is bothered by the fans, he's through in Forbes Field. Don't get me wrong. Pittsburgh people are good Joes. They just like to ribsteak you. Why, Hollywood studios used to hold world premieres in Pittsburgh. They figured if a movie got by there, it would do O.K. elsewhere."[29]

Vaughan then offered some advice to youngsters looking to improve their games. He said that when playing catch with a partner, it was better to throw each other ground balls rather than lobbing the ball in the air. As for fielding grounders, Vaughan suggested that younger players should not retreat, but they shouldn't fight it, either. It's better to move in and try to field the ball on a big hop because backing up will often result in a fielder getting a bad hop, he said. He acknowledged he wasn't the best fielding shortstop in the game and mentioned Billy Jurges of the Cubs as a talented glove man. "I was the hitter," he said. "I had to learn to hit left-handed pitching, because our lineup at Pittsburgh was top-heavy with left swingers, and all we saw were southpaws. If I had the wrist action of [Paul] Waner, I think I could have hit .400."[30]

When the Pirates visited San Francisco for an exhibition game in the third week of March, Vaughan recalled playing for Pittsburgh when the immortal Babe Ruth hit his final major-league home run while playing for the visiting Boston Braves. It occurred on May 25, 1935, and Ruth slammed three home runs and a single that day, with his final home run clearing the right field roof at Forbes Field. It was the 714th and final homer of Ruth's illustrious career, and it—along with the other two Ruth hit that day—left quite an impression on Vaughan. "I have never seen three home runs hit harder than the Babe hit them that day," Vaughan recalled. "Especially the last one."[31]

Vaughan didn't quite live up to his pedigree once the regular Coast League season began. He went on the disabled list for an undisclosed injury in late April and appeared in only 97 games for the Seals, who finished seventh in an eight-team league with a record of 84–103. In what was his final professional season, Vaughan batted a respectable .288 with an on-base percentage of .394 and an OPS of .782. In 332 plate appearances, he collected 81 hits, scored 50 runs, banged out 10 doubles, six triples and two homers while driving in 26 runs. But he could not stay healthy; in addition to his early stint on the disabled list, he suffered from a gall bladder ailment late in the season, and that's ultimately what prompted his retirement. He left the ballclub on August 29 due to his illness and returned home to Ukiah, and five days later announced his retirement.[32] Within a few weeks, though, Vaughan apparently was feeling better; a photo appeared in the *Ukiah Republican Press* on September 14 showing him and a man named George Ward proudly holding the body of a dead panther that Vaughan killed with one shot while on a hunting expedition. The 6-foot-4, 95-pound panther was killed on a ranch north of Ukiah.[33]

◆◆ 12 ◆◆

Tragedy and Triumph

His playing career finished, Vaughan turned his attention to locking up his dream ranch. That came as no surprise to those who knew him well. His mother, in an interview with the *Fullerton News Tribune* in 1967, said her son had no interest in remaining in baseball as a coach or in some other capacity. "He was a regular old farmer," Laura Vaughan said of her son.[1] On one of his trips with his friend George McDermott, who owned a meat packing plant in the Bay Area, Vaughan had heard of a ranch for sale in Eagleville, a small Modoc County town in the far reaches of northeastern California, near the Nevada border. Vaughan was familiar with the area, as his youngest child and his only son, Timothy, recalled in a 2017 interview. Timothy said that his grandfather used to go hunting in Modoc County and that Arky would accompany him. "That's where he fell in love with the place. It wasn't new to him."[2] He would continue to make periodic trips to Modoc County as an adult, as he would go hunting with friends and family. When Arky ultimately settled in Eagleville, he told a local resident named Dave Grove, who would become a close friend of both Arky's and Timothy's, "This is the place I want to live, and this is the place I want to die."[3]

When he saw the ranch that was for sale, his daughter, Patricia, wrote years later, "He knew it was the one he wanted." So on Thanksgiving Day, 1949, Vaughan and his family, which now included Patricia's not-quite-three-month-old daughter, Kathleen—yes, Arky was a grandfather at the age of 37—piled into his large Buick sedan and headed north. The 370-mile trip from Ukiah to Eagleville figured to take about eight hours. East of Alturas, the road began to climb over the Warner Mountains. At Cedar Pass, around 6,300 feet, the snow was deep, and as the Buick began its descent, a "glorious view" of Surprise Valley opened up, Patricia recalled. Four small towns comprised the valley, with Eagleville—elevation 4,642 feet—being at the south end. When the Vaughans finally reached their destination, they saw a two-story white house with a red Dutch-style roof and red trim. The town itself, at the time, consisted of a general store, a garage, a bar and restaurant, a pool hall, a town hall and a fire hall. A two-room schoolhouse accommodated youngsters in elementary grades while the high school students rode a bus to Cedarville, about 15 miles to the north.[4]

It didn't take long for the Vaughans to feel right at home in Eagleville, and Arky certainly felt at home on his new 700-acre ranch. The property contained deer as well as "geese, quail, pheasant—he had everything he wanted," Eagleville resident Henry Beeman told the *Klamath Falls Herald and News* in 1985.[5] Many of his friends and family members said he enjoyed ranching much more than performing in big-league ballparks before thousands of adoring fans. "He'd rather be out on a horse hunting fox or punching cows than playing baseball," Timothy Vaughan said. "But he had a talent [for baseball], so he went with his talent."[6] Once he finished playing, though, he didn't pay much attention to baseball. Joyce Espil Volney, who ran the general store in Eagleville, remembered one time in the fall around World Series time, a store patron ran into Vaughan and asked him who he liked in the World Series, which was broadcast on the radio. "He said he wasn't listening," Volney said. "He didn't want to talk about baseball." In fact, Volney said, Vaughan was genuinely just a quiet guy. "But when he talked, you wanted to listen. He would stand there back in the crowd, fold his arms and lean against the counter or a wall. He was a very strong man, but very quiet. He was just a joy to be around."[7]

The ranch itself, Volney said, was everything Arky had always wanted. "He had a beautiful place—one of the nicest ranches around," she said. Arky and Margaret both seemed so happy there, Volney recalled. "They were a very close couple," she said. "He was a stabilizer for her. They complemented each other. And they loved the ranch."[8]

The town took quickly to Arky and all the Vaughans. Fellow ranchers would pitch in and help each other with chores such as branding and separating, and Arky felt right at home. "They just melded into the community so easily," Volney said. "A lot of us would get together on weekends and go camping or buckarooing. He loved that little town. It kind of enveloped him. The town put its arms around him and just made him happy. He was happy with the people, happy with the ranch. It's just a tragedy what happened."[9]

Arky, Margaret, and their children didn't have a very long time to enjoy the area, at least as a family unit. In late August of 1952, not even three years after they arrived in Eagleville, it all came to a crashing halt. With summer winding to a close, there was plenty of work to be done on the ranch. On the night of August 29, Arky and Margaret spent hours baling hay—in fact, they were working well into the next morning. "It was unusual, but they wanted to finish," Volney said, because the Vaughans were planning a birthday party for daughter Mikie in the next couple of days. A friend of Arky's named Bill Wimer came by later that morning and asked Arky and Margaret if they wanted to go fishing at Lost Lake, about 16 miles southwest of Eagleville. Margaret passed, but Arky couldn't say no. Volney recalled seeing Arky at the general store on the morning of August 30, stocking up on some supplies for the fishing trip to Lost Lake. She thought nothing of the destination, as she and her husband had been at the lake with the Vaughans just the week before. "He swam across that lake and never even lost his cowboy hat," Volney said of Arky. "He was a strong swimmer."[10]

That morning at the general store, Vaughan picked up some fishing lures and a quart of milk, among other things. Young Timothy was in the store, too, and bought himself a Coke. "He was mad at me for buying that soda," Timothy said of his father. "He bought me a V-8 or some kind of juice." Wimer, Arky's fishing buddy, was a heavy-set local resident well-known to all who lived nearby. Volney, who grew up with Wimer, described him as a logger, trapper and hunting guide. "He made quite a bit trapping—beavers, muskrats, coyotes," she said. "He just kind of did his own fun things. And so did his wife. They lived frugally—and they had a deep, deep love. You never saw one without the other. For him to go fishing without her, that was an unusual thing." Unfortunately, Alma Wimer couldn't accompany her husband that day, as she had to make a trip to Alturas that night, Volney said.[11]

There are many versions of what happened the day of August 30 at Lost Lake. As best as can be pieced together, Wimer and Vaughan were out on a fishing boat in the lake that evening when Wimer stood up to cast his line, and the boat capsized. One report had Vaughan—by all accounts an accomplished swimmer—holding on to the capsized boat while Wimer was foundering. Another report, from a witness on the shore identified as Verne Wheeler, stated that as soon as the boat capsized the two men immediately struck out for shore and swam about 65 yards in the frigid water when they both went under—a mere 20 feet from the shore. That report—and others—described the lake as "bottomless."[12] Other reports had Vaughan trying to tow Wimer, who was not a good swimmer, to the shore when they both went under. Vaughan's death certificate filed in Modoc County listed the cause of death as "accidental drowning" and placed the time of death at 6:30 p.m.

But Timothy Vaughan believes his father did not drown and that the lake was not "bottomless." "He could have stood up in the water he died in," Timothy Vaughan said. "I went to that lake. I walked out in that lake. I could stand up. The part where the dam is is deep, maybe 30 feet." But where Vaughan and Wimer went under, Timothy Vaughan said, "both men could have stood up. But they didn't." Timothy Vaughan said that he was told that his father had no water in his lungs, so he believes that a combination of the frigid mountain water, the altitude—the lake sits at about 7,200 feet—Arky's body temperature, and the fact that he was experiencing some heart problems all combined to end his life. "Arky was supposed to go to the heart doctor the next day or the next week," his son said. "He'd been having trouble. When he hit that water—that ice cold water—his body locked up. He couldn't breathe, he couldn't move, he couldn't do anything. It's like a shock."[13]

Joyce Volney remembered the aftermath of Vaughan's death most vividly. Wheeler, identified as being on the shore, was actually fishing from a raft when Vaughan and Wimer went under. A report published in the September 4 edition of the *Surprise Valley Journal* in Cedarville said that Wheeler saw Wimer stand up to cast and then when Wheeler turned his back, he heard a loud splash. Wheeler turned to see the boat capsized, and then started to row toward the two men. But as he got closer, they both went under and never resurfaced. At that point, Wheeler continued on to shore, jumped in his pickup truck, and headed toward town. "He came screaming through town and lay on his horn until he got people's attention," Volney remembered. "Someone rang the church bell to try to get people to help, but it was too late."[14] The *Surprise Valley Journal* article said powerful flashlights were used to search for the bodies; Wimer's was recovered about 10 p.m. but Vaughan's wasn't recovered until nearly midnight.[15]

The town, Volney said, was crushed. "They were a big part of the community," she said of the Vaughans. "They had kids in school. They loved the ranch and the town. They added to it and we added to their life, too. For a town to lose two vital men, it was just a terrible thing."[16]

When word of Vaughan's death reached the East Coast, tributes came pouring in, and people expressed shock and extreme sadness. Audrey Smith Ifft, a Pittsburgh resident whose parents, Tom and Helen Smith, were close friends of Arky and Margaret during Arky's playing days, vividly remembered the day Vaughan died: "Daddy got the phone call—someone called him and told him Arky had been in a boating accident. And he died. Oh my God, it was really upsetting. I can remember it like it was yesterday because they were such good friends. I remember seeing my father cry. I thought, "Oh dear, I never saw Daddy that upset." My mother was upset, too. But to see a man that upset…"[17]

Harry Keck, sports editor of the *Pittsburgh Sun-Telegraph*, started his September 1 column as follows: "Nothing ever has shocked Pittsburgh baseball fans more than the tragic death by drowning in a California lake of Arky Vaughan, who for ten years never batted less than .300 as the Pirate shortstop. Arky, who rated with Honus Wagner and Glenn Wright as the best of the Pirate players at that position, always was quiet and reserved, a good, clean-living family man, and his fine character plus his proficiency as a player made him one of the most admired and respected men who ever wore the livery of the local club."[18]

Vaughan's death, *Sun-Telegraph* staff writer Chilly Doyle wrote, created a most somber mood at Forbes Field that day, which was the site of a Pirates-Cardinals game. Vaughan, Doyle noted, was one of the Pirates' all-time greats—a marvelous hitter and one of the fastest players in baseball. "He was a great team player and while he was very good-natured and [a] retiring type, the tough players 'didn't want any part' of him when he became angry," Doyle wrote.[19]

Players, managers and coaches weighed in on Vaughan's place in the game and how they felt about him personally. Stan Musial, who grew up in Donora, near Pittsburgh, noted that Vaughan was one of his favorite players and had a chance to get to know him a bit after he reached the big leagues. "He was a brilliant slugger, hustler and what a baserunner!" Musial said. Terry Moore, a coach with the Cardinals at the time of Vaughan's death and a contemporary of Vaughan's as a player, recalled how Vaughan "owned" former pitching standout Dizzy Dean. "Arky must have batted .500 against Dizzy Dean," he said. "Many times Diz would come to the bench after Arky had cleared the bases with a remark like this: 'Will some of your birds tell me how to get that guy out?'" Eddie Stanky, who was winding up his first year as manager of the Cardinals, said when he'd heard about Vaughan's death, "I felt like I had lost a brother." Stanky played with Vaughan in Brooklyn and the two roomed together during spring training—an association that gave Stanky a chance to truly get to know Vaughan. "Arky was more than a top-flight player—he was top-flight in everything."[20]

Honus Wagner, perhaps the greatest Pirate of them all and Vaughan's personal coach and road roommate during his stint with the Pirates, was shaken by Vaughan's death. "When Vaughan came to Pittsburgh, I was told to coach him and never mind anyone else," Wagner told the *Pittsburgh Sun-Telegraph*. "If I told him to do something he would do it and not ask why. He was a wonderful guy; nice to coach. He could hit, run, throw and he liked to play, which is more important. I'm sorry. It's a tough blow to his family."[21] Bill Benswanger, the Pirates president during Arky's tenure in Pittsburgh, told *Pittsburgh Post-Gazette* columnist Al Abrams that Pirate opponents had a healthy respect for Vaughan, not only because of his playing ability but his ability to use his fists. "Arky was slow to anger," Abrams wrote, "but once riled—the other guy better get out of his way."[22]

Several of Vaughan's former Dodger teammates weighed on his tragic death. Shortstop Pee Wee Reese said he didn't even feel like playing that particular day. "I kept hoping it was just a rumor, that it wasn't true," Reese told a United Press International reporter. "He was a steady, easy-going guy, and had a good long life to look forward to." Cookie Lavagetto, then a coach with the Dodgers, said, "I never knew a finer fellow or a better team man." Jackie Robinson, who broke the color barrier while Vaughan played in Brooklyn, said, "He was one of the fellows who went out of his way to be nice to me when I came in here as a rookie. Believe me, I needed it. He was a fine fellow."[23] Paul Waner, a teammate of Vaughan's both in Pittsburgh and in Brooklyn, was playing golf when told of Vaughan's drowning. Waner broke down and cried.[24]

Branch Rickey, the former Dodgers president who at the time of Vaughan's death was general manager of the Pirates, was deeply saddened by Vaughan's passing and noted that he had tried to trade for him numerous times over the years before he finally landed him. Rickey sent a Western Union telegram to Margaret Vaughan on September 1 after learning of Arky's death. "I extend my deepest sympathy to you and the family," Rickey wrote. "Arky was not only a great player, but a very fine gentleman in every respect."[25]

New York's most prestigious sports columnists weighed in on Vaughan's passing and his career. Red Smith of the *New York Herald Tribune* wrote about how the quality of play in the early 1950s couldn't come close to matching the caliber of ball that was being played during the 1930s and early '40s—essentially before Pearl Harbor. In Vaughan's youth, Smith wrote, he was a "star among stars" and rattled off some of the luminaries who played with and against Vaughan:

> He was a .385 hitter and the most valuable player in a league that included Bill Terry and Mel Ott and Babe Herman and Chuck Klein and Pepper Martin and Jim Wilson and Lloyd Waner and Rip Collins. Never since then have there been so many so good. ... In such company Arky Vaughan was one of the best for fourteen summers. Even in such company he could have been the best for seventeen summers, but for reasons which never were made entirely clear, he chose not to. ... Had he selected to play through the war against the characters who were impersonating pitchers then, there's no telling what the lifetime average would be.[26]

Down in Arky's hometown of Fullerton, the *Daily News Tribune* paid tribute to one of its shining stars. John Neubauer, who wrote a column known as "The Town Crier," recalled Vaughan's accomplishments both as a youngster at Fullerton High School and in the big leagues and called him one of the greatest athletes Fullerton ever produced. "Those who played with him will never forget Arky," Neubauer wrote. "Those who were fortunate enough to watch his inspired performances on the gridiron, court and on the diamond will never forget his greatness."[27] Neubauer noted the various leadership roles Vaughan assumed as a youngster at Fullerton High School. He added that Vaughan lacked only one thing—a colorful personality. "Those who knew him best believe he would have been one of the game's greatest heroes had he been endowed with a sparkling personality that made lesser players great."[28]

San Francisco Chronicle columnist Art Rosenbaum recalled an interview he did with Vaughan three years earlier when Vaughan was preparing for what proved to be his last professional season, with the San Francisco Seals. Rosenbaum said Vaughan offered several tips for young players, including this message: "It takes more guts to go down on a hard-hit grounder than it does to stand up to a fastball pitcher. I've done both. Don't back away from the ball. Make it come to you. Play it on the big hop. Be aggressive. Move in on a grounder before it has a chance to intimidate you on the off-hop. But don't fight it. Accept it smoothly. The big thing is to stoop low. Keep your hands soft and rubbery."[29]

Up in Modoc County, funeral services for Vaughan were held on September 2 in front of a packed turnout at St. Joseph's Catholic Church in Cedarville. Immediately afterward, the entire funeral cortege drove to Eagleville, where services were held in the Community Church for Bill Wimer. Joint graveside services then took place at the Eagleville Cemetery. Among the pallbearers for Vaughan were a former Brooklyn Dodger teammate, Augie Galan; Joyce Volney's first husband, John Espil; and her cousin, Dave Grove—one of Vaughan's closest friends in Eagleville. Galan was a frequent visitor to Modoc County and in fact had accompanied Vaughan on hunting trips there before Vaughan bought the ranch in Eagleville. Volney played piano at the funeral service for Vaughan; she reflected on something that happened a week or so earlier, when she and her husband had been up at Lost Lake with the Vaughans, and Arky had swum across the lake. When they returned from the lake, they ended up at the Vaughan house and Arky asked Volney to play the piano. "I started playing 'Danny Boy,'" she said. "And he said, 'If I die, I want you to play this at my funeral.' The next week, I was playing that song at his funeral."[30]

Margaret and her children didn't stay in Eagleville for very long following her husband's death. Margaret moved to Santa Rosa with Mikie and Judy while son Timothy—who was eight years old when his father died—was sent to boarding school for a few years, and then ultimately ended up back in Eagleville, where he lived with Dave Grove's family until he graduated high school. While he was living in Eagleville, Timothy would run into people who knew his father, and they never got tired of talking about him. Said Timothy: "It was interesting to me. I liked hearing about it—the things he did as a rancher. The fun they had, the fishing trips, the parties. Cowboys have to have parties. It was fun for me because I felt like I was part of it, a part of him. Which I always wanted to be, but never was. They really enjoyed the guy and they liked to talk about him."[31] Timothy Vaughan continued to make annual trips up to Eagleville every year to go camping and barbecuing. The number of people who remember his dad dwindled every year, but even as of 2017 there were a couple of cowboys "who rode buckaroo with my dad," Timothy said. "They're probably six or seven years older than I am—I'm 74—or maybe older. They were just young men, but they remember him. They had fun."[32]

Timothy Vaughan said he's not sure why his father felt such a connection to ranching: "It must have been something to do with being on a horse and punchin' cows. He knew every cow he had. He loved it—he absorbed cattle ranching. He just liked being a cowboy. He'd get up early—early—in the morning and go feed the cattle. Dave [Grove] said he'd feed 'em twice where others would only feed 'em once, just to be out with the cattle. He was infatuated with ranching."[33]

As the years following Vaughan's death passed, he faded into relative obscurity. Now and then his name would pop up in newspapers in Pittsburgh and elsewhere, often around All-Star Game time, as his exploits in the 1941 contest would be repeated. Sometimes if the topic of the game's fastest base runners was up for discussion, Vaughan's name would surface. Just a few weeks after his death, his name appeared in a brief article in The Sporting News that marked the occasion of Musial's 2,000th career hit. The article noted that Musial was the youngest player to reach the 2,000-hit mark since Vaughan had reached it in 1943. Vaughan was 31 when he turned that trick, a few months younger than Musial, who would turn 32 in November. However, Vaughan was in his 12th season while Musial was only in his 10th.[34] Four years later, The Sporting News had another brief mention of Vaughan, which came when Pittsburgh's Dale Long hit his 20th home run in August 1956, breaking Vaughan's team record for a left-handed hitter. "Umpire Larry Goetz congratulated Long and told him, 'You beat the record of a champion. Arky was one of the best players in baseball.'"[35]

The following year, the topic was rookies, and former Pirates great—and manager—Pie Traynor told Abrams that Vaughan was the greatest rookie he ever saw. "The first time I looked at him," Pie said, "I knew that kid had the makings of a great ball player." Abrams noted that Vaughan held the Pirate record for highest single-season batting average at .385. "When we recall that Traynor has seen some great recruits in his time—Paul Waner, Hazen Cuyler, Glenn Wright and others, one better appreciates his estimate of Vaughan."[36]

In 1964, Vaughan was mentioned in a Sporting News editorial that called for revamping the process for the Baseball Hall of Fame voting. The writer raised several issues, not the least of which was "camouflaging the identity of some players." Arky Vaughan, the editorial pointed out, "undoubtedly suffered because his name was listed as Joseph F. Vaughan."[37]

Every now and then there would be talk that Vaughan deserved to be enshrined in Cooperstown with the game's all-time greats. At the time of Vaughan's retirement from the major leagues, the Hall of Fame rules permitted players' names to be added to the annual ballot one year after their retirement, and they could remain there for 25 years. However, Vaughan's name did not appear for the first time until 1953, and he dropped off the ballot after the 1968 voting. He received just four-tenths of 1 percent of the vote the first year his name appeared on the ballot, and he never received more than 5 percent of the vote in any of his first seven years on the ballot. (Balloting by the writers took place every year until 1956; from 1957 through

1965, the writers voted every other year.) In 1964, he received 8.5 percent and then from 1966 through 1968, his percentages steadily increased—from 11.9 to 15.8 to 29 percent in his final year on the writers' ballot. That put him at No. 9 on the list of 47 players eligible for voting that year, but it was still far short of the 75 percent threshold required for enshrinement.

For whatever reason, random Vaughan fans would attempt to rally Hall of Fame support for him from time to time. For example, a Framingham, Massachusetts, resident named Ray Swanecamp mounted a one-man campaign to get Vaughan elected in 1967, to no avail. Swanecamp sent over 100 letters to newspapers throughout the country to bring the "facts" of Vaughan's career to the attention of writers who might have a vote in the Hall of Fame balloting. He also sent a letter to the Hall asking voters to consider voting in Vaughan and included a comparison of his statistics to the other eight shortstops already enshrined. "This will be Vaughan's last chance to be elected to the Hall of Fame by the Baseball Writers Association of America," Swanecamp wrote. "It would be a shame indeed if such impressive achievements as his were to go unrecognized."[38]

When that didn't work, Swanecamp went after the Veterans Committee in a similar fashion, writing to Paul Kerr—at the time the president of the Hall of Fame. Swanecamp opined that Vaughan, on the basis of games played, ranked only second to the great Honus Wagner when it came to hitting among shortstops "and as a fielder and baserunner was superior to most others including some present Hall of Famers." Swanecamp wrote that he believed Vaughan's run-in with Leo Durocher in 1943 hurt his chances of election by the BBWA. He also said that Vaughan's decision to sit out three seasons, from 1944 through 1946, severely hurt his Hall of Fame chances because he could have piled up significant numbers against the inferior pitching that prevailed during World War II. "I am certainly not trying to tell any baseball experts, as I feel you all are on the Veterans Committee, your job," Swanecamp wrote. "I am just an average baseball fan doing this in an effort to remind people of a truly great baseball figure whose untimely death came before his fifteen years of eligibility by the BBWA and as the saying goes 'out of sight, out of mind.'"[39] Swanecamp requested that Kerr and the rest of the Veterans Committee not relegate Vaughan's name to the "bottom" of the old-timers' list given that it would be his first year in that realm. Rather, he wrote, the committee should put Vaughan at the top of that list "because of his contributions to the game, and because for so many years the BBWA chose to overlook him."[40]

Swanecamp wasn't the only fan out there who believed Vaughan's accomplishments merited a plaque in the Baseball Hall of Fame. In January 1973, a man named Harry J. O'Donnell, the former director of communications for New York governor Hugh Carey, wrote to Warren Giles, then chairman of the Baseball Hall of Fame's Veterans Committee, and presented a page of statistics and other backing on behalf of Vaughan. O'Donnell also mentioned Vaughan's selection on an All-Star team that then President Richard M. Nixon and his son-in-law, David Eisenhower, had put together in late June 1972, prior to the annual All-Star Game, which was being played in Washington that year. Nixon and Eisenhower compiled two teams for each of the National and the American Leagues—one from 1925 to 1945 and the other from 1946 to the present. The president, in a narrative that accompanied the list of players he had selected, acknowledged that his choice of Vaughan for the National League's 1925–45 squad "may be a surprise to some." He admitted that sentimental reasons were partly behind the selection; he attended Fullerton High School around the same time that Vaughan did and recalled Vaughan as not only a fine baseball player but a "star football player." Nixon wrote that he believed most baseball experts would include Arky on an all-time all-star team "if he were rated solely on his hitting ability." Vaughan's fielding numbers, Nixon conceded, were not as high as some other shortstops. "But I recall reading a sports column on one occasion which pointed out that he would have had a much higher [fielding percentage] except for the fact that he covered far more ground than the average shortstop. He got to balls that most shortstops would have never reached and which would have gone through as clean hits."[41] Three months later, Nixon mailed a letter to Margaret Vaughan, congratulating her on her husband's inclusion on Nixon's all-star team. "No team would be complete without your husband's name," the letter read.[42]

A year later, Sporting News editor and publisher C.C. Johnson Spink presented a list of the 10 greatest players *not* in the Hall of Fame, as compiled by the Society for American Baseball Research, which based the list on a poll of its 125 members. The group chose one player for each position plus a right-handed and left-handed pitcher. The shortstop? Arky Vaughan. Spink pointed out Vaughan's career batting average as well as his speed, noting that he led the National League in triples three times and stolen bases once. But Vaughan did not earn the Veterans Committee vote in 1973 or 1974.[43]

In Pittsburgh, Vaughan remained mostly forgotten among many fans, although in May 1976, the Pirates honored Vaughan during a weekend series at Three Rivers Stadium. However, neither The Pittsburgh Press nor the Post-Gazette wrote anything more than a two-sentence brief to note the occasion. Nationally, The Sporting News again took up the Vaughan cause in 1977, pointing out that his numbers stacked up at least as formidably as those of several recent Veterans Committee selections, namely Earl Averill, Billy Herman, and Jim Bottomley. Columnist Leonard Koppett wrote that if those players merited selection, then so did Vaughan and Chuck Klein, among others.[44]

A change in the Hall of Fame voting rules appeared to doom Vaughan for a time. In 1977, a special committee suggested that any player who was active in 1946 or later needed to have garnered at least 100 votes during their normal eligibility period to be eligible for consideration by the Veterans Committee. For those who retired in 1945 or earlier, a simple vote of the Veterans Committee would suffice. Among the players affected by that change was Vaughan.

Neither Ray Swanecamp nor Harry O'Donnell—nor C.C. Johnson Spink, for that matter—made any headway in getting Vaughan enshrined in baseball's Hall of Fame, but they weren't the last to take up the cause. In May 1978, Wiley "Pepper" Thornton, a Dallas insurance agent who grew up in Texarkana, Arkansas, mounted a campaign to have the Hall of Fame eligibility rules changed specifically to benefit players like Vaughan, who failed to get 100 votes from the BBWA. Thornton claimed to have seen Vaughan and the Pirates play an exhibition game in Texarkana in 1938 against the Chicago White Sox when he was a teenager. Vaughan hit a towering home run that day and later, after doubling off the fence in right field, he stood on second base and tipped his Pirate cap to Thornton. Or at least that's the story Thornton liked to tell. He told his mother that day after he got home from the game and she asked, "Why do you think he did it?" Thornton responded, "Because he was looking straight in my direction and I'd been cheering louder for him than anyone else. Ask all the ones who were there."[45]

Thornton wanted to use a postcard blitz, targeting the sports desks of major U.S. newspapers, and he suggested that it could even work as a school project, with students filling out the postcards at the direction of their teachers. "I believe the rule will be changed," Thornton wrote in a letter dated May 29, 1978. Thornton's efforts caught the attention of an *Arkansas Democrat* sports columnist named Tony Moser, who devoted a column to Thornton. "Quixote He's Not, but Vaughan's Fan Charges Anyway" read the headline on Moser's column. Moser wrote: "It is not easy to figure just why a person adopts a cause as remote and unlikely as the one Thornton has embraced with heart and soul. Over the past few years, he has relentlessly taken on the National Baseball Hall of Fame, as well as a good portion of the sportswriting establishment, armed only with a pen and postage stamps."[46]

Moser contacted the Hall of Fame and spoke with Ken Smith, the hall's public relations director, who told him the rule keeping Vaughan out was being investigated and might be changed. "A lot of people really don't think this situation is fair," Smith conceded. Thornton told Moser he simply didn't understand the new rule, which only took effect in January 1978. Thornton said he talked to a number of Veterans Committee members and they agreed Vaughan deserved to be in the hall. "If they get this rule changed, things will be a lot easier," Thornton concluded. "That's really the only thing in our way now." Moser spoke with Paul Dean, a former major league pitcher and the brother of Dizzy Dean, who couldn't understand why Vaughan wasn't already in the Hall of Fame. "I pitched against Arky when I was with the Cardinals, and he was the only one who could pull my fastball," Dean said. "He could shoot a fastball out like a cannon."[47]

After the 1979 Hall of Fame vote came and went—and Vaughan remained on the outside looking in—*Pittsburgh Press* columnist Roy McHugh addressed Vaughan's situation, and specifically Thornton's campaign to change the eligibility rules. Thornton told McHugh that he had corresponded with Vaughan's widow, Margaret, for several years, telling her he would keep on working to get Arky into the Hall of Fame. But Margaret did not live to see that happen; she died on April 10, 1978, in a Ukiah hospital at the age of 65. She was buried next to her husband in Eagleville Cemetery.[48]

Thornton was relentless in going to bat for Vaughan. Not only did he hound the Veterans Committee members, but he wrote countless letters to the editor. For example, two of his letters ran in *The Pittsburgh Press* in the space of six weeks—from February 4, 1979, to March 18, 1979. In one of them, Thornton wrote that he recently had contact with former Pirate coach Bill Posedel, who told him, "If Vaughan played today he would be the highest-paid player in baseball."[49] Thornton was hardly the only letter-to-the-editor writer endorsing Vaughan's Hall of Fame credentials. The Reverend Warren E. Upton of Munhall, Pennsylvania, wrote to *The Sporting News* in May 1981 in support of Vaughan, calling his absence from the hall "a miscarriage of baseball justice." Vaughan may never make the Hall of Fame, Upton wrote, "but the Hall will be the poorer because of that omission. And one may suspect that some former shortstops, safely enshrined in the Hall, might well have collected splinters on the bench had they been on the Pittsburgh teams on which Vaughan played."[50]

While Cooperstown's doors remained closed to Vaughan in the early 1980s, he did receive recognition back in his native state, as he was inducted into the Arkansas Hall of Fame in 1980. The next year, he made it into the Orange County (California) Sports Hall of Fame. Prior to Vaughan's Orange County hall induction, in February of 1981, his old boyfriend friend, Bob Williams, questioned why Vaughan hadn't made the Cooperstown grade yet. "He had such an excellent career," he told a reporter with *The Register* in Orange County, then asked, "Do you know why not?" Williams admitted Vaughan was slow to warm up to strangers—and particularly the media. "I don't think he got along too well with you guys," Williams told *Register* reporter Steve Grimley. "He liked to let his playing on the field do the talking."[51] A few months later, in an interview with Chris Dufresne of the *Fullerton News Tribune*, John "Skeet" Steele—another one of Vaughan's closest boyhood friends—said Vaughan wasn't mysterious—"just hard to get acquainted with. He never went around with strangers." Steele said Vaughan virtually never showed an interest in talking about the sport in which he achieved so much success. "When the season was over, that was the end of baseball," he said. "Even when he retired, I never saw him listen to a game on radio or watch it on TV. But his dad, Robert, never missed a game."[52]

In Pittsburgh and elsewhere, the letter writers continued to beat the drum for the former Pirate. Charles Trunick, in a letter to *The Pittsburgh Press*, likened Vaughan to Pete Rose, who later would become baseball's all-time hit king, and said Vaughan excelled in numerous categories. "I implore the [Hall of Fame] board of directors to right an obvious wrong and put Vaughan in the Hall of Fame, where he belongs."[53]

Whether Thornton or any other Vaughan boosters had anything to do with it will never be known, but the Baseball Hall of Fame in Cooperstown did indeed alter its eligibility rules in time for the 1984 voting. The change meant that consideration could be given to 10-year players whose careers began before 1946, which opened the door for Vaughan and several other noteworthy players, including Ernie Lombardi and Enos Slaughter. However, Vaughan again failed to make the grade in '84; the Veterans Committee selected a different shortstop, Pee Wee Reese, who was Vaughan's teammate for three seasons in Brooklyn, as well as catcher Rick Ferrell. Edward H. Kelly, who wrote a column in favor of Vaughan's enshrinement in the hall, asked Reese why he thought Vaughan hadn't been selected, and Reese said he didn't know, but that "surely Arky deserved recognition by now." Reese guessed that Vaughan's defensive numbers might have worked against him, but Kelly pointed out that Vaughan's lifetime fielding percentage of .953 wasn't that far off Reese's own .962.[54]

O'Donnell, now that the eligibility rules were changed, went back on the campaign trail in support of Vaughan, writing long letters to Veterans Committee members such as Bob Fishel. Near the end of a four-page tome dated January 18, 1985, O'Donnell said the Veterans Committee was made up of "regular folks with honest, decent instincts" and therefore should allow "justice to triumph in the case of Joseph Floyd [Arky] Vaughan. Maybe all that is needed is for one of their colleagues, whom they respect, to raise the issue and appeal to their sense of fair play. My nomination for the guy to start the ball rolling is Bob Fishel! ... Dammit, Bob, let's get Arky Vaughan into baseball's Hall of Fame where he belongs. How say you?"[55]

That same month, another group that had formed in support of Vaughan—one that included Patricia Vaughan Johnson and a baseball historian named Richard B. "Dixie" Tourangeau—renewed its bid to have the former shortstop enshrined in Cooperstown. The group called itself the Committee to Elect Joseph "Arky" Vaughan to the Baseball Hall of Fame.

Tourangeau became familiar with Vaughan's story by virtue of some work he had done creating baseball calendars. Larry Rothstein, a friend of Tourangeau's, was looking at some potential calendar subjects and came across Vaughan's statistics in *The Baseball Encyclopedia*. Rothstein questioned why Vaughan, given his body of work, wasn't already enshrined in Cooperstown, and that prompted Tourangeau to take a closer look. He concluded that Vaughan certainly deserved to have his place in Cooperstown, and went about spearheading the committee's campaign.

"He had the credentials," Tourangeau said of Vaughan. "But he was a quiet guy—he was never the focal point of anything. Maybe he got into one or two fights. But he never did anything to bring attention to himself. And he died young. When you do that, you're gone from people's memories. That's the reason why he faded away."[56]

Tourangeau wrote letters over the course of several years to Hall of Fame voters, urging them to make room for Vaughan. In one of them, dated January 1985, Tourangeau wrote:

> The Vaughan Committee understands that there are underlying "politics" in the selection process of the Veterans Committee, but we believe Arky's "due" is due now. Had Vaughan not died so soon after retirement; or had he been more flamboyant a player; or had he fattened his fabulous statistics during the War Years instead of tending to his family and ranch, he would, in all likelihood, already have his bronzed profile in Cooperstown. Whether Arky receives his justice in 1985, 1986, or 1987, we are confident he will eventually receive it. We hope the Veterans Committee members will see fit to select Arky at the earliest possible opportunity—the March 1985 meeting.[57]

Not all of the Veterans Committee members appreciated Tourangeau's claim that "politics" was involved in the committee's voting. Milton Richman, sports editor of United Press International and a committee member, wrote that he would swear under oath in court that he'd never seen the slightest politics shown in any of the voting sessions that he attended. "Every committee member studies and weighs each nominee carefully and conscientiously and no worthy candidate is ever—I repeat—ever passed over because of some 'politics.' What some people seem to forget is that there are many worthwhile candidates and the Veterans Committee is authorized to elect only two each year." Richman closed his column by saying that Vaughan and at least one of his contemporaries—catcher Ernie Lombardi—both belonged in the Hall.[58]

All of the efforts by Tourangeau and the others finally paid off on March 6, 1985, when the Veterans Committee voted Vaughan and Enos "Country" Slaughter into the Hall of Fame. A Western Union telegram arrived at Tourangeau's residence and it consisted of just six words: "Thank You, Thank You, Thank You." It was signed by Bob Vaughan, one of Arky's brothers. The Vaughan family as a whole was elated to hear the news. Daughter Michaela (Mikie) Howard said she had heard rumors the Veterans Committee might tap her father that year. "But then we'd thought he would make it before and he hadn't," she told Glenn Erickson, sports editor of the *Ukiah Daily Journal*. "I'm glad it [the waiting] is over."[59]

Congratulations poured in from all points, including a note dated March 13, 1985, from Ronald Reagan in the White House:

> As a former baseball broadcaster and personal fan, I remember Arky's outstanding career with the Pittsburgh Pirates and the Brooklyn Dodgers. He endeared himself to fans everywhere as a fine-fielding shortstop, a superior baserunner, and batter who hit for power as well as for a high average and with very few strikeouts. You can be proud of this most fitting recognition for Arky. His selection for Cooperstown is a reflection of the place he has always had in the hearts of baseball fans the world over—including this one.[60]

Numerous members of the Vaughan family made the trek to Cooperstown for Vaughan's Hall of Fame induction ceremony held on July 28, 1985. Among them were daughters Patricia, Michaela, and Judith, son Timothy, brothers Glenn, Ken and Bob, and many others. Patricia accepted the plaque on behalf of Arky and spoke to the throng. "I wish that my father were here in my place," she said. "Standing here, maybe with my mother by his side, but since they deemed otherwise, I'm very proud to be representing the whole Vaughan family in accepting this." She thanked three people "who helped keep Arky's name in front of the public because he couldn't do it for himself." The first was the late Wiley Thornton, whom Patricia said "spent much of the later part of his life writing, calling, speaking on my father's behalf. And I'm sorry he couldn't be here today to see this." She then thanked two members of the Committee to Elect Joseph "Arky" Vaughan to the Baseball Hall of Fame—Colonel Mike Stevenson, who was stationed in Europe and unable to attend the ceremony, and Tourangeau.[61]

Years later, Tourangeau said he appreciated the Vaughan family's kind words regarding his role in getting Arky enshrined. "If this was 20 years ago and the Vaughan family brothers were still alive, they would tell you I got him in the Hall of Fame," Tourangeau said in a 2016 interview. "That's probably not true, but I did remind everyone about what he did." Tourangeau never called committee members, but instead relied on his written correspondence. He added: "That was my piece, my offering of information to them. My question was, if this guy had done all this, why isn't he in the Hall of Fame? I figured that's all I could do. It just struck me that because he died early, mostly, and wasn't around to be interviewed and talk about himself or anything, he was just cast aside by voters and everyone else. I thought what [the Veterans Committee] needed was a little more information and a little more prodding to put him over the top."[62]

During her remarks, Vaughan's daughter emphasized that in her father's lifetime, "He never sought fame or glory. He played baseball the way he played because he loved the game and he played the way he did everything he loved, with all his heart and soul and to the best of his ability." Patricia related something that Vaughan's old boyhood friend, Skeet Steele, mentioned and that was Arky's burning desire to get better and better at the game he loved. "And this dedication combined with his natural talent helped him to establish the statistics and records that stand till this day," she said. "And because of this, and in his induction into the Hall of Fame, the fame and the glory that he never sought are now his forever."[63]

Vaughan's family made the most of its time in Cooperstown and by all accounts had a wonderful weekend. Arky's brother Glenn at one point received word that Roy Campanella, the great Dodgers Hall of Fame catcher whose career was cut short by an auto accident, wanted to see Glenn Vaughan. "You're Arky's brother, aren't you?" asked Campanella. "I just wanted to meet you and to say that I learned more about hitting from Arky than I ever knew existed. He was the greatest!"[64]

The day following Vaughan's induction, another noteworthy man with ties to Fullerton sat and penned a letter to Patricia:

> As I listened to your eloquent remarks at the Hall of Fame, I thought back to 1927 when I was privileged to know your father. I was a substitute tackle on Fullerton High School's championship 130-pound team and remember Arky as our star halfback— fast, hardnosed and even then a real professional. I didn't know he played baseball

Patricia Vaughan Johnson, Arky Vaughan's oldest daughter, proudly displays her father's plaque at his 1985 Hall of Fame induction ceremony in Cooperstown, New York. Joining Johnson (left to right) are Hoyt Wilhelm, Enos Slaughter, and Lou Brock (courtesy National Baseball Hall of Fame Library, Cooperstown, New York).

until I read about him in the '30s when he was an All Star with the Pirates. In 1971, I selected him as the shortstop on the President's all time all star team when baseball celebrated its 100th anniversary. He would have been proud of the way his daughter represented him at the induction ceremony. Please extend my congratulations and best wishes to his brothers and the other members of his family. Sincerely, Richard Nixon.[65]

The congratulatory letters also came in from the nondescript, such as Joseph D.E. Konhauser of Minneapolis, who wrote to the Baseball Hall of Fame on July 30, 1985, and asked the Hall to forward his note to Patricia Vaughan Johnson. "I was so pleased when your father was elected to baseball's Hall of Fame," Konhauser wrote. "The recognition was long overdue." He related growing up in a small town about 40 miles northeast of Pittsburgh and his father taking him to Pirates games for the first time in 1932. "Even before I learned to spell his last name Arky was my favorite Pirate," Konhauser wrote. "Actually, he was my favorite anything and I saw him play in many games."[66]

Arky Vaughan's plaque in the Baseball Hall of Fame includes his given name, which he legally changed later in life, as well as the nickname by which he was best known among fans and those connected with the game (courtesy Pittsburgh Pirates).

McHugh wrote the day of Vaughan's Hall of Fame induction that "it taxes belief that he was not in the Hall of Fame long ago. Arky Vaughan has the credentials. Looking at them, where do you start?" McHugh pointed out Vaughan's lifetime batting average of .318 and his .385 mark that led the league in 1935 and remained the best single-season average among any National Leaguer over a full campaign. Tony Gwynn of the San Diego Padres hit .394 in 1994, but a players strike limited him to 110 games. McHugh noted that despite taking a "full cut," Vaughan rarely struck out. "He once led the league in stolen bases. Three times he led the league in walks. When he tried for an extra base he invariably made it. Going from first to third, there was no one as fast."[67] McHugh's comments were nearly identical to those of Rip Sewell, a former teammate of Vaughan's with the Pirates. "And could he ever fly around those bases!" Sewell said of Vaughan. "I never saw anybody who could go from first to third or from second to home faster than Vaughan. Like we used to say, when he went around second, his hip pocket was dipping sand. That's how sharp he cut those corners."[68]

McHugh acknowledged that Vaughan was not an outstanding defensive shortstop, but noted that he led the league in putouts or assists six times. Even without the defensive stats, McHugh wrote, "it could not be more obvious that he belonged in the Hall of Fame. Fifteen shortstops have preceded him there. With the exception of Honus Wagner, Vaughan outhit every one."[69]

One Vaughan fan—Robert E. Howell, of Emlenton—took McHugh to task for his comments regarding Vaughan's defensive shortcomings. "Vaughan made errors on balls other shortstops never would have touched. His range was amazing," he wrote in a letter to the editor of *The Pittsburgh Press*. "As for his hitting, there was a glaring omission in the article. His most remarkable statistic was that, although he was not in the Pirates' all-time top 10 players in games played or times at bat, he was in the top 10 for lifetime statistics in runs, hits, singles, doubles, triples, total bases, runs batted in and extra base hits."[70]

◆◆ 13 ◆◆

His Place
in History

It's clear that Arky Vaughan had his legion of staunch fans, many of whom were not shy about vouching on his behalf for decades after his tragic death in an attempt to persuade Hall of Fame voters that his bust deserved to be displayed in Cooperstown. But what do the experts have to say about Vaughan's ranking among the game's greatest shortstops—and the greatest players in general?

Bill James, a baseball historian who helped usher a number of statistical innovations into the mainstream, ranked Vaughan as the 39th-greatest player of all time—and the second-greatest shortstop behind only Honus Wagner. Vaughan's ranking, James noted in his book *The New Bill James Historical Baseball Abstract*, "was as much of a surprise to me as it is to you." James said that a lot of fans seem to simply forget about Vaughan when great shortstops are discussed. "I don't know how else to explain him," he wrote. James wrote that just about everyone rated Vaughan below both Joe Cronin and Lou Boudreau, who played roughly the same time that Vaughan did. "I don't see that," James wrote. "He was a better hitter than Cronin or Boudreau, he was faster—a lot faster than Boudreau." While he said just about any knowledgeable baseball fan would name Honus Wagner as the greatest of all shortstops, "almost no one, asked to name the second-greatest shortstop of all time, would turn immediately to Arky Vaughan. I believe, nonetheless, that Vaughan is the best answer to the question."[1]

James pointed to Vaughan's stellar 1935 season and noted that Vaughan's three best seasons—1934, '35 and '36—are better than the three best seasons of any other shortstop other than Wagner. During that stretch, Vaughan batted .351, was tops in the National League in walks all three seasons and scored more than 100 runs each season. He averaged 13 home runs, 11 triples and 35 doubles over that stretch. With the glove, he rated above-average in terms of fielding percentage the first two years and "dead on the league average the third season," James wrote. He also wrote that Vaughan's best five-year stretch was "far better" than the best five consecutive seasons of any other shortstop, other than Wagner.

James uses a statistical category known as Win Shares in helping to rank players. Win Shares, according to Bill James Online, "are a calculation of the number of wins a player contributed to his team. We credit each team with three Win Shares for each win. If a team wins 100 games, the players on that team will be credited with 300 Win Shares, according to their contributions at bat, on the mound and in the field. The quality of a team does not affect an individual player's Win Shares."[2] Vaughan, James wrote, had the second-best career average of Win Shares per-game of all time among shortstops, behind only Wagner. James acknowledged that Vaughan was not an exceptional defensive shortstop and said that Vaughan ranks among the bottom 25 of the top 50 shortstops when it comes to fielding. But, he said, other potential No. 2 candidates in the all-time shortstop rankings were defensively good but not great. James wrote that while many consider shortstop a defense-first position, the defensive differences between Vaughan and other potential No. 2 candidates behind Wagner could not possibly make up for the offensive advantages that Vaughan brought to the table at that position.

James elaborated on Vaughan's standing in a post to his website, billjamesonline.com, in February 2018. "It is difficult to overstate how wide-ranging Vaughan's offensive skills were; he was a lifetime .318 hitter who would be among the National League leaders at various times in everything except homers," he wrote. James noted that at age 21, Vaughan was fifth in the National League in total bases and RBIs and third in on-base percentage. The next season, he was fourth in runs scored, third in doubles, fifth in batting average, and led the league in on-base percentage. During the 1935 season, when Vaughan batted a major league-leading .385, he also led the National League in walks with 97, on-base percentage at .491 and slugging percentage at .607. The .491 on-base percentage, James noted, still stands as a Pirates franchise record and the major-league record for a shortstop.[3]

James wrote that Vaughan reached a "very, very high peak value" and was the best shortstop in baseball for eight years—from 1933 through 1940. Although he had what was considered an off-year for him in 1941—the year that Frisch chose to keep him on the bench for several stretches—he still batted .318 with a .399 on-base percentage. James pointed out that Vaughan walked away from baseball for three seasons after the 1943 campaign, when he was just 31 years old and was coming off what James termed a "tremendous season," hitting .305 and leading the National League in both runs scored with 112 and stolen bases with 20. He was still considered the NL's top shortstop at that time.[4]

James opined that Vaughan's dustup with Durocher had something to do with Vaughan's decision to stay away from the game for three seasons, despite his family's claims to the contrary. "To put this in context, a manager in that era had more power relative to a player than he does now, and managers—like all people given power—sometimes abused their power," James wrote on his website.[5] James pointed out that managers in that era would ridicule players to both the public and the media and that Durocher was one of the worst. Although Vaughan came back in 1947 and batted .325, he was gone from the big leagues after 1948. James wrote that Vaughan had to wait "an astonishingly long time" to finally gain entrance to the Hall of Fame and noted that Vaughan "never did achieve star status commensurate with his on-field performance." James said he'd be surprised if anyone else who was the best at his position for eight years had to wait 37 years to be selected to the Hall of Fame.[6]

James tried to come up with reasons why this was the case, and came up with four factors. First, he said that while there is "relatively little doubt" that Vaughan could have gotten close to 3,000 hits if he hadn't walked away from the game in 1943, he did finish with "only" 2,103 hits and "relatively modest counting numbers in other areas." This, James surmised, "no doubt lessened his historic nature."[7]

Another factor, he wrote, is that Wagner's "giant shadow" as a Pirates shortstop might have dwarfed any impressions that Vaughan might have made. Third, Vaughan's early departure from the game deprived him of what James called the "myth-making" years. "An aging player, as he nears the gold watch, sometimes benefits from three years of hagiography," James wrote, and gave several examples, including Derek Jeter. "Vaughan skipped that portion of his career," he wrote. The last factor that James mentioned was that Vaughan was not part of the Cardinals-Giants "cabal" that James said controlled the Veterans Committee voting in the 1970s.[8]

However, James said that while those factors could have shaped the way people viewed Vaughan after his career ended, he believes the perception problem with Vaughan started while he was still playing. He noted that Vaughan did not do well in balloting for the Most Valuable Player award and while he played in nine All-Star Games, he did not start every year even though his first-half performances could have warranted it. James said that one thing that worked against Vaughan is that his walk totals and on-base percentages, which are so highly valued today, "would have been entirely invisible in that era." James wrote that fans would not have known about such numbers, and even the writers generally would not have known. "The fact that Vaughan led the league in errors, in that era, would have been noted much more often than the fact that he often led the league in walks," James said, alluding to the three seasons in which Vaughan topped the NL in errors. James also pointed out that despite Vaughan's error totals, he led the league in putouts three times and assists three times, and his career fielding percentage at shortstop—.951—"is the same as Joe Cronin's and three points higher than the other Hall of Fame shortstop of his era, Luke Appling." James' final conclusion? "He just didn't break through with the public as the player that he was."[9]

Bill Felber, who has written multiple baseball books, studied what he considered to be the 24 best shortstops, not including those who played in the Negro Leagues, and after a mathematical comparison placed Vaughan as the third-greatest shortstop of all time behind Wagner and runner-up Cal Ripken. Felber looked at a factor he refers to as Wins Above Average, or WAA, which compares a player to the average major league player, and also took into consideration plate appearances in the years when their primary position was shortstop.[10]

Felber said that his No. 3 ranking of Vaughan is likely much higher than most people would view him. "I think a lot would put Ozzie Smith, Barry Larkin and a couple of other guys ahead of him," he said. "They're good, but what my system shows is basically that Arky Vaughan is underrated historically." Felber said several reasons play into Vaughan being so underrated— the fact that he played in an era before mass media exploded on the scene, and playing in Pittsburgh also worked against him when it came to achieving notoriety. "He didn't play in a big market," Felber said. "He didn't get any radio/TV exposure to speak of." And, Felber noted, Vaughan died at age 40. "He wasn't around to tout himself for very long after he retired," he said. "It was fortunate for him that he got into the Hall of Fame because, frankly, it would be very easy to overlook him."[11]

Rob Neyer, a well-known contemporary baseball writer and a former research aide to James, said he's always been struck by how quickly people seemed to forget about Vaughan's greatness. "I expect it was acknowledged in his time," Neyer said. "He never won an MVP award, but he was an all-star for the great majority of his career. And he finished in the top three of the MVP voting a couple of times. It was clear that people realized he was a tremendous player. But it does seem that he was quickly forgotten. Maybe something else was going on. It's hard to understand from this distance."[12] Neyer said the fact that Vaughan died so young—and so soon after his retirement—absolutely hurt his Hall of Fame candidacy. If Vaughan had lived longer, he no doubt would have been the focus of some media attention over the years, and been more front-and-center in the Hall voters' minds. Neyer also said that Vaughan's argument with Durocher in 1943 might also have hurt his cause with the voters. "This is purely subjective, but I think the writers of that era were more sympathetic with management than with labor," he said. "I think that rebelling against management, as he did, however briefly, hurt him in the minds of some of the writers at that time. Writers of the time felt much more so than today that if someone offered you a dollar and a uniform, you should be happy."[13]

Vaughan's decision to walk away from the game for three years also likely played into his failure to garner much support among Hall of Fame voters during his original eligibility period. Neyer explained:

> It clearly didn't help his numbers. And I think the voters always have been prejudiced against players who sort of faded away. Vaughan's retirement process was basically six years—he didn't play for three years and then he played part-time for two years and then spent a year in the minors. So you had six years where he wasn't a star anymore. It's easy for the writers watching all this to see a player fading away and thinking, well, there's not that much there. It's different if you go out on top or close to the top, playing every day, like Derek Jeter, and picking up the occasional big hit.[14]

Mark Langill, the Los Angeles Dodgers' team historian and publications editor, said Vaughan was part of several standout Brooklyn Dodgers clubs in the 1940s and certainly contributed to those teams. But he did so rather anonymously. "There's no one running around with Arky Vaughan stories," Langill said. "It's like with Burleigh Grimes—once the witnesses are gone, it's just another name. If you said the name Barney Dreyfuss 100 years ago, that's Mr. Pittsburgh. But now, who's that?"[15]

Donald Honig, a baseball historian who has written more than 40 books on the subject, said he often asked players from the 1930s and '40s about Vaughan because he was one of Honig's favorite players. All of them, he said, described Vaughan basically the same way: "He was a nice guy and a helluva player. But there are not many Vaughan anecdotes like you find with other players. I don't know if he was private, quiet, dull, or what. I just don't know. All I know is I never heard a bad word about him. From what I understand, he was just a very quiet, unassuming guy who went out and played ball. But many players were like that; especially in Vaughan's era, that was pretty much the norm."[16]

Bill Deane, a baseball historian, author and former senior research associate at the Baseball Hall of Fame in Cooperstown, New York, agreed with James in that Vaughan "did things that maybe weren't as valued back then that we understand now to be valuable things like drawing walks and showing good range even when making a lot of errors. Obviously he was an outstanding and underrated player. He had both power and speed, and that was the exception to the rule."[17]

Jay Jaffe, an author and contributing baseball writer for SI.com, in 2004 developed a system he calls JAWS—Jaffe WAR Score—that helps compare Hall of Fame candidates with those who've already gotten the Hall call. Among shortstops, Jaffe ranks Wagner No. 1 with a JAWS score of 98.1, followed by Alex Rodriguez (91.0), Cal Ripken (76.1), George Davis (64.5), Robin Yount

(62.3) and then Vaughan at No. 6 (61.8), one slot ahead of Ernie Banks and Ozzie Smith, who tied for seventh at 59.7.[18]

Jaffe said his score takes into account a player's career WAR with his peak WAR—his best seven seasons—both offensively and defensively. Jaffe said he wouldn't take Vaughan's No. 6 ranking as "the definitive be-all, end-all ranking because it doesn't incorporate postseason play, historical importance, or other subjective things you might want to consider. But it's a pretty good gauge of what he did." Jaffe said the biggest knock on Vaughan was his career length—or lack thereof. Of the top eight shortstops, all of them played at least 19 seasons except for Vaughan, who played 14—and had less than 300 at-bats in his final two seasons combined. "We're talking about a guy who walked away after his age 31 season and really only played two partial seasons after that. That's the worst thing I could say about him—he did not have a long career. But he had stellar hitting and solid glove work. Really, Wagner and [Rodriguez] are definitely the only two hitters better than him at the position."[19]

As one might expect, Vaughan's career and place in baseball history are of great interest to Pittsburgh area sports historians. Sam Reich, a local attorney and the author of a book titled *Waiting for Cooperstown*, compiled a list of the Pirates' top all-time players and placed Vaughan at No. 9. Reich rated Honus Wagner as No. 1, followed by Roberto Clemente, Paul Waner, Willie Stargell, Pie Traynor, Ralph Kiner, Max Carey, Bill Mazeroski and then Vaughan.

Reich used a point system but admitted that such systems aren't definitive. "I think they're helpful in getting clusters of players—especially point systems based on seasonal quality," he said. "They basically favor players who had longer careers and they give more premium than I believe is appropriate to less-than-great seasons." For example, Reich is not a huge fan of WAR and considers it to be substantially flawed. "The idea that you determine who's a great player by comparing them to fringe players—that would be like taking outstanding stage performers and comparing them to people in the chorus line. I believe the way to do it is you compare stars to stars and try to make a determination."[20]

As for Vaughan, Reich said, "Once you get past Wagner, I don't think there was a better-hitting shortstop in the National League. I don't think there was anyone close. His career in Pittsburgh was very impressive, but it wasn't exceptionally long, like the others' were." Reich said that in his estimation Vaughan registered five truly elite offensive seasons during his career and he was an elite hitter as a shortstop every year that he was a Pirates regular except 1941, when he played in only 106 games. Still, he batted .316 that season with an .854 OPS and slugged two home runs in the All-Star Game. Like James, Reich said he was puzzled by where Vaughan finished in the Most Valuable Player voting during his career, opining that

Vaughan's ranking wasn't commensurate with his production. Vaughan finished third in the voting twice—in 1935, when he batted .385, and in 1938 when he nearly led the Pirates to a National League pennant before the team's late collapse. But his next highest finish was 15th, which occurred twice—once in 1940 and again in his final season as a regular in 1943—and he also wound up 23rd in the voting three other times. "He wasn't always ranked nearly as high in the MVP ranking as I ranked him," Reich said.[21]

Ronald T. Waldo, a Pittsburgh author and baseball historian, said he sees Vaughan the way James does—as baseball's second-greatest shortstop ever, behind only Wagner. But he also said that Derek Jeter is "entering the equation. I say Arky is 2a and Jeter 2b after Wagner," he said. "Vaughan was a quiet player—he was not flashy, but he went out and did what he needed to do. There was a perception at times that he didn't hustle a lot. But I consider that a misconception. In regards to Pirate history, he definitely deserves a place up there with Wagner, Fred Clarke, the Waner brothers, Clemente and Stargell as one of the greats."[22]

David Finoli, a Pittsburgh author who has written more than two dozen books, has Vaughan slotted at No. 8 or No. 9 among all-time Pirate greats. "I go back and forth between him and Max Carey," Finoli said. "But if I was drafting a team, I'd take Arky in a heartbeat before Max when I think about it. He was one of the great hitters of that era—he had great gap power and he didn't strike out." Making Vaughan wait nearly 40 years to gain entrance to the Hall of Fame was a "crime," Finoli said, particularly given his run from 1934 to 1936 when he was possibly the best player in the game, or at least in the conversation. And for a five- or six-year stretch, Finoli said, he ranked among the game's elite. Those two factors, Finoli said, should have earned Vaughan more serious Hall consideration much earlier than it did.

To a large degree, it comes down to one's view of greatness. Is it very good play over a long period of time—the type of play that nets impressive numbers—or truly exceptional play, even if for a relatively short time frame? An example would be Don Sutton, who won 324 games over 23 years with five teams and never finished higher than third in the Cy Young Award voting vs. Sandy Koufax, who won 165 games over 12 years but won three Cy Young Awards and a Most Valuable Player award. "I'd rather take a guy like [Sandy] Koufax, who was superior for a short period of time," Finoli said. "And I'd classify Arky as that kind of player."[23]

At PNC Park, where today's version of the Pittsburgh Pirates play, on a section of a façade down the right field line hang 10 numbers: 1, 4, 8, 9, 11, 20, 21, 33, 40 and 42. The casual fan might have no idea what these numbers—which, at least as of the 2019 season were far too small for their lofty purpose—signify, given that no names are associated with them. The last one—42—belongs to Jackie Robinson, the former Brooklyn Dodgers star who shattered Major League Baseball's color barrier and whose number has been retired throughout Major League Baseball. Two of them belong to former Pirates managers. The other seven belong to former Pirates players—all of whom are in the Hall of Fame.

One manager is Billy Meyer, who led the team from 1948 to 1952 and compiled a 317–452 record. He is designated as No. 1. Danny Murtaugh, who wore No. 40 while guiding the Pirates to World Series titles in 1960 and 1971, is the other manager. The players—and their numbers—are Ralph Kiner (4), Willie Stargell (8), Bill Mazeroski (9), Paul Waner (11), Pie Traynor (20), Roberto Clemente (21), and Honus Wagner (33).

According to the Pirates, the Hall of Fame includes 42 players, managers and club executives who have ties to the Pittsburgh franchise, and 13 of them spent most of their time in the big leagues with the Pirates. Of the 13, 12 were players and five of them do not have their numbers or names hanging from the façade at PNC Park—Jake Beckley, Max Carey, Fred Clarke, Lloyd Waner, and Vaughan. Of the four who played their entire careers in the 20th century, Vaughan ranks No. 1 on a 162-game average in the categories of On Base + Slugging (.859), batting average (.318), RBIs (83), doubles (32) and home runs (nine). Vaughan also ranked No. 1 in career WAR with a 72.9 figure. Vaughan even ranks favorably with several of the players whose numbers *have* been retired by the Pirates. His career WAR stat, for example, trails only Wagner and Clemente and his 162-game average OPS mark of .859 trails Kiner, Stargell and Waner, and tops the others, including both Wagner and Clemente. His career stolen base total of 118 trails only Wagner and Traynor among the retired number crowd, and his per-season triples average (11) is tied for No. 4 with Clemente behind Wagner, Traynor and Waner.

Vaughan's numbers are very similar to that of Waner, the last Pirate to have his number retired. That occurred in 2007 after members of Waner's family visited PNC Park and found virtually no reminders of Waner's illustrious career. Waner played 20 seasons compared with Vaughan's 14, so Waner outranks Vaughan in terms of raw numbers in several categories. But when comparing on the basis of a 162-game average, Vaughan leads in runs (105 vs. 103), home runs (9 vs. 7), walks (83 vs. 69), stolen bases (11 vs. 7) and total bases (285 vs. 268). Waner has the edge in hits (200 vs. 187), doubles (38 vs. 32), triples (12 vs. 11), batting average (.333 vs. 318) and OPS (.878 vs. .859). The two tied in RBIs with 83 apiece.

So, should the Pirates add Vaughan's number to the list of retired digits? One complicating factor is that Vaughan did not wear just one number during his career with the Pirates. And the number he wore for the majority of his career—21—already has been retired, as it was worn by the great Clemente. However, it would not be unprecedented if the team also honored Vaughan by "re-retiring" that number; the New York Yankees recognize Bill

Dickey and Yogi Berra, both of whom wore No. 8. According to Baseball Reference, Vaughan wore No. 21 for the Pirates from 1932 through 1939, then switched to No. 3 in 1940, then wore No. 5 for part of the 1940 season and all of 1941, and he kept that number for the 1942–43 seasons while playing for Brooklyn. When Vaughan returned from tending his ranch and resumed his career with Brooklyn in 1947, he wore No. 9, which he also wore for his final season in the major leagues in 1948.

Kathleen Johnson Roberts, Vaughan's granddaughter and the keeper of much of Vaughan's baseball memorabilia, said she would love to see the Pirates retire her grandfather's number, and so would the rest of her family. "I don't follow baseball and I don't understand all of the statistics," she admitted. "But based on what I know, it would be a great way to honor him and recognize him for what he did during his playing days."

Would Arky care? "Off the top of my head, I would say no," Roberts said. "He wasn't really in it for the glory. He was in it for the love of the game—a way to do something he loved and to support his family and his other lifestyle, which was cattle ranching and being an outdoorsman. I don't think he was in it for the glory or having his name or his picture in the paper. For the family, we'd be absolutely thrilled—just like we were thrilled after people campaigned so hard to get him into the Hall of Fame. But for him, I don't really think it would matter."[24]

Chapter Notes

Chapter 1

1. Bill James, *The New Bill James Historical Baseball Abstract* (New York: Free Press, 2001), 592–594.
2. Patricia Vaughan Johnson, *"Arky": The Quiet Mr. Vaughan* (unpublished manuscript), September 1991, Microsoft Word file.
3. *Ibid.*
4. *Ibid.*
5. Steve Grimley, "Arky Vaughan: A Lone Star," *The Register* (Orange County, California), February 11, 1982, E16.
6. Johnson, *"Arky": The Quiet Mr. Vaughan.*
7. *Ibid.*
8. "San Diego Nine Wins Southland Prep Title," *Los Angeles Times*, June 9, 1929, 43.
9. "Indians Beat Whittier Nine in Hard Game," *The Weekly Pleiades* (Fullerton High School), May 25, 1930, 8.
10. Johnson, *"Arky": The Quiet Mr. Vaughan.*
11. Edward F. Balinger, "Vaughan New NL Batting Monarch Became Pirate Because Yank Scout Couldn't Be Two Places at Once," *The Sporting News*, October 24, 1935, n.p.
12. Lester J. Biederman, "The Scoreboard," *Pittsburgh Press*, May 10, 1948, 20.
13. "Schuchardt, Flyhawk, to Join El Paso," *Santa Ana Register*, January 19, 1931, 8.
14. "Vaughan Signed With Pittsburgh," *Fullerton Daily News Tribune*, January 10, 1931, n.p.
15. Edward F. Balinger, "Following the Bucs," *Pittsburgh Post-Gazette*, February 23, 1931 18.
16. Johnson, *"Arky": The Quiet Mr. Vaughan.*
17. "Rolly Meets a Rival," *Pittsburgh Post-Gazette*, March 12, 1931, 14.
18. Edward F. Balinger, "Following the Bucs," *Pittsburgh Post-Gazette*, March 11, 1931, 18.
19. Johnson, *"Arky": The Quiet Mr. Vaughan.*
20. *Ibid.*
21. *Ibid.*
22. Sec Taylor, "Demons Infield to Hold Slight Edge in Series," *Des Moines Register*, September 22, 1931, 9.
23. Louis H. Cook, "Imp Bats Smother Aviators, 11–6," *Des Moines Register*, September 26, 1931, 7.
24. Louis H. Cook, "Fog, Aviators Beat Imps," *Des Moines Register*, September 27, 1931, 15.
25. Sec Taylor, "Imps Capture Both Ends of Holiday Bill," *Des Moines Register*, September 28, 1931, 5.
26. Sec Taylor, "Wichita Homers Beat Demons," *Des Moines Register*, September 29, 1931, 7.
27. Sec Taylor, "Imps Capture Western Flag," *Des Moines Register*, September 30, 1931, 7.
28. "Each Imp Gets $177 for Series," *Des Moines Register*, September 30, 1931, 7.
29. Johnson, *"Arky": The Quiet Mr. Vaughan.*
30. Betty Allen Wagner, interviewed by Patricia Vaughan Johnson, n.d.
31. *Ibid.*
32. *Ibid.*
33. *Ibid.*
34. Johnson, *"Arky": The Quiet Mr. Vaughan.*
35. "No Buc Player in Line as Pilot," *Pittsburgh Press*, November 20, 1931, 32.
36. "Baseball Tidbits," *Pittsburgh Press*, November 21, 1931, 16.
37. "Buc Party Leaves for Minor Meet-

ing," *Pittsburgh Press*, December 1, 1931, 30.

38. Edward F. Balinger, "Baseball Gossip," *Pittsburgh Post-Gazette*, December 12, 1931, 18.

39. Volney Walsh, "Quirk of Fate Made Arky Vaughan Pirate, Not Yankee," *Pittsburgh Press*, May 8, 1935, 30.

Chapter 2

1. "Barney Dreyfuss, Owner of Pirate Club, Dies," *Pittsburgh Press*, February 5, 1932, 1.

2. "Game Loses Great Figure, Says Ens," *Pittsburgh Press*, February 5, 1932, 34.

3. Fred Wertenbach, "Dreyfuss' Death Revives Rumors of Pirates' Sale," *Pittsburgh Press*, February 5, 1932, 34.

4. "Pirate Squad Off for Camp Tonight," *Pittsburgh Post-Gazette*, February 17, 1932, 14.

5. "Pirate Reserve Material Strongest in Years," *Pittsburgh Press*, March 11, 1932, 36.

6. "Regulars and Yanigans Draw in 11 Innings," *Pittsburgh Post-Gazette*, March 12, 1932, 14.

7. "Floyd Vaughan Features in Both Contests with Sensational Fielding and Heavy Hitting," *Pittsburgh Post-Gazette*, March 14, 1932, 14.

8. "Buccos Split Double Bill at Oakland," *Pittsburgh Press*, March 14, 1932, 25.

9. "Suhr Leads Buc Hitters in Training," *Pittsburgh Press*, March 15, 1932, 29.

10. Edward F. Balinger, "Pirates of 1932," *Pittsburgh Post-Gazette*, March 17, 1932, 14.

11. Havey J. Boyle, "Mirrors of Sport," *Pittsburgh Post-Gazette*, March 18, 1932, 15.

12. "Western League Flash Impresses Gibson; Piet, Jensen, Dugas, Barbee and Swift Look Good in Exhibitions," *Pittsburgh Post-Gazette*, March 22, 1932, 14.

13. "Floyd Vaughan Visits Family in Fullerton," *Fullerton News Tribune*, March 26, 1932, n.p.

14. John B. Foster, "J.B. Foster Sizes Up Major Teams Training on Pacific Coast," *The Sporting News*, March 24, 1932, 3.

15. "Fullerton Boy Sensation of Pirate Training Camp," *Santa Ana Register*, March 29, 1932, 8.

16. Edward F. Balinger, "Meine Continues as Firm Buc Holdout," *Pittsburgh Post-Gazette*, April 2, 1932, 16.

17. "Brame and Bivin Touched for 20

Blows by Texans," *Pittsburgh Post-Gazette*, April 4, 1932, 15.

18. Chester L. Smith, "The Village Smithy," *Pittsburgh Press*, April 12, 1932, 23.

19. Edward F. Balinger, "Pirates and Cardinals Set for Opener," *Pittsburgh Post-Gazette* April 12, 1932, 14.

20. "Flashes for Pirates," *The Sporting News*, April 14, 1932, 1.

21. Betty Allen Wagner, interviewed by Patricia Vaughan Johnson, n.d.

22. Edward F. Balinger, "Pirate Rally in Ninth Downs Reds, 4–3, *Pittsburgh Post-Gazette*, April 18, 1932, 14.

23. "Pirate Club Developing Real Punch," *Pittsburgh Press*, April 18, 1932, 28.

24. "Buccaneer Bunts," *Pittsburgh Press*, April 23, 1932, 9.

25. Fred Wertenbach, "Floyd Looks Like Star in Local Debut," *Pittsburgh Press*, April 29, 39.

26. Fred Wertenbach, "Poor Mound Work Cause of Bucco Losing Streak," *Pittsburgh Press*, May 2, 1932, 24.

27. Fred Wertenbach, "Inexperience of Buc Infield May Hamper Winning Chances," *Pittsburgh Press*, May 4, 1932, 28.

28. Chester L. Smith, "The Village Smithy," *Pittsburgh Press*, May 6, 1932, 39.

29. Edward F. Balinger, "Pirates Lose Third, Bow to Phils, 4 to 2," *Pittsburgh Post-Gazette*, May 7, 1932, 16.

30. Havey J. Boyle, "Mirrors of Sport," *Pittsburgh Post-Gazette*, May 7, 1932, 17.

31. Havey J. Boyle, "Mirrors of Sport," *Pittsburgh Post-Gazette*, May 10, 1932, 15.

32. Fred Wertenbach, "Pirates Dicker for Trade with Dodgers," Pittsburgh Press May 17, 1932, 25.

33. Havey J. Boyle, "Mirrors of Sport," *Pittsburgh Post-Gazette*, June 4, 1932, 15.

34. "Chester L. Smith, "The Village Smithy," *Pittsburgh Press*, June 6, 1932, 25.

35. "Bucco Bats Big Aid to Win Streak," *Pittsburgh Press*, June 8, 1932, 25.

36. Fred Wertenbach, "Bucs Rated Real Pennant Contender," *Pittsburgh Press*, July 5, 1932, 24.

37. Edward F. Balinger, "Fisticuffs Mark Morning Win, 9–6; Take Second, 6–5," *Pittsburgh Post-Gazette*, July 5, 1932, 14.

38. Eddie West, "West Winds," *Santa Ana Register*, July 12, 1932, 6.

39. Frank Graham, "A Close-Up of Floyd Vaughan," *New York Sun*, July 28, 1932, n.p.

40. *Ibid.*

41. "The Pirates—Are They Champions?" *Pittsburgh Press*, July 28, 1932, 21.

42. Edward F. Balinger, "Baseball Gossip," *Pittsburgh Post-Gazette*, August 4, 1932, 14.

43. "Pirates Lose Fifth Straight," *Pittsburgh Press*, August 4, 1932, 1.

44. "Pirates Failure To Win Close Games Costly," *Pittsburgh Press*, August 8, 1932, 19.

45. Fred Wertenbach, "Cracked?—Nonsense, Says Manager Gibson," *Pittsburgh Press*, August 11, 1932, 22.

46. Havey J. Boyle, "Mirrors of Sport," *Pittsburgh Post-Gazette*, August 11, 1932, 13.

47. Fred Wertenbach, "Bucs Win Opener, 3–2; Giants Cop Second, 8–1," *Pittsburgh Press*, August 21, 1932, 13.

48. "Hero or Goat—No Middle Course for Him," Pittsburgh Press, August 22, 1932, 18.

49. *Ibid.*

50. Fred Wertenbach, "Vaughan Hurt, Leaves Battle," *Pittsburgh Press*, August 27, 1932, 1.

51. Chester L. Smith, "The Village Smithy," *Pittsburgh Press*, September 5, 1932, 12.

52. Ralph Davis, "New Buc Contract Coming for Gibson," *The Sporting News*, September 15, 1932, 3.

53. Edward F. Balinger, "Baseball Gossip," *Pittsburgh Post-Gazette*, October 27, 1932, 15.

54. *Ibid.*

55. *Ibid.*

56. Volney Walsh, "Honus Wagner Happy to be Associated with Pirate Baseball Club Once More," *Pittsburgh Press*, February 3, 1933, 35.

57. "Call Vaughan, Fullerton Boy, Second Hans Wagner," *Santa Ana Register*, February 16, 1933, 6.

58. *Ibid.*

59. "Pirate Star Father," *Fullerton News Tribune*, February 23, 1933, n.p.

60. Edward F. Balinger, "Baseball Gossip," *Pittsburgh Post-Gazette*, March 2, 1933, 14.

61. Volney Walsh, "Swetonic Comes Through First Test Nicely," *Pittsburgh Post-Gazette*, March 15, 1933, 21.

62. Chester L. Smith, "The Village Smithy," *Pittsburgh Press*, April 19, 1933, 25.

63. Betty Allen Wagner, interviewed by Patricia Vaughan Johnson, n.d.

64. Volney Walsh, "Vaughan's Fine Play Stands Out for Bucs," *Pittsburgh Press*, July 13, 1933, 25.

65. Al Abrams, "'There They Are, Arky,'

Latest Yell," *Pittsburgh Post-Gazette*, July 15, 1933, 13.

66. *Ibid.*

67. "'Won't Stand for That Kind of Stuff'—Gibson," *Pittsburgh Post-Gazette*, August 3, 1933, 14.

68. *Ibid.*

69. *Ibid.*

70. *Ibid.*

71. Havey J. Boyle, "Mirrors of Sport," *Pittsburgh Post-Gazette*, September 23, 1933, 15.

72. Johnson, *"Arky": The Quiet Mr. Vaughan.*

73. Volney Walsh, "New Ball Won't Hurt Pirates, Says Gibby," *Pittsburgh Press*, January 13, 1934, 20.

74. "Floyd Vaughan Holdout; Pay Cut Revealed," *Santa Ana Register*, March 2, 1934, 12.

75. Volney Walsh, "Vaughan Signs as Second Buc Squad Reports," *Pittsburgh Post-Gazette*, March 8, 1934, 26.

76. Eddie West, "West Winds," *Santa Ana Register*, March 13, 1934, 6.

77. Volney Walsh, "New League Ball Means More Speed," *Pittsburgh Press*, March 13, 1934, 27.

78. Volney Walsh, "Pie Gets Arky New Glove—He's Goin' to Town," *Pittsburgh Post-Gazette*, June 29, 1934, 37.

79. Chester L. Smith, "Vaughan Should be Northwest Mountie; 'Always Gets His Man,' Bartell Charges," *Pittsburgh Press*, May 25, 1934, 61.

80. Chester L. Smith, "The Village Smithy," *Pittsburgh Press*, June 26, 1934, 26.

81. Chilly Doyle, "Buc Shortstop Seen as Best in Game," *Pittsburgh Sun-Telegraph*, June 27, 1934, n.p.

82. Al Abrams, "Sidelights on Sports," *Pittsburgh Post-Gazette*, December 27, 1934, 15.

Chapter 3

1. "Pennsylvania and the Great Depression," Explorepahistory.com, http://explorepahistory.com/story.php?storyId=1-9-1B, accessed June 1, 2016.

2. Caroline Fellinger, in discussion with the author, July 14, 2017.

3. *Ibid.*

4. United States Census Bureau, Historical Statistics of the United States, Colonial Times to 1957, Chapter D. Labor. https://www2.

census.gov/library/publications/1960/
compendia/hist_stats_colonial-1957/hist_
stats_colonial-1957-chD.pdf?#, accessed
July 3, 2017.

5. "County Relief Cases Nearing Total of
70,000," *Pittsburgh Post-Gazette*, September
15, 1935, 3.

6. Gilbert Love, "One Out of 5 in County
on Relief Rolls," *Pittsburgh Press*, November
25, 1934, 1.

7. "320,000 in County on Relief or Pen-
sions, *Pittsburgh Sun-Telegraph*, October 9,
1938, n.p.

8. Caroline Fellinger, in discussion with
the author, July 14, 2017.

9. *Ibid.*

10. *Ibid.*

11. Hal Demich, in discussion with the
author, May 14, 2018.

12. *Ibid.*

13. *Ibid.*

14. "President Expresses 'Intense Sympathy' for Idle Marchers," *Pittsburgh Press*,
January 7, 1932, 1.

15. William G. Lytle Jr., "City Cheers
Jobless Army," *Pittsburgh Press*, January 8,
1932, 1.

16. Charles C. Alexander, *Breaking the
Slump: Baseball in the Depression Era* (New
York: Columbia University Press, 2002), 63,
101.

17. "Depression," *The Sporting News*,
December 31, 1931, 4.

18. David G. Surdam, *Wins, Losses and
Empty Seats: How Baseball Outlasted the
Great Depression* (Lincoln: University of
Nebraska Press, 2011).

19. Sports Reference LLC, "Major
League Baseball Attendance and Team
Age," Baseball-Reference.com, Major League
Statistics and Information, https://www.
baseball-reference.com/. Accessed June 3,
2017.

20. "Nation's Experts See Sports Boom,"
New York Times, December 23, 1936.

21. "Frick Sees League Facing Great
Year," *New York Times*, January 5, 1937.

Chapter 4

1. Patricia Vaughan Johnson, interview-
ing Betty Allen Wagner, n.d.

2. Edward F. Balinger, "Bucs and
Cardinals May Swing Deal," *Pittsburgh
Post-Gazette*, January 12, 1935, 15.

3. Edward F. Balinger, "Arky Vaughan

Sure to Keep Regular Job," *Pittsburgh
Post-Gazette*, January 24, 1935, 15.

4. "The Fans' Say-So," *Pittsburgh Press*,
January 4, 1935, 38.

5. Willie Q. Pryor, "Vaughan Again Holdout; Rejects Slash," *Santa Ana Register*, January 14, 1935, 6.

6. Chester L. Smith, "The Village Smithy,"
Pittsburgh Press, March 6, 1935, 29.

7. Volney Walsh, "Cold Weather Won't
Let Bucs Get Hot!" *Pittsburgh Press*, April
13, 1935, 7.

8. Chester L. Smith, "The Village Smithy,"
Pittsburgh Press, May 27, 1935, 27.

9. Art Rosenbaum, "Overheard," *San
Francisco Chronicle*, March 20, 1949, n.p.

10. Arky Vaughan, "Shortstop Must
Have Rifle Arm, Be Fast and Cover Lots of
Ground, Says Vaughan," *Pittsburgh Press*,
July 6, 1935, 7.

11. Havey J. Boyle, "Mirrors of Sport,"
Pittsburgh Post-Gazette, July 9, 1935, 14.

12. "Sports Stew," *Pittsburgh Press*, July
24, 1935, 20.

13. Dennis Bethem, in discussion with
the author, July 6, 2016.

14. Volney Walsh, "Vaughan Aims for
.400 Batting Average," *Pittsburgh Press*,
August 2, 1935, 31.

15. Sam Levy, "Sports Chatter," *Milwaukee Journal*, July 12, 1935, 9.

16. Al Abrams, "Sidelights on Sports,"
Pittsburgh Post-Gazette, August 1, 1935,
17.

17. Bill McCullough, "Arky Least Publi-
cized Sport Star," n.p., August 20, 1935.

18. Harry Grayson, "Vaughan, .400
left-handed hitter; Stars in Golf Right-
handed," *The News Journal* (Wilmington,
Delaware), August 18, 1935, 35.

19. "Vaughan, Pirates' Clouting Shortstop, Headed for Rare Circle of .400 Hitters,"
Young America, July 15, 1935.

20. Tommy Holmes, "Vaughan Is Likely
to Capture Hit Title," *Brooklyn Daily Eagle*,
August 20, 1935, 8.

21. Jack Cuddy, "Vaughan, the Pupil, May
Surpass Wagner, the Teacher," *Pittsburgh
Press*, August 21, 1935, 27.

22. Grantland Rice, "Vaughan Says
Change in Bat Helped Him Hit at .400 Clip,"
Baltimore Sun, September 5, 1935, 16.

23. *Ibid.*

24. "Vaughan Irks Traynor Now!" n.p.,
August 27, 1935, n.p.

25. *Ibid.*

26. Al Abrams, "Vaughan Sets Out to

Crack Hitting Mark," *Pittsburgh Post-Gazette*, August 20, 1935, 14.

27. Volney Walsh, "Mates Meet Cub Invasion with 'Little Poison' Out," *Pittsburgh Press*, August 31, 1935, 7.

28. Volney Walsh, "Double-Header Scheduled with Pirates as Second Game of Series is Delayed," *Pittsburgh Press*, September 9, 1935, 24.

29. "Vaughan's Average Shrinks, but He Leads League," *Pittsburgh Press*, September 29, 1935, 22.

30. Edgar G. Brands, "Greenberg and Vaughan Named as Majors' Most Valuable," *The Sporting News*, October 3, 1935, 5.

31. Johnson, *"Arky": The Quiet Mr. Vaughan.*

32. "Welcome Home!—'Arky' Vaughan!" *Fullerton Daily News Tribune*, October 7, 1935, 5.

33. "Arky Vaughan Honored by Friends at Banquet," *Fullerton Daily News Tribune*, October 9, 1935, 1, 3.

34. *Ibid.*

35. Johnson, *"Arky": The Quiet Mr. Vaughan.*

36. Eddie West, "West Winds," *Santa Ana Register*, February 13, 1936, 6.

37. "'Arky' Vaughan Shows Great Skill as Golfer," *Los Angeles Times*, February 10, 1936, 28.

38. Volney Walsh, "Cornell University Pitcher Goes to Camp with Pirates," *Pittsburgh Press*, October 15, 1935, 25.

39. Edward F. Balinger, "Vaughan, New N.L. Batting Monarch, Became Pirate Because Yank Scout Couldn't Be Two Places at Once," *The Sporting News*, October 24, 1935, 3.

40. Edward F. Balinger, "Traynor to Take Only 35 Players to Camp," *Pittsburgh Post-Gazette*, November 9, 1935, 19.

41. Grantland Rice, "'Tis a Long Trail When Arky Vaughan Sets Out After Cobb," *Pittsburgh Press*, January 5, 1936, 15.

42. Volney Walsh, "Vaughan's No Holdout Yet?" *Pittsburgh Press*, January 28, 1936, 18.

43. Edward F. Balinger, "Vaughan Joins Holdout Set, Asks More Pay," *Pittsburgh Post-Gazette*, January 28, 1936, 16.

44. Al Abrams, "Sidelights on Sports," *Pittsburgh Post-Gazette*, February 10, 1936, 15.

45. Arky Vaughan, "My Greatest Thrill," *Pittsburgh Post-Gazette*, February 12, 1936, 16.

46. *Ibid.*

47. "Sports Stew—Served Hot," *Pittsburgh Press*, March 18, 1936, 24.

48. Edward F. Balinger, "Vaughan Comes to Terms with Bucs," *Pittsburgh Post-Gazette*, February 18, 1936, 18.

49. "Traynor Sees 'Quarterback' Todd Big Help," *Pittsburgh Post-Gazette*, March 13, 1936, 20.

50. Chester L. Smith, "The Village Smithy," *Pittsburgh Press*, April 22, 1936, 26.

51. Havey J. Boyle, "Mirrors of Sport," *Pittsburgh Post-Gazette*, April 23, 1936, 18.

52. Edward F. Balinger, "Traynor Sees Four Team Race," *Pittsburgh Post-Gazette*, May 19, 1936, 18.

53. Jack Cuddy, "Vaughan Isn't Hitting—Looking for Luck Charms," *Pittsburgh Press*, June 28, 1936, 28.

54. *Ibid.*

55. *Ibid.*

56. Chester L. Smith, "The Village Smithy," *Pittsburgh Press*, May 22, 1936, 46.

57. Havey J. Boyle, "Mirrors of Sport," *Pittsburgh Post-Gazette*, June 9, 1936, 18.

58. "'Why Didn't Arky and Gus Play?' Buc Fans Ask," *Pittsburgh Press*, July 8, 1936, 23.

59. "C'mon Bucs, Let's Have Fun! Phils are Here," *Pittsburgh Post-Gazette*, July 9, 1936, 30.

60. Chester L. Smith, "Here's a Dollar, Save the Bees," *Pittsburgh Press*, July 17, 1936, 31.

61. "Sports Stew—Served Hot," *Pittsburgh Press*, July 22, 1936, 22.

62. The Old Scout, "Vaughan Holds Luck Plays Big Part in Hitting," n.p., July 29, 1936, n.p.

63. "The Benchwarmer," *Pittsburgh Post-Gazette*, August 17, 1936, 19.

64. Edward F. Balinger, "Series to Break Money Records," *Pittsburgh Post-Gazette*, October 6, 1936, 20.

65. Regis Welsh, "'I'll Trade Anyone Except Vaughan,' Traynor Says," *Pittsburgh Press*, October 30, 1936, 51.

66. John Neubauer, "Vaughan Off on Hunting Trip After Day in Fullerton; 'Homecoming' Later," *Santa Ana Register*, October 6, 1936, 6.

67. Triangle Food Store advertisement, *Pittsburgh Press*, May 21, 1937, 44.

68. Huskies Cereal advertisement, *Pittsburgh Press*, June 25, 1937, n.p.

69. Havey J. Boyle, "Bucs Reveal Cards' Demand for Dizzy," *Pittsburgh Post-Gazette*, November 28, 1936, 16.

70. Edward F. Balinger, "Traynor Hopeful of Swinging Big Deal for Buccos," *Pittsburgh Post-Gazette*, December 1, 1936, 18.

71. Julius Rottluff, interviewed by Patricia Vaughan Johnson, n.d.

72. Claire Burcky, "Arky Remains at Shortstop," *Pittsburgh Press*, March 16, 1937, 26.

73. Jack Guenther, "Takes Luck, and Plenty of It, to Win Batting Title, Bucs' Arky Vaughan Says," *Pittsburgh Press*, March 23, 1937, 26.

74. William Weer, "Sabotage is Hunted in Hindenburg Blast; Threats Revealed by Eckener; 32 Dead," *Brooklyn Daily Eagle*, May 7, 1937, 1.

75. "English Says Vaughan Is Whistling Shortstop," n.p., May 7, 1937, n.p.

76. Chester L. Smith, "Loss of Vaughan Costly Win Price," *Pittsburgh Press*, July 12, 1937, 23.

77. Edward F. Balinger, "Bees Down Pirates Twice, 5–2, 7–5," *Pittsburgh Post-Gazette*, July 26, 1937, 15.

78. "Bucs Sing 'Monday Morning Blues,'" *Pittsburgh Press*, July 26, 1937, 27.

79. Havey J. Boyle, "Mirrors of Sport," *Pittsburgh Post-Gazette*, August 12, 1937, 16.

80. *Ibid.*

81. Lester Biederman, "Bucs Gain Third Place, Trounce Cards, 7–3," *Pittsburgh Press*, August 22, 1937, 17.

82. "Lucas Faces Dizzy Dean," *Pittsburgh Press*, August 22, 1937, 17.

83. Havey J. Boyle, "Mirrors of Sport," *Pittsburgh Post-Gazette*, October 14, 1937, 18.

84. Lester Biederman, "Bucs Place Vaughan on Trading Block," *Pittsburgh Press*, December 2, 1937, 28.

85. "Traynor Here, Still Seeks Mungo," *Pittsburgh Press*, December 21, 1937, 32.

86. "Scribbled by Scribes," *The Sporting News*, December 23, 1937, 4.

87. Johnson, *"Arky": The Quiet Mr. Vaughan.*

Chapter 5

1. Chester L. Smith, "The Village Smithy," *Pittsburgh Press*, January 5, 1938, 21.

2. Johnson, *"Arky": The Quiet Mr. Vaughan.*

3. Havey J. Boyle, "Mirrors of Sport," *Pittsburgh Post-Gazette*, January 13, 1938, 18.

4. The Old Scout, "Wagner Backs Arky Vaughan," February 15, 1938, n.p.

5. Franklin Delano Roosevelt, State of the Union Address, January 3, 1938, http://www.let.rug.nl/usa/presidents/franklin-delano-roosevelt/state-of-the-union-1938.php)

6. *Ibid.*

7. Edward F. Balinger, "New Baseball Aids Hurlers, Traynor Says," *Pittsburgh Post-Gazette*, January 13, 1938, 18.

8. Lester Biederman, "Benswanger talks trade with Cubs," *Pittsburgh Press*, February 1, 1938, 23.

9. Chester L. Smith, "The Village Smithy," *Pittsburgh Press*, March 8, 1938, 23.

10. Lester Biederman, "Vaughan Signs After Long Conference; Traynor Plans to Revamp Buc Infield," *Pittsburgh Press*, March 12, 1938, 7.

11. Chester L. Smith, "The Village Smithy," *Pittsburgh Press*, March 16, 1938, 25.

12. Lester Biederman, "Brown, Brandt Bucs' Choice Against Seals," *Pittsburgh Press*, March 24, 1938, 22.

13. "Scribes Pick Yanks and Cubs for 1938," *Pittsburgh Press*, March 30, 1938, 25.

14. "Vaughan to Become Sheep Rancher; Has Small Flock," *Pittsburgh Post-Gazette*, March 18, 1938, 14.

15. Special Section, *Fullerton Daily News Tribune*, March 30, 1938, n.p.

16. "Homer Hit by Vaughan as Pirates Welcomed," *Fullerton Daily News Tribune*, April 1, 1938, n.p.

17. "Pirate Notes," *Pittsburgh Post-Gazette*, April 13, 1938, 20.

18. "Pirate Patter—P. Waner Stopped," *Pittsburgh Press*, April 14, 1938, 30.

19. Edward F. Balinger, "Pirates Win First From Cards, 4 to 3," *Pittsburgh Post-Gazette*, April 20, 1938, 1.

20. Lester Biederman, "Win Close Ones! Bucs' New Slogan," *Pittsburgh Press*, April 28, 1938, 28.

21. "Pirate Patter—All in Day's Work!" *Pittsburgh Press*, April 28, 1938, 28.

22. "Arky's Little Admirer Sees Two Games from Dugout," *Pittsburgh Post-Gazette*, May 31, 1938, 13.

23. Chester L. Smith, "Pirates Are Awake to Their Opportunities," *Pittsburgh Press*, July 14, 1938, 25.

24. Al Abrams, "Sidelights on Sports," *Pittsburgh Post-Gazette*, July 23, 1938, 11.

25. "Arky's Speed Wins," *Pittsburgh Press*, July 28, 1938, 20.

26. Havey J. Boyle, "Mirrors of Sport," *Pittsburgh Post-Gazette*, August 15, 1938, 14.

27. "Pirate Patter—Arky Most Valuable," *Pittsburgh Press*, August 20, 1938, 7.

28. Lester Biederman, "Vaughan Takes Rank with Best Shortstops," *Pittsburgh Press*, August 28, 1938, 15.

29. *Ibid.*

30. Al Abrams, "Arky Vaughan Eyes Second Batting Title," *Pittsburgh Post-Gazette*, August 31, 1938, 10.

31. Havey J. Boyle, "Mirrors of Sport," *Pittsburgh Post-Gazette*, August 31, 1938, 10.

32. Chester L. Smith, "The Village Smithy," *Pittsburgh Press*, July 14, 1938, 25.

33. Lester Biederman, "Pirates Miss Vaughan's Booming Bat," *Pittsburgh Press*, September 6, 1938, 20.

34. Havey J. Boyle, "Mirrors of Sport," *Pittsburgh Post-Gazette*, September 10, 1938, 12.

35. Edward F. Balinger, "Arky Vaughan in Shape as Pirates Face Cards," *Pittsburgh Post-Gazette*, September 10, 1938, 10.

36. Dan Parker, "Scribbled by Scribes," *The Sporting News*, September 22, 1938, 4.

37. Lester Biederman, "Rain Again Delays Pirates and Dodgers," *Pittsburgh Press*, September 21, 1938, 16.

38. "Pirate Patter—Arky Most Valuable!" *Pittsburgh Press*, September 23, 1938, 39.

39. Grantland Rice, "The Sportlight," *Pittsburgh Post-Gazette*, September 26, 1938, 15.

40. Havey J. Boyle, "Mirrors of Sport," *Pittsburgh Post-Gazette*, September 26, 1938, 14.

41. *Ibid.*

42. "Chamberlain-Hitler 'Pact' Seen as Europe Peace Key," *Pittsburgh Press*, September 30, 1938, 1.

43. "Buc Lead at Stake in Cub Game Today," *Pittsburgh Press*, September 30, 1938, 1.

44. Lester Biederman, "Bucs Bank on Klinger to Keep Them in First Place," *Pittsburgh Press*, September 28, 1938, 24.

45. Claire M. Burcky, "Hard on Nerves!" *Pittsburgh Press*, September 28, 1938, 24.

46. Havey J. Boyle, "Mirrors of Sport," *Pittsburgh Post-Gazette*, September 29, 1938, 14.

47. Edward F. Ballinger, "Cubs Down Pirates, 6–5; Take Lead," *Pittsburgh Post-Gazette*, September 29, 1938, 14.

48. Lester Biederman, "A Homer ... Then Bedlam," *Pittsburgh Press*, September 29, 1938, 27.

49. *Ibid.*

50. *Ibid.*

51. "Pirate Patter—Gloom in Clubhouse!" *Pittsburgh Press*, September 29, 1938, 27.

52. Chilly Doyle, "Pirates Stake Flag Hopes on Russ Bauer's Pitching," *Pittsburgh Sun-Telegraph*, September 29, 1938, 14.

53. Havey J. Boyle, "Mirrors of Sport," *Pittsburgh Post-Gazette*, September 29, 1938, 14.

54. *Ibid.*

55. Lawrence S. Ritter, *The Glory of Their Times* (New York: William Morrow, 1984), 344.

56. Chester L. Smith, "The Village Smithy," *Pittsburgh Press*, September 30, 1938, 3.

57. *Ibid.*

58. Havey J. Boyle, "Mirrors of Sport," *Pittsburgh Post-Gazette*, September 30, 1938, 14.

59. Lester Biederman, "Pirates Hobble Home to Face Trade Talk," *Pittsburgh Press*, October 3, 1938, 21.

60. Chester L. Smith, "The Village Smithy," *Pittsburgh Press*, November 2, 1938, 25.

61. *Ibid.*

62. *Ibid.*

63. "Pirate Fans are Learning How to 'De-Certify' Checks," *Pittsburgh Press*, October 3, 1938, 1.

64. Lester Biederman, "Honors to Pirates, but Not Pennant," *Pittsburgh Press*, December 28, 1938, 19.

65. "Art Griggs Passes Away at L.A. Home," *Santa Ana Express*, December 19, 1938, 6.

Chapter 6

1. Johnson, *"Arky": The Quiet Mr. Vaughan.*

2. Havey J. Boyle, "Mirrors of Sport," *Pittsburgh Post-Gazette*, January 11, 1939, 14.

3. Edward F. Balinger, "Dizzy Dean Checks Pirates, 6 to 2," *Pittsburgh Post-Gazette*, May 29, 1939, 12.

4. Havey J. Boyle, "Mirrors of Sport," *Pittsburgh Post-Gazette*, May 29, 1939, 12.

5. Lester Biederman, "The Scoreboard," *Pittsburgh Press*, June 1, 1939, 28.

6. Lester Biederman, "The Scoreboard," *Pittsburgh Press*, July 2, 1939, 38.

7. "Wagner's Team Winner in Centennial Game, 4–2," *Pittsburgh Post-Gazette*, June 13, 1939, 13.

8. Leslie Avery, "Lou Gehrig's Career Ended," *Pittsburgh Press*, June 22, 1939, 22.

9. *Ibid.*

10. "Gehrig Never Will Return to Ball Game," *Pittsburgh Post-Gazette*, June 22, 1939, 1.

11. Jimmy Woods, "Sportopics," *Brooklyn Daily Eagle*, July 5, 1939, 16.

12. National Baseball Hall of Fame, https://baseballhall.org/discover-more/stories/baseball-history/lou-gehrig-luckiest-man, accessed July 5, 2018.

13. Havey J. Boyle, "Mirrors of Sport," *Pittsburgh Post-Gazette*, July 5, 1939, 12.

14. Lester Biederman, "The Scoreboard," *Pittsburgh Press*, July 8, 1939, 7.

15. Tommy Holmes, "N.L. Beaten but Not Disgraced As Arky Vaughan Sprouts Horns," *Brooklyn Daily Eagle*, July 12, 1939.

16. *Ibid.*

17. Audrey Smith Ifft, in discussion with the author, August 2017.

18. *Ibid.*

19. Johnson, *"Arky": The Quiet Mr. Vaughan.*

20. Dennis Wodzinski, in correspondence with the author, April 2018.

21. Legal notice, *Ukiah Republican Press*, March 16, 1949, 6.

22. Audrey Smith Ifft, in discussion with the author, August 2017.

23. Tom Smith, in discussion with the author, June 2017.

24. *Ibid.*

25. *Ibid.*

26. *Ibid.*

27. *Ibid.*

28. Lester Biederman, "The Scoreboard," *Pittsburgh Press*, July 20, 1939, 23.

29. "Caspar Wins from Potter," *Ukiah Republican Press*, July 19, 1939, 2.

30. Edward F. Balinger, "Traynor Quits, Successor in Dark," *Pittsburgh Post-Gazette*, September 29, 1939, 18.

31. "Ring Notables at Title Bout," *Pittsburgh Press*, September 26, 1939, 25.

32. Lester Biederman, "Bucs Give Frisch Two-Year Contract," *Pittsburgh Press*, October 1, 1939, 43.

33. Lester Biederman, "Frisch Demands Daring Baseball," *Pittsburgh Press*, October 3, 1939, 27.

34. Correspondence, Arky Vaughan to Tom and Helen Smith, October 5, 1939.

35. "Many Pirates Linked with Trade Rumors," *Pittsburgh Post-Gazette*, October 12, 1939, 15.

36. Correspondence, Arky Vaughan to fan, November 2, 1939.

37. Correspondence, Arky Vaughan to Tom and Helen Smith, November 3, 1939.

38. *Ibid.*

39. Johnson, *"Arky": The Quiet Mr. Vaughan.*

40. Barbara Dawson Maple, "Arky More Colorful Than He Was Perceived," *Los Angeles Times*, September 7, 1985, 274.

41. Dan Daniel, "New National Film Short and Snappy," *The Sporting News*, November 16, 1939, 6.

42. Edward F. Balinger, "Benswanger Still Opposed to Night Ball Games Here," *Pittsburgh Post-Gazette*, November 18, 1939, 15.

43. Lester Biederman, "Pirates Turn Down Brooklyn's First Offer for Slugger," *Pittsburgh Press*, December 5, 1939, 27.

44. Havey J. Boyle, "Mirrors of Sport," *Pittsburgh Post-Gazette*, December 6, 1939, 20.

45. Al Abrams, "Sidelights on Sports, *Pittsburgh Post-Gazette*, December 12, 1939, 17.

46. Chester L. Smith, "The Village Smithy," *Pittsburgh Press*, January 8, 1940, 18.

47. *Ibid.*

48. C.L.M. "The Soap Box," *Pittsburgh Press*, January 14, 1940, 29.

49. Lester Biederman, "The Scoreboard," *Pittsburgh Press*, February 12, 1940, 21.

50. Edward F. Balinger, "Seven Contests Under Lights are Listed This Year," *Pittsburgh Post-Gazette*, January 31, 1940, 14.

51. "Vaughan Hunting Coyotes, Bobcats," *Pittsburgh Post-Gazette*, February 20, 1940, 16.

52. Lester Biederman, "Pirates' Contract Troubles Ended As Arky Vaughan Signs," *Pittsburgh Press*, March 5, 1940, 24.

53. Lester Biederman, "The Scoreboard," *Pittsburgh Press*, March 6, 1940, 27.

54. *Ibid.*

55. Havey J. Boyle, "Mirrors of Sport," *Pittsburgh Post-Gazette*, March 6, 1940, 16.

56. Bob Ray, "The Sports X-Ray," *Los Angeles Times*, March 7, 1940, 11.

57. Al Abrams, "Sidelights on Sports, *Pittsburgh Post-Gazette*, March 6, 1940, 17.

58. Lester Biederman, "Rizzo, Vaughan

Lead Pirates in Hitting," *Pittsburgh Press*, April 3, 1940, 25.

59. Lester Biederman, "The Scoreboard," *Pittsburgh Press*, April 26, 1940, 47.

60. Edward F. Balinger, "Bucs' Hustle Proves Pleasing to Frisch," *Pittsburgh Post-Gazette*, April 18, 1940, 14.

61. Lester Biederman, "Bucco Pilot Seeking New Shortstop," *Pittsburgh Press*, May 14, 1940, 22.

62. Al Abrams, "Trade Break for Me—Johnny Rizzo," *Pittsburgh Post-Gazette*, May 9, 1940, 14.

63. "Clique of Pirates Loafing on Frisch?" *Brooklyn Daily Eagle*, May 10, 1940, 17.

64. Lester Biederman, "Pirates Resent 'Foreign' Talk of Dissension," *Pittsburgh Press*, May 17, 1940, 43.

65. Joseph W. Grigg Jr., "Hitler Cheered as Genius Who Makes War Decisions," *Pittsburgh Press*, June 5, 1940, 1.

66. Lester Biederman, "The Scoreboard," *Pittsburgh Press*, June 5, 1940, 40.

67. Chester L. Smith, "National League Sticks by the Old Guard," *Pittsburgh Press*, July 1, 1940, 23.

68. Lester Biederman, "The Scoreboard," *Pittsburgh Press*, July 1, 1940, 24.

69. Edward F. Balinger, "Arky Vaughan Upholds End in Usual Brilliant Style," *Pittsburgh Post-Gazette*, July 10, 1940, 14.

70. Havey J. Boyle, "Mirrors of Sport," *Pittsburgh Post-Gazette*, July 27, 1940, 12.

71. Chester L. Smith, "Like the Dodgers, We Look Ahead," *Pittsburgh Press*, July 28, 1940, 31.

72. Edward F. Balinger, "Fists Fly as Dodgers Beat Bucs, 7–6," *Pittsburgh Post-Gazette*, July 30, 1940, 12.

73. *Ibid.*

74. Tommy Holmes, "Feud with Bucs Finds Phelps a Changed Man," *Brooklyn Daily Eagle*, July 30, 1940, 13.

75. Frankie Gustine, in discussion with Patricia Vaughan Johnson, November 1989.

76. Lester Biederman, "The Scoreboard," *Pittsburgh Press*, July 30, 1940, 17.

77. Al Abrams, "Sidelights on Sports," *Pittsburgh Post-Gazette*, July 31, 1940, 13.

78. William Nack and David Fischer, "The Razor's Edge," *Sports Illustrated*, May 6, 1991. SI.com Accessed July 11, 2018.

79. Charles F. Faber, "Willard Hershberger," *Society for American Baseball Research*, Accessed July 11, 2018.

80. "Hershberger's Suicide Hard Blow to Redlegs," *Pittsburgh Press*, August 4, 1940, 29.

81. Havey J. Boyle, "Mirrors of Sport," *Pittsburgh Post-Gazette*, August 5, 1940, 14.

82. Bill Werber and C. Paul Rogers III, "Memories of a Ballplayer," *Society for American Baseball Research*, 2001, Accessed December 19, 2019.

83. Correspondence, Arky Vaughan to Tom and Helen Smith, October 2, 1940.

84. Havey J. Boyle, "Mirrors of Sport," *Pittsburgh Post-Gazette*, December 3, 1940, 16.

85. Lester Biederman, "The Scoreboard," *Pittsburgh Press*, November 27, 1940, 16.

86. *Ibid.*

87. Lester Biederman, "Buccaneer Bosses Spike Trade Rumors Involving Vaughan," *Pittsburgh Press*, December 10, 1940, 31.

88. Chester L. Smith, "Buccaneers Can Afford to Part with Vaughan," *Pittsburgh Press*, December 12, 1940, 31.

Chapter 7

1. Chester L. Smith, "Rookie Anderson is Good in Frisch's Book," *Pittsburgh Press*, February 4, 1941, 20.

2. Paul Scheffels, "Rookie Anderson Boomed to Succeed Vaughan—Look What He Has to Beat," *Pittsburgh Press*, February 11, 1941, 26.

3. Lester Biederman, "High Purchase Price Gives Anderson High Ideas—Snubs Pirate Contract," *Pittsburgh Press*, February 16, 1941, 51.

4. Edward F. Balinger, "Vaughan Signs After Brief Confab," *Pittsburgh Post-Gazette*, March 4, 1941, 14.

5. Lester Biederman, "The Scoreboard," *Pittsburgh Press*, March 4, 1941, 25.

6. Lester Biederman, "The Scoreboard," *Pittsburgh Press*, March 3, 1941, 23.

7. *Ibid.*

8. Lester Biederman, "Vaughan's Game-Winning Homer Chokes Frisch's Rave Over Defeats," *Pittsburgh Press*, March 27, 1941, 27.

9. "Vaughan Lost for Two Weeks," *Pittsburgh Post-Gazette*, April 25, 1941, 17.

10. Edward F. Balinger, "Vaughan Set to Return to Buc Lineup," *Pittsburgh Post-Gazette*, April 29, 1941, 16.

11. Lester Biederman, "The Scoreboard," *Pittsburgh Press*, April 26, 1941, 8.

12. Billy Conn, "Handlers Keep Close

Tab on Billy Conn," *Pittsburgh Post-Gazette*, June 12, 1941, 16.

13. "More Opinions on Conn, Louis," *Pittsburgh Press*, June 15, 1941, 29.

14. "Conn Battles Louis, Cupid and Irate Father of Girl 18," *Pittsburgh Press*, June 18, 1941, 1.

15. *Ibid.*

16. *Ibid.*

17. Joe Williams, "Conn Only Boxer to Win, Lose Title the Same Night," *Pittsburgh Press*, June 19, 1941, 22.

18. Harry Ferguson, "'Joe, I Got You,' Conn Tells Baffled Louis in Ninth—Then He Made Mistake," *Pittsburgh Press*, June 19, 1941, 22.

19. "Maybe I Had Too Much Guts,' Says Conn," *Pittsburgh Press*, June 19, 1941, 22.

20. "Fancy Footwork Scores…. Billy Disappears," *Pittsburgh Press*, June 19, 1941, 1.

21. "I Can't Be Married Today, Billy Says as Crowd Waits," *Pittsburgh Press*, June 20, 1941, 1.

22. "Billy Conn Married to Mary Lou—They're Both 'Scared to Death,'" *Pittsburgh Press*, July 6, 1941, 1.

23. "Billy Conn Breaks Left Hand in Fight with Wife's Father, Title Bout Cancelled," *Pittsburgh Post-Gazette*, May 12, 1942, 13.

24. John T. Whitaker, "Yield or Face Invasion, Nazi Threat to Russia," *Pittsburgh Press*, June 19, 1941, 1.

25. Harrison Salisbury, "Decisive Red-Nazi Battle Near," *Pittsburgh Press*, July 6, 1941, 1.

26. Edward F. Balinger, "Bucs Rally in Ninth to Score Win," *Pittsburgh Post-Gazette*, June 28, 1941, 12.

27. Chester L. Smith, "Captain Arky Vaughan's Odd Experience," *Pittsburgh Press*, July 2, 1941, 24.

28. Lester Biederman, "The Scoreboard," *Pittsburgh Press*, July 1, 1941, 26.

29. Anthony G. De Lorenzo, "Americans' Power Overshadows Grand Record by Vaughan," *Pittsburgh Press*, July 9, 1941, 22.

30. "An' How!" *Pittsburgh Press*, July 9, 1941, 22.

31. *Ibid.*

32. Lester Biederman, "The Scoreboard," *Pittsburgh Press*, July 9, 1941, 23.

33. Chester L. Smith, "American Leaguers Did Two Good Jobs," *Pittsburgh Press*, July 9, 1941, 22.

34. "Demand for Vaughan Doesn't

Feaze (*sic*) Frisch," *Pittsburgh Press*, July 12, 1941, 7.

35. "All-Star Hero Warms Bench," *Baltimore Sun*, July 12, 1941, 10.

36. Havey J. Boyle, "Mirrors of Sport," *Pittsburgh Post-Gazette*, July 12, 1941, 10.

37. Chester L. Smith, "Onkle Franz Will Play Out the String," *Pittsburgh Press*, July 15, 1941, 23.

38. "DiMaggio Stopped as Yanks Win, 4–3," *Pittsburgh Post-Gazette*, July 18, 1941, 14.

39. James J. Murphy, "Frisch-Vaughan Feud May Put Arky on Block," *Brooklyn Daily Eagle*, July 18, 1941, 11.

40. "Meet the Missus," *The Sporting News*, July 24, 1941, 4.

41. *Ibid.*

42. *Ibid.*

43. Lester Biederman, "The Scoreboard," *Pittsburgh Press*, August 4, 1941, 19.

44. Johnson, *"Arky": The Quiet Mr. Vaughan.*

45. Lester Biederman, "Bucs Get 'Breather' After Pennant Dash Suffers Rude Shock," *Pittsburgh Press*, August 11, 1941, 18.

46. Frankie Gustine, in discussion with Patricia Vaughan Johnson, November 1989.

47. *Ibid.*

48. Al Lopez, in discussion with Patricia Vaughan Johnson, no date.

49. Chilly Doyle, "Chillysauce," *Pittsburgh Sun-Telegram*, August 22, 1941, 18.

50. "Bucs Trounce London, 4–1," *Pittsburgh Post-Gazette*, August 30, 1941, 11.

51. Lester Biederman, "Arky Kept Off Field," *Pittsburgh Press*, September 9, 1941, 22.

52. "Pirate Notes," *Pittsburgh Post-Gazette*, September 4, 1941, 22.

53. Havey J. Boyle, "Mirrors of Sport," *Pittsburgh Post-Gazette*, September 25, 1941, 18.

54. Chester L. Smith, "Vaughan's Days as Buc Shortstop Are Over," *Pittsburgh Press*, September 25, 1941, 23.

55. *Ibid.*

56. Al Abrams, "Sidelights on Sports," *Pittsburgh Post-Gazette*, October 8, 1941, 17.

57. Havey J. Boyle, "Mirrors of Sport," *Pittsburgh Post-Gazette*, October 14, 1941, 14.

58. Chester L. Smith, "The Village Smithy," *Pittsburgh Press*, October 25, 1941, 8.

59. Tommy Holmes, "Vaughan, Litwhiler on Brooks' Bid List," *The Sporting News*, October 16, 1 941, 1.

60. Edward F. Balinger, "Vaughan Not in Any Trade Talks—Frisch," *Pittsburgh Post-Gazette*, November 18, 1941, 14.

61. "Vaughan Can Be Had—At High Price," *Pittsburgh Post-Gazette*, November 22, 1941, 12.

62. *Ibid.*

63. Lester Biederman, "The Scoreboard," *Pittsburgh Press*, November 30, 1941, 47.

64. *Ibid.*

65. Tommy Holmes, "Dodgers Concentrate on Vaughan, Leiber," *Brooklyn Daily Eagle*, December 2, 1941, 15.

66. George Kirksey, "Ott Wants Mize for 'New Deal' Giants," *Pittsburgh Press*, December 3, 1941, 29.

67. Harrison Salisbury, "Japs Speed Troops to Indo-China; Roosevelt Sends Note to Emperor," *Pittsburgh Press*, December 7, 1941, 1.

68. Lyle C. Wilson, "U.S. Declares War!" *Pittsburgh Press*, December 8, 1941, 1.

69. Johnson, "*Arky*": *The Quiet Mr. Vaughan.*

70. Lester Biederman, "War Talk, Not Baseball, Fills Chicago as Major Leaguers Gather for Meetings," *Pittsburgh Press*, December 8, 1 941, 30.

71. *Ibid.*

72. Edward F. Balinger, "War Casts Heavy Shadow on Baseball Meet," *Pittsburgh Post-Gazette*, December 9, 1941, 20.

73. "'We'll Keep Ball Rolling,' Sports Executives Promise," *Pittsburgh Press*, December 9, 1941, 31.

Chapter 8

1. "Fletcher's Name Enters Trade Talks," *Pittsburgh Press*, December 9, 1941, 31.

2. Edward F. Balinger, "Pirates trade Vaughan to Dodgers," *Pittsburgh Post-Gazette*, December 13, 1941, 14.

3. Lester Biederman, "Pirates Trade Vaughan to Brooklyn," *Pittsburgh Press*, December 13, 1941, 7.

4. Henry Shapiro, "Russia Wins Great Victory," *Pittsburgh Press*, December 13, 1941, 1.

5. Lester Biederman, "Frisch Thinks New Players Strengthen Bucs Considerably," *Pittsburgh Press*, December 14, 1941, 52.

6. Harry Keck, "Phelps, Coscarart, Wasdell, Hamlin New Corsairs," *Pittsburgh Sun-Telegraph*, December 13, 1941, 13.

7. Chester L. Smith, "Bucs Made Good Deal For Arky Vaughan," *Pittsburgh Press*, December 14, 1941, 53.

8. *Ibid.*

9. Tommy Holmes, "Trade for Vaughan Not Dodgers' Last," *Brooklyn Daily Eagle*, December 13, 1941, 9.

10. Tommy Holmes, "Clearing the Bases," *Brooklyn Daily Eagle*, December 14, 1941, 27.

11. George Wright, "Daily Pressings," *Daily Press* (Newport News, Virginia), December 13, 1941 9.

12. J.S. Albright, "Whirlaway of Sports," *Uniontown Evening Standard*, December 15, 1941, 10.

13. Harold Parrott, "Both Sides," *Brooklyn Daily Eagle*, December 17, 1941, 17.

14. Tommy Holmes, "MacPhail is Still Willing to Deal," *Brooklyn Daily Eagle*, December 17, 1941, 17.

15. Chilly Doyle, "Quality vs. Quantity Issue in Bucs' Deal," *The Sporting News*, December 18, 1941, 7.

16. "Sports Slants by 'Pap,'" *St. Cloud* (Minnesota) *Times*, December 27, 1941, 9.

17. Chester L. Smith, "The Village Smithy," *Pittsburgh Press*, February 14, 1942, 11.

18. Lester Biederman, "Scoreboard," *Pittsburgh Press*, December 16, 1941, 30.

19. Lester Biederman, "Scoreboard," *Pittsburgh Press*, December 19, 1941, 46.

20. *Ibid.*

21. Chester L. Smith, "Primary Line of Defense Worries Onkel Franz," *Pittsburgh Press*, January 29, 1942, 20.

22. Havey J. Boyle, "Mirrors of Sport," *Pittsburgh Post-Gazette*, January 8, 1942, 14.

23. Lester Biederman, "Scoreboard," *Pittsburgh Press*, February 15, 1942, 34.

24. *Ibid.*

25. Chester L. Smith, "Pirates Could Make Trouble This Year," *Pittsburgh Press*, February 21, 1942, 11.

26. Harold Parrott, "Both Sides," *Brooklyn Daily Eagle*, January 21, 1942, 17.

27. Tommy Holmes, "Vaughan's Batting Slot is Problem," *Brooklyn Daily Eagle*, January 15, 1942, 15.

28. W. Paul Wright, "Arky Vaughan Elated Over Dodger Trade," *Fullerton Daily News Tribune*, January 31, 1942, n.p.

29. Tommy Holmes, "Arky Picks Up Pen, Writes 'Pennant,'" *Brooklyn Daily Eagle*, January 23, 1942, 13.

30. Tommy Holmes, "Vaughan Hustles to Make Good in Third-base Move," *Brooklyn Daily Eagle*, February 25, 1942, 15.

31. *Ibid.*

32. "Training Camp Briefs," *Pittsburgh Sun-Telegraph*, March 10, 1942, n.p.

33. Havey J. Boyle, "Mirrors of Sport," *Pittsburgh Post-Gazette*, February 25, 1942, 14.

34. Harry Keck, "New Third Base Job Presents Many Problems to Arky Vaughan," *Pittsburgh Sun-Telegraph*, March 7, 1942, 9.

35. Lee Scott, "Durocher Says Right Field Wall at Ebbets Field Easy Target for Vaughan," *Brooklyn Citizen*, March 13, 1942, 6.

36. *Ibid.*

37. Tommy Holmes, "Vaughan Proves Defensive Star at Third for Dodgers," *Brooklyn Daily Eagle*, April 8, 1942, 17.

38. Tom Meany, "Scribbled by Scribes," *The Sporting News*, March 12, 1942, 4.

39. "Vaughan Turns It On for Baltimore Fans," *Brooklyn Daily Eagle*, April 9, 1942, 11.

40. Tommy Holmes, "Reese, Allen Get Dodgers Off Fast," *Brooklyn Daily Eagle*, April 15, 1942, 15.

41. Al Abrams, "Sidelights on Sports," *Pittsburgh Post-Gazette*, May 2, 1942, 11.

42. "Sewell, Butcher Face Braves," *Pittsburgh Press*, May 3, 1942, 25.

43. Grantland Rice, "The Sportlight," *Pittsburgh Post-Gazette*, May 5, 1942, 15.

44. Al Abrams, "Sidelights on Sports," *Pittsburgh Post-Gazette*, May 19, 1942, 15.

45. The Old Scout, "Frisch Has High Praise for Vaughan," 1942, n.p.

46. Harold Parrott, "Both Sides," *Brooklyn Daily Eagle*, May 8, 1942, 15.

47. Harold Parrott, "Both Sides," *Brooklyn Daily Eagle*, May 6, 1942, 21.

48. "Flock Plays Under Arcs Tomorrow and Friday," *Brooklyn Daily Eagle*, June 10, 1942, 15.

49. "Medwick Nears Own Best Streak Record," *Brooklyn Daily Eagle*, June 24, 1942, 13.

50. "No Good from Raising Race Issue," *The Sporting News*, August 6, 1942, 4.

51. *Ibid.*

52. Tommy Holmes, "Daring Base Running Pays Off for Dodgers," *Brooklyn Daily Eagle*, July 25, 1942, 9.

53. Chilly Doyle, "Buc Rooters Still Bucking Over Arky," *The Sporting News*, July 30, 1942, 5.

54. Tommy Holmes, "Dodgers Fall Down—With Cards Pushing," *Brooklyn Daily Eagle*, July 25, 1942, 11.

55. John P. McFarlane, "The Sports Front," *Pittsburgh Post-Gazette*, September 29, 1942, 14.

56. Tommy Holmes, "Dodgers Seeking New Executive," *Brooklyn Daily Eagle*, September 24, 1942, 1.

57. Tommy Holmes, "Dodgers Didn't Lose Flag—Cards Won It," *Brooklyn Daily Eagle*, September 28, 1942, 9.

58. Dick McCann, "Cards with Cap 'C' Beat Bums," *The Sporting News*, November 26, 1942, 2.

59. Tommy Holmes, "Clearing the Bases," *Brooklyn Daily Eagle*, October 18, 1942, 25.

60. "Rickey Sees Flock Collapse," *Brooklyn Daily Eagle*, October 16, 1942, 15.

61. Harold Parrott, "Rickey Signs for 5 Years with Dodgers," *Brooklyn Daily Eagle*, October 29, 1942, 1.

62. "Vaughan May Quit Dodgers; 'He's Too Busy on His Ranch,'" *Minneapolis Star-Tribune*, November 20, 1942, 17.

63. "Cattle Raising Versus Ball for 'Arky' Vaughan," *Ukiah Daily Journal*, November 19, 1942, 1.

64. Tommy Holmes, "Lip Is on Probation as Dodger Manager," *Brooklyn Daily Eagle*, November 20, 1942, 17.

65. Tommy Holmes, "'Short War' Guides Rickey-Dodger Plans," *Brooklyn Daily Eagle*, November 25, 1942, 9.

66. Chester L. Smith, "The Village Smithy," *Pittsburgh Press*, November 18, 1942, 28.

67. James J. Murphy, "Walker Says He Might Quit—And Means It!" *Brooklyn Daily Eagle*, December 16, 1942, 21.

Chapter 9

1. "517 Under Reserve in Majors, with No Club Up to Limit of 40," *The Sporting News*, January 7, 1943, 2.

2. Tommy Holmes, "Possible Durocher Successor Is Mr. X," *Brooklyn Daily Eagle*, January 15, 1943, 13.

3. Tommy Holmes, "Vaughan May Play Short If Reese Goes," *Brooklyn Daily Eagle*, January 27, 1943, 13.

4. "Vaughan Enlarges Ranch for New Arrival," *Pittsburgh Press*, January 8, 1943, 33.

5. "Rickey's Talk Fails to Convince Camilli," *Pittsburgh Press*, February 21, 1943, 44.

6. Tommy Holmes, "Babe In, Kampy Out, Arky Neither, Rickey Reports," *Brooklyn Daily Eagle*, February 27, 1943, 9.

7. Harold Parrott, "Lippy Leo Rejected—and Flatbush Cheers," *Brooklyn Daily Eagle*, March 1, 1943, 1.

8. Tommy Holmes, "Only Seven Dodgers Signed for '43 Race," *Brooklyn Daily Eagle*, March 4, 1943, 13.

9. Tommy Holmes, "Flock Gets L. Waner, Glossop for Dahlgren," *Brooklyn Daily Eagle*, March 9, 1943, 13.

10. Tommy Holmes, "Vaughan Decides to Play This Year," *Brooklyn Daily Eagle*, March 14, 1943, 21.

11. Tommy Holmes, "Durocher Sees Days as Player Numbered," *Brooklyn Daily Eagle*, March 21, 1943, 25.

12. Tommy Holmes, "Camilli Says Opener Will Find Him Ready," *Brooklyn Daily Eagle*, April 6, 1943, 9.

13. *Ibid.*

14. Lee Scott, "Camilli May Be Ready to Play in Series with Yankees Friday," *Brooklyn Citizen*, April 6, 1943, n.p.

15. "Whit Wyatt Makes First Start of the Season Against Phils Today," *Brooklyn Citizen*, April 27, 1943, 6.

16. Tommy Holmes, "Dodgers, Moving Along in Stride, Shrug Off Cards with 'So What?'" *Brooklyn Daily Eagle*, May 17,1943, 9.

17. John P. Carmichael, "Spunky Ed Stanky, Cub Who 'Plays for Keeps,'" *The Sporting News*, June 24, 1943, 5.

18. Donald Honig, *Baseball When the Grass was Real* (Lincoln: University of Nebraska Press, 1975), 159–161.

19. *Ibid.*

20. "Brooklyn Players Strike, Then Swamp Pirates, 23–6," *Decatur Daily Review* (Decatur, Illinois), July 11, 1943, 10.

21. Tommy Holmes, "Leo's Tactics Stir Dodger Revolt; Vaughan Stages Sitdown Strike," *Brooklyn Daily Eagle*, July 11,1943,1.

22. *Ibid.*

23. Arthur E. Patterson, "Dodgers Revolt Against Durocher's Suspension of Newsom," *Dayton Daily News*, July 11, 1943, 25.

24. *Ibid.*

25. *Ibid.*

26. Dolph Camilli, in discussion with Patricia Vaughan Johnson, no date.

27. Tommy Holmes, "Leo's Tactics Stir Dodger Revolt; Vaughan Stages Sitdown Strike," *Brooklyn Daily Eagle*, July 11, 1943, 1.

28. Harold Parrott, "Both Sides," *Brooklyn Daily Eagle*, July 12, 1943, 11.

29. *Ibid.*

30. Havey J. Boyle, "Mirrors of Sport," *Pittsburgh Post-Gazette*, July 12, 1943, 3.

31. J. Roy Stockton, "Howley Hunts," *The Sporting News*, July 22, 1943, 8.

32. Jack Cuddy, "Brooklyn Dissension May Split Club Apart," *Pittsburgh Post-Gazette*, July 13, 1943, 24.

33. Tommy Holmes, "No Shakeup Looms as Bobo is Traded," *Brooklyn Daily Eagle*, July 15, 1943, 13.

34. Dan Desmond, "Hot-Time Table of Leo-Bobo," *The Sporting News*, July 15, 1943, 2.

35. Tommy Holmes, "Dodgers New Spirit Reflected in Boston," *Brooklyn Daily Eagle*, July 19, 1943, 9.

36. Tommy Holmes, "Wyatt Likely to Hurl Night Game Tomorrow," *Brooklyn Daily Eagle*, July 21, 1943, 13.

37. "Dodgers Eye Geary as Arky's Illness Worries Durocher," *Brooklyn Daily Eagle*, July 23, 1943, 11.

38. Dick Fortune, "Fortune Telling," *Pittsburgh Press*, July 27, 1943, 18.

39. Tommy Holmes, "Olmo Regarded First of '44 Replacements," *Brooklyn Daily Eagle*, July 30, 1943, 9.

40. Al Lopez, in discussion with Patricia Vaughan Johnson, no date.

41. Harold Parrott, "Both Sides," *Brooklyn Daily Eagle*, August 2, 1943, 9.

42. Tommy Holmes, "B.R.Quits Club for Likely Talks with McKlain," *Brooklyn Daily Eagle*, August 4, 1943, 15.

43. Al Abrams, "Sidelights on Sports," *Pittsburgh Post-Gazette*, August 14, 1943, 11.

44. Harold Parrott, "Arky to Play in 44, Flock Buys SS Hart," *Brooklyn Daily Eagle*, August 18, 1943, 15.

45. "Vaughan Enters 2,000-Hit Circle," *Brooklyn Daily Eagle*, August 30, 1943, 11.

46. Tommy Holmes, "Leo Seeks Showdown on Status with B.R.," *Brooklyn Daily Eagle*, September 30, 1943, 13.

47. "Leo Starts New Mystery," *Christian Science Monitor*, November 26, 1943, 14.

48. *Ibid.*

49. Harold C. Burr, "Leo's 'Best Contract' Demands Club Get First Consider-

ation," *Brooklyn Daily Eagle*, October 26, 1943, 11.

50. "'Leo and I Are Buddies,' Insists Dixie Walker," *Pittsburgh Press*, October 29, 1943, 39.

51. *Ibid.*

52. Jimmy Jemail, "The Inquiring Fotographer," *New York Daily News*, November 13, 1943, 11.

53. Leo Durocher, *The Dodgers and Me* (Chicago: Ziff-Davis, 1948), 176–177.

54. *Ibid.*

55. Harold Parrott, "Lip Trips Into Newsome in Travelogue and Finds Bobo's Coast-Line Familiar," *The Sporting News*, December 9, 1943, 2.

56. Tommy Holmes, "Dodgers Get Pitcher Smith for Shortstop Barkley," *Brooklyn Daily Eagle*, December 31, 1943, 10.

57. Tommy Holmes, "Draft Hasn't Hit Flock Too Hard," *Brooklyn Daily Eagle*, January 15, 1944, 6.

58. Harold C. Burr, "Vaughan Key to Our Infield," *Brooklyn Daily Eagle*, January 17, 1944, 12.

59. Harold C. Burr, "Status of 3 Aces Creases B.R.'s Brow," *Brooklyn Daily Eagle*, February 17, 1944, 12.

60. "Vaughan on Dodgers' Doubtful List," *Pittsburgh Post-Gazette*, March 17, 1944, 17.

61. Lee Scott, "Dodgers Need 'Arky' Vaughan Desperately," *Brooklyn Citizen*, March 20, 1944, n.p.

62. *Ibid.*

63. Harold C. Burr, "Vaughan's Silence Stalls Leo's Plans," *Brooklyn Daily Eagle*, March 20, 1944, 10.

64. Harold C. Burr, "Rickey Pares Dodger Holdout Crop to 6," *Brooklyn Daily Eagle*, March 24, 1944, 14.

65. Harold C. Burr, "Arky May Join Us Last Three Months," *Brooklyn Daily Eagle*, March 31, 1944, 18.

66. *Ibid.*

67. "Rickey Says Majors Should Pool Players if 4-F's are Called Up," *The Morning Call* (Allentown, Pennsylvania), March 31, 1944, 26.

68. "Arky Vaughan Quits Baseball," *New York World-Telegram*, March 31, 1944, n.p.

69. "Five Lads Are 'First' in Line for Bleachers," *Brooklyn Daily Eagle*, April 21, 1944, 1.

70. Harold C. Burr, "Dodger Pressure Seen as Breaking Down Vaughan," *Brooklyn Daily Eagle*, May 17, 1944, 14.

71. Holmes, Tommy, "Sun Comes Out— So Does Crowd," *Brooklyn Daily Eagle*, May 29, 1944, 10.

72. Harold C. Burr, "Arky Closes Door on Flock for Year," *Brooklyn Daily Eagle*, May 31, 1944, 14.

73. *Ibid.*

74. "Invaders Drive 10 Miles into Nazis' Coastal Wall," *Pittsburgh Press*, June 6, 1944, 1.

75. "Allies Smash 9 1/2 Mi. Beyond French Coast," *Brooklyn Daily Eagle*, June 6, 1944, 1.

76. "Sports Shorts," *Brooklyn Daily Eagle*, June 7, 1944, 15.

77. Al Abrams, "Sidelights on Sports," *Pittsburgh Post-Gazette*, June 10, 1944, 7.

78. Dan Daniel, "'Arky Vaughan's Retirement Baseball Calamity'—Rickey," *Pittsburgh Press*, June 20, 1944, 22.

79. Johnson, *"Arky": The Quiet Mr. Vaughan.*

80. Dan Daniel, "'Arky Vaughan's Retirement Baseball Calamity'—Rickey," *Pittsburgh Press*, June 20, 1944, 22.

81. Harold C. Burr, "Leo, Signed, Vows Better '45 Club," *Brooklyn Daily Eagle*, September 29, 1944, 15.

Chapter 10

1. Harold C. Burr, "Baseball, Football Would Be Put on Ropes by Byrnes' 4-F Plans," *Brooklyn Daily Eagle*, January 2, 1945, 13.

2. Harold C. Burr, "Rickey Favors Co-ordinating Sports Chief," *The Sporting News*, January 11, 1945, 10.

3. Johnson, *"Arky": The Quiet Mr. Vaughan.*

4. *Ibid.*

5. *Ibid.*

6. *Ibid.*

7. *Ibid.*

8. *Ibid.*

9. *Ibid.*

10. Dolph Camilli, in discussion with Patricia Vaughan Johnson, no date.

11. *Ibid.*

12. *Ibid.*

13. Correspondence with National Personnel Records Center, St. Louis, Missouri, August 2018.

14. Dolph Camilli, in discussion with Patricia Vaughan Johnson, no date.

15. Johnson, *"Arky": The Quiet Mr. Vaughan.*

16. Lyle C. Wilson, "Truman Takes Up

Fight for Roosevelt's Ideas," *Pittsburgh Press*, April 13, 1945, 1.

17. Havey J. Boyle, "Mirrors of Sport," *Pittsburgh Post-Gazette*, May 16, 1945, 12.

18. Harold C. Burr, "Leo Appeals to Boss for Vaughan's Return," *Brooklyn Daily Eagle*, May 25, 1945, 15.

19. Harold C. Burr, "Sports Shorts," *Brooklyn Daily Eagle*, June 2, 1945, 7.

20. Tommy Holmes, "Durocher Reports to His Clientele," *Brooklyn Daily Eagle*, July 31, 1945, 13.

21. Jerry Mitchell, "Flock Bans Operation on Reiser—May Trade Vaughan to Phils," *New York Post*, December 7, 1945, n.p.

22. Harold C. Burr, "Arky Shuns Call of '46 Base Hits," *Brooklyn Daily Eagle*, December 21, 1945, 17.

23. Harold C. Burr, "Herman Throws Hat on Third for Flock," *Brooklyn Daily Eagle*, February 15, 1946, 15.

24. Correspondence between Arky Vaughan and Branch Rickey, January 26, 1946.

25. Lester Biederman, "Young and Old Still Write to 'Jay,'" *Pittsburgh Press*, January 27, 1946, 32.

26. Red Smith, "Views of Sport," *New York Herald Tribune*, March 8, 1946, 25.

27. *Ibid.*

28. *Ibid.*

29. *Ibid.*

30. *Ibid.*

31. Johnson, *"Arky": The Quiet Mr. Vaughan.*

32. "'Ah Loves True Love and Leo Durocher,' Says Deacon," *Latrobe Bulletin*, February 12, 1947, 14.

33. Jeffrey Marlett, "The 1947 Dodgers: The Suspension of Leo Durocher," https://sabr.org.

34. *Ibid.*

35. Johnson, *"Arky": The Quiet Mr. Vaughan.*

36. Glenn Stout and Richard A. Johnson, *The Dodgers: 120 Years of Dodgers Baseball* (Boston: Houghton Mifflin, 2004), 127.

37. Harold C. Burr, "Robby Still Royal to Dodger Rickey," *Brooklyn Daily Eagle*, January 7, 1947, 13.

38. Harold C. Burr, "Vaughan Rarin' to Go for Flock," *Brooklyn Daily Eagle*, February 11, 1947, 17.

39. Harold C. Burr, "Vaughan Could Cure Third Base Headache," *Brooklyn Daily Eagle*, February 14, 1947, 17.

40. Harry Keck, "Sports: Memories of One of the Old Guard," *Pittsburgh Sun-Telegraph*, February 17, 1947, 16.

41. Harold C. Burr. "Dodgers in Trek to Cuban Fields; '47 Flag Hinges on Vaughan, Reiser," *Brooklyn Daily Eagle*, February 18, 1947, 13.

42. Harold C. Burr, "Arky No Ball of Fat, Dodger Scribes Find," *Brooklyn Daily Eagle*, February 19, 1947, 17.

43. *Ibid.*

44. Herbert Goren, *New York Sun*, February 19, 1947, n.p.

45. Bob Cooke, "Dodgers Make Camp in Cuba for Training," *New York Herald Tribune*, February 20, 1947, 28.

46. Leo Durocher, "Durocher Says: Papeke Has No Faults and He Plays 1st Base," *Brooklyn Daily Eagle*, February 22, 1947, 6.

47. Harold C. Burr, "Sessi, Milady Show at Dodgers' Camp," *Brooklyn Daily Eagle*, February 23, 1947, 21.

48. Herbert Goren, "Dodgers Differ on Robinson, Negro Player, as Teammate" (Muncie, Indiana) *Star Press*, March 3, 1947, 8.

49. *Ibid.*

50. Leo Durocher, "Durocher Says: Our Greatest Need Is That No. 5 Hitter," *Brooklyn Daily Eagle*, March 15, 1947, 6.

51. Matty Matthews, "'Vaughan Looks Great,' Reports Reiser," *Miami News*, March 11, 1947, 16.

52. "Durocher Hit as CYO Quits Knot-Hole Club," *Brooklyn Daily Eagle*, February 28, 1947, 1.

53. "Larry Files Charges Against Dodger Trio," *Brooklyn Daily Eagle*, March 16, 1947, 1.

54. Tommy Holmes, "My Three Weeks in a Quandary," *Brooklyn Daily Eagle*, March 25, 1947, 13.

55. Harold C. Burr, "Vaughan's Legs Cry for Major League Infields," *Brooklyn Daily Eagle*, March 25, 1947, 13.

56. Leo Durocher, "Durocher Says: Vaughan Not Hurt by 3-Year Layoff," *Brooklyn Daily Eagle*, March 26, 1947, 19.

57. Bob Cooke, "Vaughan Wins Third-Base Job with Dodgers," *New York Herald Tribune*, April 6, 1947, B1.

58. Leo Durocher, "Durocher Says: Inside Stuff on Head, Casey and Others," *Brooklyn Daily Eagle*, April 6, 1947, 23.

59. Tommy Holmes. "Rickey and Jackie Are Both on Spot," *Brooklyn Daily Eagle*, April 9, 1947, 21.

60. Harold C. Burr. "Ray Blades Favored by Rickey as Successor to Ousted Lippy," *Brooklyn Daily Eagle*, April 10, 1947, 1.
61. Tommy Holmes, "Czar Happy Throws His Weight Around," *Brooklyn Daily Eagle*, April 10, 1947, 20.
62. *Ibid.*
63. Harold C. Burr, "Robby Makes Debut with Dodgers Today," *Brooklyn Daily Eagle*, April 11, 1947, 15.
64. Harold C. Burr, "Hatten Faces Sain in Dodger Opener," *Brooklyn Daily Eagle*, April 15, 1947, 1.
65. Tommy Holmes, "Clinical Notes on Opening Day," *Brooklyn Daily Eagle*, April 16, 1947, 19.
66. Harold C. Burr, "Shotton Gets Post as New Dodger Pilot," *Brooklyn Daily Eagle*, April 18, 1947, 1.
67. "Frick Claims Cards Plotted to Shun Negro," *Chicago Tribune*, May 9, 1947, 31.
68. *Ibid.*
69. Sam Lacy, "Strike Against Jackie Spiked," *Baltimore Afro-American*, May 17, 1947, n.p.
70. Harold C. Burr, "Durocher to Help Rickey Cut 9 Dodgers Adrift by May 15," *Brooklyn Daily Eagle*, May 3, 1947, 6.
71. *Ibid.*
72. "Brook Trade Rumors Rife; Giles Still is Hopeful of Deal," *Cincinnati Enquirer*, May 8, 1947, 18.
73. Carl Hughes, "Sports Stew—Served Hot," *Pittsburgh Press*, May 5, 1947, 17.
74. "A Letter from the Home Town," *Pittsburgh Press*, May 17, 1947, 7.
75. Harold C. Burr, "Traffic Jam at Third Looms for Dodgers," *Brooklyn Daily Eagle*, May 13, 1947, 13.
76. *Ibid.*
77. Harold C. Burr, "Vaughan's Outfield Debut Becomes Pleasant Surprise," *Brooklyn Daily Eagle*, July 1, 1947, 15.
78. *Ibid.*
79. Harold C. Burr, "Reiser's Presence Tonic for Dodgers," *Brooklyn Daily Eagle*, July 11, 1947, 10.
80. Irving Vaughan, "Branca Gets 2 at Cub Expense," *Chicago Tribune*, July 11, 1947, 21.
81. Al Abrams, "Sidelights on Sports," *Pittsburgh Post-Gazette*, September 20, 1947, 12.
82. Steve Snider, "It's a 'Strong Bench' That Wins," *Des Moines Register*, September 26, 1947, 15.
83. Harold C. Burr, "Hails NL Conquest as 'Team Triumph,'" *Brooklyn Daily Eagle*, September 23, 1947, 13.
84. Dan Parker, "Dan Parker's … Broadway Bugle," *Ottawa Citizen*, September 24, 1947, 19.
85. Grantland Rice, "The Sportlight," *Miami News*, September 19, 1947, 11.
86. "Dodgers Carry 'Stronger Bench' Than Yankees," *Brooklyn Daily Eagle*, September 27, 1947, 6.
87. "Court Adjourns to See Big Game on Television Set," *Brooklyn Daily Eagle*, October 1, 1947, 1.
88. Tommy Holmes, "Yanks Nip Brooks, 2–1, as Shea Stars," *Brooklyn Daily Eagle*, October 5, 1947, 24.
89. "Player Shares Miss Record, Despite Richest Classic," *The Sporting News*, October 22, 1947, 13.
90. Gus Steiger, "Postwar Shortages Pushed Up Some Men Too Fast—Vaughan," *The Sporting News*, August 20, 1947, 6.
91. Johnson, *"Arky": The Quiet Mr. Vaughan.*
92. *Ibid.*
93. *Ibid.*

Chapter 11

1. Harold C. Burr, "Rickey Gulps Aspirin as He Tries to Decide What to Do with Vets," *The Sporting News*, October 22, 1947, 13.
2. Lou Niss, "Dodgers Sign Leo at '47 Figure—Shotton is Shifted," *Brooklyn Daily Eagle*, December 7, 1947, 27.
3. Harold C. Burr, "Not on Spot, Leo Blithely Chirps," *Brooklyn Daily Eagle*, January 7, 1948, 19.
4. Johnson, *"Arky": The Quiet Mr. Vaughan.*
5. "Dodgers Sign Robinson for About $14,000," *Hartford Courant*, February 13, 1948, 17.
6. Harold C. Burr, "Robby Maps Future After Dodger Career," *Brooklyn Daily Eagle*, February 13, 1948, 16.
7. James J. Murphy, "Dodgers Lacking 13 Player Pacts," *Brooklyn Daily Eagle*, February 20, 1948, 14.
8. "Vaughan Set for Another Year," *New York Sun*, February 25, 1948, n.p.
9. "Baseball Lifts Lid Today on 372 Exhibition Affairs," *Akron Beacon Journal*, March 6, 1948, 10.
10. Dan Parker, "Broadway Bugle," *Camden Courier-Post*, March 31, 1948, 17.

11. Harold C. Burr, "Hodges, Vaughan in Dodger Spotlight," *Brooklyn Daily Eagle*, March 25, 1948, 17.

12. Harold C. Burr, "Believe Rickey Lining Up Trade to Slice Surplus Dodger Talent," *Brooklyn Daily Eagle*, April 9, 1948, 19.

13. Arthur Daley, "Hail the Conquering Heroes Come," *Miami Daily News*, April 18, 1948, 26.

14. "4 Treatments Keep Reiser from Flock," *Brooklyn Daily Eagle*, June 3, 1948, 19.

15. Harold C. Burr, "Official Scorer's Life Not Always Soft Touch," *Brooklyn Daily Eagle*, June 6, 1948, 30.

16. Tommy Holmes, "Skipper Durocher Crosses the Bridge," *Brooklyn Daily Eagle*, July 17, 1948, 7.

17. Harold C. Burr, "Vaughan Second Gomez in his Own Quiet Way," *Brooklyn Daily Eagle*, August 22, 1948, 22.

18. *Ibid.*

19. Harold C. Burr, "Southworth Picks Sain for Series Starter on Mound," *Brooklyn Daily Eagle*, September 29, 1948, 19.

20. Johnson, *"Arky": The Quiet Mr. Vaughan.*

21. *Ibid.*

22. *Ibid.*

23. Harry Borba, "Seals Land Vaughan, Ex-Major," *San Francisco Examiner*, February 17, 1949, 30.

24. "Arky Vaughan Reports to Seals at Boyes Springs," *Santa Rosa Press Democrat*, February 24, 1949, 8.

25. Bob Stevens, "Amiable 'Arkie'—This Vaughan is a Regular Chatterbox," *San Francisco Chronicle*, March 1949, n.p.

26. "Vaughan to Make More with Seals," *San Bernardino County Sun-Telegram*, March 6, 1949, 21.

27. "Vaughan, After 14 Years in Majors, Corrects Name," *The Sporting News*, March 23, 1949, 29.

28. Arky Vaughan, "I'll Never Forget The Day," *San Francisco Examiner*, March 13, 1949, n.p.

29. Will Connolly, "Will Connolly Says…" *San Francisco Chronicle*, March 26, 1949, n.p.

30. *Ibid.*

31. Art Rosenbaum, "Arkie Remembers the Babe's Last Day When Homers Sailed O'er Fence Far Away," *San Francisco Chronicle*, March 20, 1949, n.p.

32. "Ex-Buc Vaughan Gives Up Baseball," *Pittsburgh Press*, September 3, 1949, 6.

33. "Arky Vaughan Turns from Seals to Panthers," *Ukiah Republican Press*, September 14, 1949, 1.

Chapter 12

1. Chuck Abair, "Angels Herman Buddy of Late Vaughan," *Fullerton Daily News Tribune*, April 21, 1967, C5.

2. Timothy Vaughan, in discussion with the author, June 2017.

3. *Ibid.*

4. Johnson, *"Arky": The Quiet Mr. Vaughan.*

5. Lee Juillerat, "'Arky' Finally Makes Hall of Fame," *Klamath Falls Herald and News*, March 10, 1985, 26.

6. Timothy Vaughan, in discussion with the author, June 2017.

7. Joyce Espil Volney, in discussion with the author, May 2018.

8. *Ibid.*

9. *Ibid.*

10. *Ibid.*

11. *Ibid.*

12. "Vaughan Drowns in Boat Tragedy," *Troy Record* (Troy, New York), September 1, 1952, 12.

13. Timothy Vaughan, in discussion with the author, June 2017.

14. Joyce Espil Volney, in discussion with the author, May 2018.

15. "Two Valley Men Drown in Lost Lake Saturday," *Surprise Valley Journal* (Cedarville, California), September 4, 1952, 1.

16. Joyce Espil Volney, in discussion with the author, May 2018.

17. Audrey Smith Ifft, in discussion with the author, August 2017.

18. Harry Keck, "Arky's Death Shock to Fans," *Pittsburgh Sun-Telegraph*, September 1, 1952, 14.

19. Chilly Doyle, "Pirates, Cards Mourn Passing of Vaughan," *Pittsburgh Sun-Telegraph*, September 1, 1952, 14.

20. *Ibid.*

21. "Arky Vaughan Drowns in Lake," *Pittsburgh Sun-Telegraph*, September 1, 1952, 1.

22. Al Abrams, "Sidelights on Sports, *Pittsburgh Post-Gazette*, September 1, 1952, 26.

23. "Arky Vaughan's Death Saddens Baseball World," *Pittsburgh Press*, September 1, 1952, 18.

24. Les Biederman, "The Scoreboard," *Pittsburgh Press*, September 6, 1952, 6.

25. Correspondence between Branch Rickey and Margaret Vaughan, September 1, 1952.

26. Red Smith, "Views of Sport," *New York Herald Tribune*, September 2, 1952, 24.

27. John Neubauer, "The Town Crier," *Fullerton Daily News Tribune*, September 2, 1952, 8.

28. *Ibid.*

29. Art Rosenbaum, "Hitter Vaughan Appreciated Good Fielding," *San Francisco Chronicle*, September 1, 1952, n.p.

30. Joyce Espil Volney, in discussion with the author, May 2018.

31. Timothy Vaughan, in discussion with the author, June 2017.

32. *Ibid.*

33. *Ibid.*

34. L. Robert Davids, "Musial Follows 2,000th Hit with 1,000th Run Batted In," *The Sporting News*, September 24, 1952, 13.

35. "'Soft-Touch' Tito Now Gives Hard Time to Hurlers," *The Sporting News*, August 8, 1956, 10.

36. "Al Abrams, "Sidelights on Sports," *Pittsburgh Post-Gazette*, March 12, 1957, 22.

37. "Clarify Ground Rules for Shrine," *The Sporting News*, February 8, 1964, 12.

38. Ray Swanecamp, correspondence with National Baseball Hall of Fame, January 1967.

39. *Ibid.*

40. *Ibid.*

41. Richard Nixon, White House correspondence, June 27, 1972.

42. Richard Nixon, White House correspondence, September 29, 1972.

43. C.C. Johnson Spink, "We Believe," *The Sporting News*, June 9, 1973, 14.

44. Leonard Koppett, "Veterans Committee Voting Lacks Logic," *The Sporting News*, February 19, 1977, 4.

45. Wiley Thornton, correspondence with National Baseball Hall of Fame, May 1978.

46. Tony Moser, "Quixote He's Not, but Vaughan's Fan Charges Anyway," *Arkansas Democrat*, June 7, 1978, n.p.

47. *Ibid.*

48. "Margaret Vaughan," *Ukiah Daily Journal*, April 12, 1978, 3.

49. "Arky Vaughan Put in Superstar Ranks," *Pittsburgh Press*, March 18, 1979, 24.

50. "Voice of the Fan," *The Sporting News*, May 16, 1981, 4.

51. Steve Grimley, "Arky Vaughan: A Lone Star," *The Register*, Orange County, California, February 11, 1982, E16.

52. Chris Dufresne, "The Fullerton Connection: Stars from Different Eras Share Record," *Fullerton Daily News Tribune*, August 14, 1981, n.p.

53. Charles Trunick, "Arky Deserves Induction," *Pittsburgh Press*, March 8, 1982, 12.

54. Edward H. Kelly, "How About Ernie Lombardi, Arky Vaughan for the Hall?" *Baseball Digest*, November 1984, 50–54.

55. Harry O'Donnell, correspondence with National Baseball Hall of Fame, January 1985.

56. Richard Tourangeau, in discussion with the author, June 2016.

57. Richard Tourangeau, correspondence with National Baseball Hall of Fame, January 1985.

58. Milton Richman, "Sport Parade," *Petaluma Argus-Courier*, February 4, 1985, 6.

59. Glenn Erickson, "Arky's Family Elated He's a Hall of Famer," *Ukiah Daily Journal*, March 7, 1985, 59.

60. Ronald Reagan, correspondence with Vaughan family, March 1985.

61. Patricia Vaughan Johnson, National Baseball Hall of Fame archives, July 28, 1985.

62. Richard Tourangeau, in discussion with the author, June 2016.

63. Patricia Vaughan Johnson, National Baseball Hall of Fame archives, July 28, 1985.

64. Glenn Erickson, "Vaughan Clan Treated Like Royalty at Hall of Fame," *Ukiah Daily Journal*, August 18, 1985, 13.

65. Richard Nixon, correspondence with Patricia Vaughan Johnson, July 29, 1985.

66. Joseph D.E. Konhauser, correspondence with Patricia Vaughan Johnson, July 30, 1985.

67. Roy McHugh, "At Long Last—Vaughan Getting His Rightful Place in Hall of Fame," *Pittsburgh Press*, July 28, 1985, D1.

68. Jonathan Fraser Light, *The Cultural Encyclopedia of Baseball* (Jefferson, NC: McFarland, 2005) 988.

69. Roy McHugh, "At Long Last—Vaughan Getting His Rightful Place in Hall of Fame," *Pittsburgh Press*, July 28, 1985, D1.

70. Robert E. Howell, "Remembering Arky," *Pittsburgh Press*, August 4, 1985, 58.

Chapter 13

1. Bill James, *The New Bill James Historical Baseball Abstract* (New York: Free Press, 2001), 364.
2. Billjamesonline.com, accessed May 27, 2019.
3. Billjamesonline.com, accessed May 29, 2019.
4. *Ibid.*
5. *Ibid.*
6. *Ibid.*
7. *Ibid.*
8. *Ibid.*
9. *Ibid.*
10. Bill Felber, in discussion with the author, August 2017.
11. *Ibid.*
12. Rob Neyer, in discussion with the author, June 2017.
13. *Ibid.*
14. *Ibid.*
15. Mark Langill, in discussion with the author, June 2016.
16. Donald Honig, in discussion with the author, June 2016.
17. Bill Deane, in discussion with the author, July 2016.
18. Jay Jaffe, in discussion with the author, June 2017.
19. *Ibid.*
20. Sam Reich, in discussion with the author, August 2016.
21. *Ibid.*
22. Ronald T. Waldo, in discussion with the author, May 2017.
23. David Finoli, in discussion with the author, May 2017.
24. Kathleen Johnson Roberts, in discussion with the author, June 2019.

Bibliography

Books and Articles

Alexander, Charles C. *Breaking the Slump: Baseball in the Depression Era.* New York: Columbia University Press, 2002.

Durocher, Leo. *The Dodgers and Me.* Chicago: Ziff-Davis, 1948.

Faber, Charles F. "Willard Hershberger." Society for American Baseball Research Biography Project, http:// https://sabr.org/bioproj/person/8dfc0cd0#sdendnote15sym. Accessed July 11, 2018.

Honig, Donald. *Baseball When the Grass Was Real.* Lincoln: University of Nebraska Press, 1975.

James, Bill. *The New Bill James Historical Baseball Abstract.* New York: Free Press, 2001.

Kelly, Edward H. "How About Ernie Lombardi, Arky Vaughan for the Hall?" *Baseball Digest,* November 1984.

Light, Jonathan Fraser. *The Cultural Encyclopedia of Baseball.* Jefferson, NC: McFarland, 2005.

Marlett, Jeffrey. "The 1947 Dodgers: The Suspension of Leo Durocher." Society for American Baseball Research, https://sabr.org/research/1947-dodgers-suspension-leo-durocher. Accessed May 2, 2019.

Ritter, Lawrence S. *The Glory of Their Times.* New York: William Morrow, 1984.

Stout, Glenn, and Richard A. Johnson. *The Dodgers: 120 Years of Dodgers Baseball.* Boston: Houghton Mifflin, 2004.

Surdam, David G. *Wins, Losses and Empty Seats: How Baseball Outlasted the Great Depression.* Lincoln: University of Nebraska Press, 2001.

Newspapers

Akron Beacon Journal, 1948

Arkansas Democrat, 1978

Baltimore Afro-American, 1947

Baltimore Sun, 1935

Brooklyn Citizen, 1942–1944

Brooklyn Daily Eagle, 1935–1948

Camden (New Jersey) *Courier Post,* 1948

Chicago Tribune, 1947

Christian Science Monitor, 1943

Cincinnati Enquirer, 1947

Daily Press (Newport News, Virginia), 1941

Dayton Daily News, 1943

Decatur (Illinois) *Daily Review,* 1943

Des Moines Register, 1931–1947

Fullerton (California) *Daily News Tribune,* 1931–1981

Hartford (Connecticut) *Courant,* 1948

Klamath Falls (Oregon) *Herald and News,* 1985

Latrobe (Pennsylvania) *Bulletin,* 1947

Los Angeles Times, 1929–1985

Miami Daily News, 1947–1948

Milwaukee Journal, 1935

Minneapolis Star Tribune, 1942

Morning Call (Allentown, Pennsylvania), 1944

New York Daily News, 1942–1943

New York Herald Tribune, 1946–1952

New York Sun, 1932–1948

New York World Telegram, 1944

Newark Advocate, 1937

News Journal (Wilmington, Delaware) 1935

Orange County (California) Register, 1982
Ottawa Citizen, 1947
Petaluma (California) Argus Courier, 1985
Pittsburgh Post-Gazette, 1931–1957
Pittsburgh Press, 1931–1985
Pittsburgh Sun-Telegraph, 1934–1952
The Record Argus (Greenville, Pennsylvania), 1936
St. Cloud (Minnesota) Times, 1941
San Bernardino County Sun-Telegram, 1949
San Francisco Chronicle, 1949
San Francisco Examiner, 1949
Santa Ana (California) Express, 1938
Santa Ana (California) Register 1931–1936

Santa Rosa Press-Democrat, 1949
The Sporting News, 1931–1981
Star Press (Muncie, Indiana) 1947
Surprise Valley (Cedarville, California) Journal, 1952
Troy (New York) Record, 1952
Ukiah (California) Daily Journal, 1942–1985
Ukiah (California) Republican Press, 1939–1949
Uniontown (Pennsylvania) Evening Standard, 1941
The Weekly Pleiades (Fullerton, California, High School), 1930
Young America, 1935

Websites

Baseball-Reference.com—Major League Statistics and Information, Sports Reference LLC, https://www.baseball-reference.com.
Billjamesonline.com. https://www.billjamesonline.com/appling_and_vaughan/?print=y, accessed May 27, 2019.
National Baseball Hall of Fame. https://baseballhall.org/discover-more/stories/baseball-history/lou-gehrig-luckiest-man, accessed July 5, 2018.
"Pennsylvania and the Great Depression." Explorepahistory.com, http://explorepahistory.com/story.php?storyId=1-9-1B, accessed June 1, 2016.
United States Census Bureau, Historical Statistics of the United States, Colonial Times to 1957, Chapter D. Labor. https://www2.census.gov/library/publications/1960/compendia/hist_stats_colonial-1957/hist_stats_colonial-1957-chD.pdf?#, accessed July 3, 2017.

Unpublished Manuscript

Johnson, Patricia. "Arky": The Quiet Mr. Vaughan. Last modified September 9, 1991.

Index

Numbers in *bold italics* indicate pages with illustrations

251

254 Index